SOUTH BRIDGE
CATALOGUED
R. AGRICULTURE
CHAO
48713

TO BE
DISPOSED
BY
AUTHORITY

AGRARIAN POLICY OF THE CHINESE COMMUNIST PARTY

1921–1959

Other Works by the Author

Mass Organizations in China, 1953

Agrarian Policies of Mainland China, A Documentary Study, 1957

Economic Planning and Organization in China, 1949–58, 2 vols., 1959 and 1960

AGRARIAN POLICY OF THE CHINESE COMMUNIST PARTY 1921–1959

CHAO KUO-CHUN

Visiting Professor and Head of East Asia Department, Indian School of International Studies, University of Delhi

Issued under the auspices of The Indian School of International Studies and The Institute of Pacific Relations, N.Y.

ASIA PUBLISHING HOUSE

LONDON

© INDIAN SCHOOL OF INTERNATIONAL STUDIES
NEW DELHI, 1960

Chao Kuo-chun (b. 1918)

PRINTED IN INDIA
BY PYARELAL SAH AT THE TIMES OF INDIA PRESS,
BOMBAY, AND PUBLISHED BY P. S. JAYASINGHE,
ASIA PUBLISHING HOUSE, BOMBAY 1.

FOREWORD

THIS BOOK of Dr. Chao is likely to be of very considerable interest to many people both within India and outside. As the title indicates, it is devoted primarily to an analysis of the agrarian policies of the Chinese Communist Party. But it also throws light on the broader political and economic strategy adopted by the Party over the last four decades and on the instruments it has used to bring about the revolutionary changes that have been taking place in China.

It is now almost a commonplace to say that what is required for the development of backward economies is, above all, better organization. Money, equipment, technical skill, etc. are of course necessary, but what is most important, to begin with, is the will to do the simple things that can be done without much of any of these, and the capacity to organize them.

In a sense, this is all that China has tangibly demonstrated in the course of the last decade. It seems to have lifted itself, as it were, by its own bootstraps by merely mobilizing available labour within the economy and using fairly simple and well-known techniques of production. What lends interest to the Chinese experiment is, therefore, not that something totally miraculous has been achieved—because only that which cannot be explained by human reason is truly a miracle—but that China has succeeded in doing what other countries, which have intellectually recognized the possibility, have not been able to do as yet.

This naturally makes one ask how it is that China has been able to translate into practice what has remained elsewhere a theoretical possibility. It is here that Dr. Chao's book has much light to throw.

One does not have to have a great deal of imagination to guess that the degree of organizational efficiency and power that has been attained in China in the last few years could not have been built up without employing some harsh and distasteful methods. Dr. Chao has not glossed over these, and has indeed described them in some detail in Chapter III of the book.

At the same time, it is all too easy to explain away the entire achievement of the Chinese in terms of some simple formula such as "totalitarianism." Though one cannot pronounce on matters like this solely on the basis of published material available outside China, it seems, on the face of it, improbable that breaking down an age-old structure of society, and directing forces generated by it to constructive channels, can be done solely, or even largely, through political authoritarianism.

What Dr. Chao's account brings out is that a major revolution, of the kind China has had, can be brought about only by policies based on a good understanding of the balance of forces within rural societies, of the pressures and compulsions to which different classes are subject, and of the sort of stimulii to which the mass of the people will react with hope and enthusiasm. By implication, it would seem that the power and impetus of the Chinese revolution is explained not so much by the methods used to induce, what he has referred to in one place as, the "catharsis" of the soul, but by the skill with which different elements of rural society have been used at different stages to destroy the older structure and to develop, in the process, qualities of leadership and attitudes of mind necessary for the reconstruction of society on a new basis.

Dr. Chao has traced, in considerable detail, the different stages in the evolution of the agrarian policies of the Chinese Communist Party and also the changes in its tactics from time to time. He has described the manner in which the big landlords, then the rich peasants, and finally the middle peasants were first isolated or neutralized, and then eliminated altogether as social classes. He has, however, made no attempt to speculate whether the strategy adopted by the Party could have been as successful in eliminating classes previously well-entrenched in rural society, but for the exceptional conditions prevailing in China both immediately before and after the Sino-Japanese War.

There remain some aspects of Chinese social and economic policy about which it will be difficult not to have misgivings. But, without suspending one's initial faculties, one can at least try to understand the background in which they have been adopted. Dr. Chao's book will be found to be of very great value from this point of view.

Revolutions have seldom, if ever, been repeated with the same results. One must be, therefore, careful about the conclusions one draws from the developments in China. But what China has been able to achieve in the last few years, particularly in the agrarian sector, has undoubtedly some very obvious lessons for others, and no one who reads Dr. Chao's book can fail to see what they are.

Cambridge, *May* 20, 1960 K. N. RAJ

PREFACE

THIS STUDY represents an effort to describe and analyse: (1) the background of the agrarian problem in China; (2) the genesis of the agrarian policy of the Chinese Communist Party since its foundation in 1921; (3) the major contents and results of the recent (1953–1959) agrarian programmes in China; (4) the characteristics and significance of these programmes; and (5) the problems as well as prospects of the CCP agrarian reform.

Although the desirability of the study of such a vital issue as the agrarian policy of the Chinese Communists is apparent, the meagreness of comprehensive data as well as of first-hand observations makes an accurate examination quite difficult. The situation is further complicated not only by changes in the CCP land policy during various periods in the past thirty-eight years, but also by the divergent practices in different areas at a given time. This is especially true regarding many of the historical periods when the CCP was engaged in guerilla fighting and the Nationalists' blockade prevented outsiders from learning about the Party's programmes. Furthermore, the agrarian movement itself is a complex measure embodying political, economic, social and psychological roles and functions. The agrarian question, important as it is in a predominantly agricultural country like China, cannot be isolated from other related issues such as industrialization, capital accumulation, and national economic planning.

Since the initiation of the first five-year plan by the Central People's Government in 1953, and particularly after the reorganization of statistical work on the Chinese mainland in 1955, both the quantity and quality of Peking's data on various economic sectors have shown notable improvement. In addition, qualified neutral observers such as the Indian agricultural delegation (1956), the French agronomist René Dumont (1957) and Prof. Joseph Needham of Oxford University (1959) have made public their eye-witness accounts of the developments on China's agricultural front. These detailed reports reinforce the impressions gathered from the study of current sources, especially those on the "big leap" in 1958–60, from China, namely, that the agricultural sector of China is breaking through the former stage of stagnation and has embarked on a sustained growth which the industrial sector seems to have already achieved. It is essential to examine the specific ways by which Peking effects these rapid transformations of rural China like the socialization and modernization of farming, and what problems or bottlenecks are faced by the Chinese planners. The impact of this colossal experiment in China will be tremendous not only on many Asian countries which too are primarily agricultural, but also on the world as a whole. It would also be interesting to compare the results of China's first five-year plan (1953-57) in the agricultural fields with those of India's first five-year plan (1952-56), and their respective second five-year plans. The Chinese experiences in agrarian development may also call for a reappraisal of certain aspects in some traditional Western theories on economic growth in underdeveloped countries.

The importance of the subject-matter does not necessarily guarantee the quality of the work concerning it. This study, written by one who has had neither personal participation in the CCP's agrarian movement nor an opportunity to study it first-hand, can at best only be a general survey. Many a passage in the volume will certainly need reappraisal or revision when the author gets the benefit of on the spot observations. Furthermore, the hard work, zeal, and single-mindedness of over 500 million Chinese peasants who have played a key role in the spectacular development of rural China during the past decade are not likely to be grasped in the fullest extent by any ivory-towered academic worker. It is hoped this preliminary work will soon be followed by better treatises. Here, a grateful acknowledgement is due to Dr. William Holland, Secretary General of the Institute of Pacific Relations, N.Y., and Dr. A. Appadorai, Director of the Indian School of International Studies, Delhi University, without whose encouragement this publication would not have been possible.

New Delhi CHAO KUO-CHUN
January, 1960

ACKNOWLEDGEMENTS

THE author gratefully acknowledges the permission to quote at length certain paragraphs from the following books:

Jack Belden, *China Shakes the World*, Harper & Brothers, N.Y.
Harrison Forman, *Report from Red China*, Willis Kindsley Wing, N.Y.
Theodore White and Annalee Jacoby, *Thunder Out of China*, William Sloane Associates, Inc., N.Y.

The author is also grateful for the permission to quote in this volume portions of his previous publications, with or without modifications, which appear in the following sources:

I. *Agricultural History*: 1. "Organized Leadership and Agricultural Technology in Modern China," No. 32, 1958, pp. 25–31.
II. *American Political Science Review* : 2. "Mass Organization in Mainland China," 48·3, Sept. 1954, pp. 752–65.
III. *The Annals of the American Academy of Political & Social Science* : 3. "Current Agrarian Reform Policies in Communist China," Vol. 277, Sept. 1951, pp. 113–23.
4. "Patterns of Leadership of Communist Party in China," January 1959, pp. 40–51.
IV. Center for International Studies, M.I.T. 5. *Northeast China (Manchuria) Today*, Harvard, March 1953, 131 pp.
6. *Mass Organizations in Mainland China*, Nov. 1953, 157 pp.
V. *Contemporary China* : 7. "Production and Productivity of Major Crops in China," Hong Kong Univ., August 1958, pp. 11–35.
8. "Significance and Problems of the People's Communes," Hong Kong Univ., Spring 1960.
VI. *Current History* : 9. "Chinese Land Policies," 24·142, June 1953, pp. 339–50.
10. "How Communism Works in China," 27·159, Nov. 1954, pp. 275–82.
11. "Agriculture in Mainland China," 23·185, Jan. 1957, pp. 33–42.
12. "China: United States Dilemma," Dec. 1957, pp. 332–8.
13. "Agricultural Development and Problems in China," December 1958, pp. 342–52.
14. "Sino-Indian Relations," 37·220, December 1959, pp. 354-61.
VII. *Economic Weekly*, Bombay: 15. "Agrarian Development in China," June 20, 1959, pp. 811–16.
VIII. *Encyclopaedia Britannica* : 16. "Northeast China (Manchuria)," 1960.

IX. *Far Eastern Economic Review*: 17. "Agrarian Development in China,1949–59," Hong Kong, October 1959, pp. 528–30.

X. *Far Eastern Survey*: 18. "The Government and Economy of Manchuria," 22·13, Dec. 1953, pp. 169–75; and 23·1, Jan. 1954, pp. 9–14.
19. "The 1954 National Constitution of Mainland China," 23·10, Oct. 1954, pp. 145–51.
20. "Agriculture in Mainland China," 23·185, Jan. 1957, pp. 24–31.

XI. *Foreign Affairs*: 21. "How Political Power Is Organized in China," 34·1, Oct. 1955, pp. 148–53.

XII. Harvard University, Center for Asian Studies: 22. *Agrarian Policies of Mainland China, A Documentary Study 1949–57*, Harvard Univ. Press, 1957, 276 pp.
23. *Economic Planning and Organization in Mainland China, 1949–57*, 2 volumes, Harvard Univ. Press, 1959 and 1960, *circa* 500 pp.
24. "Land Reform Methods of the Chinese Communists," *Papers on China*, Regional Studies Programme on East Asia, Vol. 5, May 1951, pp. 109–73.

XIII. *Indian Journal of International Studies*: 25. "Techniques of Economic Planning and Organization in China," New Delhi, 1960.

XIV. *Indian Political Science Journal*: 26. "Some Problems in Sino-American Relations," April-June 1959, pp. 97–113.

XV. *India Quarterly*: 27. "Current Agrarian Programmes and Problems in China," New Delhi, 12·1, Jan.-March 1956, pp. 31–53.
28. "Agricultural Development and Problems in China Today," 19·1, Jan.-March 1958, pp. 1–49.

XVI. *The Nation*: 29. "China's Tunnel to Formosa," Aug. 3, 1957, pp. 12–14.

XVII. *The New Republic*: 30. "How Peking Reaches So Many," May 12, 1957, pp. 19–21.

XVIII. *Nippon Gaisei Gaikkai*, Tokyo. 31. *Foreign Affairs Quarterly of Japan*, May 20, 1957.
32. "Agricultural Development in China," May 20, 1957.

XIX. *Nuovi Argomenti*, Rome. 33. "The Communes and the Chinese Agriculture," Sept.-October, 1959, pp. 113–38.

XX. *United Asia*, Bombay. 34. "Labour and Labour Organization in China," July 1960.

CONTENTS

Foreword by Prof. K. N. Raj v
Author's Preface vii

I. INTRODUCTION 1
A. Organizational Leadership in the Political Sphere 6
B. Organizational Leadership in the Economic Sphere 8
C. Organizational Leadership in the Social Sphere 10

II. HISTORICAL SURVEY OF THE CHINESE COMMUNIST LAND POLICY, 1921–49 14
A. The Pre-Soviet Period, 1921–27 14
B. The Soviet Period, 1927–37 17
C. The Sino-Japanese War Period, 1937–45 38
D. The Post-War Transitional Period, 1945–49 74

III. THE LAND REFORM (LAND REDISTRIBUTION) PROGRAMME, 1950–53 94
A. The General Principles in the Land Reform Movement 94
B. Major Programmes and Results 97
C. Organization and Administration in Land Reform 102
D. The Party's Role in Land Reform 113
E. General Pattern of Procedure in the Land Redistribution Movement 117
F. Perpetuating Devices of the Chinese Communists in the Land Reform 124
G. Mass Media Employed in the Land Reform 130
H. Sociological and Psychological Factors in the Land Redistribution Movement 137

IV. CURRENT AGRARIAN POLICY, 1953–59 147
A. Overall Principles 147
B. Organized Farming 150
C. The People's Communes 161
D. Crop Production and Productivity 173
E. Agro-Technical Programmes 176
F. Other Agro-Technical Programmes 190
G. Programmes on Rural Finance and Market Control 196
H. Collection and Distribution of Agricultural Products 219
I. Rural Organization and Administration 231
J. Social and Cultural Programmes in Rural China 236

V. AN EVALUATION OF THE CCP AGRARIAN POLICY 241
A. Major Characteristics of the CCP Agrarian Policy 241
B. Significant Aspects in the Current Agrarian Development 251
C. Salient Problems in Rural China 255

VI. CONCLUDING COMMENTS 282

TABLES (I to XI) 291

APPENDIX I: NPC, MODEL REGULATIONS FOR ADVANCED AGRICULTURAL PRODUCERS' CO-OPERATIVES, JUNE 30, 1956 311

APPENDIX II: CC, CCP, REVISED DRAFT PROGRAMME ON AGRICULTURAL DEVELOPMENT IN THE NATION 1956–67, OCTOBER 25, 1957 328

APPENDIX III: RESOLUTION ON SOME QUESTIONS CONCERNING THE PEOPLE'S COMMUNES, DECEMBER 10, 1958 344

APPENDIX IV: GOVERNMENT OF CHINA, FAST PROGRESS IN WATER CONSERVANCY IN CHINA, JANUARY 1960 363

APPENDIX V: JMJP, PRESS COMMUNIQUE ON THE PROGRESS OF CHINA'S NATIONAL ECONOMY IN 1959, JANUARY 22, 1960 365

Selected Bibliography 378

Index 391

NOTE

A key to the abbreviations used in this book and a table of Chinese units of measure and weight, with their Western equivalents, is given on pp. 373 and 376.

CHAPTER I

INTRODUCTION

THE IMPORTANCE of the agrarian problem in China is clearly manifested by the fact that more than 80 per cent of some 650 million Chinese reside in rural areas[1] and an estimated 33·43 per cent of the total value of industrial and agricultural output (or about 31·34 billion out of 93·75 billion US dollars) in 1959 would be derived, according to Peking sources, from agricultural and subsidiary rural products.[2]

Throughout the 2,500 years or more of recorded history of China, the significance of agriculture has been recognized. The major theme contained in a petition by Chao Ts'o (died 155 B.C.), a scholar and statesman of the Han Dynasty, was the supremacy of the peasantry over the merchant class. This was not disputed by the Chinese, even after the Western-style entrepreneur class came into existence in modern China. In the Chinese traditional division of social classes, peasants are next only to the *literati* and above the artisans and merchants. The two major political forces upon which the dynasties of the past twenty-five centuries were built were the gentry-*literati* who ruled for the emperors, and the peasants who were the chief source of taxes, *corvée*, and army recruits. However, while agriculture as such had a key place in Chinese life, the peasants, as a rule, were overtaxed, underprivileged, and overworked, and farming in modern China, by modern standards, was both backward and stagnant. It never broke out of the traditional framework. This was so in spite of the fact that chemical fertilizer was introduced in China as early as 1905. Many other modern farming techniques and tools were then known or available. But the general level of

[1] The 1953 population census of China made public in June 1954 gives the figure 582,603,417 as the number of people on the Chinese mainland as of June 30, 1953. The rate of population growth is estimated at 2·2 per cent per annum.

[2] Li Fu-Ch'un, "Report on the Draft Economic Plan for 1959," *HPYK*, No. 9, May 10, 1959, p. 15; and Chou En-lai, "A Great Decade," *HPYK*, No. 19, October 12, 1959, pp. 10-18. It was 58·5 per cent in 1952, 43·46 per cent in 1957 and 36·4 per cent in 1958—in monetary terms, in billion US dollars, 20·55, 25·62 and 28·50 respectively. The official exchange rate is 2·355 *yuan* to one US dollar.

agricultural technology in China three decades after 1905 remained very low. In farm implements, for example, Professor Ch'iao Ch'i-ming of Nanking University writing in 1944 described the 43 basic farm tools used by the Chinese peasants as "undeniably primitive" and remarked that "the agricultural technique in China has had little significant change since the T'ang Dynasty."[3] Rural studies conducted in the 1930's by Chinese and Western agronomists revealed the following facts: Through plant diseases and natural disasters, China lost each year about ¼ of a million tons of cotton or 30 per cent of the total annual production, and some 12 million tons of cereals, or more than 8 per cent of the average pre-war annual grain produce. An estimated 12 to 15 per cent of the cattle and water buffalo, 20 to 25 per cent of the hogs, and 30 per cent of the poultry died of infectious diseases each year in pre-war China.[4] Other technical deficiencies in Chinese agriculture included: inadequate soil conservation, absence of an extensive afforestation programme, defective storage and marketing facilities, ineffective flood control, and inadequate research and education on farming techniques.

To point out the low level of agro-technology in modern China is not to deny the achievements of the Chinese peasantry in many aspects of farm work. But the more significant facts were the lack of noticeable progress in agricultural technology, the higher yields of many crops in other countries, and the much greater agricultural productivity that could have been achieved through the adoption of modern farming techniques and other reforms. For example, in the period from 1929 to 1933, the average yield of rice in China was only 60 per cent of Italy's, that of wheat 48 per cent of Japan's, and that of potatoes 40 per cent of Great Britain's.[5] As to the labour efficiency of Chinese cultivators, which is another yardstick in measuring technical progress, it was estimated that in the 1930's one adult male working one year on a Chinese farm produced an average of 3,080 lbs. of grain, while his American

[3] Ch'iao Ch'i-ming, *Chung-kuo nung-ts'un she-hui ching-chi hsueh* (Socio-Economic Studies of Rural China), Commercial Press, Shanghai, 1946, p. 324.

[4] Data quoted from T. H. Shen, *Agricultural Resources in China*, 1951, pp. 64, 65, and 312; and Wu Fu-cheng, "Insect Pest Control in China," *Chung-nung yueh-k'an* (Monthly of the Farmers' Bank of China), Vol. 5, No. 4, April 30, 1944, pp. 92–102.

[5] Quoted in K'ai-ming Ch'iu's "Agriculture", *China*, MacNair, ed., 1946, p.471.

counterpart was producing 44,000 pounds, or 14 times as much.[6]

The agrarian problem in China has been an extremely complex one, with important political, social, and psychological, as well as economic and agro-technical aspects. Many of the difficulties have their roots in the traditional institutions of China and have been further aggravated by the political, social and economic dislocation and breakdown of the past hundred years.

A key factor in traditional Chinese society affecting agriculture was the dominant position of the landed gentry. This exploitative class controlled the rural administrative structure, played a decisive economic role in the countryside,[7] and had an intimate, interlocking relationship with the official *literati* class responsible for the work of government in China.

At the local level, the gentry, whose bastions were generally the traditional towns, often avoided serving as village administrative heads, partly because it was regarded as "beneath their dignity," but actually in order to avoid bureaucratic responsibility. But there was no question as to who was the real power behind the throne, for the local officials, be they small landlords, ruffians, or simple peasants, could accomplish hardly anything without the active cooperation, or at least acquiescence, of the landed gentry.

The dominance of the gentry class was further fortified by its multiple role as a leader in the clan organization, an important function of which was the management of the land rights of the kinship group. While the point of contact with the peasants might have been the pawn shops or the rice shops or money-lending agencies, further investigation usually revealed the gentry at the bottom of all these. Thus the landed gentry, together with the

[6] Gerald Winfield, "This Is China," *New York Times Magazine*, January 9, 1949, pp. 9–10.

[7] One Chinese sociologist, after field studies, wrote :

"Each member of the gentry invariably has a great amount of property. As a rule, the gentry and landlords are indistinguishable. The larger his landholding, the more powerful a gentry member becomes. Although not all the landlords belong to the gentry class, every member of the gentry is a landlord, and a big landlord." (See, Shih Chih, "The Nature of Gentry Power," in Wu Han and Fei Hsiao-tung, *Imperial Power and Gentry Power*, in Chinese, p. 158.) Another sociologist, Hu Chin-chun in an article entitled, "On the Gentry Power," states that the "Economic foundation of the gentry can only be understood by their role as landlords; most of the gentry members are landlords." Wu & Fei, p. 122.

merchants (often under the financial domination of the first group), controlled and manipulated the economic life of the peasants through rent, usurious money-lending, and the commodity markets of agricultural products and daily necessities.

Due to the combination of political and economic factors, the past half-century witnessed a gradual decline of direct gentry control in the countryside and the development instead of absentee landlordism, as the upper gentry in particular gravitated to the treaty ports and other urban centres and lived on the rent and interests of its agricultural investments. This trend was further accentuated in recent decades by the rush of merchants, bureaucrats, and militarists to buy land, thus adding both to the concentration of land ownership and to the prevalence of absentee landlordism. Land ownership was increasingly looked upon as merely an extremely profitable economic undertaking, with little personal feeling or interest in either the tenants or the land. There was also a curtailment of the gentry's on-the-spot interest in agricultural activities and improvements, and of the minor economic functions this group had performed in the countryside. As a result, the condition of the peasantry deteriorated further.

Another important factor in the decline of Chinese rural economy during the past century has been the disintegration of many handicrafts and household industries through which the peasantry supplemented its income. Here, the influx of foreign manufactured goods, aggravated by imperialistic restrictions on the Chinese tariff, and the development of western technology in the urban centres, severely undermined such rural industries.

While the figures vary, non-communist sources have estimated the percentage of full-time or part-time tenancy in pre-1949 China as ranging from 50 to 65 per cent.[8] There is also evidence of increasing land concentration during and since the Sino-Japanese war. The prevalence of tenancy had a serious effect on China's traditional rural economy.[9] Exorbitant rents, as well as numerous other burdens imposed on the tenants, greatly impeded any accumulation of savings for farm investment or improvement. In addition to these rents and other burdens, there were the agricultural taxes of the local and central governments which, with the gentry politically

[8] See T. H. Shen, *op. cit.*, p. 96.

[9] See Ch'en Po-ta, *A Study of Land Rent in Pre-Liberation China*, Foreign Language Press, Peking, 1958, p. 101.

powerful, tended to press most heavily on the overburdened peasantry. Aside from the regular land tax, which in pre-war times amounted to from five to ten per cent of the value of the annual crop yield, there were numerous surtaxes, both legal and illegal, collected by civil and military authorities. These surtaxes often amounted to many times the regular tax. It was also the practice frequently for local military authorities to "borrow" future taxes in advance.

As a result of these pressures, most of the Chinese peasants fell into debt. Dr. Lossing Buck's survey reported that 40 per cent of the farm families he investigated were in debt. Two later Nationalist government surveys, one in 1933 and the other in 1943, found that 62 to 63 per cent of the peasant families interrogated reported being in debt.[10] Worse still, most of these loans were contracted at usurious rates and not utilized for productive purposes in farming.

Superstitious beliefs and practices, such as the worship of spirits and idols, the complete resignation to fate, blind following of witch doctors, fortune-tellers and ignorant midwives, membership in mystic and secret cults and societies, and frequent sacrifices to temples or idols also seriously impeded the development of the Chinese rural economy. A field study made in a Yunnan village in 1939 revealed that one household spent about one-third of its annual income for "general good fortune," while a similar amount was spent by another family for rituals for "long life."[11] Added to the list are the elaborate and costly ceremonies, banquets and feasts given on numerous occasions like births, weddings and deaths, motivated by such concepts as ancestral worship and "face." Buck reported that "a wedding costs four months' family income and exceeds the yearly income of a hired farm labourer. Funerals cost three months' family income and dowries nearly three months' income."[12] To all this may be added the harmful effects and cost of such habits as opium smoking and gambling which prevailed in many districts, with the former more frequently found in the interior of the country.

[10] In viewing these figures, it must be remembered that Chinese peasants are generally reluctant to report their true financial predicament to "investigators" from outside the district.

[11] Fei Hsiao-tung, *Earthbound China,* pp. 101–2, 249.

[12] J. L. Buck, *op. cit.*, p. 19; also Fei's *Earthbound China,* pp. 248–9, 256, 262.

Deficiencies in the agro-technical field, too, contributed enormously to China's agricultural problem. Such things as soil conservancy, adequate irrigation, afforestation, hydraulic power, mechanization of farming, improved transportation and tools, are all essential to improving agriculture in China. It must be remembered, however, that the solution of these technical problems, and also the provision of adequate credit and marketing facilities, are linked closely with such political and economic problems as effective and honest administration, industrialization, mass education, etc.

The above has discussed briefly the conditions of stagnation in the rural economy of China prior to the establishment of the Central People's Government on October 1, 1949. However, one can still raise the question why these handicaps could not be reduced or overcome as they were in modern Japan after the Meiji period. In a number of ways, Japan was faced with greater difficulties in the nineteenth century than China was, with her poorer resources and a more rigid social system. There are, of course, many possible explanations on the question why China did not take the path of modernization as Meiji Japan did. But the most decisive single factor, in the opinion of the author, lies in organizational leadership. This is a key to the understanding of modern China's rural as well as general economic stagnation, and calls for greater elaboration. Some observations on this question may be presented under the following headings:

A. *Organizational Leadership in the Political Sphere*

The first major political impediment to agricultural progress in modern China was the absence of an efficient administration, both at the national and local levels. This factor is generally recognized, but its full implications are often underestimated in the West where effective control of the government over its territory has been taken for granted. In modern China where there was a high illiteracy rate, meagre private capital, underdeveloped village self-government, and strong traditional values, the government's role was doubly important in initiating and developing basic changes in agriculture. However, during the crucial 100 years preceding the Second World War, the impotence and political myopia of the leadership in China, not only resulted in the lack of positive reforms in agriculture, but it also entailed frequent disturbances, both external and internal, which further reduced the capital as well as the incentive of the peasants for improving farming techniques. It was estimated that between 1842 and 1911, China made indemnity payments 110 times as a result of various imperialist aggressions. While the total national receipts in 1900 were about 90 million taels, the Ch'ing government had to pay 200 million taels to Japan as indemnities from 1895 to 1900. Between 1914 and 1918, more than 477 civil hostilities were waged in China. The expenditure of warlords in Szechuan Province in 1930 was about four times the amount budgeted for hydraulic engineering for the entire nation.[13]

Other by-products of weak government were unprincipled local officials, ineffective rural programmes, and inadequate agricultural research and technical education. A few specific cases will illustrate the impact of political leadership on agriculture. In the 1930's, under the sponsorship of the National Economic Council, a canal of some 30 miles was dug near Ningsu in Inner Mongolia, which opened up 13,000 acres of cultivable land. Immediately, high military and government officials moved in and divided up the newly reclaimed area. At about the same time in the Yunting Canal region in Ninghsia Province, less than one per cent of the irrigated land came under cultivation because peasants were driven away by exorbitant taxes.[14]

Peasants in modern China often had to endure many times a year destructive wars and banditry, in the course of which crops and much property, particularly draught animals, were lost. It was reported that during a civil war in 1929, in a single county of Shensi more than 500 animal-drawn carts were commandeered.[15] Young men were impressed into the army or into labour gangs and onerous military requisitions were imposed. For example, during the seven months from April to October 1930, the average burden of military requisitions in each district of the fighting area in eastern Honan was 40 times higher than the regular land tax.[16] And it was a notorious fact that in the twenties peasants in Szechuan Province had to pay land taxes more than half a century in advance.

[13] T'ang Hsiang-lung, "How the Indemnities Were Paid Before 1911," *Collected Works on Economic History of Modern China* (Chinese), 3.2, November 1935, pp. 262–91; and the *Chinese Yearbook*, 1936–37, p. 1376.

[14] *Agrarian China*, I.P.R., 1939, pp. 31–6.

[15] Feng Ho-fa, *op. cit.*, p. 149.

[16] "Military Requisitions and Peasantry," *Agrarian China, op. cit.*, pp. 101–9.

Another important factor was that the programmes in modern China which aimed at improving rural economy lacked practical leadership. The planners and executives of these projects, being mostly urbanites, often lacked understanding or experience regarding the specific needs, capacities, apprehensions and aspirations of the villagers. Some failures were due to an indiscriminate attempt to apply Western farming methods to Chinese agriculture, irrespective of cost or local conditions. Many practical approaches, like grass-root contacts, public participation, technical demonstrations, and utilization of traditional values and symbols, which are essential in bio-technical programmes for agriculture, were often ignored. Also as a result of organizational deficiency, much useful farm knowledge and skill developed by the scientists and Chinese farmers were not properly utilized or popularized. For instance, after a decade of research, Dr. Claude Heman Barlow, a missionary who came to China before the First World War, discovered the flukeworm which constituted a major threat to the peasants' health in Chekiang. He had pursued his research even when on furlough; he swallowed 35 live but sterilized flukeworms in order to continue his study at Johns Hopkins. In 1925, Dr. Barlow published a detailed report, suggesting a number of inexpensive and simple steps for coping with the parasite. But in the generation following no concerted effort toward controlling the disease had yet been made.[17]

B. *Organizational Leadership in the Economic Sphere*

Some of the major organizational aspects of the agrarian economy of modern China which hindered agricultural development were related to the land system. The tiny Chinese farm, averaging 3·31 acres in the 30's, as compared to America's 157 acres, was further split into an average of 5·6 parcels.[18] Such small farms often made the adoption of modern agricultural techniques impractical, both because of the physical limitations and the weak financial position of such minute holdings. One American agronomist wrote that "the agricultural production and wealth per capita of China could be increased from 60 to 240 per cent if, by some magic, the average size of all Chinese farms could be raised to 13 acres.[19] The amount

[17] G. Winfield, *op. cit.*, p. 123.
[18] J. L. Buck, *Land Utilization in China*, p. 267.
[19] G. Winfield, *op. cit.*, p. 279.

of per capita farmland in modern China could not be increased overnight, but operational methods, such as cooperative farming, could have been promoted through organized leadership. Another obstacle in the land system of modern China which prevailed among more than one-third of the peasant population was the tenurial practice. The rent, which took away half or more of the principal crops, the insecurity of tenancy, the numerous services and tributes exacted from the tenants by the landlords and their agents, absentee landlordism, etc. all helped to reduce the tenants' incentive to improve farming techniques as well as their capacity to invest. One Chinese expert pointed out that one of the three major factors which discouraged a departure from the one-crop system in many areas in China was "a tenancy system that generally requires the payment of land rent in rice."[20] The absence of effective tenurial reform in modern China, and the often irrational use of rents collected, were again due more to the lack of organized leadership.

The damaging effect of modern China's agricultural system on the developing of farming technology resulted not only from the abusive nature of the taxes, but also from their bad administration. For instance, in the late 1920's in Kiangsu province, two surtaxes were collected: one under the heading of "irrigation" and another under that of "road building." The undesirability of this lay not in the fact that these taxes were imposed, but in the fact that no dam or road was ever built. Moreover these taxes were levied in spite of crop failures. Another report revealed that during the 1920's in the provinces where opium cultivation was legal, peasants who wanted to shift from poppy-growing to crops, due to a decline in opium prices, were forced to pay a fine equivalent to the amount levied on the opium poppy field; this fine was labelled "the lazy-bones tax!"[21]

Rural economic retardation in the agriculture of modern China also came from defective land management and utilization. Thus many hilly acres would have been more profitably used for grazing or forest land than for cultivation. This resulted in the eventual damage to the low lands. A survey made in 1935 showed that one type of plough and a toothed harrow were both used on the Yangtze plains for similar work, but the former was 5 times as efficient, and operated at half the cost per acre.[22] Even such basic things as

[20] T. H. Shen, *op. cit.*, p. 150.

[21] Ch'en Kung-lu, *History of Modern China* (Chinese), 1935, p. 809.

[22] Ch'ao Ch'i-ming, *op. cit.*, pp. 226, 338.

measures and weights were usually not standardized within a rural area, and no data on agricultural conditions were collected extensively and consistently.

A number of other organizations, if developed under efficient leadership, would help to develop agriculture in modern China. These include credit and marketing cooperatives, village extension systems, cottage and handicraft industries, and training in agricultural technique. On the other hand, with a defective organizational framework, even increased agricultural production through technical reforms could paradoxically result in low income to the peasants. This was amply demonstrated in China in 1932 when peasants in Eastern China suffered heavily because of bumper crops which precipitated a 40 per cent drop of the rice price, while in other areas there was a shortage of foodstuffs.

C. *Organizational Leadership in the Social Sphere*

In rural modern China, the locus of power lay, either directly or indirectly, in the landed gentry as previously pointed out. Often its members regarded themselves as the jealous guardians of tradition and were suspicious of new ideas and methods, including technical ones.[23] The kinship and familial organization in rural China also in some ways obstructed important changes in farming, because the patriarchal heads who had the undisputed authority over the more enterprising youth were in general conservative and unenthusiastic toward new farming experiments. Even the school system served, in some ways, as a hindrance to technical improvements in agriculture. Frequently both the teacher and the curriculum were symbols of archaism. Little modern farming knowledge or skill were introduced to the peasant boys. Neither was dietary or sanitary information disseminated. For example, in the *Yu-hsüeh chun-lin* or the Gem Primer, the chapter entitled "Techniques" concludes with this statement from Confucius' *Analects*: "Although these minor skills have some functions, they are useless for weighty tasks, and should not be taken up by a gentleman."

The traditional Chinese village structure also contained a number of backward and pernicious features. The unfavourable effect on progress in agriculture of such magico-religious elements as the temples, fortune tellers, and witch doctors was quite serious as

[23] See Fei Hsiao-tung, *China's Gentry*, 1953, p. 287.

previously discussed. When there was either drought or flood, many peasants went to the temples to appease the "Dragon King," instead of taking preventive or remedial measures. When insect pests became inordinately destructive, farmers burned incense at the temple of "Great Deity Chang" or, as in some Kiangsu villages, beat up a "bewitching woman." The gambling houses and opium dens indirectly contributed their share to the retardation of important improvement in agriculture. The elimination of wasteful ceremonial expenses alone might save from 5 to 7 per cent of the farmers' budget for agricultural investment.[24]

It is not the author's intention here to minimize the importance of what we might call the non-organizational factors which contributed to the stagnation of rural economy in modern China. It is also true that many organizational and non-organizational factors were closely interrelated and interacted as cause and effect. But in his opinion, in the case of an underdeveloped country like modern China, it would be more practical and more effective to assign priority to organizational leadership in breaking many vicious circles which retarded agricultural development. A few illustrations will help to elucidate this point.

Take, for example, the view that lack of capital by the rural populace of modern China with which to finance farm improvements was the primary factor which resulted in one of the vicious circles in Chinese farming. But how could there be any sizable accumulation of capital by the agricultural sector in modern China when warlords, bandits, landlords, and unscrupulous officials not only squeezed the peasants dry of surplus but kept most of them in perpetual indebtedness? Besides, with a progressive political and social leadership, many technical improvements such as conservation, reclamation, afforestation, better use of local fertilizing materials, more effective farm organization and greater farmland utilization would require little capital investment. Japan, during the same 100 years between the 1840's and 1940's, achieved far-reaching progress in farming technology by effective institutional reforms and by relying mainly on domestic resources in accumulating capital. Another concrete example is present-day India. Since her

[24] For details see Feng Ho-fa, *op. cit.*, pp. 51–6 ; Lossing Buck, *op. cit.*, pp. 468–70. Buck reported the average expenditure for funerals, CN$102, for weddings CN$127, birthdays CN$63, dowries CN$96, while the average annual income of the farm family investigated was CN$400.

independence in 1947 which made possible a popular national leadership, the result of her effort to improve agriculture has been reflected in the abolition of the zamindari system and a 38 per cent increase in foodgrain production between 1950–51 and 1958–59 (from about 53 million tons to 73 million tons), as contrasted with the stagnant conditions during the some 150 years of British rule.

For another example, take the vicious circle between the often apathetic attitude of the Chinese peasants and the stagnation in agriculture. The attitude of resignation to fate and the feeling of despair of many Chinese peasants were not inborn characteristics, but a reaction to bitter lessons of disappointment learned through many, many generations. How could the villagers of modern China be expected to harbour a strong desire for and confidence in general improvement when year after year they were frustrated by a political and social system that robbed them of the fruit of their hard labour ? The few improvements which the peasants did make in farming were not given proper recognition by the administration. As to the theory that the Chinese peasants were not attracted by material betterment or technical change because they preferred the contentment of philosophers, such an idealized picture was not supported by hard facts. Like the policeman in Gilbert and Sullivan's *Pirates of Penzance*, the Chinese peasants' lot was not a happy one.

Lastly, an issue which is often made the primary factor in tackling any basic problem of China, namely, over-population may be briefly touched on; it will be discussed more fully in a later chapter. It is true that population pressure which aggravated the under-employment and unemployment situation in rural China made some technical improvements like mechanization unprofitable. However, many agricultural programmes such as the use of better seeds and other labour-intensive projects like conservation, irrigation, afforestation, reclamation, etc. do not displace human labour. Even with respect to farm tools, it is unlikely that most Chinese peasants were aware of the population factor and deliberately refrained from adopting better equipment which would increase production and lighten their physical burden. Again, modern Japan offers a classic example which demonstrates that population growth is not an insurmountable barrier in developing agricultural technology. This, of course, assumes that with effective organizational leadership, steps will simultaneously be taken to develop secondary and tertiary occupations to siphon off the surplus working force in rural areas as well as to supply equipment to farmers.

Thus, it may be said that "organizational leadership" should be the key in analyzing the primary causes of stagnation in modern China, of agricultural development in particular, and of the rural economy in general. China was mercilessly exploited by the imperialist powers in the century following the Opium War (1840-42), but the Chinese leaders who made policy decisions, must bear the major responsibility for failing to achieve a renaissance during the century preceding the establishment of the Peking government in October 1949. And the following chapters on the CCP's agrarian programmes will serve to illustrate how decisive effective organization and leadership could be in working out ways to cope with China's complex agrarian problems and in effecting a break-through in a stagnant, backward rural economy.

CHAPTER II

HISTORICAL SURVEY OF THE CHINESE COMMUNIST LAND POLICY, 1921-1949

It is often arbitrary to divide history into stages, especially in times when tremendous socio-economic changes are involved. Yet to illustrate the major periods in the Chinese Communist Party's agrarian theory and programme, as well as to clarify the discussion, the development of the Chinese Communist land policy between 1921 and June 1950, when the Agrarian Reform Law was promulgated, is discussed here in four periods: the pre-Soviet period, 1921–1927; the Soviet period, 1927–1937; the Sino-Japanese war period, 1937–1945; and the post-war transitional period, 1945–1949. Except in the case of the first period, when the CCP had no territory under its control in which to carry out its agrarian theory and programmes, each period will be discussed from the viewpoint of the following five topical headings: (1) Party theory; (2) legislation and programmes; (3) organization and administration; (4) results and effects; and (5) general comments.

A. *The Pre-Soviet Period, 1921–1927*

Until Mao Tse-tung put his theory of agrarian revolution into practice by setting up a Soviet at Ch'a-lin, Hunan, in November 1927, the role of the peasantry in the Chinese revolution was considered subsidiary by the hierarchy of the CCP. From its formal organization on July 1, 1921, the party was under the patriarchal leadership of Ch'en Tu-hsiu, who was an academic Marxist. Ch'en Tu-hsiu maintained that:

> The Communist social revolution easily contradicts the interests of the peasants and even the landless tenants....Only when the rural proletariat starts organizing itself, then will a social revolution be possible in the Chinese rural areas.[1]

[1] Quoted by Ch'u Ch'iu-pai, "On Peasantry", *Controversial Problems in the Chinese Revolution*, in Chinese (Hoover Library), 1927, pp. 138–9.

One finds a few radical slogans in some of the resolutions between the First National Congress of the CCP in July 1921 and the Fifth National Congress in May 1927, such as the "abolition of private property,"[2] and "nationalization of land as a basic principle of the Party's agrarian programme."[3] But there were not many concrete measures for land reform beyond calling for "restriction of rent and taxation on land." The *Resolution of the First National Congress* in July, 1921, mentioned nothing about land policy. The *First Manifesto of the Current Situation* issued by the CCP on June 10, 1922, called for reduced taxes on land. The Resolution of the *Second National Congress*, in July, 1922, contained one brief section calling for the "passing of legislation limiting land rent." In the *Resolution of the Third National Congress* passed in June, 1922, there was not much about an agrarian programme. In the *Fourth Manifesto on the Current Situation* proclaimed in January, 1925, it was suggested that "a top limit should be placed on all forms of taxation . . . and an equilibrium should be established between the price of farm products and the price of those manufactured goods which are daily necessities." The enlarged session of the Central Committee of the CCP in July, 1926, resolved that "class struggle in the rural areas should not be encouraged in order to prevent a premature cleavage (with the bourgeoisie)." Thus the circular letter issued by the August 7 (1927) Emergency Conference, one of the key documents in the annals of the CCP, stated:

> Before the Fifth National Congress, the Party's leading organ paid only the least attention possible to the agrarian problem. At the Special Conference at Hankow in December, 1926, which was an important conference convened to decide the tasks of the Party after the victory of the Northern Expedition (1926–1927), not a single word was mentioned on the stand to be adopted by the Party *vis-a-vis* the agrarian problem. . . . At the Fifth National Congress of the Party (May, 1927), a resolution on the peasant question was passed but the Party leaders, like Ch'en Tu-hsiu and T'an P'ing-shan, stated that "the task of the moment was to

[2] *Manifesto of the Second National Congress*, July, 1922. The English versions of this manifesto, as well as the Resolutions and Manifestos of later Congresses of the CCP can be found in *DH*, pp. 51–164.

[3] *Resolution of the Fifth National Congress*, May 1927. English version also available in *DH*, pp. 93–7.

extend but not to deepen the revolution, and that consequently land confiscation must be postponed until some future date."[4]

Even after Chiang Kai-shek staged his treacherous *coup d'état* on April 12, 1927, the CCP hierarchy under the influence of T'an P'ing-shan continued its compromising agrarian platform in order to subordinate the peasant movement to the exigencies of retaining its coalition with left-Kuomintang elements. We have the word of no less an authority than Mao Tse-tung that the Fifth National Congress "failed to pass an adequate land programme."[5] In an attempt to woo the land-owning army officers, T'an maintained that all land belonging to officers of the army (under the leftwing Kuomintang-dominated Wuhan Government) should not be subject to confiscation. This, in effect, made the confiscation programme ineffective as the landlords frequently claimed some family relationship with army officers. Although a policy of confiscating large estates was adopted by the Fifth National Congress, the term "large estate" was defined as one exceeding 500 *mou* and not many landlords belonged to this category. As a matter of fact, when T'an P'ing-shan, one of the three CCP members serving as ministers in the Wuhan Government, resigned in July, 1927, after four months in office, he said that he "deeply regretted his inability to set the peasant movement right from excessive demands and illegal deeds."[6]

The August 7 (1927) Emergency Conference elected Ch'u Ch'iu-pai as Secretary General of the Communist Party to replace Ch'en Tu-hsiu, whose policy was condemned as "opportunist." The political pendulum then swung sharply to the left. The Conference resolved that "agrarian revolution is the crux of the bourgeois democratic revolution in China" and adopted the following programme regarding agrarian policy: abolition of rental payment to the landlord; redistribution of land; confiscation of the holdings of big and middle bureaucrats; cancellation of usurious debts of the poor peasants; prohibition of exploitative contracts; drastic reduction in taxation; and the shifting of the burden of taxes to the rich. But the new party leadership under Ch'u Ch'iu-pai and Li Li-san,

[4] English text in *DH, op. cit.*, p. 110.

[5] Edgar Snow, *Red Star Over China*, Modern Library, p. 162.

[6] Hu Hua, ed., *Source Materials* [from the study] *of the History of China's New Democratic Revolution* (in Chinese), Shanghai, 1951, p. 217. Also *DH, op. cit.*, p. 115.

devoid of experience in the peasant movement, had no understanding of mobile peasant partisan warfare. When Mao Tse-tung, despatched by the reorganized Political Bureau in the autumn of 1927 to organize the Autumn Harvest Insurrection, advocated the formation of an army of workers and peasants and the establishment of Soviets, his proposals were at first turned down by the Central Committee. Mao was reportedly reprimanded by the Central Committee for not carrying out a policy "to crush the spirit of resistance of the reactionaries." In a directive issued by the Central Committee in November, 1927, he was removed temporarily from his post as an alternate member of the Political Bureau as well as from his position as Commissar of the Front Committee. However, the August 7 Conference, by resolving to stress the role of the agrarian revolution and by sending Mao Tse-tung to organize the peasant uprising in the autumn of 1927, played an important part in bringing about the next stage of development in the CCP's land policy—the Soviet period.

B. *The Soviet Period, 1927–1937*

This period began formally with Mao Tse-tung's setting up of a local Soviet at Ch'a-lin, Hunan, in November, 1927. Ever since he had become the Secretary of the Hunan Province Executive Committee of the CCP on October 10, 1922, Mao had engaged in organizing peasants in his native province of Hunan and had written a number of articles expounding his views on the significance of agrarian revolution in the Chinese Communist movement.[7] The establishment of Soviets in Hunan and Kiangsi, and the formation of the Soviet Republic, in November, 1931, gave Mao and his lieutenants an opportunity to experiment with their theories and programmes. It is an important period because many of the CCP's later land programmes were formulated and tested at this time.

The Central Soviet in Kiangsi was terminated when the main Communist forces evacuated their bases in Kiangsi, Hunan and

[7] In the *Report on an Investigation of the Peasant Movement in Hunan*, February, 1927, one of the earliest works of Mao available, the membership of Peasants' associations in Hunan was reported to be two million. An English translation of the Report is available in *DH*, pp. 80–89, and another official version was issued by the Foreign Language Press in Peking in September, 1953.

Fukien, and started their "Long March" in October, 1934. However, a similar land policy was implemented when the Communist forces finally settled down again in Northern Shensi in October, 1935. This policy was discontinued shortly before the outbreak of the Sino-Japanese war on July 7, 1937.

Party Theory on the Land Question

During the early part of the Soviet period, roughly 1927–31, there were in effect two Party lines regarding theory on the land question, one of Mao Tse-tung and another by some in the party hierarchy. The salient aspects of Mao's basic principles during this period may be summarized as follows:

(1) The peasant fulfils a major task in the national democratic bourgeois revolution and constitutes the crux of the revolutionary movement.

(2) The three major classes among the peasantry are the rich, middle, and poor peasants. The last class, which includes the farm labourers, is the core of the agrarian revolution under the leadership of the proletariat. The middle peasants should be rallied around the poor peasants, the rich peasants should be neutralized and the landlord class eliminated. The Peasants' Association will serve as the chief instrument in carrying out the above policy.

(3) Soviets should be set up as a political regime independent of the Kuomintang and an army of workers and peasants should be organized to insure the implementation of land redistribution. The Red Army must be thoroughly indoctrinated and disciplined and should engage in mobile guerrilla warfare without costly attacks on enemy strongholds such as big cities.

(4) No mercy should be shown to the landlords and rich peasants in dividing up their land, but wanton killing and burning must be prohibited.[8]

Many of Mao's basic premises, especially the tactical aspects, did not meet with the full support of the party hierarchy under

[8] See Mao's *Report on an Investigation of the Peasant Movement in Hunan* (February, 1927); *Report of Front Committee to the Central Committee* (November, 1928); *Report to the Second All-China Soviet Congress* (January, 1934).

Ch'u Ch'iu-pai, the Secretary-General of the Party from August 1927, to September 1928. The Central Committee at that time maintained that (1) the Party's work among the peasants was only subsidiary to its urban programme,[9] (2) land was to be nationalized and private property confiscated, and (3) a terrorist policy should be pursued to "crush the spirit of the reactionaries and to create a greater proletariat." As a result, Mao Tse-tung was accused of being a "reformist" for his "moderate" agrarian tactics and was removed from the Central Political Bureau in November 1927.[10]

Mao seemed to have received *de facto*, if not explicit, vindication a year later at the Sixth National Congress of the CCP held in Moscow in September, 1928 and convened to "re-evaluate the revolutionary situation and legislate basic policies." In the *Political Report* of that Congress, agrarian revolution and the overthrow of imperialism were proclaimed to be "the two major tasks of the CCP." In the *Resolution on the Peasant Movement*, many key points such as the winning over of the middle peasants, expansion of Soviet areas, emphasis on guerrilla warfare as "a major form of struggle," organization of Peasants' Associations and promotion of the women and youth movements in the rural areas, coincided with Mao's programmes in the Kiangsi Soviet. The *Resolution on the Land Question* passed by the Congress also stated that "agrarian revolution is a crux of the Chinese revolution." Ch'u Ch'iu-pai was criticized for his "blind-actionism"[11] and was replaced by Hsiang Chung-fa as the Secretary-General of the Party. Mao himself, when looking back at the Congress in 1936, was quoted as saying:

> The resolutions of the Sixth National Congress...concluded with the approval of the emphasis on the agrarian movement

[9] Mao also fully subscribed to the theory that "the consolidation of the leadership of the working class and the CCP in the peasant movement is prerequisite to the success of the agrarian revolution" as reaffirmed in the *Political Resolution* on the Sixth Congress. But in practical consideration, he assigned much more weight to the peasants' role in the revolutionary movement.

[10] Chou Mou-chai, *Historical Development of New China*, 1949, p. 169.

[11] "Blind actionism" is the Chinese term for adventurism or putschism. Ch'u, however, blamed the lower echelon of the Party for "misinterpretation of the directives." See Li K'o-chang, "A Record of an Interview with Ch'u Ch'iu-pai," *Kuo-wen Weekly*, 12·26, July 8, 1935, pp. 1–7. This personal interview was made in a prison cell after Ch'u's capture by the Kuomintang forces on February 23, 1935. Refusing to reveal information under severe pressure, Ch'u was shot on June 18, 1935.

....With the new line adopted at that Congress, the differences between the leaders of the Party and the leaders of the Soviet movement in the agrarian districts disappeared. Party harmony was re-established.[12]

However, an intra-party difference developed between Mao and Li Li-san, who was the dominant figure of the party hierarchy immediately before and after the Sixth National Congress. The gist of the "Li-san line" was the assertion that "a new revolutionary rising tide" had arrived and "the most serious obstacle...is the guerrilla concept of the past, which [advocates] the attacking, instead of occupying, of cities and lacks the resolution to establish local Soviets in the cities."[13] Thus rebutting one of the basic strategies of Mao, Li Li-san sent out directives ordering that peasant armies in the Soviet areas should carry out all-out attacks on key cities in Hunan and Hupei. This policy ended in failure as the attacks on Changsha, capital of Hunan province, turned out to be costly and unsuccessful. Regarding an agrarian programme, the Conference of Delegates of Soviet Areas held in Shanghai in May, 1930, under the guidance of Li, advocated "collectivization of large land holdings" in its resolution.

The Third Plenum of the Central Committee, CCP, held in September, 1930, attempted a compromise stand. A report made by Chou En-lai under the pseudonym of Shao Shan criticized Li on one hand, and on the other stated that "the nationalization of land is the most thorough form of the bourgeois democratic revolution and one of the requisites for the revolutionary transformation [to Socialism]." When the impracticability of the Li Li-san line became evident, Li resigned from the Central Political Bureau in November, 1930, and soon went to Moscow "to study." Li's stand was officially repudiated at the Fourth Plenum of the Central Committee, CCP held in January, 1931, in Shanghai,[14] which resolved:

[12] Edgar Snow, *Red Star Over China*, pp. 171.

[13] Li Li-san, *New Revolutionary Rising Tide and Preliminary Success in One or More Provinces*, Report to the Central Political Bureau on June 11, 1930. English version available in *DH*.

[14] The Fourth Plenum re-elected Hsiang Chung-fa as the Secretary-General of the Party, but replaced Li Li-san, Ch'u Ch'iu-pai, Li Wei-sen (Lo Man), and Ho Chang with Ch'en Shao-yu (Wang Ming), Chang Wen-t'ien (Lo Fu), and Shen Tse-min as members of the Central Political Bureau. It also resolved to hold an All-China Soviet Congress in Kiangsi in 1931.

> As a result of Li-san's policy, the rich peasant elements have been able to infiltrate into the directing organs and have seized the fruits of agrarian revolution for their own benefit. The Collective Farm and all other premature socialistic measures proposed by Li Li-san inevitably would have further consolidated the interests of the rich peasants. The order prohibiting free business transactions and the buying or selling of land made the Soviet economic conditions even more difficult. These errors were detrimental to the alliance between us and the middle peasants.

The differences between Mao and the party hierarchy did not end with the exit of Li Li-san, but continued with Li's successors. In the words of the official Party historian, Hu Ch'iao-mu:

> In January 1931, a new "left" faction headed by Comrades Wang Ming [Ch'en Shao-yu] and Po Ku [Ch'in Pang-hsien] and characterised by its doctrinairism, made use of the cloak of Marxist-Leninist "theories" to attack the above mentioned 3rd Plenary Session from the "left." The members of this faction held the view that the chief mistake committed by Comrade Li Li-san, and the chief danger within the Chinese Communist Party at that time, were right deviations and not "left" deviations. They charged that the 3rd Plenary Session "had not done anything to expose and attack the right opportunist theory and practice which the Li Li-san line had consistently followed." They finally secured the leading positions in the central organs at the 4th Plenary Session of the Central Committee elected at the 6th Party Congress. This new "left" faction headed by Wang Ming and Po Ku completely denied the important changes which the Japanese invasion had brought about in China's domestic political situation and regarded the various cliques and middle groups in the Kuomintang as equally counter-revolutionary; therefore, they demanded that the Party should wage a life and death struggle against all of them without distinction.[15]

However, the leadership of Mao was consolidated by the following events: the election of Mao as Chairman of the Chinese Soviet Republic on November 7, 1931; the moving of the Central

[15] Hu Ch'iao-mu, *Thirty Years of the Communist Party of China*, July 1, 1951, p. 28.

Committee of the Party to Jui-chin, Kiangsi, in the autumn of 1932; and Mao's election to the formal party directorship as the Chairman of the Central Committee and its Political Bureau at the all-important Tsun-i (Kweichow province) Conference, during the "Long March" in January, 1935.[16]

Legislation and Programmes on Land Policy

The basic law on agrarian policy during the Soviet period[17] was the Land Law of the Chinese Soviet Republic passed on December 1, 1931, at the First All-China Soviet Congress at Jui-chin, Kiangsi.[18]

Before that, however, there were three other pieces of legislation on land policy which are available at present. An analysis of these reveals how the Chinese Communists adjusted their theory to reality. The earliest land law known was the one drawn up by the Hunan-Kiangsi Border Soviet in December 1928. It stipulated, among other points, that (1) all land was to be confiscated and placed under the ownership of the Soviet Government, and (2) purchase and sale of land were to be prohibited after the land was redistributed among the poor peasants.[19] The next legislation on land was the Land Law of Hsinkuo-hsien (a county in Kiangsi) dated April 1929. It also prohibited the purchase and sale of land and assigned the ownership of land to the Soviet Government, but stipulated that only the land of the landlords and public land was

[16] For some works in English dealing with the CCP during the twenties and thirties, see Benjamin Schwartz, *Chinese Communism and the Rise of Mao*, 1951; and Robert North, *Moscow and Chinese Communists*, 1953.

[17] There were, during the early thirties, more than a dozen Soviets scattered throughout China. Little detailed information was available regarding these Soviets except the Central Soviet under the direct command of Mao Tse-tung with its bases in Southern Kiangsi, Western Fukien, Northern Kwangtung and border of Kiangsi and Hunan. It was comparatively stable from 1928–1934 and covered an area of 50 *hsien* with about 15 million population.

[18] An imperfect English translation of the *Land Law of the Chinese Soviet Republic* appears in the Appendix of Yakhontoff's *The Chinese Soviets*. It contains eight articles. There also is the *Draft Land Law* circulated by the Central Committee for comment in February, 1931. It contains fourteen articles, the first eight articles are in the main the same as those of the Land Law passed on December 1, 1931 (Chinese, Hoover Library).

[19] Full text in Chinese available in Liu Kung's *Reference Materials for the Study of the Agrarian Reform Law* (June 28, 1950), Chinese, 1950, Shanghai, pp. 66–7. It has nine articles.

to be confiscated for redistribution.[20] The third document available, and preliminary to the promulgation of the Land Law of the Soviet, is the Provincial Land Law passed by the Conference of Delegates of Soviet Areas convened under the leadership of Li Li-san, in May 1930.[21] The salient aspects of its eight articles include: (1) all land of landlords was to be confiscated without compensation to be redistributed by the Soviet government; (2) the purchase, sale, rent and mortgage of land were to be prohibited; (3) all lands belonging to temples, shrines, and churches as well as public land were to be confiscated without compensation; and (4) land rented out by rich peasants was to be confiscated but the portion cultivated by them was to be exempted from confiscation.

The similarities and differences between these three laws on land policy and the operative agrarian programme in the Kiangsi Soviet can be seen in the following excerpts from the Land Law of the Chinese Soviet Republic enacted by the First All-China Soviet Congress in 1931:

1. CONFISCATION OF LAND AND OTHER PROPERTIES

All the lands of the feudal landlords, warlords, gentry, temples, and other big private landowners, were subject to confiscation without compensation, irrespective of whether they (the owners) themselves worked their land or rented them out to tenants. A significant passage of the *Land Law* stated that "it is a peculiar feature of the Chinese rich peasant that he is at one and the same time a landowner and a usurer; therefore his land shall also be confiscated. Land of the middle peasants is not to be infringed upon." The local Soviet government, "with the peasants' willingness and without hurting their religious feelings, may take steps to dispose of the land of the religious organizations and temples." The liquid and fixed assets such as houses, warehouses, draught animals, and farm implements of all the feudal landlords, warlords, and gentry,

[20] Full text in Chinese also appears in Liu Kung, pp. 67–9. It contains eight articles.

[21] A full text, in Chinese, re-translated from a Japanese source, appears in the appendix of *The CCP and The Agrarian Revolution*, n.d. (1948 ?), pp. 45–8. Ch'i Ch'i-sheng, in his articles on "The Land Policy of the Red Areas in China," *Hsin Chung-hua*, (New China), 2·10, May 25, 1934, p. 13, states that the *Provisional Land Law* was passed on September 20, 1930 after a *Land Programme* was announced in May, 1930.

and the surplus draught animals and farm implements of the rich peasants, were to be confiscated.[22]

2. REDISTRIBUTION OF LAND AND OTHER PROPERTIES

The Soviets distributed the confiscated land among the poor and middle peasants. The former owners of confiscated land were not entitled to receive any land allotment. Farm labourers, coolies, and toiling labourers enjoyed equal rights to land allotments, irrespective of sex. Each Red Army man was also allotted land. Rich peasants, when their lands were confiscated, were allotted land of inferior quality, on the condition that they should work by their own labour. It was ordered that the local Soviet governments should on no account carry out this measure (of land redistribution) by force or by mere orders issued by higher authorities, but must explain this procedure to the peasants from every point of view. The local Soviets, in conformity with the local conditions in each village, were instructed to choose the method (of land redistribution) most advantageous to the poor and middle peasants—either according to the amount of labour power in a household or according to the number of family members. In dividing up the land, not only the area of the land but also the quality of its soil, especially its productivity, was taken into consideration. Confiscated houses were assigned to poor and middle peasants or village organizations; confiscated draught animals and farm implements were either distributed to groups of poor and middle peasants, or to households, or upon the recommendation of the peasants, managed by the cooperatives.[23]

3. DEBTS, CONTRACTS, AND INTERESTS

All rent contracts and usurious loans signed by the peasants were declared null and void; peasants were prohibited from returning land or paying debts to the landlords or gentry. After land redistribution, new loans were permissible and should be repaid, but the monthly interest was limited to one per cent.[24]

[22] Articles 1, 3, 6 and 8 of the *Land Law of the Soviet Republic*.
[23] Articles 1, 2, 3, 5, 7 and 8 of the *Land Law*.
[24] Article 9 of the *Draft Land Law* and "Resolution of the Joint Conference of County and District Chairman of Kiangsi Soviet," quoted by Ch'i Ch'i-sheng, *op. cit.*, p. 22.

4. OWNERSHIP OF LAND AFTER REDISTRIBUTION

Renting, purchase, and sale of the land after redistribution were allowed, but the recipient must not be a member of a landlord or gentry family. Land after redistribution could be inherited by one's descendants. No land was to be added or subtracted on account of births or deaths.[25]

5. AGRICULTURAL TAXATION

No regulations on agricultural tax in the Soviet Area are available. According to a report written by a non-Communist writer who visited the Kiangsi areas in the spring of 1935[26] the major points regarding the agricultural tax in the Kiangsi Soviet were as follows: (1) a unified land tax replaced the numerous taxes and surtaxes of the Kuomintang rule; (2) the tax, progressive in scale, was levied on principal crops, but on each harvest; (3) the tax rates for poor and middle peasants began at three per cent for a per capita income in excess of three piculs of rice and stopped at eighteen per cent when per capita income reached fifteen piculs or more. The tax rates for rich peasants began at four per cent when per capita income reached three piculs and stopped at twenty-two per cent when per capita income reached fifteen piculs or more; and (4) taxation was suspended for one to three years for famine, agricultural improvements, reclaimed land, and the families of Red Army soldiers.

6. STATUS OF RURAL CLASSES

In the two documents *How to Analyse Class Status in the Countryside* and *Decisions Concerning Some Problems Arising from Agrarian Reform*, issued by the Soviet Republic in 1933,[27] the definitions for various class stratifications were given as:

(1) A landlord is a person who owns land, but does not engage in labour or only engages in supplementary labour, and depends on exploitation for his means of livelihood chiefly in the form of land rent, money-lending, hiring of labour or the simultaneous

[25] "Resolution of Land Confiscation and Redistribution in Kiangsi Soviet" quoted by Ch'i Ch'i-sheng, *op. cit.*, p. 21.
[26] Ch'i Ch'i-sheng, "The Land Tax in the Chinese Red Areas," *Kuo-wen Weekly*, 12.16, April 29, 1935, pp. 1–5.
[27] These two documents were re-issued with revisions in early 1948 and August 1950.

carrying on of industrial and/or commercial enterprises. (2) A rich peasant generally owns land . . . and owns better means of production and some floating capital and takes a part in labour himself, but constantly depends on exploitation for the major part of his means of livelihood. (3) A middle peasant is one who generally owns a portion of the land which he cultivates, has a certain number of farm implements, and depends wholly or mainly upon his own labour for his living. If one's income from exploitation does not exceed fifteen per cent of the total annual income of the family, he will be considered a well-to-do middle peasant. (4) A poor peasant owns inadequate farm implements and a part of the land he cultivates or has no land at all. In general, he has to rent land for cultivation and is exploited by others in the form of land rent, loan interest, and farm labour to a limited degree. (5) A farm labourer generally has neither land nor farm implements and depends wholly or mainly upon the sale of his labour for his living.

7. OTHER AGRARIAN PROGRAMMES

Local Soviet governments were instructed to promote, if circumstances permitted, the following measures: (1) reclaim uncultivated land; (2) encourage immigrants (to settle in Soviet areas); (3) improve old, and set up new, irrigation facilities; (4) develop reforestation; (5) build new roads; and (6) establish (rural) industries to develop the rural economy. All areas marked for conservation, hills, rivers, lakes, swamps, forests, pastures, and fields were to be managed by the Soviet for the benefit of the poor and middle peasants.[28]

The evaluation of the above programmes will appear in a later section.

Organization and Administration

The execution of the various agrarian programmes during the Soviet period was carried out by the Ministry of Land in the central government of the Chinese Soviet Republic, the Bureau of Land in the provincial Soviet governments, and the Department of Land in the local governments. At the village level, a great deal of the actual land reform was carried out through the Peasants' Association

[28] Articles 10 and 13 of the *Draft Land Law*.

(which excluded former landlords and the rich peasants) and mass meetings of the villagers. One of the characteristics of the land policy of the Soviet period was the preferential treatment given to farm labourers and poor peasants. Not only were they given "freedom of action," but an additional number of delegates to the Soviets was provided for the farm labourers in the electoral system set up by the Constitution of the Soviet Republic passed in November 1931.

Regarding the detailed procedure of organizing peasants to carry out land redistribution, a directive issued by the Political Bureau of the Hupei-Honan-Anhwei Soviet entitled "How to Redistribute Land" in 1931, stated:

> *Hsiang* (the rural subdivision of a county) is the unit in land redistribution, which shall be based on the mixed principle of [distributing land according to] the number of consumers and the number of labourers (in a household). The masses of the entire *hsiang* are to be mobilized to hold a mass meeting and labouring peasants with a high degree of [class] consciousness are to be elected as land commissioners. From 17 to 21 (delegates) are to be elected from each *hsiang* to form the Land Committee. Then a survey of the land will follow. The masses are to be called together by the striking of gongs to carry out a land survey together with the Land Committee. The first step is to fix the area of "public land" for the Red Army men.[29] Then all lands are to be equally and fairly distributed among the peasants, taking into consideration various factors such as the quality of the soil, the distance of the field, woods, ponds, bamboo groves, etc. Distribution of land is to be decided by majority opinion of the [village] masses.
>
> After the decisions are passed (at the mass meeting), a list containing all the names of the recipients and the amount of land to be allotted to each is to be posted at public places, soliciting comments and suggestions. If no revisions are proposed, then the land is to be divided according to original decisions . . . . Suitable measures should be adopted to meet peculiar

[29] The "public land" was cultivated by the peasants for the soldiers of the Red Army. Tools, seeds, and draught animals generally were supplied by the Soviet Government. Usually the area amounted to from three to five times that of the average land allotment in that district.

conditions of the various districts and through extensive public discussions.[30]

This general pattern of procedure was similarly described in an article entitled "The Steps and Procedure of Land Distribution in the Red Areas" written in 1935 by Ch'i Ch'i-sheng, who made some field studies of CCP land reform in the former Soviet areas occupied by the Kuomintang forces in the summer of 1933.[31] Mr. Ch'i Ch'i-sheng wrote:

> After the distribution of land, those who were allotted land and those whose land was left unchanged [such as that of the middle peasants] had to register anew and to apply for new land certificates. The major items for registration were the amount of land holding, its location, annual production, and the landowner's class status . . . . There were three kinds of land certificates: those for the rich peasants, those for the middle peasants, and those for the poor peasants and farm labourers.

The particulars contained in the three forms of land certificates, i.e. land title deeds, given as samples in the article by Mr. Ch'i are similar, except for one provision in the land certificates for rich peasants which states:

> . . . in accordance with the policy of dealing a blow to the rich peasants, allying with middle peasants, and consolidating the alliance between workers and peasants, all the land and houses of the rich peasant [holder of the certificate] are hereby confiscated. In accordance with the labour power which his family possesses, [such and such amount of] *mou* of the inferior land are hereby allotted to him . . . . This piece of land must be cultivated by himself and is not to be rented out or tilled by hired labour.

The above information seems to indicate that the Land Committees at the various levels and the Peasants' Associations were the two major instruments in administering land reform in the Soviet areas. They were aided by a number of mass organizations such as

[30] Hsi Tung, "How the Chinese Soviet Solves the Land Problem," *The CCP and the Agrarian Revolution*, (Chinese), pp. 54–5.

[31] *Kuo-wen Weekly*, 12·16, April 29, 1935, p. 4.

the "mutual-aid societies," "draught animal teams," and "rural cooperatives." Although popular participation in these organizations was encouraged, control and supervision by the party was thorough and effective.

Results and Effects

Data regarding the achievements of the Chinese Communist land programmes during the Soviet period are meagre. One obvious reason was the fluid situation in the Soviet areas. The Central Soviet in Kiangsi, comparatively stable for three or four years, had to resist five major Kuomintang campaigns between December 1930 and October 1934. The Communist forces, engaging primarily in mobile warfare, frequently shifted their bases and areas of operation. There was hardly any time for research or statistical surveys on a large scale. Some reference materials, like the report by Mao Tse-tung on his investigation of the results of land reform in Hsun-wu, a county in Kiangsi, were lost during the Long March. Such information on the results and effects of the agrarian reform in the Soviet period as can be pieced together from a few available sources, is presented in the following sections.

1. LAND REDISTRIBUTION

The available information indicates that the amount of land allotted to the peasants in land redistribution during the Soviet period varied in localities and with the class status of the recipient. The work report of the Provisional Committee of the Kiangsi Soviet, dated April 1932,[32] revealed that in ten *hsien* of Kiangsi, a total cultivated area with an annual productive capacity of 15,794,294 piculs (of rice) was distributed among the peasants. The per capita allotment ranged from six to thirty-two piculs, and the average quota was 13·4 piculs per person. Calculating from the data furnished by Dr. Lossing Buck in his book *Land Utilization in China*, which gives the average annual production per *mou* in Kiangsi as 3·7 piculs, the average land holding of the peasants in the ten *hsien* in the Kiangsi Soviet should be in the neighbourhood of 3·6 *mou*. The per capita land holding thus seems considerably higher than the figure estimated by Dr. Buck for the general area in 1937, which was 2·16 *mou* per person.[33] Possible

[32] Hsi Tung, *op. cit.*, pp. 58–9. [33] J. L. Buck, *Land Utilization in China*, p. 77.

reasons are: (1) the population in the Kiangsi Soviet region was reduced by war casualties, the fleeing of some people to the "white areas," and the execution of a number of counter-revolutionary elements by the Communists; (2) the expansion of cultivated areas through reclamation and irrigation; and (3) the increase of crop yields as a result of Soviet agrarian reform. The same work report shows that in three of the ten *hsien* the public land reserved for the Red Army constituted, respectively 0·3 per cent, 0·25 per cent, and 0·06 per cent of the total farmland. But these public lands were of the top quality.

The change in rural class status was reflected in a report entitled *Rural Investigation of Hsinkuo* (county in Kiangsi Soviet) written by Mao Tse-tung on January 26, 1931. It stated:

> The 18 landlord families constituted one per cent of the rural population and owned forty per cent of the land before the revolution. After the revolution, two landlords were executed, one imprisoned, two voluntarily divided their lands and served as local Soviet officials, and the rest fled to the Kuomintang areas. . . .The 32 rich peasant families constituted about five per cent of the rural populace and owned thirty per cent of the land. Twenty-four families were counter-revolutionary and ten of the family heads were executed. Four were imprisoned and ten cooperated with the Soviet, among whom two served as local officials. The rest fled. . . . Middle peasants made up about twenty per cent of the rural community and owned fifteen per cent of the land. On the whole they increased their holdings of the land . . . The poor peasants constituted sixty per cent of the rural population and had only five per cent of the land. They received land, a portion of the hills from which fuels were gathered, cheaper food, relief in economic burdens, better social and political conditions, and rights to elect and serve as local functionaries. . . . The farm labourers who constituted about one per cent of the rural populace got a share of land and benefits similar to those enjoyed by the poor peasants. . . .

From this report it can be seen that a number of landlords and rich peasants were "liquidated." Some reports maintain that the land policy of the Chinese Communists during the Soviet period was carried out with "great force and bloodshed," as in contrast with later periods. On the other hand, statements that the Chinese Communists wiped out every landlord and rich peasant in their areas are not substantiated by field investigations.[34] It is also evidenced in Mao Tse-tung's *Report to the Second All-China Soviet Congress*, dated January 22, 1934, on the "land investigation movement,"[35] which reported:

> According to statistics of July, August, and September 1933, 6,988 landlord families and 6,638 rich peasant families were found in the Central Soviet of Kiangsi, Fukien, and Kwangtung during the land investigation movement. 317,539 piculs' [rice] worth of land was confiscated from them. . . .

It would seem that, even though the Soviet regime implemented the policy supported by legislative provisions with vigour toward the landlord and rich peasant classes, the implementation of the measure at the village level was not as severe as the legislative provisions stipulated, possibly because of local influences and the shortage of trained cadres.

2. RURAL ECONOMIC PROGRAMMES

The rent, usurious loans, and miscellaneous surtaxes that had prevailed in former times were abolished. Unfortunately no detailed information is available regarding the results of these measures as far as the whole Soviet area is concerned. Certain data are contained in the *Hsin-kuo Report* quoted previously. It reveals that:

> On the average, rent, before the revolution, constituted about fifty per cent of the principal crop yield in the first, second, and fourth districts (of Hsin-kuo county) and sixty per cent in the third district. It was abolished after the Red Army came. . .. The Soviet government abolished all taxes and installed a unified land tax on a progressive scale. . . . Loans which were formerly made at thirty per cent or more per annum for cash loans and

[34] See, for example, correspondences by Ch'i Ch'i-sheng, who visited the Soviet areas in 1935 and wrote several articles for the *Kuo-wen Weekly* of Shanghai.

[35] The "land investigation movement" carried out in 1933 aimed primarily to check the results of the agrarian reform and to smoke out the "hidden landlords and rich peasants." For more information, see Ch'i Ch'i-sheng, "The Land Investigation Movement in the Chinese Red Areas," *Kuo-wen Weekly*, 12·7, February 22, 1935, pp. 1–6.

hundred per cent annually for loans in kind were annulled together with all old debts....[36]

A Chinese (pro-Nationalist) journalist who visited some of the Red areas after their recapture in 1933 reported that "the peasants paid a progressive land tax of from six per cent to forty-two per cent."[37] One Western writer stated that "one-fifth of the rice crop is given to the Soviets."[38] Evidence seems to indicate that agricultural tax rates varied slightly in different districts and that peasants were required to contribute labour at subsistence wages for the Soviet Government. However, compared with the taxes levied by the Kuomintang Government and made worse by grafting officials, there are reasons to believe that the tax burden of the peasants was reduced under the Soviets.

An increase in agricultural production was made the "primary task in the economic construction of the Soviet," according to Mao Tse-tung.[39] Ts'ai Ho-sheng, one of the CCP Political Bureau members in the early thirties, wrote that "crop produce in 1933 in the Soviet areas increased 50 per cent over the previous year, and in 1934 there was an increase of 100 per cent over 1933."[40] It is difficult to ascertain to what extent these increases were due to reclamation of new land, newly irrigated lands, and other improvements, and to what extent due to the enhancement of the efficiency of the peasants as a result of greater incentives and better rural conditions subsequent to the agrarian reform.

A great deal of attention was also paid to the development of rural cooperatives for the promotion of rural industries and the supplying of daily necessities. It was reported that "in September 1933 there were 1,423 cooperatives with a total capital of 305,531 *yüan* (about 100,000 US dollars at that time) in the 17 *hsien* of the Kiangsi Soviet."[41]

[36] *Mao Tse-tung Hsuan-Chi* (Collected Works of Mao Tse-tung), Chinese, Tung-pei Book Co., Harbin, 1948, pp. 67–71. (Abbreviated as *Mao* in future references.)

[37] Ch'en Keng-ya, *A Report of Inspection in Kiangsi, Anhwei, Hunan, and Hupei* (Chinese), 1935, p. 50.

[38] Agnes Smedley, *China's Red Army Marches*, p. 242.

[39] Mao Tse-tung, *Report to the Second All-China Soviet Congress*, January, 1934. (Chinese, Hoover Library.)

[40] Ts'ai Ho-sheng, "Seven Years of the Chinese Soviet," *CCP in the United Front* (Chinese), p. 43.

[41] Yakhontoff. *The Chinese Soviets*, pp. 124, 125.

Red Army soldiers were reported to have played an important role in the agrarian programme. One sympathetic writer states:

> Red soldiers worked in the fields with the peasants: They marched in "shock brigades" to the fields and, side by side with the peasants, transplanted the tender rice-shoots. . . . Chu Teh, the Commander-in-Chief, was one of a shock brigade of planters. . . .[42]

A criterion for judging the achievements of the agrarian reform of the Soviet period would seem to be an improvement in the living standard of the peasants. According to Mao Tse-tung, the economic condition of the middle and poor peasants in the Soviet areas was improved because of the following factors:

> (1) The cost of living was lowered. For example, the price of rice dropped from four [Chinese] dollars a picul before the revolution to one dollar a picul; vegetable oil from 23 dollars per 100 catties to 10 dollars; oxen from 70 dollars per head to 20 dollars; meat from 53 cents per catty to 32 cents. But the price of salt increased from 32 cents per catty to 80 cents and the cotton cloth price rose from 14 cents a foot to 32 cents. This was partly due to the Kuomintang blockade which made it impossible for the peasants in the Soviet areas to sell any surplus agricultural products to outsiders. (2) As a result of social reform, a number of expenses were saved for the peasants such as marriage expenditures which formerly cost the middle peasants as much as half of their fortune, funeral ceremonies which had cost from 60 to 100 dollars, various tributes to temples and expenses for ceremonies. (3) Other economic benefits such as reduction of interest, cancellation of usurious loans, etc., helped.[43]

Three years later, in January 1934, Mao again revealed in his *Report to the Second All-China Soviet Congress*, that:

> The living conditions of the peasants have been much improved. . . . In the past, many peasants lived on tree bark or grain husks for several months a year. This situation no longer prevails and there is no more starvation in the Soviet areas. The life of the

[42] Smedley, *op. cit.*, p. 237.
[43] Mao, *Hsin-Kuo Report* (Chinese), January 1931, pp. 79–85.

peasants is improving from year to year. They are no longer in rags. They now eat meat more regularly, it no longer being a luxury to them as in former times. In the past, most of the peasants dressed in rags, but now their livelihood is generally improved, some 100 per cent, some 200 per cent. . . .

Although with the removal of many politico-economic abuses and the promotion of agricultural production it is understandable that the peasants should be better off in the Kiangsi Soviet, one particular reason cited may be subject to review. A cause given for the betterment of the peasants' livelihood was the lowering of the price of rice. If the peasants in the Soviet region had sufficient rice to eat as reported, then the lowering of grain prices would seem to constitute a loss for the farming populace, since it affected the value they would receive for their grain surplus. Low priced food-grain benefited, however, various non-agricultural classes.

3. OTHER AGRARIAN PROGRAMMES

An important part of the Chinese Communist land policy during the Soviet period consisted of political and social programmes. The peasants were encouraged to participate in the local administration. The local government, according to Mao Tse-tung,[44] was formed in the following manner: The basic administrative unit in the rural areas was the *hsiang* (a group of villages) Soviet Council. Each Councillor lived among and looked after from 30 to 70 rural inhabitants. The quota of delegates was one for every 50 peasants (compared with workers who elected to higher Soviet governments one delegate out of every 15). Names of the electors were written on a large piece of red paper and elections were held (without the participation of landlords and rich peasants) twice each year. Any delegate who committed serious errors could be recalled by one half of the electorate or by the decision of the Council. The local government had to make periodical reports to the village voters and solicit suggestions. Mao reported that in the two elections held in 1932 and in another one in the autumn of 1933, "in many places more than 80 per cent of the electorate participated."

However, not all the provisions regarding village administration stipulated by the Soviet government prevailed in actual practice.

[44] Mao, *Report to the Second All-China Soviet Congress*, 1934, Yakhontoff, *op. cit.*, pp. 259–60.

Mao himself noted several defects in his report cited above. In one *ch'ü* (district) government, for example, among the eighteen Councillors, there were neither poor peasants nor farm labourers.

In the social reform programme the emphasis was on the elevation of the status of rural women, mass education, and the elimination of superstitious practices of the peasants. Child marriage was prohibited, and women, with reason for complaint, were granted divorces.

Mao revealed that "in many Village Councils, women constituted 25 per cent or more" of the membership.[45] But this might have been partly due to the shortage of able-bodied men, as the entire Soviet area was on a war footing. It was also reported that in 2,931 villages in Kiangsi and Fukien provinces there were 3,052 Leninist primary schools, with 89,710 pupils, and 32,388 reading groups, with a total membership of 155,371.[46] A number of improvised methods such as signboards with characters which were erected along the roadside and the "little teacher" system were adopted to boost literacy. Many boys, often as pet name called "little devils," were also very active in the campaign to destroy superstition. They demolished idols and threw away incense offered to the spirits by the older peasants. This reduction in the expenses of the peasants for temple sacrifices and other wasteful customs such as elaborate ceremonies for weddings and funerals, which sometimes cost the peasants as much as half of their annual income, helped to ease the economic burden of the rural community.

Comments on the Period

The land reform policy of the CCP during the Soviet period is characterized by its experimental nature: the few facts available show how the party's theories on the agrarian problem were adjusted and adapted to realities under the prudent guidance of Mao Tse-tung, how blunders were made earlier under the trial and error approach, and how the CCP learned a number of lessons and practices which helped the party later.

Between 1926 and 1930, at times without full support from the CCP hierarchy not to say the fierce attacks by the Trotskyites, Mao developed his theory of armed peasant rebellion as the major instrument in the Chinese revolution. As late as May 1930, the *Conference of Delegates from Soviet Areas* held in Shanghai under

[45] Quoted in Yakhontoff, *op. cit.*, p. 259. [46] *Ibid.*, pp. 274–5.

the direction of Li Li-san stated that "this Conference firmly opposes the policy that 'tillers should own their land'. . . . When the land of the landlords is confiscated without compensation and distributed among peasants, there is not the slightest intention that the land should be the private property of individuals."[47] A little more than a year later, the Land Law of the Soviet Republic made a realistic adjustment and stipulated that the peasants should not be deprived of their right to rent, purchase, and sell land.

Also, at an early stage in the Soviet period, land reform was regarded by many in the party as primarily a political instrument for winning the revolution. Thus, in 1930, two resolutions passed by a conference of local party leaders in the Soviet areas stated:

> At the present time when no decisive results are achieved in the fight between the Red and the White, the sole question is how to win over the masses, vanquish the enemy, and secure the revolutionary victory. At this moment, the criterion for all policies is the winning over of the masses, and not the development of production.[48]

There were more practical Communist leaders who realized that without the development of production neither the masses nor the revolution could be won. Fortunately, the realists prevailed. The latter's view may be represented by the following statement:

> The confiscation and redistribution of land are not sufficient to settle the agrarian problem to the complete satisfaction of the peasants. The question of scarcity of land remains. Consequently the next measure should be directed toward the amelioration of the peasants' lot and toward improved methods of cultivation by the introduction of modern agricultural machinery, improved irrigation and drainage, and selection of seeds, fertilizers and above all, the establishment of cheap credit facilities.[49]

[47] Yi Yuan, "Confiscation of the Land of the Landlords," Hung Ch'i, *The Red Flag* (underground publication of the CCP in Shanghai), 117, July 9, 1930, p. 4. (Text available at Hoover Library, Stanford.)

[48] "Resolution on the Rich Peasant Question," Joint Conference of the Front Commissars of West Fukien, June 1930; quoted by Ch'eng Shang-ch'ang in his article "The Land Problem in the Red Areas," *Kuo-wen Weekly*, 10.22, June 5, 1933, p. 3.

[49] "Resolution of the Conference of Delegates of Soviet Areas," May, 1930; quoted by Yakhontoff, *op. cit.*, p. 154.

Provisions in the Soviet Land Law of 1931 also show that adjustments were made by the Chinese Communists in the face of objective conditions. For instance the law stipulates that the "religious feelings of the peasants must be respected" and the peasants are given the right to decide on the disposal of land belonging to religious bodies and ancestral shrines.[50]

On the other hand, there existed in the Soviet period a number of measures which were later criticized by the Party leaders themselves as "erroneous and undesirable." Mao stated in December 1947 that "the policy of 'no land for the landlords and poor land for the rich peasants' (during the Soviet era) was a mistake."[51] Also the theory and practice of granting privileged treatment to farm labourers and village handicraftsmen which prevailed in the Soviet period later fell into disuse, together with such slogans as "the fundamental strength of our Party lies in the working class of the village-farm labourers, coolies and handicraftsmen." Even broadening the Marxist term of proletariat to include farm labourers, their number in the rural population was small, and the Party had to rely on the poor and middle peasants as the mainstay of its strength and power.

Significantly, many of the basic land reform premises formulated by the Chinese Communists during the Soviet period have remained in force ever since. An example is the provision that the central strategy should be to "rely on the poor peasants and farm labourers, and ally with the middle peasants." The Chinese Communists also, through their experience with land reform in the Soviet period, acquired a better understanding of the mentality of the peasants, became skilled in the technique of mass organization and mass persuasion, and accumulated administrative know-how. A number of practices such as the skilful utilization of mass organizations like the Peasants' Association, the youth corps, the women's league; the channelling of individualistic Chinese peasants into cooperative enterprises like the mutual-aid teams and the rural cooperatives; and the stimulation of incentive through emulation contests and labour heroes, all became integral parts of later CCP policy.

Viewing the land policy of the Soviet period with the benefit of twenty years' hindsight, it may be said that, blundering as it occasionally was, it gave invaluable experience to the CCP. In general it seems that the political and social features of Chinese Communist

[50] Article 6.

[51] Mao Tse-tung, *Present Situation and Our Tasks* (Chinese), December 1947.

land policy in the Soviet period—the mobilization of the masses, indoctrination of cadres, betterment of the status of women and the elimination of superstitious practices, achieved far more than the purely economic platforms, such as the increase of yield per acre of crops and the enhancement of the peasants' standard of living. The physical environment and the military situation, of course, had much to do with this outcome.

C. *The Sino-Japanese War Period, 1937–1945*

For chronological accuracy it should be pointed out that the suspension of land confiscation began in February, 1937, about five months before the Marco Polo Bridge Incident which marked the start of the Sino-Japanese War on July 7, 1937. The cessation of the land confiscation policy was officially confirmed in a statement by the CCP on Kuomintang-CCP cooperation made public on September 22, 1937. The war-time programme of rent and interest reduction lasted until December 1946, sixteen months after the conclusion of the war against Japan, although some land of Japanese and puppet officials was confiscated and redistributed, and in certain areas landlords were encouraged to contribute "voluntarily" a part of their landholdings.

Party Theory on the Land Question

During the war against Japan, the two major objectives of the CCP were the final victory over the enemy and expanding the influence of the CCP. These two goals were considered by the Party as closely linked. Land policy, which rallied most of the peasants to support the Party, constituted an extremely effective and popular means to attain such objectives. The CCP's line on the united front at that time was that "there will be several stages of development in the democratic republic and not under that of the Soviet. The firm ally of the proletariat is the peasantry, next comes the petty bourgeoisie.... The bourgeoisie is competing with the CCP for leadership in the revolution."[52]

Regarding the land policy in that era, Mao said:

[52] Mao Tse-tung, *On the Question of the Future of the Revolution* (Chinese), 1937.

It is not a policy of agrarian revolution as in the civil war [i.e., Soviet period], but rather a policy to unite all the people in a common front against Japan. The cessation of land confiscation is not because it is undesirable, but. . . to rally a greater number of people to fight Japanese imperialism.[53]

Even at an early stage of the war, Mao wrote in his *New Democracy* (January 1940):

The peasant problem is the fundamental issue in the Chinese revolution and the peasantry is the major force . . . . The new democratic republic will adopt certain necessary measures to confiscate the land of big landlords and distribute it among peasants who have little or no land . . . . It is not to build up socialist agriculture, but to turn the land into the private property of the peasants. A rich peasant-economy will also be allowed to exist.[54]

These passages indicate that the moderate land policy of reduction of rent and interest adopted during the war years was of only a transitional nature.

The resolution of the Central Committee, CCP, on "Land Policy in Anti-Japanese Base Areas," passed on January 28, 1942, was to remain the basic platform in the Communist areas until the end of 1946. It opened with the following passage:

Since the beginning of the war of resistance (July 7, 1937), the land policy carried out by our Party in the various anti-Japanese bases has been a land policy based on the anti-Japanese national united front . . . that is, a land policy involving reduction of rent and interest on the one hand, and the guarantee of the collection of rent and interest on the other.

Then the document went on to enunciate "three basic principles":

(1) That peasants (including farm labourers), constitute the basic strength in the anti-Japanese war as well as in the battle of production;
(2) That most of the landlords are anti-Japanese . . . that some of the enlightened gentry also favour democratic reforms; and

[53] *Ibid.* [54] Mao Tse-tung, *New Democracy,* Mao, p. 247.

(3) That the capitalist mode of production is the more progressive method in present-day China and that the bourgeoisie, particularly the petty bourgeoisie and national bourgeoisie, represent the comparatively more progressive social elements and political forces in China today.

A similar theme ran through Mao Tse-tung's *On Coalition Government*, a report he made to the Seventh National Congress of the CCP held at Yenan in April 1945. Under the heading "The Land Problem," Mao stated that "the policy of 'land for the tillers'[55] is a bourgeois-democratic policy, not a proletarian and socialist one." It is "the policy of all revolutionary democratic groups, not of the Communists alone." In the same report Mao elaborated on the important role of the peasants as follows:

> The peasants are predecessors of the Chinese worker, and millions of them in future will go to the cities and into factories .... The peasants are a market for China's industry. They alone can supply it with richest food and raw materials, and absorb the vast quantities of industrial products .... The peasants are the source of our armies .... The peasants, at the present stage, are the main foundation of democracy in China .... The peasants, at the present stage, are the main foundation of China's cultural movement. Divorced from the 360,000,000 peasants, are not the illiteracy elimination campaigns, universal education, popular literature, and the national health campaigns, all empty phrases ?[56]

The report concluded by stating that "the peasant's enthusiasm in production will be increased once land reform—even preliminary reforms such as reduction of rent and interest—is carried out. By degrees, when the peasants are organized, on a voluntary basis, into agricultural production cooperatives or other cooperatives, their productive power will develop. Such agricultural production cooperatives, at present, can only be ... built on the peasant's individual economic basis (based on the peasant's private property) ...."[57] The above represents the essence of the CCP's theory on

[55] This was a slogan advocated by Dr. Sun Yat-sen, founder of the Republic of China and the Kuomintang, but not carried out in practice.
[56] *Mao*, pp. 330–4. [57] *Ibid.*

the land question, which was adapted to the political conditions during the Sino-Japanese War period.

Legislation and Programmes

The general principle of rent and interest reduction was announced in the "Ten Great Policies of the CCP" on August 15, 1937, and again in the statement made public on September 22, 1937, but no detailed programme was set forth. In 1938, a directive of the Yenan Government of the Shensi-Kansu-Ninghsia Border Region stated that "in those areas where agrarian revolution (i.e., land redistribution) already has taken place, no changes shall be made. The landlords in exile are welcome to return and they will receive an equal share of land and property just as the ordinary peasants do. In those areas where land has not been redistributed, the landlords can retain their land."

The general agricultural programme for the SKN Border Region announced in 1942 was as follows:

In the economy of the Border Region, a small peasant economy still occupies an important position. Hence, the development of agriculture must be regarded as a central chain in economic construction and carried out according to a definite policy:

(1) The development of agriculture should centre on the increase of grain production. This requires the continuation of reclamation, irrigation work, the improvement of agricultural techniques, and the enhancement of yield per *mou*.
(2) More effort must be exerted regarding the production of industrial raw materials and the export of special products of the Border Region to outside areas.
(3) Protection and adjustment of labour power and encouragement of immigration (to the Border Region).
(4) Protection of forests, development of the grazing industry and other subsidiary occupations.
(5) Provision of low interest loans to the peasants (in order to) stimulate the rural economy.
(6) Unification of grain control (by the government), and strict prohibition of export of grain in order to guarantee the

supply for the military and administrative units as well as food for the people.[58]

In the Shansi-Chahar-Hopei Border Region, a similar programme was announced on January 20, 1943. This listed the following aims:

> Development of agriculture, more reclamation, prevention of land from being laid waste, expansion of cultivated areas, protection and increase of livestock, improvement of agricultural techniques such as (the use of better) seeds, fertilizer, and farm implements, digging more wells and irrigation ditches, and repairing dams in a planned manner in order to improve the soil.[59]

Other basic legislation on land reform which lasted, in general, until the end of 1946 included the *Resolution on Land Policy in Anti-Japanese Base Areas* passed by the Central Committee, CCP on January 28, 1942, the *Rent Law of the Shensi-Kansu-Ninghsia Border Region Government* of December 29, 1942, the *Rent Law of the Shansi-Chahar-Hopei Border Region Government* of February 4, 1943, and the *Consolidated Progressive Agricultural Tax Regulations* promulgated by the Shensi-Kansu-Ninghsia Border Government in 1943. The main aspects of the various agrarian programmes of the CCP during the war period are as follows:

1. RENT

Reduction of rent constituted the crux of the CCP wartime land policy, although land belonging to the "most criminal and notorious traitors" who cooperated with the Japanese was confiscated and redistributed. Rent reduction was listed as a principle in the land policy set forth by the CCP after July, 1937. Detailed provisions on rent reduction appear in the Central Committee's *Resolution on Land Policy in Anti-Japanese Base Areas*, dated January 28, 1942, which stipulated:

[58] Lin Po-ch'u, "Understanding the Policy of the United Front," *Work Report, 1939–1941* (Chinese), p. 116.

[59] Article 10, "Present Programme of the SCH Border Region," *Compendium of Current Laws and Directives of the SCH Border Region* (Chinese), 1945, pp. 2–3.

In the areas where rent has not been reduced, rent should, in principle, be reduced by 25 per cent . . . i.e., a reduction of 25 per cent from the pre-war rate for rent. No matter whether it be public land, private land, rented land or shared land, and no matter whether it be cash rent, rent in kind, unfixed rent or fixed rent, this rule applies to all. For land shared under various forms, it should not be uniformly ruled that the landlord is to obtain no more than 40 or 60 per cent, but there should be a 25 per cent reduction of the former rent, based on consideration of the labour, animal power, tools, fertilizers, seed and grain contributed by the parties. In guerilla areas or places near enemy strongholds, rent reduction may be less than 25 per cent. . . .

No rent should be collected in advance of the harvest.

Rent in arrears for many years is to be exempted from payment.

Payment of fixed rent may be postponed or reduced if all or a part of the harvest is destroyed by natural or man-made disaster.

The collection of rent by the landlord is guaranteed, if rent reduction is duly made according to law.

This programme was further elaborated in the *Rent Law of the Shensi-Kansu-Ninghsia Border Government* and the *Rent Law of the Shansi-Chahar-Hopei Border Government*, promulgated respectively on December 29, 1942, and February 4, 1943. The major points of the two laws on rent were:

Fixed rent which is calculated according to the areas of cultivated land is to be reduced by 25 per cent: share crop which is divided proportionally between the landlord and the tenant with the landlord contributing nothing is to be reduced from 25 to 40 per cent. The amount obtained by the landlord as rent cannot exceed 37·5 per cent. All subsidiary crops are to go to the tenant. Share cultivation which is divided proportionally between the landlord and the tenant, but with the former providing all or a part of the facilities for farming, is to be reduced from 10 to 20 per cent. The landlords cannot receive more than 40 per cent of the principal crops. The subsidiary produce is to be divided between the landlord and the tenant according to the contract or local customs when there is no contract. Homestead rent, which is similar to share cultivation rent except where the landlord provides additional grain and quarters, is to be reduced between

10 and 20 per cent. The landlord cannot receive more than 45 per cent of all crops, principal and subsidiary. No interest or rent can be charged on grain or living quarters lent to the tenant.

Collection of rent in advance of harvest, rent deposit, commissions for rent collectors, compulsory labour rendered by the tenant for the landlord, and exactions are to be prohibited.

Rent in arrears incurred before 1939 is considered as cancelled.

A tenant may negotiate for reduction or exemption of rent if his crops fail entirely or partially due to natural disasters.

After rent reduction is effected according to law, the tenant must pay rent to the landlord in the full amount.

These represent the general features of the rent reduction programme of the CCP land policy during the war. The degree of their implementation varied in the different areas under Communist control, and will be discussed in the section on results and effects.

2. INTEREST RATE AND DEBT

Reduction of interest was also a basic programme proclaimed in the various CCP documents after the Sino-Japanese war began. In the *Resolution of the Central Committee on Land Policy in Anti-Japanese Base Areas*, passed on January 28, 1942, it was stipulated that:

> The policy of reduction of interest rates on debts contracted before the war is a necessary policy to meet the needs of the debtors as well as to rally the creditors in the fight against Japan. One and one-half per cent per month is to be the rate in calculating the interest. If the total payment of interest exceeds the amount of the original capital of the loan, interest is to stop, and [only] the capital is to be repaid. If payment of interest is double the amount of the loan, payment of both capital and interest are to be suspended. As to the interest rate for loans contracted since the war, it can be freely decided locally in accordance with local social and economic conditions. The government should not set too low an interest rate for it may result in a slowing down of credit and harm the people's welfare.
>
> If a debtor is unable to pay the interest on debts newly contracted since the war, the creditor has the right to dispose of the collateral according to contract. All disputes are to be adjudicated by the government....

The *Regulations of Mortgage and Debt* promulgated by the Shensi-Kansu-Ninghsia Border Government on September 14, 1943, stated:

(1) Old debts and mortgage rights are considered null and void in the areas where land has been redistributed;
(2) The rate of interest is not to exceed 15 per cent per annum in the areas where land has not been redistributed;
(3) If the total interest payments equal or exceed 200 per cent of the loan, only the original loan is to be repaid; if the aggregated interest payments equal or exceed 300 per cent of the loan, the debt is to be considered as cancelled.

The *Regulations on Rent, Debt, and Interest* promulgated by the Shansi-Chahar-Hopei Border Government on February 4, 1943, contained provisions similar to those above. In addition it also stipulated that "the interest rate for new debts is to be fixed by the contracting parties." The payment of debt and interest for new loans was guaranteed by law, but the debtor, if unable to meet his obligations as a result of natural disasters, such as flood and drought, could postpone the payment of interest.

3. AGRICULTURAL TAX

Chinese Communist sources report that from 1935 to 1937 the Border Government of Shensi-Kansu-Ninghsia relied on income from the confiscated properties of landlords and gentry to meet administrative and military expenses and no tax was levied on the peasants. From 1937 to 1943 a tax in the form of "public grain" was levied on a progressive scale, but no details about the tax scales are available. In the Shansi-Chahar-Hopei Border Region, which was established in 1938, the Border Government first relied on revenue from the old land tax, customs duties, and an internal loan which was floated in the summer of 1938. Later, most of the revenue was derived from the "reasonable burden system," which was also in effect in the Shensi-Kansu-Ninghsia Border Region. The general principle of this system was that the total assessment should be allotted among the rural population on the basis of estimates of ability to pay. The Border Government assigned quotas to the *hsien* (county) which in turn held mass meetings to decide what was a fair share for each household.

In 1941 and 1943, a consolidated progressive tax system was installed in the Shansi-Chahar-Hopei Border Region and the

Shensi-Kansu-Ninghsia Border Region respectively. The principles of this tax system as it was practised in the Shansi-Chahar-Hopei area were as follows: The tax was to be paid on a "point" basis. The matter was complicated by the fact that the "point" was defined differently in different districts and periods. Districts that suffered either from natural disasters or from severe war damage could obtain some reduction of their assessment. The average rate in 1941 was 1·2 to 1·3 *tou* (one *tou* in that area at that time was equivalent to 8 kilogrammes) of millet and $1·50 (Chinese currency) plus some straw for animals per "point." In 1942 the rate varied from 1·3 to 1·8 *tou* per point. In the next two years, it was reduced to 0·93 *tou* and 0·85 *tou*, respectively. Peasant households were divided into 16 classes according to their "wealth power" (*fu-li*). One "wealth power" was equivalent to 8 *tou* (one *tou* equals to 8 kilogrammes) of millet for land whose rent was less than 20 per cent of the produce, 10 *tou* of millet for income from rent and agriculture, and 7·5 *tou* for other incomes. The tax started with the first class for one-half wealth power at 0·8 points, and progressively increased to 2·1 points for each wealth power up to the sixteenth class which included 81 wealth power or above.[60] Details regarding estimated tax burdens on the various rural classes will be discussed in a later section on results and effects. The general range of the tax burden was from 5·24 per cent to 45 per cent of income.

In the Shansi-Kansu-Ninghsia Border Region, according to *Regulations on the Collection of Public Grain and Hay* promulgated on October 23, 1943, the major provisions of the agricultural tax were as follows: A tax, in the form of grain and hay, was levied on income from principal crops and subsidiary occupations, with certain exemptions for income from cotton planting and weaving, and salt, and that of agricultural families of Red Army soldiers, immigrants and so forth. Each person, irrespective of age or sex, was allowed a minimum of 0·5 picul (or *tou*) of millet or 0·8 picul of wheat which was tax-free. The scale of the tax started from three per cent if the average yield was 0·5 picul of millet per capita and ranged up to 35 per cent if the yield per capita exceeded

[60] One *tou* was calculated as equal to 8 kilogrammes, with the average hectare producing 137 *tou*. One hectare was calculated as 17·2 *mou*. For details, see *Regulations on Consolidated Progressive Tax* of the Shansi-Chahar-Hopei Border Region, promulgated by the Executive Committee of the Shansi-Chahar Border Region Government, February 5, 1943.

4·6 piculs. The amount of tax levied was subject to audit and review by the Examination Committee composed of delegates from the peasantry and local governments. The tax-payers could appeal to the village, district and county governments if they deemed the tax levy too high. The decision of the county government was final.

No detailed information is available regarding the tax system used in other Communist areas during the war, but the programme adopted in the above two major Border Regions was presumably followed, perhaps with minor modifications to suit local conditions.

4. PROGRAMMES REGARDING CERTAIN SPECIFIC PROBLEMS

The *Resolution of the Central Committee on Land Policy in Anti-Japanese Base Areas* of January 28, 1942, also contained provisions regarding "special types of land problems." It stipulated:

> Land belonging to landlords who have fled a given area is not to be confiscated, no matter where the landlord in question may be.
>
> Clan land and group land are to be managed by a control committee organized by the clan or society concerned. The income from such land shall be used for the benefit of the clan or the society or for the local community as a whole.
>
> School land shall be reserved as a source of educational funds, to be managed by an educational fund committee set up by the government or by the local inhabitants.
>
> Land that belongs to a religious group (Christian, Buddhist, Moslem, Taoist or other sects) shall undergo no changes.
>
> Uncultivated public land is to be distributed by the government to families of Red Army personnel, refugees, and poor peasants....

5. OTHER AGRARIAN PROGRAMMES

In addition to the above programmes, a number of other measures were undertaken to increase agricultural production and to win greater support from the peasants. Peasants were given various incentives, in the form of rewards and recognition, to engage in more intensive farming and to raise certain types of crops such as cotton. Peasants were encouraged to organize themselves into mutual-aid teams and cooperatives to achieve more efficient utilization of manpower and farming implements. Steps were taken to improve credit and marketing facilities. Rural industries, especially weaving, animal husbandry and salt production were fostered—especially when the Kuomintang intensified its blockade after the New Fourth Army incident in January, 1941. Certain agro-technical improvements, such as seed selection, pest control and animal breeding were carried out but on a rather limited scale due to the lack of equipment and technical personnel.

As a part of the land policy, a number of political, social, and educational reforms were implemented. Local governments were elected, and Peasants' Associations, People's Militia and other mass organizations were organized to give the peasants a greater sense of participation in their own welfare programmes and defence. These local organizations, which were under the close supervision of the CCP both by means of policy directives and through the action of cadres, also gave the party more effective control of the area. Social and educational programmes mainly took the form of village schools, discussion groups, discouragement of superstitious and wasteful practices, and the advocacy of equal rights for women.

Organization and Administration

The basic local administrative bodies in the Communist areas during the war were the *hsiang* (administrative unit embodying several villages) and the *ts'un* (natural village) offices.[61] *Hsiang* and *ts'un* officers were elected by the *hsiang* and *ts'un* councillors, who in turn were elected by direct ballot of the eligible voters at the village congress (*ts'un-min tai-hui*). The village congress was the highest depository of power at the village level, usually meeting twice a year. If some *ts'un* were too small, then the *hsiang* organ administered directly.

The tenure of Council members was one year, the retiring members were eligible for re-election. The Council met once a month, but extraordinary sessions could be called upon the request of one-tenth of the village voters or by one-fifth of the Village Councillors or by the Village Office. During the period of recess of the Village Council, a Standing Committee served as the executive. The major functions of the Council were (1) election or dismissal of the responsible staff

[61] There were, in 1941, 1,065 *hsiang* consisting of 6,703 *ts'un* with a population of 1,352,175 in the Shensi-Kansu-Ninghsia Border Region, according to the *Work Report of the Shensi-Kansu-Ninghsia Border Region Government 1939-1941* (Chinese), p. 15.

of the Village Office, (2) formulation of the "Common Pledge" of the villagers, (3) approval and supervision of the execution of the village budget, (4) disposal of the public properties of the village, such as the public land, (5) initiation or termination of village work and public affairs programmes, (6) discussion of village problems and petitions from villagers, and (7) supervision of the work of the village office and the implementation of the Council's decisions. The Councillors enjoyed legal immunity while the Council was in session, unless they committed criminal offences or treason. A Councillor could be impeached for delinquency in his duty or illegal deeds by the special group of voters to whom he was responsible.[62] But the Chairman and Vice-Chairman of the Council, who were concurrently the Chief and Deputy Chief of the Village Office, and those who were elected as officials of the Village Office could only be recalled by a decision of the Village Congress or by a resolution of the Council.

The Village Office was composed of a Chief, a Deputy Chief, and from seven to ten members responsible for various functions such as secretarial, civil, financial, educational, security, industrial and military affairs. They were all, except in the case of the security and military officials,[63] elected by the village council. The appointment of the Chief and the Deputy Chief, who were concurrently the Chairman and Vice-Chairman of the council, had to be approved by the *hsien* (county) government. The village office generally met twice a month. Its major functions were: (1) to carry out instructions from higher administrative organs; (2) to put into effect the resolutions passed by the village council and the villagers' congress; (3) to promulgate and implement the "Common Pledges" of the village; (4) to increase production; (5) to investigate and register land, population, and other social conditions in the village. All members of the village office except the Chief and the Secretary remained engaged in farming and received no remuneration unless it was deemed absolutely necessary. In case administrative funds provided by the Border Regional Government were found to be

[62] Village voters were divided into groups according to their residing locality and personal relations. Each group elected one Councillor who was responsible to the group which elected him.

[63] The Security and Military officials who were responsible for intelligence and military affairs during the war — especially for the activities of the People's Militia—were appointed by the Eighth Route Army.

insufficient, an additional appropriation not exceeding two piculs of grain might be collected by the Village Council for expenses.

The Peasants' Associations that played a key role in the village administration during the Soviet period were not emphasized in the Border Regions during the Sino-Japanese war. Mutual-aid teams, also called labour exchange groups, and rural cooperatives, however, continued to be extensively organized in the Border Regions. The organization of the mutual-aid teams, which were especially active in the Shensi-Kansu-Ninghsia Border Region, where population was comparatively sparse, was described by one Western reporter as follows:

> A group of eight, ten, or a dozen neighbours and farmers get together and exchange their labour power by working together on one man's field today, the next man's field tomorrow, and so on 'til all have been cultivated. Should one man have more land than his neighbour, the scale is balanced by a supplementary contribution of, say, a son's manpower, or an extra portion of food contributed to the pool. No one is under compulsion to join a labour exchange brigade, but few refuse since the scheme has proven itself profitable. Wives also participate in the labour exchange by taking turns in preparing the group's meals. In this way, the other wives are given time in which to engage in cooperative spinning and weaving.[64]

In addition to labour, animal power, and farm equipment, techniques were also pooled. Labour exchange was also utilized in other rural work such as irrigation, reclamation and fishing.

Rural cooperatives consisted of consumers' cooperatives and producers' cooperatives; the former supplied the daily necessities such as salt, matches, cloth, farm tools and other goods at lower than market prices; the latter included weaving, dyeing, cotton seed oil production, pottery, and other subsidiary industries. The cooperatives also served as agencies for the collection of public grain (tax), rural credit, and depositories for savings. Cooperative shares could be bought with cash or by contributing agricultural products or labour. Each member of a cooperative could buy an unlimited number of shares, but had only one vote.

At the village level, there were also a myriad of mass organizations, such as the youth corps, women's league and children's corps,

[64] Harrison Forman, *Report From Red China*, pp. 62–3.

aiming to achieve more thorough mobilization of the peasants and more effective control of the villages by the Border Region administration. Traditional village institutions such as kinship and family organizations and religious establishments were utilized after certain modifications. For example, peasant households were encouraged to form "family councils" to plan and discuss farm work.

Results and Effects

1. LAND REDISTRIBUTION

Two years before the arrival of the Red Army under Mao Tse-tung in Northern Shensi in October 1935, a land programme similar to that of the Kiangsi Soviet was carried out in the area by the guerilla units under Liu Tzu-tan and Kao Kang.[65] Even after the cessation of the land confiscation policy in 1938, both public land and the land of those who were traitors was distributed among the poor peasants. It was reported that "somewhere between 10 to 20 per cent of the land" in the Shensi-Kansu-Ninghsia Border Region had been redistributed.[66] As a rule, however, landlords, even absentee landlords, were allowed to retain their land, although land that had already been redistributed was not returned. The central programme, as pointed out previously, was for reduction of rent and interest.

2. RENT, INTEREST AND TAXES

The central feature of rent reduction was a 25 per cent reduction of the amount collectable by the landlord, and the rent after reduction was not to exceed 37·5 per cent of the main crop. While there are no comprehensive reports available regarding the results of rent reduction, there are indications that in some areas the stipulated rent reduction was not fully carried out. A directive issued by the Shansi-Chahar-Hopei Border Region government dated October 28, 1943, stated that "in many areas rent reduction has not been realized." It urged the party cadres in the villages "to organize the peasants to carry out the provision that rent must not exceed 37·5 per cent of the principal crops."

The regulations limited the interest on old debts to 15 per cent per annum, although on new loans the interest rate could be higher. Mao Tse-tung reported that "in order to encourage the old

[65] See Edgar Snow, *op. cit.*, p. 222.

[66] George E. Taylor, *The Struggle for North China*, p. 112.

inhabitants to lend (to the immigrants), for each *tou* (one-tenth of a picul) of grain loaned in the spring 1·3 *tou* will be returned after the autumn harvest."[67] It was 30 per cent interest in about eight months. This reflects the fact that the Border Government was not in a position to supply the peasants with all the credit they needed. It also indicates that the Border Government was aware of the danger of accelerating inflation by granting large amounts of cash credit to the peasants without the backing of goods.

The estimated amount of "public grain" collected as tax in kind[68] in the various Border Regions during the Sino-Japanese war period (1937–1945) appears in the table on page 53.

The tax was on total agricultural income (with a few exceptions); hence the burden on principal crop yields must have been greater. The high tax burden in 1939 (and probably also in 1940) was mainly to meet the tightening of the blockade by the Kuomintang and to pay back the grain "borrowed" in 1938. "Public hay" to feed animals and for other uses was also collected by the SKN Border Region Government. In 1941 and 1942 the amount of hay collected totalled, 11,818 and 7,274 (metric) tons respectively.

According to Michael Lindsay, the tax burden on the various rural classes in the Shansi-Chahar-Hopei Border Region in accordance with the progressive agricultural tax rates of 1944 was as follows:

> Tax on small farms [0·84 hectare, one hectare equals about 2·47 acres]: 5·24 per cent of the income after paying rent, assuming there were five members in the household. If there were only one member, the tax would be 14·6 per cent.

[67] Mao Tse-tung, *Economic and Financial Problems* (Chinese), p. 24.

[68] From 1937 to 1943 an agricultural tax under the name of "public grain for national salvation" was collected. From 1937 to 1940, quotas were allotted to the tax-paying rural households in public discussions. The major burden fell on landlords and rich peasants. From 1941 on, a system of progressive rates was adopted and peasants paid in accordance with their incomes. The "Regulations for the Collection of Public Grain for National Salvation," promulgated in October, 1943, in the SKN Border Region contain the following salient points: (1) the tax applies to all agricultural income, including proceeds from subsidiary industries, and (2) tax rates range from three per cent for five piculs of grain per capita in a household to 35 per cent for a per capita income of 46 piculs or more. In 1943 the unified, progressive agricultural tax was adopted. The rates start with a minimum base of four per cent and end at 35 per cent. See *Collection of Policies and Laws of the SKN Border Region* (Chinese), Vol. 2, pp. 214–39.

TABLE 1

ESTIMATED AMOUNT OF AGRICULTURAL TAX IN KIND IN BORDER AREAS DURING THE SINO-JAPANESE WAR PERIOD (1937–45)*

Region	*1938*	*1939*	*1940*	*1941*	*1942*	*1943*	*1944*	*1945*
I. Shensi-Kansu-Ninghsia Border Region								
1. Amount of grain collected as tax (1,000 piculs at 110 pounds each)	10	50	90	200	160	180	160	125
2. Percentage of tax in total grain production	0·78	3·63	6·29	13·33	10·69	11·25	9	7·8
II. Shensi-Suiyuan Border Region								
1. Amount of grain collected as tax (1,000 piculs)	..	..	..	404·43	163·2	219·5	205·6	324·5
2. Percentage of tax in total grain production	..	..	..	24·6	17·4	19·61	19·35	21
III. Shensi-Chahar-Hopei Border Region (Peiyueh Region)								
1. Amount of grain collected as tax (1,000 piculs)	104·45	117·16	180·48	221·27	211·37	220·68	210	350
2. Percentage of tax in total grain production	6·27	7·12	9·71	14·98	13·62	10·07	8·9	..

* Li Ch'eng-jui, "Agricultural Tax System and Tax Burdens in Several Revolutionary Bases During the Sino-Japanese War," *Ching-chi yen chiu* (Economic Research), No. 2, 1956 (April 17, 1956), pp. 108–9.

Tax on medium large farm [2·66 hectares and 57·9 per cent of the rented]: 15·2 per cent of income after paying rent. With one person in the household, 18·9 per cent.

Tax on very large farm [5·16 hectares, 43·8 per cent of land rented]: 20·5 per cent of income after paying rent. With one person, 22·4 per cent.

Tax on landlord [about 17·4 hectares, receiving rent at the maximum rate of 37·5 per cent of the crops]: 45 per cent of income.[69]

A directive regarding the burdens on the peasants issued by the Shansi-Chahar-Hopei Border Region Government on April 28, 1945, stated that the tax burdens on the various rural classes were as follows: landlord, 52 per cent; rich peasant, 18 per cent; middle peasant, 10 per cent; and poor peasant, 4 to 5 per cent.

From the above we find that the landlords in the Communist areas were the most heavily taxed: they had paid about ten per cent of their crop yield in the form of land tax in pre-war days and from 20 to 25 per cent when the land tax was collected in kind by the Nationalists after 1941.[70] Also, the landlords could no longer pass their taxes on to the peasants through various exactions such as rent deposits and increases in rent, as they usually had done prior to the Communist period. Poor peasants and farm labourers, who in the Nationalist areas had to pay from 50 to 70 per cent of their crops as rent[71] were much better off in the Border Region areas.

The tax system of the border regions during the Sino-Japanese war period (1937–45) was helped considerably by the frugal living standard of the local cadres. They were given 1·1 to 1·65 pounds of food grain per day, one summer dress each year, one winter dress every two or three years, and a small allowance for food and personal expenses. The average annual salary for a local cadre was from 660 and 880 pounds of rice—or in term of 1956 value, between 80 and 110 *yuan* or 34 and 47 US dollars.[72]

[69] Michael Lindsay, *The Tax System in a Chinese Communist Area*, pp. 5–8. Here one hectare is calculated as 17·2 *mou* which is larger than the usual 15 *mou* hectare, or the local *mou* is smaller in area.

[70] Calculated from Wang Hiao-wen, *The Land Problem of China* (Chinese), p. 48; *China Year Book of 1948*, 1338; and Fei Hsiao-tung, *Earthbound China*, p. 208.

[71] Meng Nan, *The Problem of Land Reform in China* (Chinese), p. 23.

[72] Li Ch'eng-jui, *op. cit.*, p. 101.

3. RECLAMATION AND IRRIGATION

Mao Tse-tung reported an increase in grain production in the SKN Border Region amounting to about 68,182 (metric) tons between 1937 and 1942, and that one-sixth of this increase came from the reclamation of waste land amounting to 3 million *mou* during these six years.[73] One foreign reporter observed that "during the last five years (1940–1945) reclamation has added one million acres to the 1·5 million acres of land that had formerly been under cultivation in the entire Border Region. The army alone with its 40,000 to 50,000 garrison troops has contributed about one-third of this new source of food and wealth."[74] However, it should be noted here that many areas opened up were marginal lands, which may not be economically profitable to operate after a period of fifteen to twenty years. The opening up of hill-side land has a more serious effect in that the removal of wood and grass causes floods which, in turn, destroy the farms on the plain and in the valley. A great amount of the uncultivated land was opened up by immigrants whose number totalled 125,000 in the period from 1937 to 1943.[75] These refugees were helped by the Border Government which supplied them with land, equipment and seed, and exempted their newly reclaimed land from taxes for three years.

Irrigation was one of the major agrarian programmes in the Border Regions, but unfortunately only scant data are available. It was reported that the area of land benefited by irrigation projects increased from 801 *mou* in 1937 to 8,010 *mou* in 1939. The goal of an additional 10,000 *mou* of irrigated land failed to materialize because of floods.[76]

4. MUTUAL-AID TEAMS AND RURAL COOPERATIVES

In the Border Regions during the war, mutual-aid teams were not only desirable as a means of increasing efficiency but necessary as more and more able-bodied men became engaged in military activities and a great quantity of farming equipment was destroyed. According to a report by Mao Tse-tung, "experience in the

[73] Mao Tse-tung, *Economic and Financial Problems, op. cit.*, p. 15.
[74] Gunther Stein, *op. cit.*, p. 166.
[75] Mao Tse-tung, *Economic and Financial Problems, op. cit.*, p. 13; and Gunther Stein, p. 166.
[76] *Work Report of the SKN Border Region Government, 1939–41, op. cit.*, p. 44.

Shensi-Kansu-Ninghsia Border Region has shown that two persons working in a labour exchange group equal three persons working individually in productive endeavour. Some labour exchange groups that ploughed, winnowed and harvested collectively, raised their production 200 per cent."[77] Another writer observed that "the labour exchange system was encouraged in order to increase efficiency in production. Already 24 per cent of the Border Region's 338,760 agricultural labourers had been organized and it was expected that this figure would be almost doubled by the end of 1944."[78] One Communist source stated that "in the 26 *hsien* in the Shansi-Chahar-Hopei-Border Region, there were 38,500 labour exchange groups with 230,000 peasants in 1944 which amounted to about 28 per cent of the rural labour. These groups not only engaged in farming, rural industries, trade, transport and household work, but also in education and public health, and propaganda activities."[79] Another report revealed that "in Northwest Shansi in 1944, 146,550 peasants out of 391,788, or 37·4 per cent, joined labour exchange groups. In some villages, the percentage was as high as 96 per cent."[80]

One of the important aspects of the CCP land programme in the Border Regions was the setting up of cooperatives whose activities covered a wide range of enterprises. Their major operations centred on the production and distribution of essential goods for the peasants such as cotton yarn and cloth, towels, salt, vegetable oil, flour, farming equipment, and seed. No detailed information is available regarding the activities of the cooperatives in the Communist areas during the war. Lin Po-ch'ü reported in January, 1944, that "24 per cent of the productive labour in the villages (of the Shensi-Kansu-Ninghsia Border Region) joined the rural cooperatives in 1942 and there were 260 such cooperatives in 1943."[81] In the SCH Border Region it was estimated that "there were over 9,000 cooperatives in Hopei province (in 1942), east and west of

[77] Mao Tse-tung, *On the Cooperatives* (Chinese), a report made at the Cadre Workers' Convention of the SKN Border Region in October, 1943.

[78] Harrison Forman, *op. cit.*, p. 85.

[79] Chao Lien-tse, *The Mutual Aid of Labour in a New Democracy* (Chinese), p. 19.

[80] Mu Hsien, *Bird's-eye-view of the Shansi-Suiyuan Liberated Area* (Chinese), p. 65.

[81] Lin Po-ch'ü, *Report to the Border Region Government*, January 6, 1944, pp. 27 and 30. The membership of cooperatives in the SKN area was reported by Mao Tse-tung as 140,218 in 1942. Mao Tse-tung, *Economic and Financial Problems* (Chinese), p. 57.

Peiping-Hankow Railway." A directive on cooperatives issued by the SCH Border Region Government on February 10, 1944, stipulated, among other things, that "the capital of the cooperatives be supplied by the government in the form of grain to be returned in instalments within five years. Peasants may buy cooperative shares with cash, savings bonds, or commodities such as grain, farm produce, and livestock. More than half of the capital of a cooperative must be invested in productive enterprises."

The major functions of cooperatives in the Border Regions can be classified into four general categories: (1) to provide for the peasants everyday necessities such as cloth, vegetable oil, and matches at a discount price; (2) to foster subsidiary occupations in the rural areas; (3) to extend loans in the form of grain, seed, and farm implements; and (4) to organize transport teams, in order to effect better distribution of needed commodities and an adjustment in market prices. The last two functions were a part of the credit and marketing systems in the Communist areas, which will be discussed in the following section.

5. CREDIT, MARKETING, AND SUBSIDIARY INDUSTRIES

Although comprehensive data are lacking, isolated reports indicate that the credit and marketing facilities in the Communist areas during the war were imperfect, due largely to the war.

Rural credit was offered both in cash and in kind and was managed mostly through cooperatives. There were four types of rural loans according to the "Regulations on rural credit" promulgated by the SKN Border Region Government in March, 1943: (1) credit for farm production (the purchase of oxen, tools, seed, fertilizer, and cotton) and for the promotion of commercial crops; (2) credit for farm implements, and the transport of daily necessities and agricultural products; (3) credit for subsidiary occupations and industries such as weaving, vegetable oil pressing, grazing, and trade; and (4) credit for irrigation and the building and maintenance of dikes, wells and canals.

Interest on long-term loans (longer than one year) was ten per cent per annum, and on short-term loans one per cent per month. The ordinary time limit for loans was generally one year, but repayment could be postponed or exempted if natural disaster made repayment at the stipulated time impossible. The "Regulations on loans for grain production" promulgated by the SCH Border Region

Government on February 4, 1941, stipulated that peasants could apply for loans in grain to develop production. The interest rate for such loans to cooperative members was fixed at ten per cent per annum and for ordinary peasants at one per cent per month. Repayment was to be made in grain in instalments after each harvest.

According to a report of Lin Po-ch'ü, the total amount in cash loaned to peasants exceeded 30 million dollars *pien-pi* (Border Region currency: the rate of exchange with the Nationalist currency in June 1944 was eight *pien-pi* to one CNC dollar).[82] Mao Tse-tung reported in his *Economic and Financial Probelms* that in 1942, 1·58 million *pien-pi* were lent to the peasants in the seven *hsien* in the Border Region. This sum, together with one million *pien-pi* contributed by the peasants themselves, bought 2,672 oxen and 4,980 farm tools. The total amount of rural credit scheduled for 1943 was 20·1 million *pien-pi*. Mao also emphasized the following points in the extension of rural credit:

(1) Preference should be given to those households that possess labour and land but are short of oxen or equipment;
(2) Farm implements and oxen should be purchased by the Border Government from outside of the Border Region and loaned to the peasants;
(3) Credit should be extended in a planned manner to those areas where there are lands to be reclaimed and peasants who have labour power and are in urgent need;
(4) Credit should be managed by the local administration or cooperatives that have the confidence of the villagers;
(5) The procedure for obtaining loans should be simplified, and complicated steps such as the filling out of applications should be avoided;
(6) Three million of the twenty million *pien-pi* earmarked for rural credit (in 1943) should be for cotton and wheat planting;
(7) Rural credit should be granted to meet the timely needs of the peasants, i.e., when planting is about to start.[83]

[82] Lin Po-ch'ü, *Report to the Border Region Government* (Chinese), January 6, 1944. In 1943, millet was sold at 2,100 *pien-pi* a picul, which was 300 catties (about 330 pounds) according to the weight system in Northern Shensi.

[83] Mao Tse-tung, *Economic and Financial Problems*, p. 39.

Like rural credit, many operations of storage, transportation and distribution were undertaken in a crude manner by the cooperatives. There were no modern methods of storage and packing. Transportation facilities in the modern sense were extremely limited in most Border Regions, as the Communist forces had to destroy many railways and highways to harass the Japanese. However, there did exist an underground network of communications, and a small quantity of medical supplies, tools, information, and even ammunition trickled in from enemy-held territory. On the whole transportation between villages and border areas was in the traditional style—by wheelbarrow, cart, beast of burden, and more often, by human carriers. This inadequate transportation and communication system was reflected in a report of Lin Po-ch'ü in 1942 in which he said:

> Communication facilities in the Border Region are too primitive. It is difficult to make use of materials that are even a few score of *li* (one *li* is about one-third of a mile) away. The transport expenses on salt and foodstuffs often exceed their original cost. Although we are not yet in a position to use modern transportation, at least roads should be built extensively for (mule-drawn or bullock) carts.[84]

In 1945 there were only twenty trucks in the SKN Border Region, according to one report.[85] Here cooperatives again played an important part by organizing caravans of donkeys, mules, horses, and bullocks for the transportation of salt and other essential goods and raw materials. In 1943, 530,000 donkey loads of salt were handled by the cooperatives. Conditions in less stable guerilla areas were even worse; there an inter-regional flow of goods was at a minimum. The double blockade of the Border Regions by the Japanese and the Kuomintang made smuggling a very important, albeit dangerous, undertaking.

This difficult situation, however, helped the development of those rural subsidiary industries that produced daily necessaries. Forced to choose between self-sufficiency (often on a subsistence level) and destruction, and driven by the desire for self-preservation reinforced by Messianic zeal for their cause, the Communists made great progress in supplying themselves with essential commodities such

[84] *Work Report of the SKN Border Region Government, 1939–1941, op. cit.* pp. 53–4. [85] Israel Epstein, *The Unfinished Revolution in China*, p. 269.

as grain, cotton cloth and vegetable oil. For instance, only 55 per cent of the cotton yarn used in the SKN Border Region in 1940 was produced locally, whereas in 1943 it was claimed that the import of cotton yarn was no longer needed.[86] In the Shansi-Suiyuan Liberated Area cotton weaving looms were reported to have increased from 13,000 in 1941 to 81,762 in 1945, in addition to 12,834 native-style looms. Peasant women engaged in weaving and textile manufacturing numbered 125,180 and supplied around 75 per cent of the needs of the area.[87] About 470,000 pounds of cotton seed oil were produced in the SKN Border Region in 1942.[88] The grazing industry's progress in the SKN Border Region was reported by Mao Tse-tung as follows: oxen, donkeys, and sheep increased from 70,000, 50,000, and 500,000 in 1937 to 202,914, 137,001, and 1,724,203 respectively in 1941.[89] The export of salt, which was a special product of the SKN Border Region, increased from about 7,000 tons in 1938 to 38,000 tons in 1943; and 3,700 donkeys were engaged in full-time salt transportation that year.[90] The silk industry had considerable importance in the rural economy in the SKN Border Region. In An-ting *hsien* alone, 3,585 peasant families were engaged in the silk industry in 1942. They produced about 40,000 pounds of silk cocoons during that year, valued at $60,000 *pien-pi*.[91]

Some of the other important subsidiary occupations as illustrated in the First and Second Agricultural Exhibitions held respectively in January 1939 and January 1940 at Yenan were: timber, fruit, preserved food and wild animal hides.[92]

6. AGRICULTURAL PRODUCTION AND PRODUCTIVITY

As a result of war destruction and the blockade, the levels of production and productivity in the Communist areas during the war fell below the pre-war average. The only exception, perhaps, was the SKN Border Region which was comparatively stable between 1937 and 1945.

The degree of general decrease of productive facilities and production in the guerilla areas was reflected in a report by Mu Hsin on the Shansi-Suiyuan Liberated Area:

[86] Israel Epstein, *op. cit.*, p. 269. [87] Mu Hsin, *op. cit.*, pp. 74–5.
[88] Mao Tse-tung, *Economic and Financial Problems, op. cit.*, p. 53.
[89] *Ibid.*, pp. 8–9. [90] Lin Po-ch'ü, *op. cit.*, p. 26.
[91] Mao Tse-tung, *Economic and Financial Problems, op. cit.*, p. 54.
[92] *Work Report of the SKN Border Region Government, 1939–1941, op. cit.*

When the Shansi-Suiyuan Liberated Area Administration was set up (in 1940), the conditions in Northwest Shansi as compared with the pre-war period (1937) were as follows: rural labour was reduced by 33 per cent; oxen, by 60 per cent; donkeys and mules, by 80–90 per cent; sheep, by 60 per cent; cultivated land, by 16 per cent; agricultural production, by 33 per cent; and cotton production, by 97 per cent. Other rural industries were all badly mauled.[93]

The North China Year Book of 1945 reports that the cultivated area of wheat, millet, and nine other crops in Hopei, Shansi, Shantung, and Northern Kiangsu was reduced by 16 per cent between 1937 and 1941. In some of the Japanese-occupied areas, as much as 25 per cent of the cultivated land was abandoned. The cotton area in North China had decreased by 78 per cent by 1940, and the yield per *mou* of dry land had declined by 30 to 60 per cent between 1940 and 1942. The decline of productivity per *mou* of irrigated land was 60 per cent in those three years and as much as 80 per cent as compared with 1937.[94]

The above indicates that during the war, the agricultural production and productivity in Communist areas, except in the SKN Border Region, were below the pre-war average. In the SKN Border Region, grain production reportedly almost doubled from 1937 to 1944 (from 1·1 million piculs to 2 million piculs). As no pre-war data were given, there is no means of comparison. A number of factors contributed to this increase of agricultural produce in the SKN Border Region. The role played by reclamation, irrigation, immigration and the organization of peasants into mutual-aid teams have been mentioned previously. The other important factors that helped to increase food production were the Eighth Route Army and the expansion of the territory of the Border Region. According to one American writer, the Border Region garrison in 1943 achieved 79·5 per cent self-sufficiency in grain, vegetable, uniforms and paper. By 1943 the Army had reclaimed 215,000 *mou* of land and hoped to have 824,034 *mou* under the plough by the end of 1944.[95] Communist forces in other areas were also engaged in production work. In Central Hopei, each soldier

[93] Mu Hsin, *op. cit.*, p. 62.

[94] Quoted by Chang Hsi-chang, *Land Policies in Communist China* (mimeographed pamphlet in English, 1947), p. 4. [95] Harrison Forman, *op. cit.*, p. 74.

was required to cultivate one *mou* (i.e., 1/6 of an acre) of land annually. All troops when not fighting pledged themselves to help the peasants in their fields for at least three days of each agricultural month.[96] Other government institutions also raised farm produce. In Yenan alone, government organizations cultivated 35,893 *mou* of land, and produced 6,011 piculs of grain and 19·2 million pounds of vegetables in one year. The area of land reclaimed by various government organs, excluding the army, totalled 113,414 *mou* in 1939.[97] In the Shansi-Suiyuan Liberated Area, the total area reclaimed by the army and other government institutions in 1944 was reportedly 150,000 *mou.*

From the spring of 1940 until the end of the war in August, 1945, there seemed to be little territorial change in the SKN Border Region. But between 1939 and 1940, the population jumped from 600,000 to 1,400,000. In 1945 the population was reported to be 1,500,000.[98] Of course this additional population included the influx of students and other non-agricultural personnel.

From the data furnished by the *Work Report of the Border Region Government* in 1941, total grain production in the period from 1937 to 1940 increased by 58 per cent, while the area of cultivated land increased by 16·8 per cent.[99]

7. AGRO-TECHNICAL IMPROVEMENTS

Scattered reports indicate that the Chinese Communists did not achieve any spectacular results in the field of agro-technical programmes. Although the importance of agro-technical improvements was realized by the Border Region Government, factors such as war, blockade, shortage of technical personnel and industrial backwardness made any substantial progress all but impossible. As mentioned previously, considerable work accomplished in the Border Regions regarding irrigation involved primarily human labour. As part of the conservation programme of the SKN Border Region, 292,535 trees were planted in 1937, 482,852 in 1938, and 1,392,160 in 1939. In 1940, 524 "public forests" were set aside as preserves.[100]

[96] Israel Epstein, *op. cit.*, pp. 278–9.

[97] Mao Tse-tung, *Economic and Financial Problems, op. cit.*, pp. 168–74.

[98] *Work Report of the SKN Border Region, 1939–1941, op. cit.*, p. 57; Gunther Stein, *op. cit.*, p. 177.

[99] *Ibid.*, pp. 44–5. [100] *Ibid.*, pp. 44–50.

The Agricultural Exhibitions held at Yenan from 1938 to 1945 showed many "improved crops"—more than seventy types of millet, seventy types of bean and a number of improved cotton seeds, fruits and vegetables.[101] There was also in Yenan an experimental farm which had 300 *mou* of land and fifty employees. The farm was divided into three departments: experimentation, veterinary, and dairy products. Animal vaccines were made at the farm and several improved crops were reported to have been developed. It was reported that one type of millet was pest-resistant and had a 10 per cent higher yield than ordinary millet; one breed of corn had a 50 per cent increase in yield; some improved potatoes were 25 per cent higher in yield; and several new types of vegetables and fruits were produced.[102] Animal breeding stations were set up to develop and distribute improved breeds of donkeys and sheep. Technical advice regarding pest control, prevention of animal diseases, and farming techniques was given to the peasants through government agencies.[103] In the Shansi-Chahar-Hopei Border Region, 344,229 agricultural implements were produced by arsenals and cooperative workshops in 1940 and 1941. Fragmentary as the above reports are, they are given here to indicate the general lines along which the Chinese Communists worked in the agro-technical field during the war.

8. EFFECTS OF CHINESE COMMUNISTS' WAR-TIME LAND POLICY ON RURAL STRATIFICATION AND STANDARD OF LIVING

Although no land redistribution policy was carried out in war-time in the various Communist areas (except in the SKN Border Region from 1935–1937), the Communists reported that their rent and interest reduction programme had resulted in an increase of the middle class in the rural areas. An investigation of a "typical village" in the SKN area showed that during the war years the number of rich and middle peasant households had increased from 68 per cent to 88 per cent, while poor peasant and farm labourer households had decreased from 32 to 12 per cent. Per capita land holding of the various rural classes was reported as on page 64.[104]

[101] *Ibid.*, pp. 51–2.
[102] Huang Yen-pei, *Return From Yenan* (Chinese), pp. 33–4.
[103] Mao Tse-tung, *Economic and Financial Problems, op. cit.*, p. 47.
[104] Israel Epstein, *op. cit.*, p. 271.

Class	*Average land holding in acres*	
	1936	*1942*
Farm labourer	0	1·3
Poor peasant	4·7	6·7
Middle peasant	7·0	17·0
Rich peasant	10·0	18·0

One foreign observer reported that "in a typical village (in the SKN Border Region) from 1936 to 1942, the number of families of landless labourers decreased from 14 to 1; the number of poor peasant families fell from 48 to 15; that of middle peasant families rose from 44 to 94; and that of rich peasant families from 2 to 15; while the total number of households in the village increased from 108 to 125."[105] In the Shansi-Chahar-Hopei Area, an investigation of 35 villages in 1943 showed the following changes in class composition:[106]

Class	*1937*		*1942*	
	% in households	*% in landholding*	*% in households*	*% in landholding*
Landlord	2·42	16·43	1·91	10·17
Rich peasant	4·50	21·93	7·88	19·56
Middle peasant	35·42	41·69	44·31	49·14
Poor peasant and farm labourer	47·53	19·10	40·95	20·12

Although comprehensive data are lacking, the available information from Communist sources indicates an apparent gradual trend towards the equalization of landholdings in the Communist areas during the Sino-Japanese War.

In addition to political and social reforms which will be discussed later, the CCP sources reported that the majority of the peasants in the Border Regions improved their lot economically. However,

[105] Gunther Stein, *op. cit.*, p. 163.
[106] Ti Ch'ao-pei, *Peasant Problem in Post-War China* (Chinese), p. 7.

information available also indicates that the living conditions in the SKN Border Region were not without hardships. In 1940 and 1941, the situation was especially trying as a result of the KMT blockade. Mao Tse-tung described that period as follows: "We were almost without clothes, vegetable oil, paper, or vegetables. The soldiers had no shoes or socks, and the cadres spent the winter without blankets."[107] One foreign observer also reported that there was a drop in the standard of living in the Communist army from 1939 as 100 per cent to 88 per cent in 1940 and to 84·2 per cent in 1941. The turning point seemed to have reached in 1943 when the army's living standard went up to 125 per cent compared with that of the previous year.[108]

Some reports described the "betterment of the peasants' lot" in other Communist-held territories during the war. One writer claimed that "in the Shansi-Suiyuan Liberated Area, from 1940 to 1944, 100 out of 1,961 middle peasant households were raised to the status of rich peasants and 1,993 out of 3,378 poor peasants became rich or middle peasants."[109] In general, however, it seems reasonable to assume that no spectacular rise in the peasants' living standards was realized in the Communist areas under the strain of fighting and blockade. It was from many of the political and social measures undertaken by the Communists that the peasants benefited most.

9. OTHER AGRARIAN PROGRAMMES

(*i*) *Village administration.* The organization and functions of basic local administrations such as the *hsiang* and *ts'un* Offices and Councils have been discussed previously. According to one survey, in the *hsiang* Councils in the eight *hsien* of the SKN Border Region, Communist councillors constituted 19·8 per cent of the membership, and after the 1942 *hsiang* Council elections, it was claimed that the three-thirds system[110] prevailed everywhere.[111] It was reported that in 1944, among the 9,967 candidates elected to the district Councils, 7,490 or 75·6 per cent were non-Communists. The class composition of these councillors was reported to be as follows:

[107] Mao Tse-tung, *Economic and Financial Problems*, *op. cit.*, p. 2.

[108] Harrison Forman, *op. cit.*, p. 74.

[109] Mu Hsin, *op. cit.*, p. 40.

[110] The "three-thirds system" provided that in all levels of government in the Border Regions, one-third of the officials should be Kuomintang members, one-third Communists, and one-third independents.

[111] *Regulations and Policies of the SKN Border Region*, *op. cit.*, pp. 20–1.

landlord and gentry, 1·8 per cent; rich peasants, 7 per cent; middle peasants, 24·4 per cent; poor peasants, 55·6 per cent; tenant farmers, 0·5 per cent; farm labourers, 5·1 per cent; handicraftsmen, 3·9 per cent; and merchants, 1·7 per cent.[112] In fifty-five administrative villages investigated, the average percentage of rural classes represented in the *ts'un* Councils was described as follows: middle peasants, 44 per cent; poor peasants, farm labourers and rural workers, 38 per cent; landlords and rich peasants, 17 per cent; and merchants, 1 per cent. Among the *ts'un* chiefs, 32 per cent were middle peasants, 54 per cent poor peasants, and 14 per cent landlords and rich peasants. Women councillors constituted about 10 per cent.[113]

Regarding the details about village elections in the Border Region, one American observer gave the following eye-witness account:

> The Election Committee of eleven sat in a clearing examining the voters' qualifications. The Committee was composed of one rich peasant, one middle peasant, three poor peasants, two farm labourers, three women, and a primary school teacher. Of the 620 prospective voters whose names were posted on a bulletin board, only three were declared unqualified. One was feeble-minded and the other two were not yet 18 years old.[114]

While the Chinese Communists encouraged popular participation in administration and allotted one-third of the representation to Kuomintang members, controlling power lay in the hands of the Party. Whether through sympathy with the Communist programme or the Communists' control of the mass organizations from which most of the "non-partisan" members were elected, the Communist Party never had to worry about deviations from its basic platform in the various administrations. The cadres at the village level were mostly new recruits after 1937.[115] Most of them had only been educated as far as the middle school level. However, their honesty and hard work enhanced the effectiveness and popularity of the administration.

[112] Israel Epstein, *op. cit.*, p. 247. [113] Mu Hsin, *op. cit.*, pp. 19–20.

[114] Harrison Forman, *op. cit.*, pp. 98–9.

[115] In 1944 there were 11,500 on the government pay roll in the SKN Border Region, including 3,300 in the educational institutions. Seventy per cent of the lower class cadres joined after the war (July 7, 1937). *Collection of Policies and Regulations of the SKN Border Region* (Chinese), Vol. 2, pp. 9, 17.

(*ii*) *Village mass organizations.* There are little statistical data available regarding the organizational strength of the mass organizations in the villages such as the youth corps, the women's league, the mutual-aid teams, the people's militia, and others. But reports indicate that they were extensively organized. The people's militia, consisting of several million men because of wartime needs, played an especially important role in the Border Regions. These village forces served not only as auxiliary and guerilla units, but as an adjunct of the agrarian programme such as the production-increase movement. Backed by about 1·5 million regular Communist troops, they greatly helped in the implementation of the land policy among the peasantry in the Communist areas during the Sino-Japanese War.

(*iii*) *Social and educational reform programmes.* The social reforms in the rural areas under Communist control during the war centered on the improvement of the status of peasant women, the abolition of undesirable customs and habits such as superstitious practices, opium-smoking and gambling, and the reform of loafers in the villages. These programmes formed an integral part of the agrarian reform of the CCP and helped to provide greater incentive for the increase of agricultural production.

Women's right to inherit property, chiefly in regard to land, was guaranteed.[116] They were given equal rights with men to participate in political activities, and many of them were elected to village administrative offices. Monogamous marriage was made the rule, as in the Kuomintang areas; but unlike their Kuomintang counterparts Communist officials kept no concubines or mistresses. Divorce was made easier for the peasant women, but it was not encouraged.[117] Also discouraged were the practices in the rural districts of keeping slave-maids and child daughters-in-law. The elevation of the status of peasant women came mainly from their better economic position as a result of property inheritance, from subsidiary occupations such as weaving, and from increased opportunity to receive education. Girls and even adult women were given every encouragement to join the village school or reading classes. Literacy enhanced both their social mobility and prestige.

[116] For more details, see *Regulations on the Women's Rights to Inheritance* (Chinese), SCH Border Region Government, June 15, 1943.

[117] For more details, see *Marriage Law* (Chinese), SKN Border Region Government, March 20, 1944.

The strengthening of the position of village youth had a great deal to do with the important role played by the people's militia and the hard and often dangerous work undertaken by young village officials. Old peasants were generally too weak or timid for such jobs and power gradually shifted into the hands of more vigorous young peasants. Even village children joined in defence and productive work when they were not at school. Many of the "little devils" distinguished themselves in village security work and in agricultural odd jobs such as the removing of pest insects and picking up of animal manure for fertilizer.

Another social programme in the Border Region publicized both by the Communists and outside observers was the reform of *Erh-liu-tze*. *Erh-liu-tze* is a colloquial term for the "loafers" in the Border Region who were undesirables because of such bad habits as opium-smoking, gambling, and thieving. Harrison Forman gave a vivid description of the measures used by the Communists to transform these social "incurables" into productive peasants. One report stated that the number of *Erh-liu-tze* in the SKN Border Region was reduced from about 30,000 in 1935 to 400 in 1945.[118] Mao Tse-tung describes the methods used to "mobilize" these loafers in the following manner: (1) educate and convince them that production work will result in a better living for them; (2) assign each of them a definite task and check them regularly; (3) organize peasants to offer them assistance and supervision; (4) mobilize the villagers to encourage and persuade them; (5) give them the income and products from their work; and (6) offer every help in solving their difficulties through the government.[119] Side by side with the reform of these "social wastrels," steps were taken to weed out many of the factors responsible for their bad habits, such as opium-smoking, gambling, prostitution, and superstitious practices.

Education in the Border Regions was closely co-ordinated with agricultural production work. Two directives on education, issued respectively by the SCH and SKN Border Region Governments on November 11, 1943, and April 18, 1944, both stressed that "education must unite with the production movement," and emphasized the propagation of farming knowledge and techniques. To achieve the above objective a number of educational devices

[118] Harrison Forman, *op. cit.*, p. 71.

[119] Mao Tse-tung, *Economic and Financial Problems*, *op. cit.*, p. 29.

besides the regular village school were utilized. Among these were evening classes, newspaper reading groups, night schools, family reading units, and vocational training classes. Villagers were encouraged to study wherever they could—at home, in the fields as well as in school. Various media were used to persuade the masses to adopt better farming methods and to increase their efforts. Notable among these means of propaganda and education were the "blackboard" newspapers, lectures, exhibitions, personal interviews, group discussions, story telling, village dramas, and the folk dance known as *yangko*. "Blackboard" newspapers were bulletins written either on a board or on the wall. They publicized government directives on agriculture and announced the results of "emulation contests" between mutual-aid teams as well as between agricultural labour heroes. Drama teams formed by villagers utilized many of the traditional techniques, but with new themes such as the commendation of labour heroes and the merits of increasing production. The plots often depicted local personalities and the dialogue used was colloquial and simple. One drama team of Yenan, the "Resistance Drama Club," gave eighty performances in four months to more than 50,000 spectators in 1940.[120] The "July Drama Club" of the Shansi-Suiyuan Liberated Area acted before an audience of more than 3,000,000 from July 1939 to January 1945 in 1,500 performances.[121] The *yangko*, which will be discussed further in a later section, was an indigenous folk dance popular among the peasants in China. It was a form of song or dance or drama, or a combination of these. As it was simple, easy to learn, and colourful, its popularity spread far and wide. The *yangko*, like the other propaganda media, was modified both in form and in content to depict the life of the peasants, and to publicize the Communist agrarian programmes in simple and realistic style. Many *yangko* lauded the deeds of the more famous agricultural labour heroes of the Border Regions.

The labour heroes were those peasants who were chosen, generally by election, for their special achievements in various aspects of agriculture—crop production, irrigation projects, reclamation, cotton cultivation, and so on. They were given public acclaim as well as material rewards to stimulate others to higher incentive and greater production.

[120] *Work Report of the SKN Border Region Government, 1930–1941, op. cit.*, p. 76. [121] Mu Hsin, *op. cit.*, p. 92.

The above-mentioned political and social reforms were closely co-ordinated with other land programmes. They formed an integral part of the Communists' effort to transform the traditional, backward agrarian system and to increase agricultural production. Many of these measures, as we shall see, have been retained in the land policy of the Chinese Communists in the post-war period.

Comments on the Period

The wartime agrarian policy of the Chinese Communists was designed to attract support from all rural classes for the war effort and for expansion of power by the CCP. Thus the landlords' "civil, political, and property rights were guaranteed as well as those of the peasants."[122] Collection of rent and interest was also guaranteed, after the carrying into effect of rent and interest reduction stipulated by the Border Region Government. In the village administration, all elements, including the Kuomintang and the gentry, were represented and the policy of limiting the Communists' seats to one-third was generally observed. This moderate programme was, however, of a transitional nature rather than a long-term policy. This was made clear in the major writings of Mao Tse-tung of this period, such as *New Democracy* (January, 1940), *Economic and Financial Problems* (December, 1942), and *On Coalition Government* (April, 1945). The conciliatory nature of the land programmes served chiefly to win over the upper and middle classes in the rural as well as urban areas until the peasants were sufficiently organized and mobilized. At the beginning of the war, popular understanding of Communism was not yet widespread among the peasants in North China, partly because of propaganda by the Kuomintang, partly because of the extreme measures implemented by the Communists during the Kiangsi Soviet period, and partly because of the traditional conservatism of the Chinese rural community. The advocacy of a moderate, practical policy together with a number of other moves which will be discussed in the following sections, helped the Communists to expand their influence in China from about a score of *hsien* in 1937 to about one-fourth of the mainland at the end of the war in August, 1945.

[122] See *Resolution of the Central Committee on Land Policy in Anti-Japanese Base Areas* (Chinese), January 28, 1942.

With their eyes on political needs and their fingers on the public pulse, the Chinese Communists put increasing emphasis on their demand for national resistance against Japan; and an anti-Japanese united front was finally established after the December Twelfth (1936) Sian Incident, when Chiang Kai-shek was released by his kidnappers Generals Chang Hsüeh-liang and Yang Hu-cheng, reportedly upon the advice of the Chinese Communists. The first sentence of the *Resolution of the Central Committee on Land Policy in Anti-Japanese Base Areas* dated January 28, 1942, stated that "since the beginning of the war of resistance (July 7, 1937), the land policy carried out by our Party in various anti-Japanese bases has been a land policy based on the anti-Japanese national united front." The shift from the land confiscation policy to rent and interest reduction was attributed to the fact that "most of the landlords are anti-Japanese." Peasants were organized into Peasants' National Salvation Associations. The composition of the CCP itself was also undergoing a change in the war. Ninety-three per cent of its membership, which totalled 1·2 million at the end of 1944, joined after the war began, and ninety per cent of these new recruits were peasants. Many of them came to the Party not after having read the theories of Marx, Lenin, Stalin and Mao Tse-tung, but in the course of liberating their homes from the Japanese and reforming the social life of their villages. This nationalistic tinge of the CCP was also manifested during the war in many other ways.[123] When Mao Tse-tung was asked whether the Communists were Chinese first or Communists first, he replied, "Without a Chinese nation there could be no Chinese Communist Party. You might just as well ask what is first, children or parents?"[124] The strong nationalistic flavour at Yenan was reported by many observers who visited there during the Sino-Japanese War.

The skilful utilization of the nationalistic sentiments of the Chinese rural populace during the anti-Japanese war was only one of the practical approaches taken by the Chinese Communists to expand the power and popularity of the Party. Throughout, in legislation and directives, there was a constant reminder that adjustments must

[123] For example, the term "Soviet" and "Red Army" were dropped after 1937 and replaced by "Border Region" and "8th Route Army". The Marx-Lenin Institute at Yenan was changed to the Party School. Lu Hsün, the late dean of Chinese writers, replaced Gorki as the name of another academy in the Communist capital.

[124] Gunther Stein, *op. cit.*, p. 118.

be made and attention paid to specific local conditions and needs. This pragmatic approach is reflected in the "Outline for the Simplification of the Administrative Structure" promulgated by the SKN Border Region Government in March, 1943.

> First . . . good ideas and good policies are results of investigation and studies of actual conditions. Without familiarity with the circumstances, without understanding the actual needs of the people and the situation of the lower administrations, without careful studies and gathering of information, there can hardly be good ideas and good policies. Mistakes of subjectivism will be committed. Second, the thorough realization of the policies. . . . To accomplish them, it is both necessary to handle and utilize skilfully the cadres and to make periodical checks on the policies, decisions, and effects. Assistance should be given to overcome the difficulties encountered by the lower administrations, mistakes rectified, and timely rewards and encouragements given. Third, past experiences should be utilized for the training and directing of lower cadres as well as the administrative heads themselves. The bureaucratic practice of unrealistic planning, alienation from the people, formalism, red tape, and issuing orders instead of explaining and persuading must be avoided. . . .[125]

As previously described, in the SKN Border Region, which was the most stable area under Communist control during the war, grain production increased by about 58 per cent between 1937 and 1940. As the amount of cultivated area was raised by 16·8 per cent during the same period and more farm labour was available as a result of the influx of immigrants, it may be assumed that the enhanced agricultural yield was not primarily due to agro-technical improvements in agriculture. Marketing facilities were poor, but the dearth of farm credit was partially remedied by the extensive organization of mutual-aid teams, although the problem was not wholly solved. Due to the pressing need for manpower in the war, the question of rural underemployment temporarily faded into the background. However, it is only fair to point out that during the war, with constant pressure from the Japanese army, with a tight blockade set up by both Japan and the Kuomintang, and with no industrial cities in the

[125] *Collection of Policies and Laws of the SKN Border Region*, Vol. II (Chinese), pp. 15–16.

Communist areas, there was little possibility for providing materials, equipment, and technicians necessary to develop scientific farming.

When the Chinese Communists began to expand their land reform programme outside the SKN Border Region, the shortage in trained cadres became more acute. Although the various training centres and schools at Yenan turned out a few thousand graduates annually, they were soon swallowed up by the vastness of the North China plain. A report of the SKN Border Region Government pointed out that "personnel at the lower level is comparatively weak."[126] Another directive of the SCH Border Region Government, dated February 25, 1944, complained that "in some guerilla areas not yet consolidated, the village administration is still in the hands of the feudal elements, loafers, and even traitors."[127] The problem was further aggravated by the fact that the training period for the cadres was generally short, ranging from a few months to two years. Because of years of isolation due to the blockade, it was often difficult for the Communist cadres to keep abreast of current world events. Theodore White, in his description of the Yenan leaders, said:

> They knew their own country thoroughly and understood the villages....they knew precisely what the peasants' grievances were and precisely how those grievances could be transmuted into action....Their ignorance of the outside world was sometimes shocking. They knew little of high finance, protocol, or Western administration; their understanding of industry, Western engineering, and international commerce was primitive....But they knew down to the last detail the impact of the Western world on China and how they planned to harness the energy and technology of the West for the benefit of the peasant.[128]

The CCP had many capable political leaders, but not enough trained specialists such as technicians and economists at that time. Also, disciplined indoctrination, although yielding efficiency, at times dampened the initiative of certain individuals. P'eng Chen, member of the Central Committee, said:

[126] *Collection of Policies and Laws of the SKN Border Region, op. cit.*, Vol. 2, p. 9.

[127] "Directive on the Strengthening, and Reformation of Village Administrations" (Chinese), *ibid*.

[128] Theodore White and Annalee Jacoby, *Thunder out of China*, p. 229.

Some of the cadres in the Party have a dishonest attitude: when one thing is said to be good, then everyone says it is good; bad, they all say it is bad. They are like a kite directed by the wind, without its own stand or its own principles. Another undesirable attitude is to give orders arbitrarily.[129]

D. *The Post-War Transitional Period, 1945–1949*

Among the four periods covered this one is the shortest spanning about five years from August 1945, when the Sino-Japanese War ended, to June 1950 when the new Agrarian Reform Law was promulgated. But this transitional period is the most complicated one, embodying many shifts in the land policy of the CCP. There were four major changes during this stretch of five years. The first stage which lasted from August 1945 to December 1946 was, on the whole, a continuation of the wartime programme of rent and interest reductions. The second stage which lasted from December 1946 to October 1947 was characterized by the compulsory purchase of "excess land" of the landlords. The third stage which lasted from October 1947 to the spring of 1948 was the most radical in the post-Soviet period, and was expressed through the Land Law of October 10, 1947, calling for land redistribution and the elimination of the rich peasantry as a class. The fourth stage which lasted from the spring of 1948 to June 1950 showed a swing back to moderation, with the reduction of rent and interest again becoming the order of the day in the new liberated areas.[130] Also, due to the transitional nature of this period, some aspects can only be discussed briefly, as comprehensive data are not available.

Party Theory on the Land Question

A major shift in Party theory came in this period, when the 2nd Session of the 7th Plenum of the Central Committee, CCP, officially announced that "the centre of gravity of Party work is shifted from

[129] P'eng Chen, "Equal Division of Land and Reorganizing Our Ranks," a report made to the Land Conference of the SCH Border Region, (1947), *Fight for the Purification of Party Organization* (Chinese), p. 11.

[130] This term generally covers those new areas that came under the control of the CCP from the autumn of 1947 onward.

rural areas to the cities."[131] This was closely tied in with political and economic considerations. Politically, this decision reflected the continuous effort of the CCP to reconcile the Marxist theory of leadership by the urban proletariat with the fact that the CCP came to power mainly through the strength and support of the peasants. Economically, the CCP must also have realized that, with the taking over of metropolitan cities like Tientsin, Peking and Shanghai, as well as the increasing needs of reconstruction and rehabilitation and the forthcoming industrialization programme, the economic and financial needs which were formerly sustained principally by agricultural produce could not be met successfully without greater industrial production. However, inasmuch as China is predominantly agricultural, agrarian policy continued to receive top attention from Party leaders.

Before this pronouncement in March 1949, there were a number of tactical changes in the line of the CCP regarding land policy, although the overall theory which gave the peasantry a primary role in the Chinese revolution (in principle under the leadership of the workers) persisted. Briefly, from August 14, 1945, when Japan surrendered, to the spring of 1948, the principles of the CCP land policy gave an increasingly important role to the poor peasants and hired farm labourers. Provided with the legal sanction of the Land Law of October 10, 1947, not only the landlords' but also the rich peasants' properties were confiscated for redistribution without compensation. Poor Peasants' Corps (including farm labourers) were designated as the "legal executive organ" in carrying out the land reform. During the winter of 1947-48, the poor peasants were encouraged to give no quarter to the landlords and rich peasants; as a result, a number of the latter were subject to harsh treatment. Even the properties of some middle peasants were infringed upon in what was later labelled "ultra-leftist errors." In the spring of 1948, after Jen Pi-shih's speech on January 12, 1948, in which he emphasized the importance of middle peasants and criticized the use of physical violence against the landlords, the line was again reversed to moderation. Beginning with the fall of 1948, land redistribution ceased and reduction of rent and interest

[131] The resolution was made public on March 23, 1949 at Shih-chia-chuang, near Peiping. At that time, a number of large cities like Kirin, Loyang, Kaifeng, Tsinan, Changchun, Mukden, Tientsin and Peiping were successively occupied by the Chinese Communist forces.

became the order of the day until June 1950, when land redistribution was again enforced. That this moderate measure of the 1948–50 period was only of a transitional nature was reflected in an editorial of the *Yu-hsi jih-pao* (*West Honan Daily*) of August 24, 1948, which stated that "it (the carrying out of rent and interest reduction) is because the preparatory work of agrarian reform in the greater part of Central China still has not progressed to the fullest extent, and not because the policy of agrarian reform (i.e., land redistribution) is incorrect nor because the territory of Central China is unsuitable for agrarian reform. . . . We must have the proper environment and must complete the preparatory work; the most important part being that the peasants must possess a high degree of political consciousness and confidence in the success of the revolution." This implied that when the power of the CCP was consolidated and the peasants properly indoctrinated, land redistribution was to be carried out. The overall slogan during this transitional period was enunciated by Mao Tse-tung as "to rely on poor peasants, co-operate with middle peasants, eliminate the feudal system of exploitation in a planned, discriminate manner, and develop agricultural production."[132]

Legislation and Programmes

Following the various shifts in tactics during this period, the emphasis in the programme varied too, although the principal goal of increasing agricultural production and organizing the peasants remained paramount throughout.

For about fifteen months following V-J Day (August 14, 1945), the wartime programme of rent and interest reduction remained the general guiding principle. However, several measures were adopted by the CCP to satisfy the increasing demand for land by the poor peasants and farm labourers now that the common enemy of Japanese imperialism was removed. Land belonging to the Japanese government or its officials or to the Japanese puppet regime or its officials was confiscated and redistributed. According to one report, such "public land" in certain areas in the Northeast constituted from one-third to one-half of the total cultivated area.[133] Large land holdings which belonged to landlords who cooperated

[132] Mao Tse-tung, *Speech at the Cadres' Conference of the Shansi-Suiyuan Liberated Area* (Chinese), April 1, 1948.

[133] *Handbook of New Democracy*, 1947 (Chinese, Hongkong), pp. 82–3.

with the enemy were also expropriated. On May 4, 1946, a directive was issued by the Central Committee of the CCP ordering that landlords' land should be redistributed among the landless, with the landlords allowed to keep a larger-than-average share of land. It also warned against trespassing upon the properties of the rich peasants. On December 21, 1946, the Draft Law for government purchase of landlords' land in the Shensi-Kansu-Ninghsia Border Region was promulgated and soon similar programmes were adopted in other Communist areas. The salient features of the Draft Law were as follows:

(1) All land of the landlord over and above the following reservations for himself and his family may be purchased by the government with land bonds payable in grain and redeemable in ten years. In general, the landlord's household shall keep land to the extent of 50 per cent more than the per capita land owned by the middle peasant household in the same locality . . . . Landlords who contributed to the anti-Japanese War may keep 100 per cent more than the per capita average of land owned by the middle peasants . . . . Land cultivated by the owners' household, irrespective of size, is not subject to government purchase.

(2) Land owned by rich peasants is not subject to government purchase.

(3) Prices for the land (to be purchased) shall be fixed jointly by the *hsiang* administration, the *hsiang* Peasants' Association, and the landlord in question. The price of the land to be purchased is to be progressively reduced when the area becomes larger.

(4) Surplus houses are subject also to purchase by bonds.

(5) For land belonging to religious establishments and clans, the local inhabitants shall decide whether it should be purchased or not.

(6) Land purchased by the government shall be distributed to landless peasants and peasants with little land at a price which is 50 per cent of the original purchase price. This half-price shall be paid by instalments within ten years. Peasants who are too poor to pay may be exempted from all payment at the recommendation of the district

government and with the approval of the Border Region Government.[134]

Under the double pressure of an increasing clamour of the peasants for more land and the need for obtaining a greater effort from the poor peasants who formed the backbone in the CCP's political and military struggle against the Kuomintang, the pendulum of land policy continued to swing to the left. In September 1947, leading cadres who engaged in land reform work were called upon by the Central Committee of the CCP "to review past experiences and to formulate new policies." The result was the Land Law, passed on September 13, 1947 was promulgated on October 10, 1947. The salient points in this legislation are as follows:

(1) Land ownership rights of all landlords as well as those of all ancestral shrines, temples, monasteries, schools, institutions and organizations are all abolished. (Articles 2 and 3.)

(2) The village Peasants' Association is to take over the landlords' draft animals, farm implements, houses, grain and other properties and also to requisition the surplus portions of the above properties of the rich peasants. They shall then be redistributed to peasants and other poor people who are lacking in these properties. An equal portion is to be allotted to the landlord. (Article 8.)

(3) Land deeds shall be issued to those who receive land. They shall be allowed to freely manage, but not sell and rent out, the land under specific conditions. Land contracts as well as debts incurred before the promulgation of the Land Law are declared null and void. (Article 11.)

Following the enactment of this Law, the winter of 1947–48 witnessed a series of radical measures in the form of "struggle meetings" and "settle account" mass gatherings which often resulted in harsh treatment of the landlords and rich peasants. The poor peasants were granted undisputed power, and in their excitement, the properties of many middle peasants were infringed upon. Sensing the dissatisfaction of the middle peasants and the confusion

[134] For details, see *Draft Law for Government Purchase of Landlords' Land* (Chinese), Appendix II; Chang Hsi-chang, "Land Policies in Communist China," February 1948, a mimeographed pamphlet in limited distribution, pp. 16–20.

caused in the villages, the Communist leaders exhorted the cadres to "safeguard the interests of the middle peasants" and warned against "ultra-leftist deviations."[135] At the end of 1947, the Central Committee reissued the two documents of the Kiangsi Soviet days (1933) on the classification of the status of various rural classes, with certain modifications. Following their general principles, the late Jen Pi-shih gave definitions of the various rural classes in his speech of January 1948 as follows:

(1) Landlords: those who possess much land, do not labour themselves — especially those relying on exploiting the peasants' land rent — or concurrently engaged in usury and profit without working;
(2) Rich peasants: those who possess much land, ploughing animals, and farm implements, participate themselves in the principal farm labour, and at the same time exploit hired labour;
(3) Middle peasants: those with land, ploughing animals, and agricultural implements, labouring themselves and not exploiting or only slightly exploiting others;
(4) Poor peasants: those with little land, agricultural implements, etc., labouring themselves and at the same time selling a portion of their labour power; and
(5) Farm labourers: those who do not possess land, ploughing animals or agricultural implements and sell their own labour power.

Jen further elaborated upon the delicate but all-important question of differentiating rich from middle peasants by saying that "those engaging in slight exploitation such as hiring others to herd cattle or sheep, hiring part-time labourers or labourers on a monthly basis or even one full-time labourer or so, or perhaps renting out a little land or making small loans, from which the income does not exceed 25 per cent of their gross income, are still considered middle peasants or well-to-do middle peasants." This was an evidence of the moderate trend adopted by the CCP hierarchy in land policy

[135] See Mao Tse-tung, *Present Situation and Our Tasks* (Chinese), December 25, 1947; Jen Pi-shih, *Some Problems in the Agrarian Reform* (Chinese), January 12, 1948; and Mao Tse-tung, *Speech at the Cadres' Conference of the Shansi-Suiyuan Liberated Areas* (Chinese), April 1, 1948.

as the provisions in the reissued 1933 document allowed only 15 per cent in ordinary cases for the income from exploitation for the middle peasants.

Echoing this new tune, the Central Committee on February 22, 1948 issued a directive "On Land Reform and Party Purification Work in the Old and Semi-old Areas." It divided the Communist areas into three categories: the "old areas," the "semi-old areas," and the "new areas," according to the degree of consolidation. "In the first category," the directive stated, "the land reform is comparatively thorough. . . and there should be no more land redistribution but only an adjustment of land made through mutual consent. In the second category, the land reform has not been thorough . . . and land redistribution should be effected if the majority of the peasants so demand it. Consent of the middle peasants must be obtained when their land is affected and not more than one-quarter of their land should be taken. In the third category, land reform is very inadequately carried out or has not been undertaken at all. In these areas, the policy of confiscating excess land plus other properties of the landlords and the rich peasants should be implemented. The properties of middle peasants must not be touched without their consent."

In the period from April 1948 to June 1950, during which the Communists crossed the Yangtze River and gained control of East, Central, South, Southwest, and Northwest China, the moderate land policy continued. A number of directives were issued by the Central Committee as well as by regional party organs. The major ones available are: *Directive on Land Reform* (CC, CCP, February 22, 1948); *Directive on Land Reform and Party Purification* (CC, CCP, May 25, 1948); *Outline for the Reduction of Rent and Interest* (Central China Bureau, CCP, October 8, 1948); *Outline for Reduction of Rent and Interest* (Political Department, Kwangtung-Kiangsi, Human-Border Region Forces, June 1949); *Provisional Regulations for Rent Reduction in the New Areas in East China* (East China Bureau, CCP, September 1949); and *Regulations for Rent and Interest Reduction in the Central-South Area* (Military and Political Committee, Central-South China, February 1950). The key points of these official pronouncements, which followed in general the programme of the Sino-Japanese War period, may be summarized as follows:

(1) Rent was reduced by 25 per cent, and the total amount of rent could not exceed 37·5 per cent of the crop yield.

(2) Rent in arrears was declared null and void; rent deposit as well as other forms of extortions were prohibited.

(3) Old debts were to be calculated at an interest rate ranging from 15 to 30 per cent per annum. If interest payments equalled or exceeded the loan, no more interest was to be paid; if the interest payments doubled the loan or more, the debt was considered cancelled.

(4) Investments by landlords and rich peasants in industry and commerce were to be protected. If such properties were infringed upon by mistake, they were to be returned.

(5) Clan land was to be managed by the village community, and land belonging to religious organizations was to be protected.

(6) The Peasants' Associations were designated as the official organ to carry out the programme of reduction of rent and interest.

The shift toward moderation is discernible in these documents. For example, the Directive of the Central Committee regarding land reform issued on May 25, 1948, stated:

> The direction of work should be shifted from land redistribution to unifying all the labouring people in the villages and organizing the landlords and rich peasants to develop agricultural production together. . . . Only in those areas where conditions are ripe is land redistribution to be carried out. . . . The question of land redistribution must not be raised in those districts where only slight difference in land holding exists between the poor and the middle peasants. In these districts the central task should be the recovery and development of production.[136]

That this conciliatory gesture represented a temporary withdrawal is seen by the fact that land redistribution continued to be enforced in the "new areas" in the Northeast and North China, where the hold of the Communists had been consolidated. This fluid policy of adjustment to circumstances was also reflected in the fact that, although the government stipulated that "no land redistribution would be carried out before the summer harvest of 1952 in the six provinces of Kwangsi, Yunnan, Kweichow, Szechuan, Sikiang, and Suiyuan,"[137] land redistribution was implemented in the winter

[136] Mao Tse-tung, *Speech at the Cadres' Conference of the Shansi-Suiyuan Liberated Area, op. cit.*, pp. 23–7.

[137] Government Administrative Council (Central People's Government), *Directive on Land Reform and Taxation in Kind in the New Liberated Areas* (Chinese), February 28, 1950.

of 1951–52, when the Communists found they were in a position to do so.

Regarding the programme of agricultural taxation, no information is available on the agricultural taxes collected in the early stages of this period. Presumably the progressive agricultural tax instituted during war-time was continued, with local variations. The rate of agricultural tax for the year 1948 was reported by Communist sources as 20 per cent of the agricultural income of the peasants.[138] This indicates that the fighting against the Nationalists necessitated a heavier tax scale. Peasants in the liberated areas reportedly paid about 10 per cent of their income as agricultural taxes in the latter years of the Sino-Japanese War. The directive of February 28, 1950, issued by the Government Administrative Council ruled that "the average (of agricultural taxation) must not exceed 17 per cent of the total agricultural yield, and the additional public grain levied by the local people's governments must not exceed 15 per cent of the amount collected by the Central People's Government." The tax was collected on a progressive scale, and the maximum rate reached 60 per cent and, in special cases, 80 per cent. The actual results of tax collection will be discussed later.

Other programmes in the land policy, such as the movement to increase agricultural production, the organization of peasants, especially the youth and women, mass education, propaganda, and indoctrination programmes, were similar to those carried out during the Sino-Japanese War, except that now the main target of attack was the Kuomintang. One significant development also occurred during this period. In February 1950, the *Directive for Dealing with Agricultural Land in the Suburbs of Cities of Old Liberated Areas* was issued by the Government Administrative Council. One of the provisions stated that "in the interests of municipal construction and development of industry, the suburban farmlands (confiscated from the landlords) shall be placed under state ownership." The land then was redistributed among the poor peasants, but the government retained the right to repossess it and collected agricultural taxes from the cultivators. Although the nationalization of land under State ownership is not in immediate prospect, this move is interesting to be noted as a possible signpost to future developments.

[138] Reported by Po I-po, Chairman of the North China regional government at that time, *Chun-chung* (*The Masses*), 2·42, October 28, 1948, p. 2.

Organization and Administration

From August 1945 to October 1947, when the Land Law was enacted, the organizational structure in the villages in the Communist areas followed in general the pattern during the Sino-Japanese War. Local administration was primarily managed by the *hsiang* and *ch'ü* governments elected by the villagers. The People's Militia continued to serve as an auxiliary force to the regular Communist army, and other mass organizations such as the mutual-aid teams, reading groups, drama and *yangko* teams continued to be organized, with functions similar to those that they had had during the war. There was, however, one new feature: the Peasants' Associations received increasing attention and powers. In the *Regulations for the Purchase of the Land of the Landlords* made public in December 1946, the Peasants' Associations were given a one-third voice together with the *hsiang* government and the landlord in question in determining the price of land to be purchased by the government. From the autumn of 1947 to the spring of 1948, the Poor Peasants' League became an all-powerful organ in matters dealing with land reform. It was officially stipulated in the Land Law of October 10, 1947 (Article 5) that:

> The legal executive organs of reform of the agrarian system shall be the village peasants' congress and the committees elected by them; the assembly of the Poor Peasants' League organized by the landless and land-poor peasants of the villages, and the committees elected by it; *ch'ü*, *hsiang*, provincial and other levels of the peasant representatives' congresses and the committees elected by them.

The predominant position assigned to the poor peasants can be seen from a report made by the Mao Tse-tung to the Central Committee on December 25, 1947, in which he said:

> In order to resolutely and thoroughly carry out the agrarian reform, not only Peasants' Associations and the committees elected by them should be organized to represent the vast masses of farm labourers, poor peasants, and middle peasants, but first of all the Poor Peasants' League which includes the poor peasants and farm labourers and the committees elected by it must be

organized. They are to be the legal executive organs for agrarian reform, and the Poor Peasants' League should be the core in leading all struggles in the rural areas.[139]

As stated previously, during the winter of 1947–48, cases were discovered in Communist areas where the poor peasants confiscated not only the industrial and commercial investment of landlords and rich peasants but the properties of some middle peasants as well. These extreme actions led to discontent and confusion not only among the middle peasants but also among the poor peasants. After this, the CCP directives frequently reminded the cadres of the necessity of having the participation of middle peasants in the village administration. "Two-thirds of the seats in the village administration were allotted to middle peasants in the old areas, and one-third of the seats in the new areas."[140] The Poor Peasants' Leagues were no longer organized in the areas that came under Communist control after 1948, and those in the old areas were incorporated into the Peasants' Associations. After the establishment of the Central People's Government in October 1949, peasants were encouraged to form *hsiang* and *ch'ü* people's representatives conferences or peasant representatives conferences to be the depository of power at the village level, with the local people's governments as the administrative organs. In the new areas, the authority to execute land reform was first vested in the Peasants' Association, and later in the *hsiang* and *ch'ü* people's representatives' conferences. The organization and functions of these local power structures will be discussed more fully in the section on the current land reform programme of the CCP.

To relieve the shortage of administrative personnel and trained cadres in land reform, a great number of young men and women were trained in various areas. From March 1947 to October 1948, more than 200,000 middle school students in the Northeast were reported to have joined training schools or various branches of the administration. In North China, 15,559 students were admitted to the three newly established colleges in the spring of 1949. In East China, more than 30,000 entered the Communist institutions in the summer of 1949. Many of these trainees later served

[139] Mao Tse-tung, *Present Situation and Our Tasks*, *op. cit.*, p. 8.
[140] Jen Pi-shih, *Some Problems in the Land Reform* (Chinese), January 12, 1948, p. 8.

as cadres in the rural areas for land reform. Special schools and classes were also set up by local governments at various levels to train personnel for land reform work. The training period was generally short—from three months to two years.[141]

Results and Effects

In the period from 1945 to 1950, because of its transitional nature and the continuous fighting of the Communist and KMT forces, data are very scanty regarding the concrete results of the various programmes in the CCP land policy. The available information on what was done in this transitional period may be summarized under the following headings:

1. LAND REDISTRIBUTION

According to one source, the "land redistribution plan was carried out in many areas in North and Northeast China even before July 1946." In four of the six Border Regions visited by Mark Gayn in 1947, land distribution, according to him, was "nearly completed."[142] But in general, landlords were allotted more land than the middle and poor peasants in that period.[143] In the winter of 1947–48 the process of land redistribution was accelerated after the enactment of the Land Law in October 1947. One of the results was that a number of extreme measures were taken against the landlords and rich peasants by the poor peasants as well as by many cadres. This was admitted by Jen Pi-shih in January 1948, when he said:

> The correct criterion for the demarcation of class standing has not been grasped and the class standing of many people has been determined incorrectly. . . . Now I cite a case from the Shansi-Suiyuan Area, to elucidate on the seriousness of this danger. The number of landlord and rich peasant households should be less than 8 per cent, but the number of landlord and rich peasants

[141] For more information on the training of cadres by the Chinese Communists, see *New China News Agency* bulletins March 18 and 20, 1949; *NYT*, July 4, 1949, p. 1; and *HCJP*, July 28, 1949, p. 4.

[142] Chang Hsi-chang, *op. cit.*, p. 10.

[143] *Ibid.*, pp. 7–8. Cases quoted by Chang show that in one region, "landlords" (numbering 11,052 households) got an average of 121 *mou*, which was about five times the holding of a middle peasant in the same region.

households in Tsaichiai (an administrative village in Hsinghsien county, Shansi) exceeded 8 per cent by nearly twofold. . . . It may be positively stated that in other villages of the Shansi-Suiyuan area, in North China, East China, Central China, the Northeast, and the Shensi-Kansu-Ninghsia Border Region, there is sure to be quite a number of cases of incorrectly determining class standing like that which took place in Tsaichiai, or instances more or less similar to this.[144]

Revealed in the criticisms by the CCP leaders as well as in non-Communist reports were a number of cases in which the properties of middle peasants were wrongly confiscated and many landlords manhandled by local cadres.[145] This often caused discontent among the middle peasants and certain confusion in the rural areas.

After the spring of 1948, the middle peasants were given a greater voice in the management of land redistribution and village administration. In many villages, households were reclassified according to the standards enunciated in the speech of Jen Pi-shih. The properties "erroneously dealt with" were returned to their original owners. Illegal corporal punishment of landlords was "strictly prohibited." Meanwhile in the old areas, redistribution of land continued, though in a milder manner. According to one *NCNA* bulletin dated April 23, 1950, "land redistribution has been completed in the Northeast and in about 76 per cent of the total area of Shansi, Chahar, Hopei and P'ingyuan provinces."

2. RENT AND INTEREST REDUCTION PROGRAMME

No comprehensive reports are available regarding the land reform in the new areas where rent and interest reduction was in effect between the summer of 1949 and the summer of 1950. Available information concerning results regarding reduction of rent in early 1950 varies with different areas. In some districts the landlords were hard pressed and even beaten when their tenants demanded the refund of rents paid in 1949 or before. In some districts where the peasants were so afraid of the landlords through years of undisputed domination, they returned secretly part of the rent refund to which

[144] Jen Pi-shih, *op. cit.*, pp. 2, 4.

[145] For sample cases, see Liu Shao-ch'i and others, *Typical Experiences in Land Reform and Party Purification* (Chinese), pp. 6–40.

they were entitled. Even in old areas, renting out of land in small quantities was permitted under special conditions by the Communist authorities.[146]

Debts contracted before the Communist take-over were calculated at rates which were generally between 15 and 30 per cent per annum, irrespective of the originally agreed-upon interest rates. New loans were made at whatever rate was arrived at by mutual consent of the parties concerned. This also indicates that as a result of the policy of cancelling old debts, opportunities for peasants to secure loans from private sources were at times reduced. The Peking Government initiated extensive credit programme to supply the peasants with means of production as well as cash.

3. AGRICULTURAL TAXATION

Po I-po, member of the Central Committee, CCP, in a report of August 1948 said that "the agricultural tax on the average must not exceed 20 per cent of the total agricultural income." This was higher than the stipulated agricultural tax in Communist-held areas during the war. One *NCNA* bulletin dated February 20, 1949, stated that "the public grain (tax in kind) in the new liberated areas in Honan. . . was, on the average, less than 15 per cent of the agricultural income." Another report stated that in the year 1949 the peasants in the Northeast paid a total of 2·3 million tons in tax, about 5·7 million tons less than what they paid under the Japanese and puppet rule.[147] The reported 2·3 million tons of grain paid as tax were about 16 per cent of the total reported grain production, and the percentage would be lower so far as total agricultural income is concerned. However, there are indications that peasants in East, Central, South and Southwest China in the months immediately after the Communist take-over, paid higher taxes than did their compatriots in the old areas. For instance, one Chinese economist wrote in January 1950 that "the average tax burden on the peasants in the new liberated areas was about 20 to 25 per cent of the agricultural income—which was more than the stipulated rate."[148]

[146] Kao Kang, *Speech to the Conference on Rural Work in the Northeast* (Chinese), December 10, 1949.

[147] *Ibid.*

[148] Nan Han-ch'en (General Manager of the Central People's Bank), speech to the Shanghai banking circle in January 1950.

4. AGRICULTURAL PRODUCTION

With the fighting gradually ended on the mainland, with more accurate reporting on acreage and yields, and with the various programmes set up by the Chinese Communists to stimulate production, there seems to be no reason to doubt Communist reports that the total agricultural output of 1949 and 1950, 109 and 125 million metric tons respectively, showed increases over the previous post-war years. These figures were short of the pre-war peak production of 139 million tons of grain, excluding soybeans. But there is also an indication that grain production fell short of the planned goal for 1949. For example, in the Northeast, the most stabilized area in mainland China, Kao Kang (at that time Chairman of the Northeast People's Government) admitted that only approximately 90 per cent of the 1949 agricultural production goal was realized, netting a total of 14·5 million tons (metric) of grain. (This figure does not include 2 million tons of subsidiary crops.) Production in other less consolidated areas such as South and Southwest China for 1949 probably fell short of the planned goal also, since the mainland in that year suffered the worst flood and drought since 1931. Figures for agricultural production for the years 1945–48 in the various Communist areas show a slow but steady increase. These data are not included here because (1) they cover only small areas and are spaced over long intervals, and (2) they may not be representative of the other areas in general. By 1952, foodgrain production reached 154 million tons and other crops, in general, had reached or surpassed pre-war levels.

5. RURAL CREDIT AND MARKETING

Information on credit and marketing facilities in the rural areas under Communist control during this period is rather meagre and scattered. On March 5, 1949, the North China People's Government announced the rural credit plan for North China for 1949. It is quoted here not so much to evaluate its effects on the rural areas as to present some relative criteria regarding the priorities assigned to the various rural programmes at that time. The plan for rural credit totalling 564 million dollars in the people's currency (*jen-min-pi*)[149] gave the following allocations: 44·6 per cent for

[149] The official rates of exchange between the people's currency (*jen-min-pi*) and the American dollar announced by the Peking government at different periods were: May 31, 1949: 1,040 *yuan*; March 13, 1950: 42,000 *yuan*; January

irrigation and equipment; 20 per cent for subsidiary industries; 11·4 per cent for livestock; 8·8 per cent for state farms; 4·4 per cent for cotton planting; 3·4 per cent for chemical supplies (pest control, fertilizers, etc.) in agriculture; 1·7 per cent for afforestation; and 5·7 per cent for other purposes. The credit, with the increase of production as its primary goal, was divided into two categories: general loans for equipment, fertilizer, seeds, draught animals, etc. managed by the People's Bank (established on December 1, 1949) through the rural cooperatives; and the special loans which were for irrigation projects, afforestation, livestock, cotton planting, etc. managed jointly by the People's Bank, technical institutes, and local administrations. Most of these, however, were also managed through the rural cooperatives. General credit was given for a short period of about eight months at an interest rate of six to twelve per cent per annum. The special loans were extended for a longer period of two to three years, at an interest rate of 2 to 3 per cent per month.[150] Available information indicates that the loans were short of actual needs.

Marketing facilities for rural products were very much limited as a result of fighting between the Communists forces and the Nationalists. Things improved a little during the latter stage of this transitional period. At the end of 1949, more than 80 per cent of the railways were in operation; and inland water navigation along the Yangtze and other navigable rivers was resumed on a limited scale. But for most agricultural produce, the market was limited to neighbouring districts during this period. The distribution of essential goods such as foodstuffs in the cities and cloth in the countryside was conducted by State trading companies and cooperatives.

Other programmes like the organization of mutual-aid teams, the setting up of village women and youth leagues, and the promotion of bio-technical and educational improvements followed the general pattern discussed in the previous sections on war-time programmes. Available reports regarding concrete results of these programmes during the earlier stage of this period are fragmentary.

6 to December 6, 1952: 20,240 *yuan*; December 6, 1952: 23,430 *yuan* and since February 1955, 2,355 new *yuan*.

[150] *Hua-ch'iao jih-pao* (*China Daily News*), New York, March 12, 1949, p. 1.

Comments on the Period

Because of the changes of policy toward the various rural classes as described in the section on legislation and programmes, confusion sometimes resulted in certain districts. For instance, immediately after the enactment of the Land Law on October 10, 1947, the various regional Party and administrative organs called for the "confiscation of all the properties of the landlords and all the surplus properties of the rich peasants, the assignment of supreme power in the disposition of confiscated properties to the poor peasants and farm labourers, and the overthrow of the landlord class without mercy."[151] As a result, not only were some villages turned into a turmoil, but errors were committed in classifying the peasants. In a report by a Communist cadre[152] it was revealed that in the thirty-three "administrative villages" in an area in Shansi, 106 middle peasant households were wrongly classified as rich peasants, twenty-six middle peasants as landlords, five middle peasants as "former landlords," fifty-one peasants as "bankrupt landlords," and forty-three rich peasants as landlords. This was attributed by the writer to the "mistakes" of the local cadres and to the fear of the cadres of being accused of "protecting the landlords."

This transitional period also saw a number of cases of extremities against the landlords committed by the poor peasants and cadres. These illegal acts, called "irregularities and deviations" by the Communist leaders, were especially in evidence during later 1947 and early 1948. They were reported by Communist sources to be "rectified" after the spring of 1948. But in the new liberated areas south of the Yangtze, there were still reported cases of "illegal punishment" inflicted upon the landlords. Cases of excessive assessment of agricultural taxes and severe treatment of former Kuomintang village officials were reported by some foreign observers in certain areas during this period.[153] A cause of confusion

[151] See the various articles in the pamphlet *Struggle for the Purification of the Organization of the Party* (Chinese), pp. 1–63.

[152] T'an Cheng-wen, "How the Land Reform Has Been Carried Out in Tunghsien, Shansi," *Typical Experiences in Agrarian Reform and Party Purification* (Chinese), p. 7.

[153] For example, see G. William Skinner's "Aftermath of the Communist Liberation in Chengtu Plain," *Pacific Affairs*, 24·1, March 1951, pp. 61–76. The author observed that immediately after the Communist occupation of Szechuan, the agricultural taxes were heavy and the quota was later reduced.

during the winter of 1947–48 was the vagueness in the definition of various rural classes. The situation improved after Jen Pi-shih redefined rural class status in his speech on January 28, 1948, and by the promulgation of the detailed "Decisions on the Differentiation of Rural Classes in the Countryside" in August 1950, which will be discussed later.

One of the important trends that emerged at the end of this period was the greater power and prestige attained by the middle peasants. In general, middle peasants, who possessed relative economic independence and do not exploit others, were the productive members of the rural community. There was discontent among many of them during the 1947–48 period when the poor peasants in many rural districts acted arbitrarily and infringed upon their interests. The situation was described by Jen Pi-shih in January 1948:

> According to available information, in many places of the liberated areas where the agrarian reform movement has been set in motion, a "leftist" tendency to encroach on the interests of the middle peasants and to exclude the middle peasants has occurred. This kind of tendency is manifested in the following questions: (1) the class-standing of some middle peasants has been determined incorrectly . . . and they have had their possessions confiscated. (2) (This erroneous tendency) is expressed in not wanting the middle peasants to take part in managing affairs. The middle peasants doubt that they are still needed . . . . (3) (The erroneous tendency also) is expressed in not giving consideration to the middle peasants on the question of public duties, especially in the increase of the middle peasants' burdens. In some places, it has been discovered that only the poor peasant-farm labourer group decides and makes decisions on the apportioning of the public grain tax; and, because after agrarian reform the landlords and rich peasants are not in a position to meet their responsibilities, the public grain burden is placed on the middle peasants and even the delivering of public grain is apportioned more to them. . . .

Jen Pi-shih concluded that the middle peasants could be "united very well" when their rights were safeguarded and they were given opportunities in the management of village affairs. Similar themes ran through subsequent directives and programmes of the Chinese Communists on land policy. There were also a number of important measures which were taken during the early stage of this period and later discarded as "incorrect." One was the confiscation of the industrial and commercial investments of the landlords and rich peasants. This was discovered to have a disruptive effect on the rural economy, as these enterprises had to be operated as a unit; also, those who had savings no longer dared to invest them in industry and commerce. The second was the confiscation of the "hidden treasure" of the landlords and rich peasants, such as gold, silver, jewelry and personal belongings. The owners generally hid these items, and when the peasants tried to unearth them, confusion and disorder often resulted. The third was the confiscation of the "surplus properties" of the rich peasants. This discouraged the peasants in general from saving or from investing, for fear of being later labelled as rich peasants. These measures were after 1948 officially "abolished."[154]

Finally, an important shift of policy by the CCP occurred during this period. This was, as officially announced by the 2nd Session of the 7th Plenum of the Central Committee, CCP on March 23, 1949, "the shift of the centre of the Party's work from rural areas to urban cities." The implications of this significant event have been discussed in the section on the CCP's theory on the land problem in this period. A basic reason for the shift can also be seen from the following excerpt from Mao's *On People's Democratic Dictatorship*, written on July 1, 1949, to commemorate the 28th Anniversary of the CCP:

> The grave problem is that of educating the peasant. The peasant's economy is scattered. According to the experiences of the Soviet Union, it requires a very long time and careful work to attain the socialization of agriculture. Without the socialization of agriculture, there will be no complete and consolidated Socialism. And to carry out the socialization of agriculture, a powerful industry with state-owned enterprises as the main component must be developed. The State of the people's democratic

[154] For more detailed information, see Jen Pi-shih, pp. 10–18; Mao Tse-tung, *Speech at the Cadres' Conference of the Shansi-Suiyuan Area, op. cit.*, April 1, 1948; Liu Shao-ch'i, *On the Agrarian Problem*, June 14, 1950; and *The Agrarian Reform Law*, June 28, 1950.

> dictatorship must step by step solve this problem of the industrialization of the country. . . .

The emphasis was now shifted to industrializing China, and agriculture would bear the major direct and indirect burden in the process of accumulating capital and developing exports in exchange for capital goods.

CHAPTER III

THE LAND REFORM (LAND REDISTRIBUTION) PROGRAMME 1950–1953

THE LAND REFORM or land redistribution programme, vigorously carried out in the first few years of the Central People's Government, had a tremendous impact on all the major aspects of rural China. Seldom were so many people (half a billion) so deeply affected by any movement within so short a period. Institutions and values that had prevailed in China for centuries were swept away or transformed during this stupendous political-social-economic revolution. The practice of redistributing land had, as preceding sections described, prevailed in small areas of China prior to 1950. But only between 1950 and 1953 was the land reform carried out all over the Chinese mainland; and elaborate organizational as well as propaganda techniques were developed. Although the land reform served only as a transitional measure, paving the way for later cooperative and collective farming, it constituted an indispensable step with which the ground was laid for the building of a new rural system. It might have seemed in 1950 that Peking was taking a devious route to promoting collectivization by first dispersing land ownership among millions of tenants and farm labourers. But it would have been very difficult, if not impossible, to carry out the programme of collective farming immediately, bypassing the gradual (three-stage) process of individual ownership, mutual-aid teams, and cooperative farming. Furthermore, without breaking the hold of the landed gentry class, which was socially reactionary and economically unproductive, effective reforms would have been impossible, as many an abortive reformist movement in modern China demonstrated.

A. *The General Principles in the Land Reform Movement*

The overall guiding tenets of the CCP's land reform policy during the period 1950 to 1953 were laid down in two basic documents, namely, the Common Programme of September 1949 and the

Agrarian Reform Law of June 1950. In the Common Programme, adopted by the CPPCC on September 29, 1949, it was stipulated that:

> The agrarian reform is a prerequisite for the development of the productive power and the industrialization of the countryside. ... the right of ownership over the land obtained by the peasants (during the land reform) shall be protected (Art. 27).

It also described the central task of the government in those areas where agrarian reform was completed as "the organization of the peasants and the development of agricultural production as well as subsidiary occupations" (Art. 34). Similar themes are found in the Agrarian Reform Law adopted on June 28, 1950, which contains the following basic points: "(1) Land ownership of the landlord is abolished; (2) Investment and other properties of the landlords and rich peasants in connection with industry and commerce are protected by law; and (3) A rich peasant is allowed to retain land cultivated by himself and by hired hands, his other properties, and rented-out land which does not exceed the amount tilled by his own household" (Art. 1, 4 & 6). In the implementation of the agrarian reform programme, the principal stategy is said to be "reliance on poor peasants and farm labourers, uniting with middle peasants, neutralization of rich peasants, and the systematic development of agricultural production."[1]

This policy of preserving the rich peasant economy was changed later. It serves to illustrate that land policy, like many other policies of the Peking Government, is adapted to political needs at a given time. The tactical line in the "rural class policy" during the transitional period of socialist transformation was, according to Teng Tzu-hui, "to rely on the poor peasants (including the newly-elevated middle peasants), solidly to unite with the middle peasants, and gradually to proceed from restricting to finally wiping out exploitation activities of the rich peasants."[2]

At the same time, the Communist leadership repeatedly emphasized the "subordination of the peasantry to the leadership of

[1] Liao Lu-yen, "Great Victory of the Land Reform Movement in the Past Three Years," October 1, 1952, *HCJP*, October 22, 1952, p. 6.

[2] Teng Tzu-hui (Director, Rural Work Dept., Central Committee, CCP), "Rural Work During the Transition Period," *op. cit.*

the working class," as well as the ultimate goal of industrializing and socializing China. However, in China rural inhabitants still constitute over 80 per cent of the total mainland population of over 600 millions, and only 33 per cent of the national income was derived from modern industries in 1954. Thus the peasantry remains the major source of strength of the CCP. For example, despite persistent efforts of the party to raise the number of workers among its 12 million members (in 1956), more than 70 per cent of the membership still came from the peasantry. At the same time, the Party leaders continue to emphasize the importance of agriculture in the overall development of the Chinese economy. Thus the agrarian reform of the CCP is multi-functional. In addition to its economic role of stimulating greater agricultural production and productivity, it is co-ordinated with the political objectives of the party: to indoctrinate the masses with Marxist-Leninist-Maoist teachings and to organize the individualistic peasants in order to facilitate the implementation of government policies. It is also designed to transform the traditional Chinese village into a highly organized community, thus preparing the farmers, organizationally and psychologically, for eventual collectivization.

A basic step during the period of land redistribution was the redefining of class status for various peasant households. These *Decisions Concerning the Differentiation of Rural Class Status*[3] were adopted on August 4, 1950. They stated the following:

(1) Landlord: "One who owns land, but does not engage in labour or only engages in supplementary labour, and depends on exploitation for his means of livelihood. Exploitation by the landlords is chiefly in the form of land rent, money lending, hiring of labour, and other ways."

(2) Rich peasant: "One who owns better means of production and some floating capital and takes part in labour himself, but is constantly dependent on exploitation for a part or the major part of his means of livelihood."

(3) Middle peasant: "One who depends wholly or mainly upon his own labour for his living. If his income from exploitation does not exceed 25 per cent, he shall be considered a well-to-do middle peasant."

[3] The "Decisions" are a revised version of similar legislation passed by the Kiangsi Soviet Government in 1933. The new provisions are more lenient in their treatment of landlords, rich peasants, and middle peasants.

(4) Poor peasant: "One who, in general, has to rent land for cultivation, and is exploited by others in the form of land rent, loan interest, and hired labour."

(5) Farm labourer: "One who generally has neither land nor farm implements, and depends wholly or mainly upon the sale of his labour power for his living."

(6) Status of peasant household: "Under ordinary circumstances, a family is considered as being engaged in labour if one family member is engaged in essential labour for one-third of a year. A family is considered as being engaged in supplementary labour if one member is engaged in essential labour for less than one-third of a year or if he is engaged in labour, but not in essential labour, for one-third of a year. . . . Essential labour means labour employed in the main forms of agricultural production such as ploughing, planting, reaping and other major items of labour in agriculture."

B. *Major Programmes and Results*

The confiscation of the land and other rural properties of the landlord, to be distributed to the peasants who have little or no land, constituted up to 1953 the major feature in the land reform in mainland China. *The Agrarian Reform Law* of June 28, 1950, stipulates the following provisions regarding the redistribution of rural wealth:

(1) For landlords: their land, draught animals, farm implements and surplus grain and surplus houses in the countryside were to be confiscated; but other properties such as cash, jewellery, investment in industry and commerce, etc. would be protected. They would be given an equal share of land and means of production during the redistribution of land (Articles 2, 4, and 10).

(2) For rich peasants: land owned and cultivated by themselves or by hired labour as well as other properties were to be protected from infringement. Small portions of land rented out by rich peasants might also be retained. If the portions of land rented out by rich peasants exceeded the amount of land worked by them or by hired labourers, these portions would be requisitioned (Article 6).

(3) For middle peasants, including well-to-do peasants: their land and other property were to be protected from infringement (Article 7).

(4) For poor peasants and farm labourers: they would receive a portion of the confiscated or requisitioned land and other means of production in a unified, equitable and rational manner. When rented land was drawn upon for distribution proper regard was to be given to the tiller who might get slightly more land than those who originally had little or no land (Articles 10 and 12).

(5) For rural land belonging to ancestral shrines, temples, monasteries, churches, schools, institutions and other public land: the land was to be requisitioned, but appropriate measures were to be worked out by the local people's government to solve the financial problems of schools, orphanages, homes for the aged, hospitals, etc. if they were dependent upon income from the above land. Some or all land owned by mosques could be retained by them subject to the consent of the Moslems residing in the area (Article 3).

The following table shows the development of land redistribution on the Chinese mainland (excluding Sinkiang and Tibet) from June 1950, when the *Agrarian Reform Law* was put into effect, up to the spring of 1953:

ESTIMATED DEVELOPMENT OF LAND REDISTRIBUTION PROGRAMME IN CHINA*

Period	*Rural population affected (in millions)*	*Rural population still unaffected (in millions)*
June 1950	178 (out of roughly 500)	322
February 1951	339	161
September 1951	400	100
September 1952	463	37
November 1952	494	6
Spring 1953	497	3

* Not including Sinkiang, Tibet and Taiwan. Data adjusted according to announcement of the national census in 1954 which gave the total rural population of mainland China at about 500 million.

The land redistribution programme on the entire mainland was basically completed in 1953, except in districts where minority groups dwell such as in Sinkiang, Tibet, Inner Mongolia and certain regions of the Northwest. In those temporarily exempted districts, reduction of rent and interest was carried out as an alternative to land redistribution. The average per capita amount of land received by the peasants in north Manchuria was about 7 *mou* (one *mou* equals approximately one-sixth of an acre), in south Manchuria, 3 *mou* ; in Honan province (Central China), 2 to 3 *mou*; in Hunan and Hopei provinces (South and North China, respectively), from 1 to 2·5 *mou*[4] and in East China, from 1·5 to 2 *mou*.[5]

This minute division of the land, especially in areas south of the Yangtze River, is not conducive to agricultural development. Small farms are not only less efficient but a handicap to modern farming, which includes the use of machinery. The efforts of the Chinese Communists to organize the peasants into cooperative and collective farming indicate that land redistribution was only a transitional means rather than an end. On the other hand, it is perhaps true that no economic, political, or social reforms could be successfully implemented without removing first the power of the landed gentry. The idea of transforming the large estates of landlords immediately into cooperative or collective farms would not be a practical one, as the century-old urge of Chinese peasants to own land was too deep-rooted to change overnight. It must also be pointed out that in pre-Communist days the land was minutely divided because the landlords usually rented out land to many tenants in small parcels.

Peking sources claim that land redistribution, which gave new hope and incentive to the peasants, together with other related reforms, was a basic factor accounting for the improvement of the rural economy in China. Some reports indicate, however, that the carrying out of the land redistribution programme at the grass roots was not without irregularities and difficulties. For example, when a sample check was made by the Land Reform Committee of the then Military and Political Committee of Central-South China (now abolished) in December 1950, it was found that of the districts where land reform had been carried out, only 20 per cent were considered as "successful." Thirty per cent of the districts investigated were described as "unsuccessful," and the remaining 50 per cent somewhere in between.[6] Other reports indicate that

[4] Lin Feng, "Financial and Economic Construction and the Taking-Over Work," *HY*, 1·1, November 1949, p. 89.

[5] Lin Jui-lung, "Report on Agrarian Reform," *CFJP*, November 29, 1951, p. 1.

[6] *JMJP*, December 20, 1950, p. 2.

persons accused of committing various "crimes and counter-revolutionary activities" were subjected to harsh treatment and that some of them were killed at mass meetings, especially in South China, even though such violent methods were strictly prohibited by the *Agrarian Reform Law* and other official directives on land reform.

The Communist land reform aimed at eliminating landlords as a class, and the treatment accorded to the estimated "20 million landlords" was often severe. The "Provisional Regulations on the Supervising and Reforming of Landlords in the Central-South Area," which were promulgated on August 18, 1952, reflected the general policy towards the landlord after the agrarian reform was launched in China. The salient points of these Regulations are as follows: (1) Landlords who commit counter-revolutionary activities or who do not engage in any proper profession may be placed under house arrest or forced to labour in the local district or elsewhere; (2) Landlords who are able-bodied and possess no other skills must do farm work. They cannot sell or rent the land allotted to them to others; (3) Landlords who do not have enough manpower in their households may hire some farm labourers or rent out land, with the approval of the local Peasants' Association; (4) Landlords who are literate or possess professional skill may engage in professions other than farming but must report their whereabouts to the local village government; (5) Landlords who have surrendered their rural properties in accordance with the law may invest the rest of their properties in agriculture, industry or commerce; and (6) Landlords who behave well after the agrarian reform for five continuous years may change their status according to the nature of their current profession and with the approval of the village people's representatives' congress and the county people's government.[7] The above provisions indicate that the general policy of the Chinese Communists toward the landlords is to punish those who oppose the agrarian programme and make those who acquiesce in work be productive.

The *Agrarian Reform Law* also stipulates that "after agrarian reform is completed, the people's government shall issue title deeds and shall recognize the right of all landowners to manage, buy, sell, or rent out land freely. All land contracts made before the reform of the agrarian system shall be null and void" (Article

[7] Chinese text of these Regulations appear in *HCJP*, September 4, 1952, p. 4.

30). The work of surveying land and fixing yield per *mou* was made one of the key programmes in the agricultural work since 1951 by the Central People's Government. The basic points of the programme are contained in the "Outline to Carry Out the Work of Land Survey and (Agricultural) Production Evaluation in the Agricultural Taxation (Programme)," promulgated by the Ministry of Finance, on July 5, 1951. The major points of its nine Articles are: "(1) In old areas where land has been surveyed and annual production estimated, permanent records should be set up after checking or re-investigation either in 1951 or before the end of 1952. (2) In new areas where agrarian reform has been carried out, land surveying and production evaluation work should be done in coordination with the land reform and the issue of new title deeds. Old land records and old personnel in land taxation work should be efficiently utilized when the above work is done through the mobilization of the masses. The timetable for these areas is from three to four years (i.e., before 1956). (3) In new areas where agrarian reform has not yet been carried out, the quality of the land should be evaluated and unregistered land ("black land") checked during the movement of rent reduction. Land deposits are to be refunded. A preliminary evaluation of agricultural production of individual farms should be made and these estimates should be readjusted when agrarian reform is initiated. (4) "Committees on Land Survey and Production Evaluation" are to be organized at provincial and county (*hsien*) levels and "Committees on the Investigation and Evaluation of Agricultural Tax" set up at *hsiang* (administrative village) and *ts'un* (natural village) levels. (5) Detailed procedures are to be drawn up by Regional Administrations in accordance with the general principles laid down in this Outline."[8] A directive on agricultural tax work in 1953 announced the cessation of the land survey and production ascertainment work in areas where such work had not been completed. Probably some peasants were upset by repeated changes in tax rates. This point will be discussed more fully later.

In the report by Liu Shao-ch'i the statement was made that "poor peasants, farm labourers, middle peasants and others make up 90 per cent of the rural population and possess only 20 to 30 per cent of the land." A recent Peking source gave the following figures on the class composition in rural China before the land

[8] Chinese text in *HY*, 4·3, July 1951, pp. 678–9.

redistribution: poor peasants and farm labourers, 70 per cent; middle peasants, 20 per cent; rich peasants, 5 to 6 per cent; landlords, 4 to 5 per cent. The same source gives the following estimates for early 1955: ex-landlords, 3·5 per cent; old rich peasants, 4·5 per cent; new rich peasants, 2 per cent; old middle peasants, 20 per cent; new middle peasants, 50 per cent; poor peasants, 20 per cent. Since these figures depend upon definitions of terms, they cannot be easily evaluated from outside.[9]

C. *Organization and Administration in Land Reform*

A myriad of administrative and mass organizations were established by the CCP, not only as originating and propagating agencies for the planning, implementation, and checking of land redistribution programmes, but also as indoctrinating and controlling organs to direct the rural population towards the goals set up by Peking. Among the major objectives were these: to increase agricultural production and productivity; to promote cooperative and community living; to effect centralized control politically; to create grass-roots channels through which social and ideological transformations could be made; and to spread Marxism-Leninism-Maoism. Almost all the villagers, from the children on up, became members of one or more organized group activities. The activities, particularly the holding of meetings, were so numerous that they sometimes left both the cadres and the participants exhausted. On the other hand, these group activities offered new stimuli and new outlets for the peasants, particularly the more active and the more capable. The rural masses, cemented together by skilled organizers and guided toward the same goals, had become a new powerful force. The following section describes the major political and mass organizations in the rural areas in Communist China. The village party cell, which is generally the locus of power, and the planning board, will be discussed in a separate section on the role of the party.

1. THE PEASANTS' ASSOCIATION

The Peasants' Association, defined as "a mass organization formed by the voluntary will of the peasants," was officially designated

[9] *The Economic System of Chinese Society* (Chinese), China Youth Publishing House, *NDYL*, June 1951. Also, editorial *JMJP*, June 30, 1950, p. 1.

as "the legal executive organ for the reform of the agrarian system in the rural areas."[10] The basic organizational unit was the *hsiang*. The functions of the PA were stated to be: "(1) to unite farm labourers, poor peasants, middle peasants, and all anti-feudal elements in the villages, to carry out systematically anti-feudal social reforms and to protect the interests of the peasants; (2) to organize the production work of the peasants; to set up rural co-operatives; to promote agriculture and subsidiary occupations; and to improve the livelihood of the people; (3) to protect the political rights and cultural welfare of the peasants; and to participate in the construction work of the people's democratic regime." The organ which exercises the authority of the PA at the various levels was the Peasant Representatives' Congress (PRC). When the Peasant Representatives' Congress was not in session, the PA Committee, whose members served as executive organ, was elected by the Peasant Representatives' Congress.

In practice, however, the organization of the PA was by no means as simple as the provisions show. Due to the traditional lack of opportunity in rural China for self-government and public service, peasants were often lethargic and ignorant as to how to begin. The Communists train these individualistic peasants, who were often apathetic partly due to their bitter experiences under the KMT regime, for collective action and self-government through intensive propaganda, practical programmes that were attractive to the villagers (such as group discussion on better and larger crops), and the help of "positive elements."[11] Sometimes a small group was first organized under names such as "production group," "self-helping team," or "PA preparatory group," which served as nucleus for the later organization of the PA. The "key points" in organizing the PA, according to a Communist cadre in land reform,[12] were: (1) that great care must be taken in selecting the first group of "positive elements," who are to be the backbone of the PA; (2) that the middle peasants must be won over so that the

[10] Articles 1 and 3; *General Regulations for the Organization of the Peasants' Association*, GAC, July 1950. Chinese text in *HY*, 2·4, August 1950, pp. 796–7.

[11] Some of the difficulties in organizing a PA are discussed in Tao Wei-lien's "Land Reform Begins in the Newly Liberated Areas," *CWR*, October 22, 1949, p. 12; also Li Yen-nien, "How To Start and Develop Mass Movement," *HY*, 1·3, January 1950, p. 728–9.

[12] Li Yen-nien, p. 729.

poor peasants will not be isolated;[13] (3) that practical measures must be implemented to suit specific local needs, with periodic checking on the fitness and progress of the cadres and of the programmes.

The details of setting up a PA varied, of course, in different areas. However, the following report, describing the founding of a PA in a *hsiang* in South Kiangsu, may serve as an illustration. The arrival of PA members from the various villages was heralded by *yangko* teams, amidst drums and gongs. The meeting ground, with an elevated platform at one end, was in open air. Portraits of Mao Tse-tung and Chu Teh were hung at the centre of the platform, and colourful posters with such slogans as "Chairman Mao is the lighthouse of the people," "Peasants are of one family," "Solidarity is strength," etc. were widely displayed. The attendants, numbering about 1,000, were divided into sections each with a leader. After the meeting was opened by the firing of firecrackers, the presidium, which consisted of work-team leaders, local peasant leaders, and some old people who were mostly parents of Communist soldiers, asked the section leaders to expel any "landlords, despots, and bad elements" from the meeting. There followed short speeches explaining the key aspects of agrarian reform and the necessity for an increase in production, and the usual agitation. After the election of officials for the Preparatory Committee of the *hsiang* PA, the meeting was concluded with a *yangko* play, which dramatized how poor peasants in a certain village became well-to-do after land reform by working through mutual-aid teams and the adoption of better farming methods.[14]

Peking sources reported that there were, in September 1952, 88 million members in the Peasants' Associations of East, Central-South, Southwest and Northwest China.[15] Although the total membership of the PA in areas south of the Yangtze River increased rapidly between 1949 and 1952, the PA served as a transitional device to mobilize the peasants during the land redistribution

[13] To woo the middle peasants, one-third of the seats in the PA Committee and the PRC are often allotted to them; the rest goes to the poor peasants and farm labourers. See Miao T'a, "New Face of the Villages Near Tsingtao," *HY*, 1·5, March 1950, 1219.

[14] See Ch'en Chung-i, "Villages in Kiangnan in Turmoil," *CW*, 4·10, September 10, 1949, p. 10, and other reports.

[15] Ten Ying-ch'ao, *The Women's Movement in New China*, October 1, 1951; and Liao Lu-yen, *op. cit.*

movement. There was no large-scale expansion of the PA after 1952. With the land redistribution programme completed by 1953, the village governments, local people's representatives' congresses, and organized farming groups (cooperatives, people's communes, and experimental collective farms) took the place of the PA.

2. THE NEW LOCAL ADMINISTRATIVE STRUCTURE

The organization of the provincial, municipal and county governments still basically followed the "General Regulations for the Organization of the Provincial, Municipal and *Hsien* People's Governments" promulgated by the Government Administrative Council in Peking on January 6, 1950. The major provisions contained in the above documents are summarized as follows: (1) The people's representatives' congresses at the various levels shall elect the heads of the respective local governments. The congress is the repository of power; but when it is not in session, the corresponding people's government is the organ of administrative power. (2) The resolutions of the people's representatives' congresses, if found to be contradictory to regulations promulgated by superior administrative organs, may be revised or annulled by the superior people's governments. (3) The tenure of the members of the provincial people's government council, including the provincial chairman and deputy chairman, is two years. The tenure of the members of the municipal and county governments is one year. Council members are eligible for re-election.[16] Under the *hsien* and the municipal government is the *ch'ü* (district) people's government (for class A districts) or the *ch'ü* office (for class B districts). Officials of the *ch'ü* people's government are elected by the *ch'ü* people's representatives' congress with the approval of the *hsien* people's government. The *ch'ü* office, which governs sparsely inhabited districts, is composed of officials appointed by the *hsien* people's government. Under the *ch'ü* administration is the *hsiang* (administrative village) people's government. It usually embodies several natural villages and is the basic administrative unit. The members of the *hsiang* people's government are elected by the *hsiang* people's representatives' congress, upon approval of the *ch'ü* people's government. The tenure for the *hsiang* official is one year. The

[16] The Chinese texts of the "General Regulations for the Organization of the Provincial, Municipal and *Hsien* People's Governments" appear in *HY*, 1·4, February 1950, pp. 866–8.

delegates of the *hsiang* people's representatives' congress are elected directly by the village (*hsiang*) voters.[17]

On March 1, 1953, an Election Law was promulgated governing the election of the National People's Congress and the people's representatives' congresses at various levels. According to the provisions of this Law, people's representatives' congresses at local levels would be established in the following manner: "(1) Each *hsiang* will select from 15 to 35 delegates, in accordance with the population, to form the *hsiang* people's representatives' congress; and (2) Each *hsien* will elect from 100 to 350 delegates, in accordance with the population, to form the county people's representatives' congress."[18] The *hsiang* and market-town people's representatives' congresses in rural areas are elected directly. All higher people's representatives' congresses are elected indirectly by the people's representatives' congress immediately below. Men and women 18 years old and over are qualified voters. "Unreformed landlords" are among those who are deprived of their right to vote. [After 1957, most *ch'ü* level organs have been abolished, and many villages have been amalgamated under the people's communes.]

From the above it may be seen that one of the basic characteristics of the administrative structure in China is the high degree of centralization. Although the people's governments at the various levels are directly or indirectly elected by the voters, the final authority usually rests with the superior administration. The CCP labels this "democratic centralism," which is the basic principle enforced in all political and mass organizations.

3. PEOPLE'S MILITIA AND PEOPLE'S TRIBUNAL

During the land reform movement, the people's militia and the people's tribunals were the major instruments for wielding the power of the State in dealing with any opposition to the redistribution of land. The fact that resistance to the land reform existed was admitted by Premier Chou En-lai, who said in 1950 that

> Among the landlord class there are those who are now inventing "theories" in opposition to land reform and the land reform law.

[17] The Chinese texts of the "General Regulations for the Organization of the *Ch'ü* and *Hsiang* People's Governments and *Ch'ü* and *Hsiang* People's Representatives' Congresses" appear in *HY*, 3·4, February 1951, pp. 756–8.

[18] Full text of the *Election Law* appears in *HCJP*, March 12, 13, 14, 16, and 17, 1953, p. 3.

> We must firmly disprove such "theories" and strengthen our publicity about the main contents of the land reform law and make them generally known in these areas where we are preparing to carry out land reform and especially in the villages. There are other landlords who are now dispersing their land and property, killing cattle and destroying farm implements, houses, arable land and trees. Such unlawful acts must be firmly prevented and punished.[19]

Since the summer of 1950, and especially after the winter of 1950–51, harsher punishment had been meted out to those in rural China who were guilty of sabotage activities.

In a village where land reform was being carried out, the people's militia was usually organized simultaneously. The reasons given were that there must be protection against the landlords, who often possessed private arms, if not guards, and that the village must be safeguarded from bandits or thieves, especially during the harvest. During the Sino-Japanese War period (1937–45), the people's militia in Communist areas played an important role as an auxiliary force of the Communist regular armies in harassing the enemy by laying mines and by other guerrilla tactics. But the militia also served some other important functions. The militia, numbering some 10 million in 1953, was and still remains the reserve force of the People's Liberation Army. Also, through organizing the people's militia for local protection, arms customarily hoarded or kept by rural secret societies were collected and controlled by the government through the local forces.

According to Article 1 of the *General Regulations Governing the Organization of the People's Tribunals* promulgated on July 20, 1950:

> The people's tribunal is created for the protection of the revolutionary order and the promotion of the enforcement of the people's government's agrarian reform policy and the laws and regulations pertaining thereto. The duty of such a people's tribunal is the employment of judicial procedure for the punishment of local despots, bandits, special agents, counter-revolutionaries and criminals who violate the law and order pertaining to agrarian reform . . . . It shall also undertake the

[19] *HY*, 2·6, October 1950, p. 1220.

> disposal of cases involving disputes over the demarcation of land lots in the course of agrarian reforms, and other matters connected with agrarian reform.[20]

The people's tribunal was organized with the *hsien* or municipality as the unit and with branches in the *ch'ü*. Generally, it moved about the villages in circuit court fashion. It was presided over by a committee of judges, half of whom were elected by the *hsien* People's Representatives' Congress or by popular organizations and half of whom were appointed by the *hsien* or municipal people's government. The accused could engage a defence counsel and the use of third degree methods was "strictly prohibited." The sentences of the tribunal, if the accused was found guilty, might range from fines to death. The sanction of imposing any sentence exceeding 5 years imprisonment belonged to the provincial people's government.

In some instances, when a regular people's tribunal had not yet been formed, the people's tribunal was composed of local cadres and such representatives of the village mass organizations as the PA for the trial of "despot-landlords." This was done to legalize the verdicts passed at the "anti-despot" meetings and to restrain the avenging peasants from physical violence. The people's tribunals were especially set up to deal with cases arising from agrarian reform and were different from the people's courts, which formed a part of the regular judicial system.

After the Chinese forces entered the Korean fighting, the Peking authorities intensified their "public security" campaign. In July 1952, the Ministry of Public Security promulgated the *Regulations on the Control of Counter-Revolutionaries*. Among those defined as "counter-revolutionary" were members of some secret societies and despotic landlords in the rural areas. In August of the same year, the "Committees on Public Security and Protection" were extensively organized throughout China. The masses were encouraged to "check, watch, supervise and report on counter-revolutionaries and spies."[21] The encouragement of people to check on each other might have strengthened internal order, but it could also create an atmosphere of apprehension among some people. Communist leaders explained that "our judicial

[20] *HY*, 2·4, August 1950, p. 799.

[21] *HCJP*, July 30, 1952, p. 4; *HCJP*, August 27 and September 8, 1952, p. 4.

work must serve political ends actively and must be brought to bear on current central political tasks and mass movements."[22]

4. EDUCATIONAL AND CULTURAL ORGANIZATIONS IN RURAL AREAS

As mentioned previously, the Chinese Communist land reform (redistribution) was an integrated and co-ordinated programme with political, economic, and social functions. The educational programme, besides teaching literacy, was also instrumental in indoctrinating the peasants and propagating government programmes such as the promotion of modern farming knowledge and techniques. The social and recreational functions often were used to stimulate the peasants to greater productive effort, to propagate propagandist themes, and to serve as channels of emotional release. Greater enthusiasm for agrarian programmes on the part of the peasants was aroused by making available to them the much coveted opportunity of receiving education, which was monopolized in the past by the *literati*-gentry class.

(*i*) *The village school and the winter school.* These educational institutions constituted a part of the regular channels of propagating and even implementing land reform programmes. Usually the teacher or teachers of the village school were key members of the *ts'un*, *hsiang*, and *ch'ü* people's governments. Often the village teacher was the person with the highest degree of literacy among the village inhabitants and the central source of information regarding the world outside.

Primary schools in rural China varied both quantitatively and qualitatively with the size and economic condition of the village. Their methods of operation also differed. Some held classes only in the evening, thus permitting the adult students and elder children to engage in agricultural work; some gave both day and night courses; some had no school house, and the teacher gave lessons by visiting the peasant households at designated times. However, there were some principles which guided them all: (1) schooling must not hinder farm work; (2) lessons must be practical for the peasants and immediately applicable; (3) students must not be compelled to study; (4) pupils should adopt the "little teacher" system and teach those who were unable to come to school.

[22] Quoted from speech by Shen Chün-ju, Chief Justice of the Supreme People's Court, see *NYT*, August 29, 1952, p. 2.

The curriculum consisted generally of the 3 R's, talks on political and current affairs, and basic knowledge for securing large and better crops as well as for other agricultural activities.[23]

The development of primary schools between 1949 and 1953, as reported by a Peking source,[24] is shown in the following table:

DEVELOPMENT OF PRIMARY SCHOOLS

Year	*No. of primary schools*	*No. of pupils*
1949	346,789	24,391,000
1950	383,647	28,923,900
1951	502,189	43,154,400
1952 (estimates)	551,942	50,000,000
1953 (estimates)	500,000	51,500,000

The 1952 figure for the number of pupils attending primary schools was estimated to represent about 65 per cent of all the children of school age on the Chinese mainland at that time.

The village school and its teacher played a significant role in the land reform. If a primary school existed in the district where land reform was being carried out, the teacher served as a source of information and advice and was usually consulted by the cadres of the work team in the initiation of the programmes. At the same time, the teacher was "re-educated" and the curriculum gradually "reformed." If there was no village school at the time of the land reform, the work team often began the mass education in the form of reading classes. As the land reform work progressed, the inhabitants of one or several villages were encouraged to organize a regular primary school or a winter school, which then became the centre of a number of activities. It often was used as the headquarters of such cultural and recreational activities as the village drama and *yangko*; it was also the propagating agency for government policies, a demonstrating ground for new farming techniques and tools, and the sponsor of social reforms such as the abolition

[23] For more information on the operation of the village schools, see Pao Sha-ying, *Experiences of Teaching in Villages* (Chinese), 1949, pp. 1–84; and Wang Chung-ch'ing, "Report on the Winter School Movement in Shansi in 1949," *HY*, 2·2, June 1950, pp. 421–2.

[24] Kuo Lin, "Primary Education in the Past Three Years," *Jen-min chiao-yu* (*People's Education*), Peking, No. 33, January 1953, p. 29.

of superstitious practices, sanitary improvements and equality of women. The teacher, who served as one of the key members in the local administration, reported the reactions and comments of his adult students to the cadres.

The winter school followed the same general principles, except that it operated only in winter when the peasants were not engaged in farm work, and consequently was more extensively established. In some districts in the "old areas" like Shansi and Shantung, it was reported that each *hsiang* had an average of two winter schools.[25]

The land reform programmes were co-ordinated with the three general fields of study in the winter school—current affairs, farming knowledge and techniques, and the "3 R's." The lessons, in addition to reading, writing and arithmetic, included talks on the salient aspects of the Agrarian Reform Law, methods of insect control, use of better farming methods, and the omnipresent propaganda line. The school teacher often served in various odd capacities, such as instructor of *yangko*, writer of family correspondence, general medical adviser, and painter of posters and decorations for festivals.

According to Peking reports, the total number of students attending the rural winter schools in China was as follows: 1950, 22,217,914; 1951, 42,183,281 and 1952, 50,000,000.[26]

(*ii*) *The village drama groups and* yangko *teams.* Next to the village school with its related programmes such as the winter school, newspaper reading groups, discussion classes, etc. (which will be discussed in the section under village administration), the important instruments among the cultural and educational organizations during the agrarian reform movement were the village drama group and the *yangko* team.

Both during and after the land redistribution, the village drama group played a significant role from the propagandist and psychological point of view. A directive on village drama groups issued by the Commissioner of the Tai-hang Region (South Shansi and North Honan, an administrative region now abolished) in 1947 stated:

[25] Wang Chun-ch'ing, *op. cit.*, p. 415. For information on the organization, function and operation of the winter schools, see "Directives on Winter School," *SCH*, pp. 381–98; and *Chiao-yu kung-tso che shou-ts'e* (*Handbook of Educational Workers*), Hongkong, 1950, pp. 39–43, 46–65, and 101–06.

[26] Lin Han-ta, "Spare-time Education for Workers and Peasants in the Past Three Years," *Jen-min chiao-yu* (*People's Education*), No. 33, January 1953, p. 16.

> Village drama groups . . . must study carefully local conditions, reflect the opinions and sentiments of the peasants, give praise to progressive elements in the villages, bolster the peasants' courage to struggle, enrich the cultural life of the peasants, and guide village work toward progress. Hence, cadres of the drama groups should, first of all, maintain close liaison with the masses and coordinate their work with the key programmes (in the land reform). The performance (of plays) should precede the actual land reform programmes (i.e., the reform programme should first be propagated by drama before it is actually carried out) and prepare the peasants (psychologically) for it. Cadres of the drama groups should participate in certain planning and reviewing of rural work, and local administrations should continuously supply the groups with material and information (for their production of plays) . . . to produce plays in coordination with the central programmes in the land reform. . . . The main work of the drama groups is propaganda and agitation.[27]

(Ch'en) Huang Mei, one of the leading Communist writers, listed 4 points that were essential for the development of village drama groups:

> First, their performances must not interfere with farming or hinder production. Second, the plays must be closely co-ordinated with the major programmes (in land reform) that are being carried out in that particular area . . . reflect the reality, portray real people and events, sing the praises of the model deeds of labour heroes. Third, administratively the groups must obey the direction of the local administration, and financially, they should be self-supporting. Fourth, the plays should be short and attractive, and in writing a play, the preferences and needs of the people must be kept constantly in mind.[28]

The effect of the village drama groups grew with their number.[29] They were popular among the villagers because the events dramatized were often familiar ones and sometimes the whole community participated in the acting. There were occasions when a drama

[27] *NU*, pp. 33–6. [28] *NU*, pp. 180–9.

[29] In the 42 counties in Hopei, for example, there were more than 1,800 drama groups in the summer of 1950. See *HY*, 2·4, August 1950, p. 803.

group had been dispatched to areas where the cadres found the peasants too indifferent or conservative to be "mobilized."[30] In cases where a drama group performing in rural areas was composed mainly of students or artists, they were told to learn from the native inhabitants their colloquial expressions, mannerisms, and even "moods."[31] The content and functions of the plays as a medium in the Communist agrarian reform will be further discussed in a later section.

One of the common sights in a Chinese village during the early 1950's, especially in the "old areas," was a group of people, old and young, dancing and singing the *yangko*. The major reasons why the *yangko* was vigorously propagated in China are the following: (1) it is one of the few indigenous—hence, nationalistic—art forms which are well adapted to group activity; (2) it is simple, easy to learn, and widely known among the peasants; (3) it is suitable for numerous occasions—there is a great degree of elasticity in the form, the number of participants, and the accompanying musical instruments. These same qualities make the *yangko* an ideal instrument of propaganda and indoctrination.

In the land reform, *yangko* teams were used on innumerable occasions—in heralding a mass meeting, celebrating the conclusion of a mass meeting, carrying out specific programmes, comforting the labour heroes, in parades, as recreation, etc. Its popularity may be seen from the number of *yangko* teams in Communist China. For example, in the spring of 1950, there were 2,300 *yangko* groups in the two counties of Shihchiachuang and Tientsin (Hopei province) alone.[32]

D. *The Party's Role in Land Reform*

There were two major channels through which the Chinese Communist Party guided and controlled the direction and execution of the land reform: through party directives and through party cadres, many of whom were concurrently leaders of government organs as well as of mass organizations at all levels. At the policy-making level, often the substance of party decisions is later found

[30] Mu Tse, "The People Are Overjoyed After Their *Fan-shen*," *NU*, pp. 4–6.

[31] For discussions on the organization, function, training, and analysis of village drama groups, see some 14 articles on rural drama groups in *NU*, pp. 1–19, and pp. 61–114.

[32] *HY*, 2·4, August 1950, p. 803.

embodied in government laws and regulations. For example, Mao Tse-tung stated in his report to the 3rd Session of the 7th Plenum of the CC, CCP on June 6, 1950, that "there should be a change in our policy toward the rich peasants, a change from the policy of requisitioning the surplus land and property of the rich peasants to one of preserving a rich peasant economy in order to further the early restoration of production in the rural areas. This change of policy will also serve to isolate the landlords while protecting the middle peasants and those who rent out small plots of land." Eight days later, when Liu Shao-ch'i, heir-apparent to Mao Tse-tung, reported on the problems of agrarian reform to the National Committee of the People's Political Consultative Committee (PPCC), the preservation of a rich peasant economy was explained and this point was then embodied in the *Agrarian Reform Law* formally promulgated by Central People's Government upon the recommendation of the National Committee of the PPCC, on June 28, 1950.

Tung Pi-wu, then a Vice-Premier of the Central People's Government, gave a very illuminating analysis of the "relations between the Party and administrative authority machinery" in a report on the strengthening of work regarding the people's representative conference on September 23, 1951. His statements are significant and they are quoted at length below:

> Through the work of members of the Party in administrative authority machinery, the latter are made to accept the policies of the Party, and to turn them into the policies of the State. In any administrative authority machinery where there are more than three members of the Party, they will be organized into a Party cell to ensure the leadership of the Party in said organization. ... The Party is assuming the administrative authority of the State. But the Party does not directly control the affairs of the State, and it is incorrect to say that the Party and the State's administrative machinery are one and the same.... Many examples from the leadership of the Central People's Government by the Central Committee of the Party deserve to be emulated by comrades of the Party. The Central Committee has never once issued an order to the Central People's Government. All the laws and orders issued by the Central People's Government have been in keeping with the decisions of the Party, and many important

documents and proclamations had first been drafted by the Party (there has not been a single document which has not been prepared or at least considered first by the Party), the drafts being then brought before the National Committee of the Chinese People's Political Consultative Conference, of its Standing Committee for discussion, after which it was passed on to the Central People's Government Council or the Government Administrative Council for further discussion and adoption....This procedure must be properly extended to all areas in the country.

The correct relationship between the Party and the administrative authority machinery of the State should be as follows: (1) The Party should issue proper directives to [the Party members in] the administrative authority machinery on the nature of the tasks to be carried out and the proper course to follow in their implementation ; (2) Through the administrative authority machinery and their subsidiary departments, the policy of the Party should be enforced, while the operations of this machinery should be supervised; (3) Loyal and capable cadres (Party members or candidates of the Party) for work in the administrative authority machinery should be selected and promoted.[33]

The above passage indicates that the Communist Party is not only the engineer of all major administrative programmes but also serves as supervisor and controller in the execution of such programmes.

At the implementation level, local party organs and even the provincial and regional headquarters often issue directives to elucidate and/or elaborate on the government decrees regarding various agrarian policies. Such directives and decisions are binding upon the party members, many of whom are heads of the local governments as well as of the popular organizations. This decisive role of the party in the administrative ladder runs from top to bottom. Thus, it would be very difficult, if not impossible, for a county magistrate to initiate a project that is opposed by the Party secretary of that particular county. In *ch'ü* (district), *hsiang*, (administrative village) and *ts'un* (village) governments, it is not uncommon to find that party cadres either concurrently serve as administrative heads or hold actual power while local peasants are elected local chiefs. In a booklet entitled "How Should the Village

[33] *JMJP*, Peking, January 20, 1952.

Party Branch Lead the Masses in Production?" (issued by the Propaganda Department of the Liaotung Provincial Committee of the Communist Party), it was suggested that (1) all important village programmes should be discussed at the meetings of the village party branch; (2) decisions reached at these party meetings should be put into effect through party members serving in the village administration, but there must be no open interference with village administrative affairs by the party branch; (3) in case party members are not holding positions in the village office, the party should try to win over the village officials as well as the villagers to support party decisions.[34]

At the same time it must be pointed out that, by the election of local officials and by critical discussion of administrative programmes through such institutionalized channels as the people's representatives' congresses, the rural masses are now able, within the framework of Communist Party direction, to participate in public affairs.

The party exercised its control and influence from the very beginning of the land reform programme. The leaders of the work teams which were dispatched to initiate the land redistribution programme were as a rule party cadres supported by organs of the State, such as the militia and the army. After the land reform got under way, the party's control was further strengthened by the systematic absorption of the most active, capable and popular elements among the peasants into the Youth League and the Party.

Agricultural "labour heroes" were often enlisted into the Communist Party. These village Party cadres in turn were assigned to lead programmes sponsored by the Party, such as the mutual-aid teams and agricultural producers' cooperatives. The Party members enjoyed great prestige and better opportunity for promotion in local administrations. By indoctrination and training, by controlling the mass organizations, by serving the villagers as a source of help and comfort, by personal exemplary deeds, and by integrating active elements among the peasants into the Party, the CCP had firm and effective control at the grass-roots level for agrarian and other programmes. In fact, the Party was so well-established in areas

[34] "How Should the Village Party Branch Lead the Masses in Production?" (Chinese), Propaganda Department, Provincial Committee, Liaotung, Communist Party of China, published by Hsin-hua Book Co., Peking, November 1949, 77 pp.

like the Northeast that the CCP leaders exhorted the cadres in 1950 to allot at least 50 per cent of the seats in the People's Representatives' Conferences to non-Party members.[35]

E. *General Pattern of Procedure in the Land Redistribution Movement*

Agrarian reform in terms of land redistribution was basically completed on the Chinese mainland in 1953. It is, however, interesting to make a detailed study of the procedures and methods employed in the initial period of the movement, since it has had a profound effect on some 500 million Chinese in rural areas. The specific techniques of land reform used by the CCP vary with local conditions, political expediency, and the quality and quantity of the cadres available in a particular place at a particular time. The directives and speeches of Communist leaders in China invariably stress the necessity to adopt flexible methods in accordance with the local conditions, and warn against arbitrary and mechanical application of regulations regarding land reform. However, a general pattern of procedure is discernible. The salient aspects at the local level may be described as follows.

The Preparatory Stage

Between the government's decision to effect land reform in an area and the actual realization of that programme, weeks or even months may be required to recruit and train cadre workers and to discuss problems in detail. But so far as the village is concerned, this epoch-making change in the agrarian system begins with the arrival of the "work-team" group. These groups vary in name (work-team, rural service corps, land reform team, etc.) and in number (from a few to dozens), but generally they concentrate on one or several demonstration villages or districts as a team under the leadership of veteran cadres who are experienced in working among the peasants and are, as a rule, Party members. Members of the group are usually drawn from party organs, political workers in the People's Liberation Army, students, government staff workers, and members of the Cultural Work Corps. The "Cultural Work

[35] Kao Kang, "Speech at the Forum on Rural Work in the Northeast," *HY*, 1·4, February 1950, p. 953.

Corps" men, who are specialists in all kinds of propaganda work—giving speeches, painting cartoons, producing *yangko* dances and staging plays (propaganda media which will be discussed in later sections)—play a key role on the team. Either each "work-team" contains men who are trained propagandists, or special propaganda groups circulate among the villages. The work-teams come to the villages usually after harvest time or shortly before harvest, so that the cadres can help the peasants do the harvesting and can have time to learn the detailed conditions of the district.

The initial work of the work-team in the village consists of a series of co-ordinated measures—propaganda, education, interviews, investigation, discussion, training and organization. The cadres, living among the poor peasants and offering various services, gradually gather data from those who have suffered a great deal in the past and are honest and sincere. This "investigation" work relies heavily on personal interviews and group discussion. Simultaneously, the villages are bombarded with intensive propaganda—personal "explanations," colourful posters, *yangko*, plays, ballads, etc.—to "heighten their class consciousness." Some of the favourite slogans are: (1) "The peasants are poor because the landlords exploit them," (2) "Land reform will result in better livelihood for the peasants," (3) "Good days will come when the peasants organize themselves, overthrow the landlord as a class, and work hard for greater production," and (4) "The poor are of one family and should help each other." Propaganda is not only carried out in interviews and group discussions but also through welfare programmes such as night classes on the elimination of pest insects, winter subsidiary industries and "reading classes." Through group activities, individual talks, and meticulous investigation, the cadres systematically rally around them the "positive elements" among the poor peasants and farm labourers, who will be the key members in later village organizations and the cadres of new work-teams when the land reform is expanded to other areas. Invariably the Communist cadres are told that the discovery and organization of "positive elements" are prerequisites for the success of the land reform in the district.

However, there are variations in the above-mentioned pattern. Sometimes the work-team upon arriving strikes cymbals and beats drums to a mass meeting of all village adults at which propaganda speeches are delivered and the important features of the land reform programmes are explained in the local, colloquial dialect. Sometimes, after a short period of propaganda work, peasants, with the "positive elements" as a nucleus, are encouraged to form a Peasants' Association without going through the intermediate steps described in the following section. But this procedure is considered hasty and undesirable by the Communist hierarchy. In all cases, directives from party and government organs remind the cadres to be constantly on the alert in the initial stage of the land reform and to watch out for the following: (1) lest the agents of the landlords and "local despots"[36] pose as "positive elements" and subvert the land reform programme; (2) lest elements of the former local administration or gentry infiltrate into the new village leadership; (3) lest old and new cadres compromise with, or become corrupted by, the landlord-gentry through bribery or threats; and (4) lest over-zealous cadres and peasants take the law into their own hands and take "rough measures" against landlords, "local despots" and peasants accused of oppressive or subversive deeds.[37]

The Iconoclastic Period

The second step—after the "positive elements" have been rallied together and indoctrinated, the peasants "awakened" by propaganda and agitation, and information regarding the district has been collected—centres on the breaking down of the traditional power-structure in the village and the power-image in the minds of the peasants. The key features in this period are mass meetings to accuse and punish the "local despots" and mass meetings to define class status.

The anti-despot meetings may be convened under different names, such as "speak bitterness" meetings, "settle-account" meetings, or simply "struggle" meetings, but the general characteristics are the same. First, the cadres, after careful discussion and planning, pick up one or several "local despots"—the number picked as a target

[36] "Despots" are defined, in the *Decisions Concerning the Differentiation of Class Status in the Countryside*, as "those who have proved on the basis of substantial evidence to have committed such crimes as relying on or organizing a reactionary force to play the tyrant in a locality or using force or their influence to oppress and rob the people resulting in a heavy loss of lives and properties of the latter."

[37] Various reports on the land reform appear in *JMJP*, December 20, 1950, p. 2; Jack Belden, "The 'Overturning' of Sesame Garden Village," *The Reporter*, January 3, 1950, pp. 8–16; and *NYT*, February 13, 1951, p. 4.

at one time is never large, and the accused are generally landlords unpopular for their exorbitant rent, usurious loans, or other oppressive deeds; or former local officials notorious for extortion, bribery or other exactions. Second, while the cadres go around the village to collect data on the atrocities of the accused, various means, such as house-top loudspeakers, "black-board newspapers," *yangko* and plays are employed to publicize the accusations. Third, a mass meeting of all villages is convened, with the accused lined up on the platform. The chairman of the presidium, usually a local cadre, announces the major charges in detail. After the victims, relatives of the victims and other attendants are invited to air their grievances, the accused is asked to answer the charges or, if he pleads guilty, to sign a paper admitting his misdeeds. Finally, at the climax of the peasants' agitation, the chairman announces the closing of the meeting with an assurance that "justice will be dealt by the people's tribunal" and a string of propaganda slogans. In an article in *People's China* of July 16, 1950, the author describes the opening address of an "accusation meeting" as follows: "The time has come to spit out all of your bitterness, fellow-villagers! Speak out all your grievances, and hold nothing back. We have nothing to fear. The government, the army and the militia all belong to us labouring people now. We need never again be afraid of these rich scoundrels and loafers." The writer goes on to say that after the despot was given a four-year prison sentence, "the village now begin to realize how powerful they are as a collective force, powerful enough to prevent their feudal oppressors from ever regaining their former authority. Conditions are ready now for starting the actual work of land distribution."[38] Sometimes the "guilty party" is paraded with a high paper hat after the meeting; sometimes sentence is passed not by the people's tribunal but by the peasants attending the meeting; and sometimes the accused is man-handled or even killed by the enraged victims—all these practices are now prohibited by the Agrarian Reform Law (Article 32) as "illegal."[39] If there is no "local despot" or notorious landlord in a village, then several villages or even districts may jointly hold

[38] Lao Dunne, "A Village Uproots Feudalism," *PC,* 2·2, July 16, 1950, pp. 21–2.

[39] For reports on the detailed proceedings of a "speak bitterness" meeting, see "The Anti-Despot Struggle in South Kiangsu," *HY,* 1·1, November 1949, pp. 175–8.

an "anti-despot" mass meeting. Such a meeting may last from several hours to several days; but usually it is held at a time when the peasants are not busy with their farm work.

Although the charges brought against the accused are generally true,[40] a key function of these "condemnation" meetings is psychological. Thus a Communist cadre writes: "Speak bitterness (meetings), in order to achieve definite objectives and functions, must heighten the class-consciousness of the masses and strengthen the thoroughness of our work . . . there must be careful preparation, i.e., peasants must be psychologically mobilized . . . there must also be leadership, i.e., the masses must be skilfully organized and channelled into practical action through these meetings."[41]

Although Party directives stress the spontaneity of the peasants at these struggle meetings, and as a rule, the bitterness towards the landlord-despot is genuine, some reports indicate deliberate planning and even manipulation of these struggle meetings by the cadres. For example, one professor reports that "we are instructed by our leaders to scatter among the crowd at the meeting. Our tasks are: when the peasants are at a loss as to how to argue with the landlord, we should give the peasants some ideas to speak up; when the peasants become incensed and want to resort to rough measures, we should exhort them to be calm. . . . "[42] It seems from the above illustrations that a primary function of these struggle meetings is to strengthen the confidence of the peasants in their new power and to prepare them psychologically for further aggressive action against the classes identified as enemies. At the same time, these meetings, like many other activities in the land reform programme, serve as an instrument of indoctrination of the new cadres—to reinforce their

[40] Not only do the cadres usually pick up the truly notorious ones for effectiveness, but the atrocious nature of the "local bosses" in rural China exceeds often the worst assumptions. Professor Feng Yu-lan wrote in May 1950: "Formerly I thought that stories describing these despots who set up private dungeons, killed at will, commandeered properties and raped women, allied with the authorities and dealt shadily with bandits, happened in novels. Now (after engaging in land reform work in Honan) I realize they are not only true, but happened frequently. In many counties in Honan some despots are kings in area under their control. . . . When they murder, they eliminate the whole family in order to 'cut off the root'. . . . " *HH*, 2·5, May 16, 1950, p. 24. [41] Ch'en I-cheng, *op. cit.*, p. 1224.

[42] See "Lessons (Learned) in My Participation in the Land Reform," by Professor Feng Yu-lan, *HH*, 2·2, April 1, 1950, p. 23.

hatred of the enemy and to enrich their techniques of handling the masses.[43]

Another important feature of this period was the holding of meetings to define the class status of the village adults. This is an all-important step, as the fate of the villagers is determined by their class status. The amount of land and equipment allotted to each poor peasant or farm labourer depends on the quantity available in that area for redistribution. The share is not equal quantitatively or even qualitatively, as adjustments are made according to quality of land, distance of the field, and other specific conditions. Landlords are allotted a similar share and tenants have priority to the land they are cultivating. Landlords and rich peasants are barred from becoming members of the Peasants' Association, but after the completion of land reform, rich peasants (the landlord class being eliminated) may become members upon the approval of the PA membership.[44]

The principles for the determination of class status are stated in Art. 31 of the *Agrarian Reform Law*:

> It shall be determined by democratic estimation and decision at the village peasant congress and peasant representatives' congress under the leadership of the village people's government, by the method of self-assessment and public discussion. If any person concerned is not a member of a Peasants' Association, he should, nevertheless, be invited to participate in the estimation and decision at the meetings and to argue his case. The estimation and decision must be reported to the *ch'ü* (district) people's government for ratification. Where any person concerned, or any other person, does not agree with the result, an appeal may be lodged with the county people's tribunal which shall pass judgment and carry it into effect.

But as the land reform process was accelerated by the Communists during 1950–51 in the "new areas," the classification was usually determined at mass meetings of village adults with the help of the work-team cadres before the organization of the Peasants' Association and the Peasant Representatives' Congresses.

[43] See Chu Tsun-huang, "Speak Bitterness (Meetings) Educated Me," *HH*, 2·6, June 1, 1950, p. 29.

[44] *General Regulations for the Organization of the PA* (Chinese), July 1950, Art. 4.

From reports describing land reform proceedings in North, East, Central, and South China,[45] the general pattern of procedure in determining the class status of villagers may be described as follows: first, the cadres of the work-team explain to the villagers in detail the status of various rural classes with some concrete examples from a few local households. Second, mass meetings are called during which the class status of those who have anything to do with land is discussed and then defined. The first group to be classified is either the landlords or the poor peasants, with each person entitled to argue his own case. Whether the principle of *Tzu-pao kung-i* (i.e., each individual defines his own class status and then it is discussed and approved by the attendants of the meeting) is followed or class status is decided by the meeting, all are encouraged to give information so as to make class "differentiation" accurate. Those whose class status is not agreed upon by the peasants will wait for clarification by higher authorities. In some instances, the occasion for ascertaining the class status of the landlords is combined with the "speak bitterness" meeting of the peasants. Third, after the status of each household is approved by the mass meeting, a preliminary list is posted in the village for a few days, during which comments and complaints may be presented to the organ in charge of class differentiation. Fourth, after consideration of the comments and suggestions regarding the preliminary list, a revised list is submitted to the higher authority (usually the *ch'ü* administration or the provincial committee for agrarian reform) for approval and then publicly promulgated in the village.

Then comes the stage of action. After the "surplus properties" of landlords have been registered and the "surplus land" of landlords and some rich peasants has been surveyed, these lands are divided among the poor peasants and farm labourers through public discussion and approval of individual requests. The final step takes the form of a celebration meeting, which is often combined with the

[45] Professor Feng Yu-lan, "Mass Line in Agrarian Reform Work," quoted by *HCJP*, April 14, p. 2; Jao Shu-shih, "Conclusions on the Experiences of the Model Experiments in the Agrarian Reform in East China," *JMJP*, December 20, 1950, p. 2; *Letter to All Honan Peasants*, by the 1st Congress of Peasant Representatives of Honan Province, March 21, 1950, *HY*, 2·1, May 1950, p. 85; "Report to Chairman Mao on Agrarian Reform in Kao-chao *Hsiang*, Hunan," *JMJP*, October 8, 1950, p. 2; and "Land Reform in the Five *Hsiang* Near Canton," *HCJP*, February 6, 1951, p. 5.

issuing of new title deeds to the land.[46] This occasion is generally utilized as another opportunity for propaganda and indoctrination, and also of mobilization and planning for greater agricultural production. The people's government at the county level or above may, "in accordance with the local land situation, set aside part of the land to be nationalized and used for agricultural experiments or as state model farms for one county or more. Such land may be rented to peasants for cultivation until the farms are established." (Art. 15, *Agrarian Reform Law.*) With respect to land in suburban areas which formerly belonged to the landlords and which has been nationalized, peasants who are cultivating the land under a "certificate to use nationalized land," pay only an agricultural tax. Such land may be taken back, with compensation to be paid by the government, for the expansion of industry or other projects.[47]

The above is only an overall picture of the land reform procedure at the initial stage. In reality, of course, there are many variations on this general theme. In some villages, no "anti-despot" meetings are held. In some districts, peasants may become so bitter against some landlords that they take the law into their own hands and commit atrocities. In still other districts, peasants are sometimes so afraid of the landlords that they secretly pay rent as usual or return confiscated properties which have been allotted to them.

F. *Perpetuating Devices of the Chinese Communists in the Land Reform*

Certain sources report questionable conduct by some cadres during and after the land reform on the Chinese mainland, such as the use of power to revenge personal grudges, haste, and misinterpretation of government laws and regulations. Some of the measures the Chinese Communists are taking to deal with such abuses include mechanisms for recruiting and training new cadre workers, sample checking and re-checking of agrarian programmes in the villages, criticism and self-criticism

[46] Art. 30 of the *Agrarian Reform Law* stipulates that "after agrarian reform is completed, the people's government shall issue title deeds and shall recognize the right of all land owners to manage, buy, sell or rent out land freely. All land contracts made before the reform of the agrarian system shall be null and void."

[47] *Directive on the Disposal of Suburban Agricultural Land in the Old Liberated Areas, HY,* 1·5, March 1950, p. 1215.

meetings and the *cheng-feng* (roughly, correction of erroneous tendencies) movement.

1. THE RECRUITING AND TRAINING OF CADRES

"The most important preparation for land reform is the preparation of cadres," Chou En-lai declared in October 1950. This training of cadres is a continuous process before, during, and after the land reform. According to a bulletin of the *NCNA*, dated December 11, 1950, over 176,000 persons had been trained to carry out land redistribution work in 1,200 *hsiang* in East China. The trainees included "members of various democratic parties, large numbers of young intellectuals, and rural personnel."[48] Correspondence from Huiyang (county in Kwangtung), which appeared in the *Hua-ch'iao jih-pao* (*China Daily News*, New York) of January 11, 1951, states that "the first training class for land reform, after 14 days' intensive and enthusiastic study, was concluded on December 24, 1950. Four hundred trainees, consisting of local cadres of the county and of military units stationed at Huiyang, and positive elements among the peasants, were sent to four 'experimental' *hsiang* in four groups after a mass meeting where pledges were made."

For the training of peasant cadres for land reform (particularly land redistribution) work at the village level, the "study" period is generally a short one, varying from several days to a few weeks. The trainees are as a rule poor peasants, middle peasants, and farm labourers. The following report illustrates how the actual training of peasants works: at Shukow *ch'ü*, Hsi-hsien, Anhwei, 344 peasants (312 poor peasants and farm labourers and 32 middle peasants, including 20 peasant women) were trained in 18 days in August, 1949, with training classes lasting from 2 to 3 days at each *hsiang*. At the end of the training period, the committee responsible for the training made 5 recommendations: (1) the poor and middle peasants must be encouraged to come voluntarily after individual interviews and group discussions; (2) if discussions touch on their sufferings and problems, the trainees will speak up about their difficulties and needs; (3) positive elements can be discovered through the above discussions; (5) concrete methods and salient points of the programmes which the peasants are asked to carry out must be explained to the trainees at the

[48] For a detailed description of the training of work-teams, see Wang Hsiao-shih, *op.cit.*, p. 13.

meetings of the training period; (5) continued assistance and training should be given to the trainees when they return to their respective villages to carry out their work.[49] In areas where land redistribution has been completed, cadres at the *ts'un* and *ch'ü* levels are called up successively to receive additional training after the farming season.[50] In addition to the peasants, cadre workers for land reform are also recruited from among students and by re-educating personnel who served in the KMT administration. The 8 disciplines stipulated by the East China Military and Political Committee on July 22, 1950 for the cadres who engage in land reform are as follows:

> (1) Enforce strictly the laws and directives of the people's government regarding agrarian reform, of which there must be no infringement; (2) support resolutely agrarian reform, with no favouritism toward the landlords; (3) serve the public with integrity, never pocketing any proceeds (from land redistribution) or accepting bribes; (4) respect the democratic rights of the people, listen to opinions and criticisms of the masses, never cheat or oppress the people; (5) discuss all important issues with others, never making decisions on one's individual judgment alone or implementing programmes arbitrarily; (6) act in accordance with legal provisions; never indiscriminately arrest, punish, beat, or kill; the use of third degree methods or any measure of an illegal nature is prohibited; (7) obey strictly the directives of the superior organs; do not pay mere lip service; (8) observe strictly the system of asking for instruction (when encountering difficult cases) and report the results (when a programme is carried out); do not falsely report the conditions, and do not act without co-ordinating (with other districts).[51]

The problem of shortage of personnel in the various fields of agrarian programme and of current training of rural cadres will be discussed in a following section.

2. INSPECTION TEAMS

Inspection teams are organized at all administrative levels to check the results and effects of the land reform. The central

[49] "The *Fan-shen* of the Peasants in Kiangnan," *HY*, 1·1, Nov. 1949, p. 171.

[50] *Directive on the Rural Work This* (1949) *Winter in the Old Areas* (Chinese), Northeast Bureau, CCP, October 8, 1949.

[51] *TU*, pp. 144–5.

government sends inspection teams to the provinces; for example, the Central Agricultural Inspection Corps headed by Li Shu-cheng, then Minister of Agriculture, toured the provinces in May and June 1950. Inspection teams are sent to the villages periodically by the provincial and *hsien* people's governments. In some provinces, a Joint Bureau of Production is set up, composed of representatives from the Agricultural Bureau, the provincial research institute, the People's Bank, the cooperatives, the Youth League, the Women's Federation, the provincial newspapers, etc. to deal with the following work: inspection, liaison with local administrations, instruction in farming techniques, and collection and compilation of data regarding agricultural conditions in that province.[52]

At the local level, inspectors are generally dispatched to do the following: review and improve the implementation of such specific programmes as the definition of rural class status, the introduction of new seeds or tools and the planting of crops which are being promoted by the government (such as cotton), examination of the accomplishments and style of work of the local cadres, checking reports and data submitted by the local administrations, collecting suggestions from, and information regarding, the local peasants and cadres.

3. THE *cheng-feng* RECTIFICATION MOVEMENT

Cheng-feng, a movement "to correct undesirable tendencies" in the various spheres of CCP activities, was launched in the spring of 1942 with three speeches by Mao Tse-tung at Yenan.[53] According to Mao, undesirable tendencies in learning take the form of subjectivism; in the party, that of sectarianism; and in literature and art, that of formalism. The second *cheng-feng* period was from late 1947 to 1948, and another one started on July 1, 1950, the 29th anniversary of the CCP. The objective of *cheng-feng*, as stated officially in an editorial of the leading Party organ, *Jen-min jih-pao* (*People's Daily*), is "to improve the organization of the Party and to remould its style of work—these are dual aspects of one central task, that of raising the political quality

[52] Hua Shu, "Glorious Achievements in the Agricultural Construction of New China," *HK*, 1·8, October 10, 1950, p. 17.

[53] *Correcting Undesirable Tendencies in Learning, the Party, and Literature and Art*, February 1, 1942; *Opposing Party Formalism*, February 8, 1942; and *Speech at the Forum on Literature and Art at Yenan*, May 2 and 23, 1942.

of the Party to facilitate the consolidation of unity with the masses of the people." But the *cheng-feng* movement has two further functions: to reassert the Leninist concept of the party as a highly centralized, highly disciplined group and to eliminate and prevent any deviation within the party, whose membership jumped from 40,000 in July 1937 to 6·5 million in 1955.

The *cheng-feng* movement has been closely co-ordinated with the land reform work. For example, the activities of the *cheng-feng* below the *hsien* level in Honan province, which lasted from July to October, 1950, were carried out in three phases. First, the Provincial Committee of the Party sent cadres to hold discussions and meetings with the veteran cadres of *hsien* and *ch'ü* on various agrarian reform problems. Second, the cadres of *hsien* and *ch'ü*, after their conferences with the Provincial (Party) Committee representatives, went to the *hsiang* and *ts'un* for planning and discussion with the local cadres, especially the new ones. Third, after a certain period, village programmes were checked and improved by cadres from *hsien* and *ch'ü*.[54] In a directive issued by the Honan Provincial Committee (of the CCP), it was stated that:

> The crux of the (*cheng-feng*) movement is to develop criticism and self-criticism through the re-examination of work so as to increase efficiency and improve the style of work. Reports should be made only after detailed investigation, and must be concise and clear. The reports (made at the discussion meetings) should contain both principles and concrete illustrations, discussions, and explanations. In analyzing a problem, comparisons should be made between desirable and undesirable cases from practical experience, with the emphasis on the commendation of the meritorious. In criticizing the bureaucracy and formalism of others, the speaker must not forget to check on his own work and conduct. Cadres should constantly solicit advice and comments from the non-Party members of the *ch'u* and *hsiang* People's Representatives' Congresses.[55]

Several points are emphasized in most of the reports and "model" cases of *cheng-feng* in Chinese publications. The movement must be closely co-ordinated with local problems; discussions and reports must be concise and offer practical solutions to the

[54] *JMJP*, October 19, 1950, p. 3. [55] *JMJP*, October 19, 1950, p. 5.

problems raised; the cadres must take the lead in criticism and self-criticism; detailed investigations must be held and data collected before *cheng-feng* conferences are to be convened.

In connection with the various aspects of the *cheng-feng* movement, a later and similar event was the "three-anti" movement and its subsequent development, the "five-anti" movement in 1952. The first movement was a campaign "against corruption, waste and bureaucratism" and the second a movement against "bribery of personnel in the government and in public organs, smuggling and evasion of taxes, stealing of State property, doing shoddy work and using inferior materials on government contracts, and espionage to obtain economic information from government sources to be used for market speculation."[56] These movements were proclaimed "successfully concluded" by the Central People's Government in July 1952.

Like the agrarian reform movement, the "three-anti" and "five-anti" movements are of basic political, economic and social significance, and their long-run impact and results in both urban and rural areas are far-reaching. Politically, these movements further weakened the power and influence of the business class, strengthened the control and prestige of the Communist Party, and reduced the chances of Party members being influenced by material temptations. Socially, according to the Communists, it aimed at "bringing about a complete liquidation of the dirt and poison of the old social order and the establishment of a new moral code of integrity and thrift."[57] The political and social effects of these movements were basic and profound, and their repercussions have been particularly great in the economic field in general and in commerce in particular.

Another party reform movement similar to the "*cheng-feng*" was initiated in April 1953. The movement, concentrating on rural areas, was officially named the "Re-adjustment of the Organization of the CCP" and the "rectification" campaign. It aimed at expelling "undesirable elements" from the party and at making it more difficult to obtain membership in the party by setting up more rigid requirements. According to a report in the *New York Times* of April 8, 1953, the North China Bureau of the CCP announced

[56] Liu Tsun-ch'i, "Movement to Eliminate Corruption, Waste and Bureaucratism in China," *PC*, March 16, 1952.

[57] "Order on Three-anti and Five-anti Movements," *NCNA*, March 11, 1952, Peking.

two sets of measures dealing with problems affecting members of the party and cadres in areas where the "re-adjustment programme" was under way. The first set of provisions dealt with economic issues, such as hiring of farm labourers, the issuance of loans, members' engaging in business activities, and the renting out of land. The second dealt with political issues connected with corruption, waste and "commandism." Expulsion was meted out to party members who were guilty of the following offences:

(1) Any member who, after having been educated by the party, still persists in the employment of labourers, engages in their exploitation and thereby is transformed into a rich peasant or any other exploiting element; (2) Any member who derives his main income from the operation of commercial enterprises and who is considered to have the status of a capitalist; (3) Any member who derives his main income from loans at usurious rates; (4) Any member who derives his main income from renting out land and has been transformed into the status of a landlord; (5) Any member who buys land for renting out or for cultivation with hired labour.

The provisions also reportedly stipulated a number of exemptions under which party members might employ hired farm labourers. These included sickness, disability, old age, weakness, and occupation in other useful production work. Under the heading of corruption, members were threatened with expulsion if they acted individually or collectively through illegal means to encroach on and steal State and public property for self-aggrandizement and self-profit. Waste was defined in the provisions as unnecessary expenditure of State or public property or excessive spending in expenditures. The directive states that party members who "arbitrarily detain, fine, or beat persons who violate the law" should be regarded as erroneous for having used force and "commandism."[58] (The most recent rectification campaign during 1956-58, will be discussed in a later section.)

G. *Mass Media Employed in the Land Reform*

This study does not purport to present a detailed analysis of the various forms of mass media used in the agrarian programmes in

[58] *NYT*, April 8, 1953, p. 3.

China, as many aspects of such media are rather technical in nature. Following are some of the major types and functions of the media utilized by the Chinese Communists in the land reform movement. It is interesting to note that extensive use has been made of both traditional (often with modifications) and modern media.

(*i*) *Musical forms.* The telling of stories in simple tunes, usually by the blind, has always been a common sight in Chinese villages. Many such singing artistes are now organized and trained to sing new songs praising the labour heroes and various agrarian reform programmes. Instruments like the fiddle, lute, and flute are used, and while the themes and expressions are new, many traditional forms are employed with innovations.

Yangko, which literally means the "planting song," is one of the most common and effective media used by the Chinese Communists and has already been discussed. It is simple—the basic dance step is 3 steps forward, 1 step backward. It is popular—more than a hundred varieties can be found throughout China proper. It is flexible—it may be danced by a few or a few hundred, may be performed as a dance, song, or drama, or a combination of these, as the occasion demands and it may be accompanied by a number of native instruments—cymbals, drums, flutes, etc. It is interesting—new colourful costumes have been added to the original bright and enchanting peasant drapes donned for festivals—especially when it is danced with waist drums or on stills. Because *yangko* is an attractive form of group activity, it is used on many occasions to serve numerous psychological, propagandistic, cultural and political purposes. The *yangko's* role in the Communist agrarian reform programmes is reflected by the titles of some of the more popular *yangko ch'ü* (drama) such as *Hsiung-mei k'ai-huan* (Brother and Sister Reclaiming Land), *Pien-kung hao* (Mutual Aid Is Good), *Chung Wan-tsai ch'i-chia* (Chung Wan-tsai [name of a former village idler] Becomes Prosperous), and *Pai-mao-nü* (The White-Haired Women). Since *Pai-mao-nü* is generally agreed to be the most successful and most frequently performed *yangko* play thus far, a brief analysis of its plot and propaganda themes is presented as a representative study of *yangko* drama.

Pai-mao-nü, in its present version,[59] is a collective work by three writers, Ho Ching-chih, Ting I, and Wang Pin, with 92 songs

[59] 1946 edition, put out by the *Hsin-hua* (New China) Bookstore in Kalgan.

composed by Mao K'o, Chang Lu and Ch'u Wei. The plot, divided into 6 scenes, has been summarized by Jack Belden as follows:

> The heroine of the play is the daughter of a tenant farmer. Seized by the "dog legs" (i.e., lackeys) of the landlord when her father cannot pay his New Year's debts, she is forced to become a maidservant in the landlord's home. There she is constantly beaten by the landlord's wife . . . and finally raped on a dark night by the landlord's son. Made pregnant, she threatens to reveal her shame to the whole village. The landlord's son, who is about to be married, and the "dog leg" bind up the girl and throw her in a closet and make ready to murder her. An old woman servant, who many years ago had been brought to the landlord's home under much the same circumstances, releases the girl who flees in the night. The landlord's son and "dog leg" pursue her into the mountains. The girl evades capture by taking refuge in a rocky glen where she gives birth to a baby, her hair turning white in the process. She is adopted by guerrillas who eventually free her home village and bring the landlord's son before a speak bitterness meeting.[60]

Even from this simplified version of the play, one can clearly see that such things as the struggle against the despot-landlords, the redistribution of land, the abolition of social injustices (the slave-maid system) have been skilfully dramatized.

Min-ko are folk songs. Many of the *min-ko* tunes are now sung with new words, serving like other traditional art forms as a propaganda medium.[61] Communist writers and artistes have also written a number of new songs and poems following the style of *min-ko*.

(*ii*) *Drama.* It is traditional in China during festivals, especially in the Lunar New Year period, for the peasants either to enact a play themselves or to employ professional performers. The Chinese Communists have encouraged the villagers to organize drama groups and to produce plays with such new themes as a story about a local labour hero or the dramatization of the success of a certain land reform programme. Many traditional Chinese "operas" have also been revised, with the assistance of the leading actors

[60] Belden, *op. cit.*, p. 210.
[61] Ai-Ch'ing, "Wang Ting-yu and His Songs," *MI*, pp. 25–32.

such as Mei Lan-fang. Many popular "operas" including the *Assassination of the Tiger General*, *Lady Precious Stream*, *The Monument of Li Ling*, *The Fisherman's Revenge*, *The Tale of the White Snake*, etc. have been given new interpretations and expressions.

Occasionally modern drama troupes also visit the villages; however, they are generally organized not at the village level, but by the Cultural Corps of the *hsien* or provincial people's government. There were in 1953 some 70,000 part-time dramatic troupes on the Chinese mainland.[62]

(iii) Publications, press, and pictures. Besides the books, newspapers, periodicals and pamphlets published for the masses, some of the most common visual media used by the Communists in rural China are cartoon books, "black-board" newspapers (including "wall-papers"), and posters.

The cartoon books contain stories in pictures with explanatory phrases in simple language. Between 1950 and 1954, 90 million copies of serial picture books and 11 million cartoons were printed. The common themes of these stories can be seen from the titles of some of 136 "popular artistic readers" listed in the *Hsin-hua* Bookstore catalogue (1950)—"The Joy of *Fan-shen*," "Labour Changed Men," "The Reform of An Idler," "An Oppressed Woman Peasant" and others.

"Black-board" newspapers are news bulletins written either on a large piece of black-board or on sheets posted on the walls of public buildings, and hence are sometimes called "wall-papers." They are "issued" periodically, perhaps every two or three days in simple colloquial language. The "black-board newspapers" serve not only as a source of information about government programmes and village activities, but also as an outlet for public opinion, since the peasants are encouraged to write criticisms, comments and suggestions on them. They are also used frequently to announce the progress made on a certain project or programme, so that greater competitive spirit can be aroused between villages and groups.[63] It is reported that in many "old areas" there is a "black-board newspaper" in every village.[64]

[62] "Cultural Centres and Houses of Culture," *PC*, No. 9, 1954, May 1, 1954, p. 29.

[63] Ho Ting, "Labour Hero Chang Fu-kuei," *HY*, 2·1, May 1950, p. 90.

[64] "Cultural Life in the Villages of 'Old Areas' of North China," *HY*, 2·4, August 1950, p. 803.

Posters, in the form of felicitous phrases written on coloured papers, or of pictures symbolizing good omen, have been traditionally popular among the peasants, especially during the Lunar New Year Festival. They have been used as decorations for doors, windows, rooms, and even stables. Peking Government now not only makes posters in the old designs with new themes but also distributes posters of a new type. For instance, the picture of Mao Tse-tung is now sometimes found in the place once occupied by the God of Earth, and decorative pictures of tractors and the like have replaced the old drawings of phoenix and *ch'i-lin* (male and female mythical animals like unicorns).

Another medium which is skilfully exploited is the traditional almanac published each year primarily for peasants. Its circulation of 3 million in North China and the Northeast alone (in 1952) is greater than that of any of the "popular readers." The Chinese authorities have issued a new "Almanac for Peasants," retaining many such old features as the notes on seasonal changes, festival days in the lunar calendar, etc. But they have replaced unscientific portions (notes telling the readers when and when not to take a bath, when "withered grass becomes fireflies" and when "birds dive into water and turn into frogs" etc.) with seasonal farming information, propaganda slogans, basic sanitation rules, and so on.

(*iv*) *Audio-visual aids*. Movie houses on the whole are still to be found more in cities and towns than in villages. According to Kuo Mo-jo, it was planned that 700 projection teams be set up in 1951 to show movies in both urban and rural areas. Another report, in December 1952, stated that 1,800 mobile projection teams gave film shows to 140 million people in rural areas and in factories from urban theatres in 1951.[65] But lantern slides are shown either on a screen or in a box to peasants and soldiers by circuit teams. The content of these slides is closely co-ordinated with current agrarian reform programmes. Often the pictures on the slides are drawn on the spot so that local stories and personalities may appear in the show. These slides were used extensively during and after the Sino-Japanese War and found to be very popular among soldiers and peasants.[66]

Radio broadcasting as a medium for mass persuasion has been receiving increasing attention. A *New York Times* dispatch from

[65] Yu Chi-tung, *op. cit.*, p. 34.

[66] "A New Propaganda Tool—the Slides," and "A New Weapon in the Literature and Art Front," *NU*, pp. 157–78.

Hongkong dated January 21, 1951 reported that according to the Peking radio,

> Chinese Communists have built up a vast propaganda network through which the voice of Peiping will be heard by virtually half of China's vast population. . . . When the nation-wide network is in full operation, the Communists will be able to make their line of thought known to the country's 450,000,000 inhabitants within 24 hours. . . . Even the smallest villages (will be reached). This is the first time in Chinese history that rural districts have received such special attention.[67]

To reach as many peasants as possible, the Chinese authorities also distributed mimeographed sheets of news and other materials monitored from Peking broadcasts to be read by the local cadres to the villagers over housetop loudspeakers, in discussion groups, at the village school, and through various group activities in the village.

It was reported in December 1952 that over 3,573 receiving stations had been organized in areas which had no daily newspaper registered. Special monitors take notes of important news and government decisions and relay them. The Central Radio Station broadcast a dictation service which, in 1953, served over 1,000 rural newspapers in remote areas inaccessible by the telegraph.[68]

During the land reform, the telephone was another medium that enabled the local leaders at the *hsien* and provincial levels to keep close and constant contact with the local cadres and to cope quickly with any problems. The important role assigned to telephone communication was reflected in Liu Shaoch'i's statement (June 1950) that "administrative leaders must keep close contact with local cadres by telephone communication regarding developments in the agrarian reform."[69]

(*v*) *Group activities.* In addition to the use of such traditional activities as festival gatherings, village celebrations, and local markets and fairs, the Party has developed a myriad of other group activities. Some of these have been described previously: the village mass organizations, "the family council," drama and *yangko*

[67] *NYT*, February 7, 1951, p. 4. [68] Yu, Chi-tung, *op. cit.*, pp. 34–5.
[69] Liu Shao-ch'i, *On the Agrarian Reform Law*, June 14, 1950.

teams, mutual-aid brigades, etc. These activities and organizations are designed not only to facilitate the implementation of the agrarian reform and other programmes but also to break down the traditional individualism of the peasants.

One of the most common collective activities in the new Chinese village is the "reading group." These groups are organized informally to suit the convenience of the peasants. Anywhere from 3 to 10 peasants may meet at a time when they are not occupied with work—during the lunch hour in the field, rainy days when little farming can be done, evenings in the home—and study together. Either the village teacher comes to teach at a pre-arranged time and place, or one of the group members serves as the "little teacher." The primary objective of these "reading groups" is to learn a few dozen to several hundred characters for practical use; but the text (newspapers, textbook for peasants,[70] primary school textbook, local news sheet, or phrases made up by the village school teacher) generally contains some "current events," "political common sense," and "basic knowledge for farming." In this way, these groups also serve as propaganda and indoctrination channels. In certain districts, they are called "newspaper reading groups," a name which explains itself.

In some rural areas, discussion classes or groups are organized extensively. Discussion generally centres around methods and techniques for agricultural improvement, important problems in the specific locality, and current events. When a specific programme is being promoted, propaganda agents are sent from *hsien* or *ch'ü* administration to conduct special sessions among the discussion groups. Lectures and exhibitions are presented by circuit teams

[70] One *Textbook for Peasants,* available at the Harvard-Yenching Library, was compiled and published by the "Peasants' Association of the Shensi-Chahar-Hopei Border Region" in September 1945. On the cover, these words were printed: "This textbook is issued to *ch'ü* cadres and some *ts'un* cadres who are responsible for its safe-keeping. It must not be lost. The various *ch'ü* should set up a time to have it returned." The major themes of the text may be seen from the topical headings for the 8 chapters listed in the table of contents: (1) Who supports whom?; (2) To realize *fan-shen,* (we) must ourselves rise and fight; (3) 25 per cent reduction of rent and the guarantee of tenancy rights; (4) Why carry out the policy of rent and interest reduction?; (5) The solutions to some concrete problems; (6) To achieve victory in the struggle, (we) must first of all organize; (7) To participate in the local government, to participate in the armed forces; and (8) The mutual-aid team. 38 pp.

sent from the central or provincial government. Talks, demonstrations, and pictorial displays on various farming problems (pest control, irrigation improvement, better seeds, public health) are presented, enlivened by entertainment programmes like *yangko*, lantern slides, or plays and mixed with the usual propaganda themes. In many villages a "cultural and recreational centre" is established.

At the end of 1953, there were about 2,470 "houses of culture," 4,560 village cultural centres, and 18 mobile cultural service teams. From July to September 1952, 6,000 cultural houses and centres organized 148,000 lectures, reports and discussions on various subjects with a total attendance of 46 million persons. In addition, they held more than 20,000 exhibitions on different themes which were visited by more than 56 million people. Some 20 million people came to read materials in their reading rooms and libraries.[71] A "house of culture" usually includes a library, a music room with some native instruments, a reading room where games like Chinese chess are provided, and a playground for children. The propaganda value of these centres can be seen by their propaganda posters and the types of activity sponsored by them. Often such a centre forms a part of the village school, and the teacher as a rule assumes a key role in its management and planning.[72]

The above deals only briefly with the media most frequently used by the Chinese cadres in their intensive and extensive propaganda campaign in connection with the land redistribution programme. There are also numerous specific media that are popular in some districts or areas but are little known in other parts of the country. These local media, although effective within their area of popularity and utilized by the Communists, are too numerous to be discussed here.

H. *Sociological and Psychological Factors in the Land Redistribution Movement*

Conflicts Aroused During Land Reform Between Old and New Values and Beliefs

In the land reform led by the CCP, there are a number of aspects that, in varying degrees, are at variance with the traditional values

[71] "Cultural Centres and Houses of Culture," *PC*, May 1, 1954, p. 29.
[72] *Kuang-ming jih-pao*, Peking, October 31, 1950, p. 2.

and beliefs of the Chinese peasants. The fight against landlords conducted in the violent Marxist class-struggle manner is regarded by some peasants as contradictory to the ethical norm of moderation and the golden mean taught by the Confucian school. The digging of irrigation ditches may be looked upon with suspicion as flouting the superstitious beliefs of "wind and water." Social and educational measures in the agrarian programme, such as the granting of equal rights to women, abolition of witch doctors, whittling down of the power of the patriarchal head, etc. often arouse the passive if not overt opposition of the conservative elements in the villages. On those matters regarded by the Party as basic, such as the overthrow of the landlord, the programme has been carried out with vigour and persistence. But on many of the minor aspects, the Chinese Communists have been tactful and cautious. For example, a special directive issued by the Kwangtung Provincial People's Government on March 1, 1951, reminded the cadres who were engaged in land reform work that "the elimination of superstition among the people is a long-range educational task and it cannot be done by simply demolishing the temples and idols, which only arouses antagonism of the people and plays into the hands of the landlords". Article 20 of the *Agrarian Reform Law*, which stipulates that "all graveyards and woods surrounding the graves must remain intact during the confiscation and requisition of land," serves as another illustration of how the CCP adroitly avoids clashing with such deep-rooted customs as ancestor worship.

On the whole, in dealing with firmly established mores and traditions, the Communists employ methods of persuasion through propaganda, indoctrination, training and education. When these persuasive approaches fail, however, it is not uncommon for coercive methods to follow. Some of the major techniques and skills used by the Party in its programme of mass persuasion in the land reform programme are discussed in the following section.

Technique of Mass Persuasion Utilized by the Chinese Communists in Land Reform Movement

The methods used by the CCP for "psychological mobilization," considered as "of equal importance to the redistribution of the land," may be described under two general categories: persuasion and pressure. Mao Tse-tung said in June 1950:

> The people's democratic dictatorship has two methods. To the enemy it uses the method of dictatorship; namely, it does not allow him to take part in political activities, compels him to obey the law of the people's government and to work and remould himself into a new person by labour. To the people it does not use compulsion but the democratic method. Namely, it allows them to take part in political activities, does not compel them to do this or that, but through democratic methods educates and persuades.[73]

The following illustrates the way the Party utilizes psychological and sociological techniques and skills:

1. PERSUASION

Traditional Chinese ethics and political philosophies emphasize persuasion. One of the requisites in the Confucian theory of the "mandate of heaven" (i.e., popular moral support for a regime) is the carrying out of *jen-cheng* (benevolent administration) by the government. The *Four Books* repeatedly enjoin "golden mean" and "benevolence." The Party is aware that these traditional values are influential among the Chinese population, and emphasizes that its policy toward all but the "leaders of the reactionaries," is the "reform" through education and training. Many non-Communist Chinese are sympathetic to such CCP programmes as the reform of village idlers, beggars and prostitutes, the abolition of the "child daughter-in-law" practice and equality for women, because they possess a strong moral flavour. The following are techniques most frequently used by the Communist cadres in persuading the peasants that it is both desirable and necessary to support the agrarian reform.

(*i*) *Presentation of rational justification.* In addition to the Marxist theory on agrarian revolution and on rent, landlordism is branded as the major source of all China's ills in popular literature and statements. Liu Shao-ch'i, in his speech *On the Agrarian Law* of June 14, 1950, remarked:

> The concentration of land in the hands of a few is the root of the poverty and backwardness of our nation and the cause of its having become the object of aggression and oppression. It is also the basic obstacle to the achievement of democracy,

[73] Mao Tse-tung, *Report to the National Committee of the CPPCE* (Chinese), June 23, 1950.

industrialization, independence, unification, and prosperity in the country. Unless we change this situation, the victory of the Chinese people's revolution cannot be consolidated, the productive force in the rural areas cannot be set free, the industrialization of New China cannot be realized and the people cannot enjoy the fundamental gains of the revolution.

In the villages, the concepts of Marxism are translated into colloquial language, and the peasants are told that the landlords are rich and powerful because the poor peasants work like beasts of burden to support them. A number of "basic questions" is presented by the cadres of the work team to the peasants, for example, "Who cultivates the land but who takes away two-thirds of the harvest?" "Why do the peasants toil endlessly but starve while the landlords live well without working?" and "How can the land be returned to those who are its rightful owners?"[74]

The peasants are also told that they have both the right and duty to shoulder political responsibilities and to increase production because "the labouring masses are now the masters of New China." The first paragraph in the *Letter to the Peasants of Honan* by the First Peasant Representatives' Congress of Honan Province (in 1950) illustrates this general approach. It begins with "Now the world is changed! Chairman Mao of the Communist Party has led the People's Liberation Army to liberate us and the people's government is set up. We labouring people are the masters now. . . ." [75] Together with these honours, the peasants are told, come certain duties such as the payment of tax in kind, the increase of production, and reform of the "peasant mentality," by which is meant the "conservatism" and "individualism" of the peasants. Thus "psychological mobilization" serves a triple purpose: (1) it appeals to peasants' enthusiasm by offering incentives and definite objectives; (2) it creates group consciousness through class differentiation and collective activities; (3) it aims at reducing internal contradictions by emphasizing "moral obligations" and by presenting long-range and immediate compensations.

(*ii*) *Rewards and compensations*. Notable among the long-term rewards and compensations offered by the Party are

[74] See Ch'in Feng, "The *Fan-shen* of the Peasants and the 'Homecoming' of the Land," *CW*, 5·2, January 21, 1950, p. 13; and Li Ch'ing, p. 12.

[75] *HY*, 2·1, May 1950, p. 83.

security, prosperity, peace, national honour and personal prestige.

Security is offered to the peasants in the form of better land utilization which in rural China is a source of prestige as well as a means to improve one's livelihood. The peasants' desire to own land is also recognized during the land redistribution movement. The *Common Programme* provided that "in the areas where agrarian reform has been carried out, ownership of the land acquired by the peasants must be protected" (Article 27). The Agrarian Reform Law stipulates that "after agrarian reform is completed, the people's government shall issue title deeds and shall recognize the right of all owners to manage, buy, sell, or rent out land freely" (Article 30). The "Directive on the Issue of Land and House Title Deeds" issued by the provincial people's government of Honan on April 8, 1950, emphasizes that "the issue of land title deeds . . . protects the land ownership of the peasants and stimulates the peasants to greater production. It must be regarded as a political task, not merely as a procedural matter."[76] The deep-rooted desire of the peasants to own land was utilized in Party propaganda to facilitate the land reform programme and to win support for other policies of the CCP at the initial stage of transition.

Peasants are told that the land reform will result in the economic betterment of the peasants. In government reports, newspapers, periodical articles, and slogans, cases after cases are presented showing how poor peasants have improved their standard of living as a result of land reform. For example, one report in 1950 claimed that in 28 villages in Shansi, Hopei and Chahar provinces, 1,439 out of 1,865 households of poor peasants (i.e., 80 per cent) improved their standard of living and became middle peasants.[77] A *NCNA* bulletin (May 11, 1950) stated that

> By 1949, the total area of cultivated land had expanded by more than 2 million hectares; the average output per hectare had increased from 750 kilograms in 1947 to 910 kilograms in 1948. With state trading companies and cooperatives buying surplus

[76] *HY*, 2·3, July 1950, p. 561.

[77] Editorial of *JJ*, quoted in *HY*, 2·4, August 1950, p. 801; also *NCNA* bulletins of May 11, and July 17, 1950, entitled, respectively, "The Living Standard in the Northeast Rises," and "Poverty Becomes Prosperity in the Village After Land Reform."

> grain directly from the peasants and supplying them with industrial goods, exploitation by the middlemen has been minimized. In 1949 the same quantity of grain was exchanged for four times the quantity of cloth offered in 1946.

Reports like this, which are circulated continuously in the areas of land reform, have an effective psychological impact on peasants who are traditionally harassed by debts and semi-starvation.

"Peace" and "stability" are among the rewards promised by the Party. They are doubly attractive in view of the past, which as far back as the peasant's memory goes has been filled with official corruption, fighting and military atrocities. The argument is also presented to the peasants that the only way to attain and keep peace is by the "thorough liquidation of the landlords as a class and the defeat of the KMT, which is backed by the foreign imperialists."

The Communist cadres, in their psychological warfare against the landlords, also make use of nationalism and personal prestige. Thus the peasants are informed that land reform will make China "a truly independent, strong, united, progressive and prosperous nation, free from the oppression and exploitation of feudal and imperialist elements." They are also told that China will be a first-rate power when she is industrialized and that industrialization is feasible only after agrarian reform. The Korean war was used to reinforce patriotic enthusiasm for greater agricultural production. Land reform also enables the peasants to "*fan-shen*" (turn-over) and makes them, together with the workers, the "masters of New China." As masters of the country, it will be an honour to pay taxes, to serve as soldiers and to elect, and be elected to, local people's governments.

In addition to these long-range attractions, certain immediate rewards and compensations are given the peasants either in the form of material gains or in honour and prestige. This is done most commonly through the election of "labour heroes."

The labour heroes in agriculture are peasants who have made outstanding contributions in various agricultural activities—in mutual-aid teams, farm production, irrigation projects, fertilization, use of new techniques and equipment, etc. Those who are elected labour heroes not only receive material rewards (draught animals or farm implements), but are showered with honours and recognition. At the Representatives Conference of Labour Heroes of Workers, Peasants and Soldiers, held in Peking between September

25 and October 1, 1950,[78] the delegates were greeted personally by top government leaders including Chairman Mao Tse-tung, entertained by various mass organizations, and cheered by the populace wherever they went. The labour hero movement in the villages is closely co-ordinated with the land reform programme. Indeed, one may get a general picture of the agrarian programme from the titles bestowed on rural labour heroes: mutual-aid, irrigation, promotion-of-new-cotton-seed, tractor-running labour heroes. The overall goal is generally greater production. The initiation of a labour hero movement with a new title could indicate the direction of a new government programme. The election of labour heroes at the village level often takes place at a mass meeting during which there is discussion of the various candidates. Those elected (who are generally members of mutual-aid teams or agricultural producers' cooperatives) at the meeting are presented with colourful banners and rewards in kind. Sometimes they are paraded through the village and their deeds are dramatized by *yangko* or plays.

Another example of the Party's coordination of reward with propaganda is the distribution of relief grain. When the village poor are called together to present their claims for the relief grain, the occasion is used to "heighten the class consciousness" of the attendants by pointing out that their poverty and suffering are due to the feudal and imperialist elements and by reminding them that only the adoption of conservation methods, better seeds and modern farming can produce larger crops and prevent further catastrophes.

(*iii*) *The utilization of traditional values.* While many traditional beliefs and values in rural China such as the peasants' strong belief in fate, and worship of witch doctors are discouraged and uprooted, some of the deeper customs, such as ancestral and temple worship,[79] are diplomatically and temporarily left untouched. A number of traditional cultural values prevailing in the rural society of China are

[78] Among the 414 labour heroes attending the Conference, 178 were elected from rural areas.

[79] One news item in the *HC* of March 5, 1951, reports: "The people's government of Kwangtung province sent directives to cadres engaged in land reform in which it was pointed out that the abolition of superstitious practices among the people could not be achieved overnight. . . . The indiscriminate destruction of idols and abolition of temples will only cause the antipathy of the people . . . and should be corrected."

skilfully exploited. There is, for example, the use of the "family council" in the land reform. Realizing the peasants' strong family sentiment and reverent attitude toward the patriarchal head, the Party encourages the villagers to hold "family councils," usually with the male head as chairman, to plan farming and division of labour.[80] Following is the usual procedure of a "family council." A detailed plan is first drawn up, after discussion among the members of the family, which assigns a work-schedule to each member of the family. The plan is then posted in the household, and rewards or criticisms are given to the individuals in accordance with their work. At subsequent meetings, adjustments are made according to the actual progress of the work. The principle advocated by the cadres is that while the opinions and judgments of the old should be respected, the young people, especially the women, should be free to speak up critically, in the interest of attaining efficiency and greater production. From this it can be seen that the "family council" is useful in many ways: to increase production through collective planning and activities, to secure more rights for women and youth, and to provide incentives for greater efficiency through competition and rewards.

(*iv*) *Catharsis.* The "speak bitterness" meetings, an integral part of the land reform procedure in China, afford an opportunity for emotional release among the peasants, largely through the accusation and punishment of the "landlord-despots." *Yangko* is another medium for providing emotional release. Such other devices as the criticism and self-criticism meetings, plays, etc. serve similar functions in varying degrees.

2. PRESSURE

The CCP came to power through armed insurrection, and the force of the state is in evidence. Expounding the Leninist concept of the state, Mao Tse-tung announced to the whole nation that:

> The army, police, and courts of any state are instruments for classes to oppress classes. To hostile classes, the State apparatus

[80] For more information regarding the "family council," see *Household Planning, the Family Council, and the Reform of the Village Idlers* (Chinese), Shansi-Chahar-Hopei Border Region Government, 1948, 44 pp.; also "The Democratic Family of Kuo Fu-kuei," *HY,* 1·4, February 1950, pp. 954–5.

> is an instrument of oppression. It is a weapon of violence and not of benevolence....We certainly are not benevolent toward reactionaries and the reactionary classes.[81]

In the land reform, the landlord class is made the target of attacks. The cadres are told that "a peaceful surrender of the landlord class is not possible without struggle."[82] Since the summer of 1950 and especially after February 1951, numerous editorials, speeches and directives demanded the "punishment of unlawful landlords and other counter-revolutionary elements."[83] On February 20, 1951, *Regulations for Punishment of Counter-Revolutionary Elements* were announced which extended the penalties of death and life imprisonment to a long list of counter-revolutionary offences. Mme. Shih Liang, Minister of Justice, subsequently made a speech instructing law enforcement agencies to "combine labour with re-education for prisoners." The punishment imposed on those found "guilty of sabotage and espionage" in the land reform serves as a warning to other villagers, especially the landlords. The people's tribunals and the village militia, as pointed out in previous sections, are the principal instruments of punishing the criminal elements as well as the strong symbols of the power of the State.

In addition to physical punishment, there is also social pressure, intensified by propaganda and indoctrination. An article written by the well-known Professor Feng Yu-lan states:

> Following land reform, the social values in the rural areas also have changed. At Chang-i village near Peking I heard a woman abusing her husband with these words: "You are a landlord! a rich peasant! a local despot!" "Landlord" used to be a laudatory term, but it has now become a derogatory one.[84]

Other reports show that some peasants confessed in tears at self-criticism meetings to having "hidden land" as well as to other illegal deeds. Many former landlords joined group-farming together

[81] Mao Tse-tung, *On the People's Democratic Dictatorship*, July 1, 1949.
[82] Henry Lieberman, *NYT*, February 7, 1951, p. 4.
[83] See editorials, *JMJP*, October 21, 1950; *CF*, October 13, 1950; and *Directives on the Suppression of Counter-Revolutionary Activities*, GAC, July 23, 1950.
[84] Feng Yu-lan, "My Gains from Participation in the Land Reform," *HH*, 2·2, April 1, 1950, p. 24.

with poor peasants.[85] There were even cases of children reporting to the cadres against the "criminal acts of their parents during the land reform."[86] Such group pressures vary in direct proportion to the intensity of the Party's organizational and propaganda work in a rural district.

[85] Mu Ch'ing, *HY*, 2·4, August 1950, p. 806.

[86] Li Hsin, "Comrade, Our Public Grain Is Watered," *CW*, 5·3, January 28, 1950, pp. 10–11.

CHAPTER IV

CURRENT AGRARIAN POLICY, 1953–1959

A. *Overall Principles*

THREE BASIC features stand out regarding the current agrarian policy in China—formulated and directed by the CCP. First is its utilization as a major medium to accumulate capital for China's economic growth in general and industrialization in particular. The annual rate of accumulation in the first five-year plan period (1953–57) was reported at 21·6 per cent, and the national income increased in that period at an average rate of a little less than 10 per cent annually. The value of national income of China for 1957 has been estimated as about 95 billion *yuan*. Peking data put the estimated national income for 1958 and 1959 at, respectively, 127·3 and 154·8 billion *yuan*, or 54·05 and 65·73 billion US dollars. The percentage increase for these two years was 34 and 21·6 per cent, respectively.[1] One Western scholar estimated in the October 1956 issue of *Foreign Affairs* that "India today is taxing only about one per cent of her agricultural output for economic development, whereas China is appropriating over 25 per cent of her agricultural output for that purpose."[2] Whether or not these respective percentages estimates are exact, there is no doubt that in China the rate of saving in the agricultural sector for reinvestment is high. The increase in the value of agricultural products in 1958 over the preceding year has been estimated at 25 per cent, at a total of 67·1 billion *yuan*. Second is that the agrarian programmes in China today as exemplified by the people's communes are multi-purposeful and multi-functional —serving, concomitantly, a host of roles and functions in the

[1] Li Fu-chun, "Big Leap in Our Nation's Socialist Construction," *HPYK*, No. 19, October 12, 1959, p. 30; *The Statesman*, Delhi, January 24, 1960, p. 8, and *NYT*, January 24, 1960. Joan Robinson and Solomon Adler, *China: An Economic Perspective*, Fabian Society, 1958, p. 5; and Yang Po, "Some Interpretations on the Ratio Between Consumption and Accumulation in the National Income," *HH*, No. 20, October 18, 1957, p. 24.

[2] Mathew J. Kust, "Economic Developments and Agricultural Surplus," *Foreign Affairs*, 25·1, October 1956, pp. 105–15.

political-organizational, economic-technical, and social-cultural fields. The agro-technical improvements and the rural financial programmes are certainly important. But equally significant are the social reforms, such as the mass education programme and the breaking down of the peasant's traditional fatalistic attitude, and the political changes, such as the organized participation of the villagers in public activities, and the removal of the domination of the landed gentry. These efforts combined have brought to the peasant an awareness that his lot can be improved and a resolution to strive resolutely for such betterment. As a United Nations report points out: "Economic progress will not be desired in a community where the people do not realize that progress is possible. Progress occurs only where people believe that man can, by conscious effort, master nature."[3] Third is the emphasis assigned to the socialization of rural China, including the collectivization and communization movement, and the effort to mould the traditional Chinese villages into a highly organized unit following the ideological pattern of Marxism-Leninism. An important instrument in the intensive organization and propaganda work is the mass organizations—the Youth League, the women's federation, and the children's corps. They form an effective and unique network for social engineering, communication, and indoctrination. The meaning and impact of the current agrarian programmes in China cannot be adequately understood or evaluated solely from economic approaches. For instance, when the economic and ideological considerations do not coincide in a particular agrarian measure in a locality, the political factor was often made predominant.

The above three basic features are discernible in the fundamental laws governing the agrarian (and other) policies of the nation. As early as September 1949, the Common Programme stated that "The agrarian reform is the necessary condition for the development of the productive power and the industrialization of the country." (Article 27) The National Constitution stipulated (in September 1954) that "Partial collective ownership by the working masses is a transitional form by means of which individual peasants, individual handicraftsmen and other individual working people organize themselves in their advance toward collective ownership by the working masses.... The promotion of producers' cooperatives is the chief

[3] U.N. Department of Economic Affairs, *Measures for the Economic Development of Under-Developed Countries*, May 1951, p. 13.

means for the transformation of individual farming and individual handicrafts." (Article 7) In the *Revised Programme for the Development of Agriculture*, 1956-67 (October 25, 1957), it was pointed out that "agricultural cooperativization opens up a most broad path for developing the productive forces in our nation's agriculture.... The peasants should be educated to unify the concepts of loving the country, the cooperative, and the family." (Preamble) Similar passages may be found in the drafts of the first and second five-year plans.

It is significant to note that more emphasis has been put on the agricultural sector by the Peking government since 1956. The second five-year plan (1958–1962) assigns greater weight to agriculture and its related fields than did the first five-year plan. After a month-long conference on national planning in July and August 1957, Chia To-fu, Vice-Chairman of the State Economic Commission announced that there would be a 33·1 per cent (later revised to 40 per cent) more investment in agriculture in 1958 over 1957. In monetary terms, the total State investment in agriculture in 1958 was scheduled at 3 billion *yuan* or 870 million US dollars. The scheduled national budget for 1958 was about 33 billion *yuan*, but the actual figures came to approximately 41·8 billion *yuan*. Investment in industries directly related to agricultural production was also expanded.[4]

Some writers describe collectivization as the primary or ultimate goal of the CCP's agrarian policy. It seems, however, more accurate to say that collective farming and the communes are envisaged as a means of attaining such goals as the socialization of the rural community, more efficient utilization of rural resources (including manpower), and the development of agricultural production. Even in organized farming, an area the CCP has always held with firm conviction, the flexibility of the Party's policy is evident. Thus Premier Chou En-lai recommended in his speech on the second five-year plan on September 16, 1956: "Cooperative members should be encouraged to engage individually in agricultural subsidiary occupations which do not necessarily require unified operation by the APCs." The ceiling for the amount of acreage an APC could set aside as private lots under individual management was increased from 5 per cent of the average amount of cultivated land for each

[4] *NYT*, August 23, 1957, p. 2; Li Hsien-nien, "Final Accounts for 1958 and National Budget for 1959," April 21, 1959, *HPYK*, No. 9, May 10, 1959, p. 20.

person in a particular locality to 10 per cent in 1957. However, by the end of 1958, practically all the 120 million peasant households had joined the people's communes and the means of production in agriculture (land, farm implements, draught animals, etc.) had come under joint ownership. These facts make it desirable for a student of the Chinese agrarian problems refrain from sticking to doctrinaire approaches in judging the trend or tempo of the CCP's agrarian policy.

B. *Organized Farming*

The term organized farming as used here includes mutual-aid teams, agricultural producers' cooperatives (APCs), collective farms (called "higher-stage APCs" in mainland China), and the peoples communes. The major features of these various types of organized farming are summarized in Table I. The quantitative development of Peking's organized farming programme in the past 10 years is indicated in Table II. (A discussion on the latest development in China's agriculture, the people's communes, can be found at the end of this section.)

The mutual-aid teams and APCs, although designed only as transitional forms leading eventually to collectivization, played a vital role. As the CC, CCP's *Decisions on Mutual-Aid and Cooperativization in Agricultural Production* of February 15, 1953 point out:

> Cooperativization and mutual-aid at present means collective labour practised on the basis of an individual economy (private ownership of property by peasants); its future is collective and socialist farming.

Both organizationally and psychologically, it was easier for the peasants to make the shift from cooperative to collective farming, than from individual to cooperative farming. Thus, one of the advantages attributed to cooperative farming by Teng Tzu-hui in his Report to the rural work conference of the CC, NDYL, on July 15, 1954 was that "cooperatives can easily be accepted by the peasant, and can also gradually reform the system of peasant private ownership." Up to June 1958, virtually all of the 120 million or so peasant households in China had become members of about 750,000 higher-stage APCs or collective farms. The various aspects regarding mutual-aid teams and the lower-stage APCs have been touched upon in preceding sections, as well as in a number of recent publications in English.[5] This section therefore will center on discussing the contents, significance, and problems of the collectivization movement.

Collectivization of farms has always been the professed goal of the CCP, and it is a part of the "general line of the state" made public by Mao Tse-tung in 1953. The tempo of the collectivizing programme after June, 1955, was greatly stepped up. Among the possible reasons for such an accelerated pace and its timing are the following: First, the industrial sector of China's economy had been growing very rapidly, and it was thought that an accelerated collectivizing programme would facilitate a greater coordination of agriculture and industry by the State. Second, a good harvest was already in evidence by July 1955, and Peking might have thought the acceleration of collectivization could be more effectively accomplished in a bumper-crop year. Third, a new polarization of rural classes had been coming about in some localities when Mao Tse-tung delivered the now famous report on July 31, 1955, "On the Cooperativization of Agriculture."

The CCP obviously deemed it politically necessary and economically beneficial to organize the peasants into larger farming units within a short time. Hence, it assigned priority to the resolving of problems of the poor peasants who were numerically the majority, politically the least resistant to organized farming, and productively the most handicapped. This policy is explained in the Resolution of Agricultural Cooperativization[6] adopted by the CC, CCP on October 11, 1955:

> The better-off middle peasants (that is, the upper sections of both the old and new middle peasants) have better farm tools

[5] For a discussion of the mutual-aid teams and the agricultural producers cooperatives in China prior to 1956, see S. B. Thomas, "Communist China's Agrarian Policy, 1954–1956," *Pacific Affairs*, June 1956, pp. 141–56. Solomon Adler, *The Chinese Economy*, 1957, pp. 105–11; and Chao Kuo-chun, *Agrarian Policies of Mainland China: A Documentary Study (1949–1956)*, Harvard University Press, 1957, pp. 54–120.

[6] The "general line of the state" appears officially in the revised Constitution of the CCP adopted on September 26, 1956. It is described as "the gradual realization, over a considerably long period of time, of the socialist industrialization of the state, and the gradual realization of the socialist transformation by the state of agriculture, handicrafts, and private industry and commerce." *Ta-kung pao*, Hongkong, September 29, 1956.

> and draught animals, their land is managed more carefully, the output of their land is higher, or they derive a bigger income from subsidiary occupations. First we should organize the poor peasants and the lower section of the middle peasants....

Thus if the poor peasants, the weak link in the production line in the Chinese agriculture, can be made more productive through the pooling of land, capital and manpower, the entire rural economy would become more dynamic.

Fourth, larger farming units (i.e., higher-stage APCs and now the communes as compared to 120 million individual peasant households) are considered more desirable for a number of economic and political reasons. They include a more rational use of farm plots, greater amount of capital, more effective promotion of large irrigation projects, and facilitation of carrying out of government programmes. Teng Tzu-hui, member of the CC, CCP and specialist on the agricultural problem, made the last point quite clear in a recent statement:

> Individual peasants cannot be directly controlled by the State plan. They formulate their production plans according to their own requirements and particularities; they cannot formulate plans according to the requirements of the State.[7]

Fifth, the specific conditions in the agriculture of China during 1954 and early 1955 explain in part why Mao Tse-tung decided to accelerate the collectivization movement in the summer of 1955. The goal for grain production increase for the years 1953 and 1954 was not reached, and there were shortages of certain industrial crops like cotton, soybean, and oil-bearing crops in 1954. The collectivization programme aimed to facilitate the overall economic planning and the increase of agricultural production.

An APC of the higher-stage (i.e., collective farm) is defined in the *Model Regulations for Advanced APCs* promulgated on June 30, 1956 as "a socialist, collective economic organization formed by working peasants on a voluntary and mutually beneficial basis, with the guidance and help of the Communist Party and the People's Government." (Article 1) The APC "shall convert the chief means of production owned privately by its members into the collective

[7] *HY*, November 1955, pp. 9–13.

property of the cooperative." The members are organized for "collective work, and the cooperative applies the principle of 'from each according to his ability, to each according to his work,' giving equal pay for equal work, irrespective of sex or age." (Article 2.)

The above provisions are important because they not only laid down the guiding premises for the APCs but also helped to stimulate greater production effort of the members. The women and youths in the villages were given greater incentives to participate in farming work, now they were entitled to equal remuneration for the same kind of work. The legal stipulation guaranteeing voluntary joining or withdrawal, together with the three-stage approach (mutual-aid, cooperative and collective farming) in reorganizing the traditional form of Chinese agriculture, played a major role in mitigating the disrupting effects, both physical and psychological, during the transformation. It is true that various forms of encouragement existed for the Chinese peasants to join and remain in the APCs, but the announcement of the voluntary principle helped to reduce tension among the rural populace during collectivization.

The major operational rules as contained in the major directives on the APCs may be described as follows:[8] (Many of these practices are continued in the people's communes.)

First, peasants who join the APCs must turn their land, draught animals and large farm implements over to the cooperative as contributing shares, and their values, after group discussion and evaluation, were compensated in term of cooperative shares or shares plus cash instalments (in three years or more), to the owners. In case the indigent members were still unable to pay up the share funds after getting loans from the bank out of the poor peasants' cooperative fund, the members could decide in general meeting or congress whether payment should be deferred or reduced. No interest was charged on share funds paid by instalment or deferred. Household goods, odd trees, poultry, small domestic animals, simple farm tools, and means of production for family subsidiary jobs might remain as private property. In 1957 and early 1958

[8] See NPC, *Model Regulations for Higher-Stage APCs*, June 30, 1956; CC, CCP, "Directive on the Production Management Work of the APCs," *HPYK*, No. 19, October 10, 1957, pp. 136–7; CC, CCP, "Directive on the Mutual Benefit Policy in the APCs," *HPYK*, *op.cit.*, pp. 137–8; Teng Tzu-hui, "On the Problems of Hog Raising and the Expansion of Production in APCs," *Chung-kuo ch'ing-nien*, (Youth of China), No. 22, November 16, 1957, pp. 2–4.

peasant households were encouraged to raise domestic animals, especially hogs partly on an individual basis. Original owner or owners of fish ponds, orchards, and mulberry groves for which large investment was made, may be entitled to special bonuses.

Second, the APCs were allowed to set aside a portion of the farmland as private lots to grow vegetables, etc. The amount of such plots allocated to each household depended on the number of persons in a household and the quality of the land. The maximum amount of these private holdings came to 10 per cent (5 per cent before 1957) of the average amount of cultivated land for each household in the locality concerned in early 1958.

Third, the cooperative must set aside a certain amount of its annual income as reserve and welfare funds. The reserve fund was to be used for expanding production, for storing seed and fodder, and for increasing the fixed assets of the cooperative. It must not be diverted to other uses. The welfare fund was for improving the cooperative's cultural and welfare services. It too must not be used for other purposes. A member who withdrew from the cooperative could not make any claim on the reserve fund or welfare fund.

Fourth, the APC was required to organize members into field production brigades and subsidiary occupation brigades or groups in accordance with the scope of its production, division of labour and of occupations arising from the needs of production, and the conditions of its members. It might appoint people to take charge of book-keeping, technical management, livestock, common property and other special jobs in order to implement the system of individual responsibility for production tasks. The suitable number of peasant households in each production brigade or group was described as around 20 in 1957.

Fifth, the production brigade was the basic unit of labour organization in the cooperative and its members were organized on a permanent basis. The field production brigade assumed responsibility for cultivating a definite area allotted to it and was given draught animals and farm tools for its regular use. The subsidiary occupation brigade or group was responsible for specific subsidiary occupations and was allotted, for its regular use, the tools employed in such occupations. In organizing members into production brigades and assigning work, the APC took into consideration the size of the land allotted to the brigade for cultivation, the quality of this land, the crops suited to it, and the distance between it and members' homes.

The cooperative's leadership had the responsibility to see that the labour power, the skill of the members and the ability of the leaders of the brigade measure up to the jobs given to it. Similar considerations were given while organizing members into subsidiary occupation brigade or group, or assigning them work.

Sixth, the brigades for production and subsidiary occupations might again be sub-divided into teams or groups. During 1957–58, the "three-responsibility" system was advocated. Specific quotas were assigned, after group discussions, to the production or side job brigades in the following three areas: labour, production and finance (cost). The brigades in turn were to agree on specific targets in the above three fields with the teams or groups or even households under them. The types of work which could more suitably be done by the cooperative as a whole and other works of special requirements were arranged differently. One directive pointed out that there should be in each production task two sets of targets—one lower than the normal production figure, which also served as the norm in the "production responsibility" system; another higher than the normal production figure, which served as the planned goal. Special bonuses were given when the planned goal was reached or overfulfilled by a production group or brigade. In evaluating the work performed, both quantity and quality were taken into consideration.

Seventh, every cooperative was called on to draw up work plans. At the same time as it worked out annual and seasonal production (also labour) plans and mapped out particular stages of field work for the various production brigades, it calculated how many work-days would be needed to fulfil its production targets.

Plans on fiscal and financial matters were prepared in a similar way. The cooperative estimated, according to the needs of production and the judgment of the members themselves, the number of work-days a member would be required to put in in a year, a season, or during a particular stage of field work. In assigning work-days to members, the cooperative took into consideration their different physical conditions and made due allowance for women members and their actual need for doing household work. When a member finished the number of work-days he or she was required to do, the time left would be at his or her own disposal.

Eighth, the policy of frugality and self-sufficiency was repeatedly emphasized. In November 1957, a directive called for the reduction of administrative personnel who were not engaged in production work—from 1·5 to 2 per cent in the Model Regulations of APCs to a maximum of one per cent. APCs were encouraged to attain "four sufficiencies"—in capital, seeds, fertilizers, and raw materials. Former handicraftsmen and peddlers now joining the APC could enroll in handicrafts cooperatives or marketing cooperatives so that their special skills might be fully utilized.

Ninth, the APCs were constantly reminded of the top importance of production increase and basic construction work in the fields of crop yields, livestock raising, subsidiary occupation, and transportation development. The following were specifically listed as chief measures to increase agricultural production in the APCs:

(1) build irrigation works; conserve water and soil;
(2) use improved farm tools and gradually bring about the mechanization of agriculture;
(3) increase the supply of manure and other fertilizers by all possible means and make better use of them;
(4) use improved strains of crops;
(5) suitably and systematically enlarge the area under high-yield crops;
(6) improve the soil; level and terrace arable land;
(7) make rational use of all arable land and increase multiple cropping acreage;
(8) improve farming methods: practise deep ploughing and intensive cultivation;
(9) eliminate and prevent insect pests, plant diseases and other natural calamities;
(10) protect and breed more and better livestock; and
(11) reclaim wasteland and enlarge the area under cultivation according to plan if the work of water and soil conservation is not affected.

Every cooperative is exhorted to exert energetic efforts to learn the most efficient farming methods and do its utmost to find the best ways of increasing output and putting them into practice.

It is too early to make a conclusive evaluation of the complex effects of collectivization on agriculture as well as on the peasants in China during this period, but the issue is too vital to be bypassed. One Chinese report states that "according to investigations in many areas, about 80 per cent of the APCs in 1956 reported increased output over 1955, and 75 per cent of the cooperative members received greater income than the previous year."[9] Development of the APCs also resulted in greater utilization of rural labour power. The average number of work-days of a Chinese full-time agricultural worker was estimated as 172 days a year in Dr. Buck's surveys conducted in the 1920's. The average number of work-days for an able-bodied male in the APCs in Shansi province in 1956 was around 250 days (and woman labourer, 120 days).[10] Although we do not know whether the definitions of these terms employed in the above statistics are identical or whether the national average work-days for the APCs in 1956 was lower than 250, available evidence indicates that labour utilization in the APCs was much more intensive. This in turn facilitates the expansion of subsidiary occupations to supplement income from cultivation and the undertaking of large-scale projects such as conservation work. As a result, there developed a shortage of labour in many rural districts in the winter of 1957–58. A survey of 26,935 APCs in 1955 yielded similar results. As these reports do not indicate whether the APCs surveyed are representative of the regional differences in grain production levels, or to what extent government aid to the APCs contributed to their better showing, further details are needed. From the economic and technical viewpoints, there are reasons to support the premise that organized farming, if carried out with the cooperation of the peasants, will help to resolve a number of problems in Chinese agriculture including the minute parcellization of cultivated land, inefficient use of farm implements, draught animals, and manpower, inadequacy in funds or labour to undertake long-range projects such as large-scale irrigation, underemployments and the shortage of farm hands during busy seasons. As an American agronomist pointed out :

> Without any change in technology whatsoever, production and wealth per capita could be increased from 60 to 240 per cent if,

[9] Ho Wei, "Consolidate Further the Socialist Front in Rural Areas," *Cheng-chih hsueh-hsi* (Political Study), No. 8, August 13, 1957.

[10] See Ishikawa Shigeru, "Effects on Productivity of Collectivization in China," *Keizai Kenkyū* (Economic Research), Tokyo, 8·4, October 1957, pp. 371–6; also Mu Yu, "The Superiority of the Higher-Stage APC," *HH*, No. 3, February 3, 1957, p. 20.

by some magic, the average size of all Chinese farms could be raised to 13 acres.[11]

However, a number of operational or technical matters must also be considered in evaluating the impact of collectivization on agricultural production in China. These practical issues which can often be both challenging and urgent for the specific APCs involved, may include the following: What should be the most desirable size for APCs in a certain rural area ? How should the remuneration for each APC member be calculated accurately according to the quantity and quality of his work ? What is the proper method of compensation for land and other properties brought into the APC by the members? What are the suitable proportions of income to be distributed and to be reserved as sinking funds? How to train a sufficient number of managerial, accounting and technical personnel to meet the expanding needs of the APC? How is the best division of labour to be realized, and the productive power of APC members maximized but not over-taxed? What agro-technical improvements are to be carried out, and when? How to develop within the resource limitation of a particular APC, additional sources of income to meet the growing need of operating funds? Many of these considerations also have their application concerning people's communes.

Several measures contained in three directives on the APCs issued in September 1957 by the CC, CCP aimed to tackle a number of the above questions. One directive dated September 15, 1957, called on the APCs to establish coordinated management and control, clear division of labour, and the drawing up of concrete quota assignments for production as well as fiscal workers. Another directive said that village handicraftsmen and peddlers now joined the APCs should be allowed to form supply and marketing teams or handicraft production groups in order to utilize their skills. The directive of September 14, 1957, also shows an awareness of possible drawbacks of over-sized APCs.

Regarding another major source of complications in the APCs—the insufficiency of trained personnel for managerial or technical work, a very significant move was made by Peking in 1957, which directed school graduates who could not enter an institution of a

[11] Gerald Winfield, *China, the Land and the People*, 1948, p. 279. Dr. Winfield's estimates are based on Dr. Buck's data on the efficiency and production of large-size farms versus small-size farms in China surveyed during the 1930's.

higher level to work in the rural areas. In December 1957, it was reported that 3,080,000 students in 21 (out of 28 at that time) provinces and municipalities had joined agricultural production.[12] As more and more "educated peasants" come into existence, the far-reaching impact of such a movement on the agro-technical as well as social transformation of the Chinese villages cannot be overestimated. Still another problem involves the quality of many of the functionaries in the APCs. Some were too rigid or impatient in their effort to popularize collective farming. A few even became corrupt by their new powers over hundreds of rural households. Aiming to cope with this situation, a directive of CC, CCP of September 14, 1957 emphasized that all members of the APCs should have the right to freely criticize the shortcomings and errors of the cadres at general sessions of members or meetings of production teams. The increasing influx of students into the rural districts since mid-1957 is also helpful to the leadership in the APCs.

The impact of collectivization goes, of course, beyond the economic and technical fields. The APC movement is also affecting the social structure in the Chinese villages. For example, peasant women have become economically more independent than before because the APCs initiate more varieties of work in which they can engage and often provide nurseries for their children. These social effects, although they cannot be discussed in detail here, have undoubtedly had a tremendous impact on Chinese rural society.

The managerial and operational problems faced by many APCs in China have been discussed previously. A number of overall problems in connection with the collectivization and communization movement in China will be brought up in the chapter on evaluation of the CCP agrarian policy in general. In addition, several other organizational problems are revealed in Chinese sources. For example, Teng Tzu-hui, in his speech on the "Current Situation in Agricultural Cooperativization" of May 7, 1956, listed three shortcomings:

(1) Waste and faulty planning;
(2) Negligence of industrial crops and subsidiary occupations; and
(3) Defective organization due to "rapid advance of the movement."

[12] *HCJP*, September 17, 1957, p. 3.

This question of how to achieve collectivization quickly, but not at the expense of the quality of the collective farms, is a most challenging one. There are also issues which cannot be resolved entirely by the APCs themselves. These include the need for more capital investment (such as chemical fertilizer and insecticides), better marketing facilities, appropriate prices for some agricultural products, and a suitable amount of agricultural produce purchased by the State.

Complex as the problems of APCs (now the communes) in China are, there is no *a priori* reason to believe that collectivization must lead to the disruption of the Chinese agriculture. It is true, as pointed out in the "Decisions on Mutual Aid and Co-operativization in Agricultural Production" by the CC, CCP on February 15, 1953, that "the peasants' enthusiasm for production in the field of individual economy was inevitable after the agrarian reform (i.e., land redistribution)." However, there are several factor counterbalancing this. First is the great desire of the Chinese peasant to improve his material and social welfare. When the APCs, through more rational utilization of manpower, means of production, and agro-technical know-how, achieved improvement in the economic as well as communal life of the peasants, more villagers would naturally support collective farming. Second is the step-by-step way through which collectivization was promoted in mainland China. The mutual-aid teams and co-operatives paved the way, organizationally and psychologically, for collective farms in China—in contrast to the collectivization process in the Soviet Union. Furthermore, the rich peasant group was never very strong in China and a tradition of many rudimentary forms of mutual aid among the Chinese villagers helped the promotion of cooperative farming. Third, a great number of peasants, probably the majority, never enjoyed secured ownership of their land, either because they were tenants or because their land was mortgaged to the debtors. Now they could retain the ownership of their land even as members of the APC, and legally they are free to withdraw from the collective farms if they so wish. True, there existed various kinds of pressure on the Chinese peasants to join and remain in the APCs, but psychologically it made a considerable difference when they were given the right to disengage themselves from organized farming—a right more than 24,000 farm households exercised in Kwangtung province in the year 1956.

Co-operative and collective farming exists today in a number of non-Communist lands like India, Israel, Jamaica, British Guiana and Iraq.[13] Many non-Communist leaders have come out in support of organized farming in specific areas. Prime Minister Jawarharlal Nehru wrote in 1951 that "The co-operative principle should be applied to the exploitation of land by developing collective and co-operative farms (in India)."[14] The Nagpur Convention of the Indian Congress Party in January 1959 came out in favour of co-operative farming. A report published by the Food and Agricultural Organization of the U.N. in 1950 pointed out that co-operative farms could contribute greatly to the improvement of the land tenure system and the better use of the land in the Caribbean countries.[15] Collective farming, like atomic energy or gunpowder, may be used with varying results. Its application depends a lot on the manner it is introduced, how it is managed, and the overall political-economic-social institutional reforms that accompany it.

C. *The People's Communes*

Background

The people's commune movement which was to sweep the Chinese countryside and basically transform the rural community in 6 months had its embryonic origin in April 1958. At that time, 27 small APCs in Suip'ing county, Honan province began amalgamating their 9,369 households and formed the Weihsing or Sputnik Joint Co-operative.[16] But they had not mapped out any deliberate goals for future expansion. After the first few federated APCs proved successful, a number of others followed. The real impetus came when Mao Tse-tung, during his inspection trip in Shantung province in August that year (after the Peitaiho Conference ?), advised a township where the farmers wanted to group several cooperatives into a State farm that it would be better if they organized themselves in the form of a commune. His suggestion was followed, and after

[13] United Nations, *Land Reform*, 1951, p. 82.

[14] Jawaharlal Nehru, *Discovery of India*, 1951, p. 376.

[15] FAO, *Co-operatives in the Caribbean*, Washington, 1950, p. 15.

[16] See Wu Chih-pu, First Secretary of Honan Provincial Committee, CCP, "From APCs to People's Communes," *Hung-chi* (Red Flag), No. 8, September 16, 1958.

that the movement spread like wild fire.[17] At the end of 1958, 99 per cent of some 120 million peasant households were communized. Instead of 740,000 APCs with an average of about 160 households, there were in September 1959 about 24,000 people's communes, averaging over 5,000 households in each. The only area where the communes have not started (as of 1959) is Tibet, which is an Autonomous Region of China.

The Party's decision to promote the organization of communes may be prompted by a combination of ideological, political, economic, and social considerations. As stated in the "Resolution on Some Questions Concerning the People's Communes," adopted by the CC, CCP (Sixth Plenary Session) on December 10, 1958:

> Marxist-Leninist theory and the initial experience of the People's communes in our country enable us to foresee now that the people's communes will quicken the tempo of socialist construction and constitute the best form for realizing the following two transitions in our country: firstly, the transition from collective ownership to ownership by the whole people in the countryside; and secondly, the transition from socialist to Communist society.[18]

Marx and Engels wrote in the Communist Manifesto in 1848: "The theory of the Communists can be summed up in the single sentence: Abolition of [bourgeois] private property."[19] The commune movement is envisaged to facilitate a more thorough transformation of property relations in rural China, and with it, the super-structural mentality of conservative, self-centred individualism among the peasantry. Although the communes are regarded as a long-range policy of the CCP, the complete socialization of rural communities is envisaged as a gradual process. Thus the same Resolution points out:

> In the future Communist society, the people's communes will remain the basic unit of social structure, but the completion

[17] Liu Yi-hsing, "People's Communes, A New Stage," *China Reconstructs*, December 1958, p. 9.

[18] This very significant document appears in a number of English publications, including *China Today*, No. 13, December 27, 1958, New Delhi.

[19] Marx-Engels, *Selected Works*, vol. I, p. 47.

of this whole process will take a long time—from 15, 20 or more years counting from now (1958).

Politically and administratively, the communes reinforce the overall planning and direction by the government. They also help (together with decentralization of industries and commerce since 1957) to form semi-autonomous centres of administrative-economic-social activities. This is conducive to local developments, and the bureaucratic structure is streamlined–for example, the *hsiang* (village) administration is combined with the commune and comes directly under the *hsien* (county) guidance. Strategic-wise, in an age of thermonuclear weapons when national headquarters of politico-economic direction may be wiped out or neutralized in a matter of few days if not hours, a dispersed system of national organization is extremely meaningful. Furthermore, through the integration of townships with the villages under the commune, the gap between urban and rural populations, and its resultant contradictions, are reduced.

Economically, the people's communes, by pooling greater resources including manpower together in a more effective manner, are envisaged as instrumental in the promotion of large-scale and divergent economic-social programmes in the countryside such as big irrigation projects, more intensive farming, development of subsidiary as well as industrial undertakings, and the propagation of technical-cultural activities. These multiple endeavours had already been initiated by many APCs since 1956, but they found their labour force, capital, time, and other resources inadequate to cope with such comprehensive programmes. It was pointed out in a Resolution of the CC, CCP on August 29, 1958 that "the establishment of people's communes with all-round management of agriculture, forestry, animal husbandry, side-occupations and fishery, where industry (the worker), agriculture (the peasant), exchange (the trader), culture and education (the student) and the military affairs (the militia-man) merge into one, is the fundamental policy to guide the peasants to accelerate socialistic construction, complete the building of socialism ahead of time, and carry out the gradual transition to communism." A survey in the summer of 1958 showed that the number of factories, workshops, and mines set up by the people's communes totalled 700,000 and the value of their output accounted for some 10 per cent of the national total . . . .

Forty per cent of the communes had set up special transport teams.[20]

Socially and culturally, the communes are expected to effect basic changes in the social structure, personal relationships, and value systems in the villages. For example, through the establishment of common dining halls and creches, peasant women are freed from many daily chores so that they now have much more time (and energy) for production work or education. By the propagation of literacy and technical training, the peasants acquire modern farming methods and greater social mobility. Thus the marginal productivity both in the economic and social sense is enhanced.

The origin of the people's communes may have been spontaneously developed by the peasants, but the subsequent policy of Peking to give the movement firm support must be based on many of the above considerations. The decision of the Party to accelerate the organization of communes in the summer of 1958 may also be timed with the situation that a bumper harvest of major crops was assured, which would facilitate, materially and psychologically, the changeover from APCs to the communes. As mentioned previously, the decision of the Party to step up the tempo of collectivization in the summer of 1957 was also done at a time when the prospects of a good harvest were more or less certain.

The Organizational Aspects of the People's Communes

The governing principle for the communes, like for other organizations in China, is "democratic centralism"—that is, the decisions on major actions are taken after popular discussions and consultations with the masses, but the resolutions once made must be observed by all and the superior organ retains the power of veto over the subordinate organs.

Operationally, with regional variations, the organization of the communes is generally divided into three levels: First, the Commune Administrative Committee which is the guiding body on all important matters; second, the administrative district (or production brigade), which serves as an intermediary link between the commune policy-making body and the basic-level units; and third, the production teams and the production groups under them. Of course

[20] *People's Communes in China,* Foreign Languages Press, Peking 1958, pp. 2–3; and *JMJP,* September 25, 1959.

there are regional or local variations to this general organizational pattern.

The Administrative Committee, the leading organ, is elected by the congress of the commune. It includes representatives of all production brigades as well as important village groups such as the women, youths, old people, cultural and educational workers, medical personnel, technicians, traders, and employees in local industries. It decides on all policy matters concerning the commune and supervises the work of intermediate and basic-level units. Under the Administrative Committee are the departments and commissions in charge of specific functions, such as agriculture, water conservancy, animal husbandry, rural industry, communications, commerce, rural finance, cultural-educational affairs, agro-scientific research, and the militia. The Committee members are generally elected for a term of two years, but are eligible for re-election.

The administrative districts (sometimes called production brigades) are organized with a division of labour similar to that of the Administrative Committee. They are in charge of various localities within a general area covered by a commune which as a rule embodies a township with several *hsiang* or administrative villages. (Since the total number of *hsien* [county] and *hsiang* in China in 1958 was estimated to be, respectively, 1,750 and 80,000, the average number of people's communes in each *hsien* should come to about 14, with each commune covering 3 or 4 *hsiang*. The number of *hsiang* may have been further reduced in 1959). These administrative districts operate on a basis of economic accounting, with its gains and losses calculated on the basis of the commune as a whole. They enjoy considerable autonomous powers in such matters as the organization of production work, investment in capital construction in the district within the allocated funds, and welfare amenities.

The production teams are the basic units that attend to various agricultural and related activities, including farming, subsidiary jobs, livestock raising, forestry, and local industries. They also run nurseries, kindergartens, canteens, local militia, village schools, and agro-scientific research. Each production team elects a leader, several deputy leaders, and other members. The total number varies with the size of the commune. Their tenure, like that of the membership in the production contingent, is one year with eligibility for re-election. Under the production teams, numbering more than 3,000,000 in the fall of 1959 there are the production groups.

At each of the above-mentioned three levels, a supervisory committee is elected to evaluate and check the accounts and work of the different units. At the *hsien* level, a Federation of Communes is formed to co-ordinate the work among the various communes.[21]

Other important operational aspects of the commune include the following: (1) Various programmes concerning production, exchange, distribution, consumption, and investment (accumulation) are planned by the commune in co-ordination with the overall plans of the state and of the province. (2) The minimum needs of the members, mainly in the form of food and clothing, are supplied free. Certain communes provide, in addition, medical treatment, maternity care, housing, education, wedding and funeral expenses, electricity, etc. under a gratis system. In principle, between 20 to 30 per cent of the income of commune members comes from such free-supply category, the rest is drawn as wages. The wage income for commune members in 1958 came between 3 *yuan* (minimum) and 20 *yuan* a month. (3) The wage system is based on the contribution made to production and community welfare by each member of the commune. The wage scale is at present generally divided into 6 or 8 grades, the highest grade may be four or more times as the lowest one. However, social incentives, expressed in terms of group effort working for a better future and *esprit de corps*, are vigorously emphasized through education, propaganda, and group discussions. The remuneration for labour or technical contributions is distributed directly by the commune to each member, including women and youths, thus enhancing their economic independence and social status. Bonuses are paid to members who over-fulfil their assignments. (4) All means of production such as land, farm implements, and draught animals are converted into common ownership in the commune. But the means of livelihood owned by the members, including clothing, furniture, personal savings in the banks or credit co-operatives, and small number of domestic fowls remain their personal property. Members can also retain individual trees around their houses, small farm tools, small instruments, as well as continue to engage in certain small-scale household side occupations as long

[21] See "Draft Regulations of the Weihsing (Sputnik) People's Commune," August 7, 1958; *People's Communes in China*, pp. 161–80; and section V, *Resolution on Some Questions Concerning the People's Communes*, CC, CCP, December 10, 1958.

as these do not hamper their taking part in common labour.[22] (5) The general pattern of income distribution among the communes is reported as: 30 to 50 per cent as consumption for the members; 20 to 40 per cent as accumulation, including about 5 per cent as public welfare funds and another 5 per cent as grain reserve; 20 per cent as operational expenses, including around one per cent of administrative fees; and approximately 10 per cent as taxes to the government. The average rate of accumulation among the APCs during 1953–57 has been estimated as 10 per cent.[23] (6) In the communes, each male member gets two days' leave every month with pay, and women members, three days. Sick leave is extra, and during child-birth, the mother gets 48 days' vacation, and (7) a system of "production responsibility" is adopted, assigning specific duties to production contingents, production teams, and individuals. There are quotas for various categories of work such as production, investment, cost, labour and administrative personnel. Bonuses are offered for over-fulfilment of these quotas.[24]

Salient Effects of the People's Communes

It is still too early to evaluate the full impact of the communes on rural China in general and on the Chinese agriculture in particular. However, there are a number of aspects about which some preliminary comments may be offered. These may include the effect of people's communes on farming, the rate of accumulation of capital in the agricultural sector, and the marketing (distribution) process in the countryside, their political significance, and their role in the socio-cultural development in China's countryside.

Farming methods have been undergoing drastic changes in China ever since the establishment of the Central People's Government on October 1, 1949, and especially after the stepping up of the cooperative movement in the autumn of 1955. But the introduction of communes is accelerating a number of novel measures in agriculture. For example, the division of labour among the villagers is now done on the basis of several *hsiang*, if not the entire county.

[22] See section IV, *Resolution on Some Questions Concerning the People's Communes*, December 10, 1958.

[23] Yang Po, "Correctly Deal with the Question of Accumulation and Consumption in the Communes," *JMJP*, January 9, 1959, p. 7.

[24] *JMJP*, February 17, 1959, p. 1.

The variety of economic activities and the utilization of resources, including manpower, are also greatly extended. The communes, partly through the release of women-power from household chores, have facilitated the implementation of the 8-point code of agricultural improvement, much of which calls for greater labour intensity. These eight programmes are: irrigation, use of more fertilizer (mainly manure and compost at present), deep ploughing and soil improvement, seed selection, close planting, plant protection (pest and disease control), tool innovations, and better field care and management. In 1958, for instance, between 60 and 70 million acres of cultivated area (out of a total of some 280 million acres) were added to irrigation, 20 million acres deep-ploughed, and tens of tons of fertilizer (mostly manure) were reportedly used on each acre of farmland (compared to 6 tons in 1957).[25] All these necessitated the employment of a great deal of labour force. As a result, there was a shortage of rural labour in the fall of 1958 and in 1959. That this helps to resolve a basic problem of many underdeveloped countries, namely, surplus agricultural labour in the form of under-employment, unemployment, and disguised unemployment needs little elaboration.

The communes also put resources, particularly land and labour, under more rational planning and use—such as the allocation of different types of crops to suit various soil conditions, more intensive farming, and greater ability to take risks in trying out new methods, tools, or crop strains. In each village now there is at least one experimental plot on which numerous farming experiments are conducted. This has a direct bearing on the enhancement of yield per acre of major crops in China in 1958 and 1959. At present, it is possible to find rice fields producing as high as 5 tons per acre, or wheat plots at one ton per acre. The long-range blueprint of agriculture, as envisaged by the Chinese planners, is to reduce the prevailing cultivated area to one-third, and divide the other two-thirds equally between afforestation, gardens, or orchards and leaving the land in fallow to build up soil fertility.

The second significant effect of the communes concerns the distribution and marketing system in rural China. The communes are now incorporating in their departmental structure, the functions of supply marketing cooperatives and credit cooperatives. It is no longer necessary to have separate organizations at the village level

[25] See *Ts'ai-cheng* (Finance), No. 11, October 24, 1958, p. 10.

for government purchase of major rural products or the extension of state loans to farmers. Prior to the introduction of communes the quota allocation of foodgrains among the rural households according to their actual consumption required tremendous amount of checking work, time and personnel. Now the communes are taking over the work of supplying of the food needs of the rural inhabitants, in the form of common dining halls. The government can concentrate on the task of unified purchase of major crops to ensure the supplying of food and raw materials to urban centres. The communes are also, as previously mentioned, changing the income distribution pattern in the rural sector. Instead of an average of 10 per cent of agricultural income used for investment during the first five-year period, the proportion allocated as accumulation came to about 30 per cent in 1959. In 1958, the total estimated amount of accumulation by the communes came to 10 billion *yuan*.[26] At the same time, cost (such as the quantity of coal needed for cooking) is reduced as a result of collective management. The marketing facilities in the countryside are helped by the extensive building of roads (150,000 kilometres added in 1958), the internal adjustment of supply and demand in commodities within a commune, and the construction of granaries.

A related development in the rural economy after the propagation of communes is the effect on taxation programmes. The agricultural tax system, reorganized in 1958, is now based on a proportional scale, though it continues to be mainly levied in kind in the form of staple crops (discussion on the new tax system can be found in a later section). With the rapid increase in per acre yields and attainment of food sufficiency in China, a less cumbersome form of tax in cash and a more egalitarian progressive scale may be desirable. Also certain forms of taxes such as the industrial-commercial tax (consolidated in September 1958 to include commodity tax, commodity circulation tax, business transaction tax and stamp tax) on a number of items will bring a decreasing yield in the future as the communes are striving for self-sufficiency in many products and the supply system within a commune does not involve commercial transactions. The amount of retail sale in foodgrains (3 per cent in tax rate) is one obvious example. Other taxes may generate greater income, such as those on local industrial goods and on

[26] See *Ts'ai-cheng* (Finance), No. 11, October 24, 1958, p. 10; and *JMJP*, October 14, 1959, p. 60.

subsidiary produce. According to one preliminary sample survey, the tax burden on the income in rural China in 1958 was as follows: industrial tax, 7 per cent of the total value of industrial products in the countryside; commercial tax, 9 per cent of the total value of commodities in circulation; agricultural tax, 15 per cent of the value of agricultural products; tax on forestry products, animal husbandry, fishery, and subsidiary occupations, 5 per cent of the value of these enterprises. Taxes on special items like wine had special rates.[27] With the rapid expansion of local industries and side occupations, some adjustments in the tax structure and value would seem to be in order.

On the political and administrative side, the communes facilitate the elimination of some intermediary local government organs such as the *ch'ü* (district) people's council, as the *hsiang* administration has now come under the direct jurisdiction of the county (or *hsien*). There is now a greater coordination of the administrative and economic programmes at the *hsiang* level, because the communes are operated under an integrated command. Due to the enlarged scope of planning for farming and other activities, the number of *hsiang* and even *hsien* is reduced.

Equally important is the impact of communes in the socio-educational fields in rural China. With greater resources at the communes' command and with the labour force more effectively organized, the development of mass education, agro-technical training, and other social reforms are accelerated. In 1958, the number of enrolment in primary schools increased from 64 million (1957) to 86 million, and that of secondary and technical schools from 7·08 million to 15 million. In early 1959 there were over four million nurseries taking care of about 37 million children or 90 per cent of children of pre-school age. In addition, 110,000 maternity homes were set up and 61 per cent of child births was delivered by modern-type midwifery in 1958. There were also over one million recreation clubs and half a million libraries in the countryside. At the end of 1958, there were 3·4 million nurseries, 150,000 old people's homes, 3·4 million community dining halls, 60,000 cultural stations, 500,000 clubs and 130,000 amateur dramatic groups.[28] The long-range impact of these social-cultural programmes cannot

[27] *Ching-chi yen-chiu* (Economic Research), No. 10, October 17, 1958, p. 10.

[28] *China Today*, No. 4, January 24, 1959, p. 7; and *JMJP*, September 25, 1959.

be over-exaggerated. The investment in these social overheads (services) is bound to enhance the marginal productivity of the rural economy sooner or later.

Some Problems Regarding the People's Communes

A few problems regarding the communes have been brought out in previous discussions. In general, current problems may be grouped into three categories: (1) organizational-administrative; (2) economic-technical; and (3) social-cultural.

Regarding organizational and administrative problems, it is relevant to note that the average size of people's communes is about 30 times that of an APC, the programmes undertaken by a commune have been vastly expanded to include industrial and commercial activities, and the time taken to regroup 740,000 cooperatives into some 26,500 communes was about 6 months. That the Peking leaders are not unaware of these problems can be seen in the fact that the winter of 1958–59 and spring of 1959 were set aside as a period for consolidating the communes. In the *Resolution on Communes* by the CC, CCP passed on December 10, 1958 it was stated: "In order to promote the consolidation of the people's communes and ensure an ever bigger leap forward in industry and agriculture in 1959, the Party committees of the provinces, municipalities, and autonomous regions should, in compliance with the requirements put forward in this resolution, make full use of the five months from December 1958 to April 1959 to tide up the people's communes in their areas by doing educational propaganda, checking over, and consolidating them."[29]

The managerial issues, such as the effective division of labour among various undertakings of the communes, proper remuneration of members for their work, both quantitatively and qualitatively, the suitable allocation of income between distribution (consumption) and accumulation, and the setting up of accurate but simple accounting procedures, will be of great importance to the successful operation of a commune. Furthermore, there are questions which go beyond these organizational factors. For example, what amount should be taxed by the state and how much resources should be left at the disposal of the communes? What are the items that may be retained by members as private property? These involve political decisions.

[29] Section VIII, *op. cit.*, p. 19.

In the economic and technical spheres, the basic question is how to coordinate the multiple enterprises within a commune and how they can be most effectively integrated with the overall national plans and regional developments. Within the commune, the question of what agro-technical improvements are to be emphasized and at what time call for close attention. In addition, the fast expansion of crop yields has intensified the problem of storage, packing, processing, marketing, and price adjustments. At the end of 1958, the load on transportation facilities in China was very heavy, and consequently, the supply of certain agricultural produce became tense in a number of urban or mining areas.[30] The desirability of making adjustments in the existing tax systems in rural areas has been mentioned previously.

In the social-cultural fields, several problems also claim attention. The collective system of living in people's communes has drastically changed the conditions of community life, family living, and even personal relationships among the villagers. For instance, peasant women are now freed considerably from household burdens like cooking, mending and taking care of children, and are getting rewards for their labour directly from the Commune Committee. But then the question is how to strike a balance between the liberation from the burdens of daily chores which bound the rural women and the need of children for personal affection of their mothers. On this point the Resolution of the CC, CCP (December 10, 1958) directed that "nurseries and kindergartens should be run well . . . so that the children are willing to stay there and the parents are willing to put them there. The parents may decide whether the children need to board there, and may take them back home at any time they wish." The arrangement to have the commune dormitories built in such manner that the nucleus family members can live together as a unit is certainly a step in the right direction. The better organization of labour power and the promotion of divergent social and educational activities by the communes will have a tremendous impact on the social structure and values in rural China. Equality and welfare among men will remain an abstract idea if there do not exist broad educational opportunities, economic equality between the sexes, and vertical social mobility. Parallel to group discipline and community welfare, there must also be encouragement for the commune members to develop their

[30] *The Statesman*, New Delhi, December 21, 1958, p. 6.

personality as well as to give expressions to their individual aspirations.

D. *Crop Production and Productivity*

The development of major food and economic crops, livestock, and certain subsidiary produce in China from 1950 to 1959 is summarized in Tables III to VI. The achievements, particularly in the cases of rice, wheat, and cotton, has been very impressive. For example, the production of rice increased from an estimated 48·6 million tons in 1949 to 71 million tons in 1952 and about 113 million tons in 1958; that of wheat, from 13·8 million tons to 18 million tons and some 29 million tons, during the same period; that of cotton, from 444,000 tons in 1949 to 1·3 million tons in 1952 and 2·13 million tons in 1958. This accomplishment is even more pronounced when one takes into consideration the fact that in 1949 grain production was reportedly only 74·6 per cent of the pre-war average, cotton, around 52 per cent, and livestock and farm tools were depleted by 16 per cent and 30 per cent respectively.[31] The production of grain and cotton in 1959 estimated at 270·5 and 2·41 million tons respectively, was achieved in spite of the extensive floods and a long period of drought in many areas in China in that year.

The increase of agricultural production has always been regarded as a central task by Peking, and increasing weight is being assigned to it due to the need for more agricultural products to meet the rapid pace of industrialization. The various measures adopted by the Peking Government to develop agricultural production may be grouped into four general categories: First, those which contribute to the expansion of crop acreage—conservation, reclamation, and encouragement of multiple cropping practices. Second, those which aid the enhancement of yield per hectare—irrigation, afforestation, water and soil conservation, use of better seeds, application of more fertilizers, new farm implements, and technical training of the peasants. The cultivation of more high-yielding crops, like corn and potatoes, also helps to increase the yield per unit of land. Third, organizational measures like the establishment of cooperatives and people's communes, which are designed to enhance mass enthusiasm, to raise labour efficiency, and to improve the marketing systems. Fourth, ways and means which help to reduce crop losses

[31] Li Shu-cheng, *Great Achievement in the Agricultural Production of New China in the Past Three Years,* September 18, 1952.

and wastes, including the control of plant or animal pests, better storage facilities, and a host of other methods to practise greater economy in the use of agricultural produce.

Details about the various programmes in the first three categories will be discussed in separate sections of this volume. The fourth category, often underestimated or neglected by Western observers, plays an important role in the agricultural production programme of Peking. For example, the percentage of extraction loss in the processing of coarse grain into retail grain in the pre-war period was estimated to be more than 20 per cent,[32] while the current rate is reportedly about 14 per cent. The number of feasts for festival or other celebrations has been cut down drastically, and wine-making which in the pre-war era is said to have consumed 11·5 per cent of all the rice and wheat produced in 1946,[33] has also been curtailed. Various substitutes have been introduced to replace grain as animal feed. The campaign to exterminate rats and sparrows (initiated in 1955) is another effort to save foodgrains. An official of the Ministry of Grains wrote in August 1955 that 470,000 rats were killed between January and May 1955, and an estimated 7,000 tons of grain were saved.[34] In 1958, 1·88 billion rats and 1·96 billion sparrows were wiped out.[35] The estimated annual consumption of grain for a rat is about 20 pounds, and for a sparrow, 5·5 pounds. One *NCNA* news bulletin, dated December 1, 1956, reported that "to minimize waste, many APCs in Shensi are rethreshing their wheat ears, and it is estimated that an additional 33,000 tons of wheat will be obtained throughout the province."[36] When such cases are multiplied on a nation-wide scale, the effect is bound to be considerable.

Another qualitative standard in evaluating the agricultural production in China is crop productivity (yield per unit of land). Again progress is more pronounced in the three major crops of rice, wheat, and cotton. Their productivity (pound per acre) in the years 1949, 1952 and 1958 through estimates, is as follows: Rice, 1,688, 2,147, and 3,050; Wheat, 573, 651 and 957; and Cotton, 143, 208 and 380 (1959 preliminary estimate).

[32] Hua Shun-nien, *On the Control of Foodgrains*, Taipei, 1953, p. 112.

[33] Hua Shun-nien, *op. cit.*, p. 170. [34] *JMJP*, August 9, 1955, p. 2.

[35] *JMJP*, December 31, 1958, p. 1. It has been estimated that in India, at least 4 billion rupees of foodgrains were lost annually to various kinds of pests, rats, monkeys, and stray cattle. *The Times of India*, November 19, 1958, p. 6.

[36] BBC, "Summary of World Broadcasts," Part V, *Economic Supplement* No. 247, January 3, 1957, p. 8.

The following table showing yields (in pounds per acre) of rice, wheat, and cotton in some other countries gives a comparative picture:

*Country**	*Rice*	*Wheat*	*Cotton*
India (1958)	946	790	100
Italy (1956)	4,170	1,600	160
Japan (1956)	3,759	1,860	116
U.S.A. (1956)	3,144	1,200	410
China (1958)	3,050	957	380 (1959 est.)

* Data taken from FAO, *Yearbook, 1957*, pp. 33–4; 48–9; and 130–1. Indian data from charts at the Exhibition of Agricultural Development, Indian Agricultural Research Institute, 1958, and other current sources.

The above statistics indicate that China has done well in raising the level of productivity for rice and cotton, compared to other countries which achieved high yields. In wheat, the per-acre yield is still not up to the highest level in the world. A number of crops including soybeans, potatoes, jute, kenaf, and sugarbeets did not reach the planned productivity at the end of the first five-year plan —that is, in 1957. However, both the production and yield per acre of practically all crops exceeded the planned goals after the "big leap" in 1958. (See Tables III and IV and Appendixes). The qualitative aspects of agricultural products should at the same time be considered. They include the utilization value of a particular crop such as the sugar content of sugarbeets and the fibre quality of cotton, and the food value (calorie content as well as preferential values in local food habits) of different grains. The quality of sugarbeets, for example, deteriorated in certain areas like Heilungkiang in 1956, and adversely affected sugar production.

There is, in addition, the problem of balanced development among the various sectors of agriculture—especially among the three major areas of foodgrains, industrial crops, and subsidiary occupations. Up to 1956, the attention of Peking planners was focussed on the increase in production in foodcrops and cotton. As a result, a number of other crops and side jobs did not get adequate emphasis. Measures have been taken since 1956 to rectify the situation, but it will take time to fully develop some important subsidiary products. The goal in 1959 aimed to raise the income from subsidiary (non-farming) occupations to 30 per cent of the total income of the peasant households.[37] The number of livestock in China at the end of 1957 did not reach the planned goals in most cases. The amount of tea produced in 1957, for instance, was only 70 per cent of the pre-war level, and that of domestic cocoons, less than one half.[38] This may partly be due to the extensive natural calamities which occurred in 1956, when an estimated 38·33 million acres of cultivated land were affected in varying degrees and 12 million tons of grain lost.[39] With the big leap forward in agricultural production in 1958, the light industries have now to catch up.

Barring the unlikely event of a world conglomeration, a continued growth in China's crop production may be expected—due primarily to the following factors: First, Peking planners are assigning greater weight in agricultural investment and in industries closely related to agricultural production. Second, many agro-technical improvements, like conservation, irrigation, afforestation, and the use of more chemical fertilizers, will begin increasingly to take a cumulative effect. Third, rural reorganizational measures like the collectivization of farms and communization have been completed without much disruption of the rural economy. Fourth, a series of non-economic programmes like the despatching of students into the villages, mass education, the "cultural-technical revolution" and rural health programme will exercise a positive influence directly and indirectly on the development of agricultural production. Fifth, the Chinese peasants have fostered a spirit of confidence and cooperation under the skilful organization of the CCP. Other relevant factors which may substantially affect agricultural production like rural taxation, pricing policy for farm products, and marketing control, will be brought up in other sections.

E. *Agro-Technical Programmes*

The term "agro-technical" is used here to describe a myriad of biological and technical measures to promote agricultural development. These include conservation, irrigation, reclamation, afforestation,

[37] *Ta-kung pao*, February 3, 1959, p. 1.

[38] Statistical Bureau, *Implementation of the National Economic Plans in 1956*, *op. cit.*, and *Hua-ch'iao jih-pao* (China Daily News), November 13, 1957, p. 1.

[39] *Liang-shih* (Foodgrain), monthly, Peking, No. 7, July 1957.

the use of better seeds, more efficient application of fertilizers, anti-pest controls, modern farm implements, and plans to develop technical training and research. They also include the dissemination of traditional farming knowledge and practices which have proved effective in specific rural areas of China but are yet to be popularized in other regions where conditions are favourable. The major developments in the agro-technical fields reported in China for the past decade are summarized in Table VIII.

Emphasizing the importance of agro-technical measures does not mean other non-technical programmes are unimportant or the former can be isolated from the latter. As Dr. Solomon Adler points out:

> The line of demarcation between technical and economic and, for that matter, social progress is necessarily arbitrary. Better tools and equipment and improved methods of cultivation are both the cause and effect of higher standards of living and advances in literacy and public hygiene. The combined effect of all three types of change is cumulative, each tending to reinforce the other.[40]

It is significant to note that when Vice-Premier Li Fu-ch'un, delivered a speech on the results of the first five-year plan on December 7, 1957, among the eight topics listed by him to promote agricultural development, all except the first (on greater investment in agriculture) deal with agro-technical programmes. And the 8-point agricultural code enforced since 1959 all deal with agro-technical improvements. Brief discussions of these programmes shall be made under the following headings:

Conservation and Irrigation (See Appendix IV)

At all the major rivers and their tributaries in China, systematic water and soil conservation work has either begun or will start soon. In the fall of 1959 six major conservation projects and 30,000 minor works were in progress. For example, the Sanmen Gorge Project was started in April 1957, marking the first step of a comprehensive 15-year plan. It is estimated when the first phase of the Plan is completed in 1967 (now probably before 1963), more than five million acres of land will be added to irrigation, 21 million acres of land improved in irrigation, and an additional 2·73 million

[40] Solomon Adler, *The Chinese Economy*, 1957, p. 139.

tons of grains produced.[41] Up to 1958, the State had invested 608 million US dollars in the Huai River project, and constructed earthwork amounting to 1·6 billion cubic metres in the first 8 years.[42] Similar programmes are being started on the Yangtze, Pearl River, Heilungkiang, and Liaoho.[43] Preliminary conservation works have been completed at the Huai River, and Haiho (including the Yungting River near Peking) in 1957. Between October 1955 and September 1956 alone, more than 610,000 channels and dikes, 2·6 million reservoirs, and 4·5 million wells were built.[44] As a result, about 60 million acres of irrigated land were added during the first five-year plan (1953–57), which was about three times more than the original planned goal. Between 1955 and 1957, 26,447 canals were dug and 6,000 sluice gates built.[45] The 1958 plan, according to Vice-Premier Teng Tzu-hui, called for an additional 6·7 million acres of irrigated land and improvement for over 7 million acres of land already irrigated.[46] But actually about 67 million acres were made available for irrigation in 1958. The proportion of irrigated acreage expanded from 16·3 per cent in the total cultivated area (or 72 million acres) in 1949 to about 60 per cent (or 165 million acres) at the end of 1958.[47] Equally important is the fact that the number of conservancy engineers and technicians jumped from 5,360 in 1950 to 31,280 in 1956. While there were only a small number of students in conservancy studies prior to 1949, about 1,800 annually graduated from university conservancy departments and 1,000 from technical institutes or schools in China in the past several years.[48] In 1958, a total of 50 billion cubic metres of earth and stone works was completed in irrigation projects and the figure for 1959 was about 13 billion cubic metres up to September of that year.[49]

[41] See Teng Tzu-hui, *Report on the Multiple-Purpose Plan for Controlling the Yellow River*, July 18, 1955; Foreign Languages Press, Peking, 1955, pp. 42–4; also *NCNA* bulletin quoted in *The Statesman*, New Delhi, November 3, 1959, p. 6.

[42] Quoted in Charles Bettelheim, "China's Economic Growth," *Economic Weekly*, Bombay, November 29, 1958, p. 1497; and Appendix IV.

[43] See "Red China Plans to Tame Yangtze," *NYT*, November 24, 1957, p. 22.

[44] Fu Tso-yi, "Evaluation of Conservation Work in 1956 and Plan Policies and Tasks in 1957," *Chung-kuo shui-li* (Conservation of China), No. 5, May 14, 1957.

[45] *China Reconstructs*, November 1958, p. 9.

[46] *HCJP*, September 13, 1957, p. 1.

[47] NCNA, June 28, 1958.

[48] Fu Tso-yi, *op.cit.*, *HCJP*, October 5, 1957, p. 2.

[49] Ch'en Cheng-jen, "Rapidly Start a Higher Advance in Irrigation Work," *JMJP*, December 27, 1958, p. 1; and *China Today*, January 30, 1960, p. 15.

Regarding the development in water and soil conservation, a very significant report appeared in the *People's Daily* of November 17, 1957. This article told about the progress made in two *hsiang* in Yu-hsien of Honan province during 1956 and 1957, where the local APC members developed small irrigation projects, built terraces and water-holding pools on the hills, and accomplished an 80 per cent survival rate in the trees planted. As a result, the low land was completely protected from the floods for the first time in 1957 and water was assured during a drought. This accomplishment concerns only a small area (two administrative villages) in Honan, but what makes the event extremely meaningful are the following factors: (1) It shows that hilly, poor land can be made fertile and productive by effective water and soil conservation; (2) The achievement was made primarily by the villagers themselves, relying on local resources; (3) The benefits were immediate—while investment in one *hsiang* amounted to 3,350 *yuan* (2,845 *yuan* in labour at 0·45 *yuan* per labour-day, and 500 *yuan* in the form of government aid), the direct income from the conservation work was estimated at 3,490 *yuan* a year later (in 1957); (4) The various projects were helped by sending several cadres (in 1956) to study at Ta-ch'uan-shan (a hilly *hsiang* well known for its achievement in conservation work) in Shansi —about 300 miles away, and (5) The experiences gathered in the local conservancy work in Yu-hsien are being popularized in turn in other rural districts.[50] When these local improvements are multiplied on a national scale, even with occasional failures or blunders, the effect on China's agricultural development should be tremendous.

The above reported progress is an impressive one and labour-intensive projects like conservancy and irrigation suit the particular characteristic of the Chinese agriculture—great manpower resources and inadequacy in capital and advanced technology. However, there exist also a few problems in the conservation programmes in China. Sometimes the conservation plans were too ambitious or drawn with incomplete understanding of the local conditions and needs. For example, the plans (in 1957) for the Haiho basin would have involved four reservoirs with a total capacity of 7·5 billion cubic metres, requiring an investment of 360 million *yuan*. But the average volume of flow of the Piho basin on the main upper stream of Haiho for quite a number of years in the past had been only 3·1

[50] The report also appears in *HPYK*, No. 24, December 25, 1957, pp. 78–9. It is co-authored by Sung Hai-yen and Ch'eng Shih-sha.

billion cubic metres.[51] Greater attention needs to be paid on the qualitative and technical aspects of the projects. It helped agricultural production when more than 5 million wells were dug between 1950 and 1956 (3 million in 1956), but hundreds of thousands of wells were imperfectly built. Also it is desirable to accord greater encouragement to small-scale and medium irrigation projects which may be undertaken mainly with local resources. Better coordination is desirable between conservation or irrigation and other programmes like afforestation, soil improvement, and the accumulation of river mud as manure. The success of conservancy works depends partly on whether they are carried out timely—for example, in winter and spring before the floods develop and when the peasants are not too busy.[52] The managerial ability and technical competence of the leaders who guide the conservation work constitute, just as in many other agro-technical programmes, a key element for success.

Reclamation and Afforestation

Chinese sources estimate the total amount of "reclaimable land" at some 266 million acres,[53] slightly less than the 280 million acres of cultivated area in 1958. Even if some 10 per cent of this arable land is reclaimed, it would contribute substantially to the agricultural production of China. However, as Prof. Ma Yin-ch'u pointed out in a speech on July 3, 1957, "among the 'waste land' some are barren, some lack water, and some are grassland needed by minority groups."[54] During the first 5-year plan period (1953–57), the original goal of land reclamation of some 6·3 million acres was fulfilled over 200 per cent, but the per capita land holding of the nation decreased slightly (2·7 *mou* in 1953 versus 2·6 *mou* in 1957), due to population growth. It is true that the labour-intensive nature of reclamation projects which require little capital or advanced technology makes advantageous use of the abundant manpower of China. But reclamation cannot be regarded as a panacea to the need for greater crop production in China, both due to the cost factor (estimated at 40 to 50 *yuan* per *mou* or averaging US $115 per acre) and the limited amount of good arable land. Even when opening up

[51] See, CC, CCP and State Council, "Decision to Launch a Campaign for Building Irrigation Projects and Accumulating Manure in Coming Winter and Next Spring," *Kuang-ming jih-pao* (Brilliance Daily), September 25, 1957.

[52] *Ibid.* [53] *Shih-shih shou-ts'e* (Current Events Handbook), September 10, 1955.

[54] Ma Yin-ch'u, *op.cit.*

readily accessible "wasteland" for reclamation, care is needed to study the soil conservation situation in a particular locality. Significantly, both in the revised programme for agricultural development, 1956–67, and Li Fu-ch'un's report on the direction of construction in the 2nd 5-year plan (1958–62) of December 7, 1957, reclamation is listed as the last item in some 10 measures designed to enhance agricultural production. The utilization of hilly lands for the cultivation of non-foodcrops like tea, tung trees, bamboo and mulberry deserves attention. The amount of land to be reclaimed by the State farms in the 12 years following 1956 is set at around 14·5 million acres. Since 1958, the emphasis has been on the raise of yield per acre, and the long-range plan aims to devote one-third of the current cultivated area for crops, the rest to be divided between planting of trees or flowers and leaving the remaining one-third in fallow.

At the moment, reclamation may still occupy an important role in the agricultural development of China. Organized and planned resettlement for reclamation of wasteland began in earnest in 1956. The reclamation work by State farms also was accelerated in that year. By 1956, the 454 large State farms and ranches expanded their arable land holdings to 2·27 million acres. Up to February 1957, about 100 million acres of wasteland in China had been surveyed.[55] The amount of small plots of wasteland which could be reclaimed by peasants nearby was estimated at approximately 16·67 million acres. The amount of foodgrains yielded from the 1·1 million acres reclaimed in 1956 was estimated to be 285,000 tons.[56] In 1956 alone, 433,000 persons migrated from more densely populated areas of Shantung, Honan, Hopei, Peking, Tientsin and Shanghai for reclamation work in Heilungkiang, Kansu, Tsinghai, Kiangsi, Inner Mongolia, and Sinkiang. In addition, in the provinces of Kwangtung, Fukien, Liaoning, Kirin, Chekiang, Kiangsu and others, a total of over 292,000 people were resettled in areas within the respective provinces.[57] The population in Tsinghai province alone increased from 1·4 million in 1949 to 2·3 million in 1958.[58]

[55] *NCNA* bulletin, February 25, 1957.

[56] *NCNA* bulletin, June 14, 1957.

[57] *NCNA* bulletin, December 27, 1956. Another bulletin of June 14, 1957 gave the number of migrated persons in 1956 as 660,000.

[58] *The Times of India*, New Delhi, March 18, 1959, p. 1.

Peking has offered various assistances to the settlers. The travelling expenses needed for moving their homes, the building of new houses, roads, bridges, and the sinking of wells were taken care of through State investments. Additional government loans were extended to help them in solving their difficulties in production and livelihood, and about 70 per cent of the funds spent by the State consisted of investment for which no repayment was called. In 9 settlement areas, including Heilungkiang, Inner Mongolia, Kansu, and Tsinghai, the State had invested over 110 million *yuan* by the end of 1956. The government also bought in that year 500 tractors for the settlers to use in their reclaiming work.[59]

There are other labour-intensive programmes in agriculture which stand much less chance of having unfavourable side effects. Afforestation is one of them. According to a *NCNA* report in 1958, trees were planted on a total area of 46 million acres in the first 5-year plan period—which is three times above the original target. This is reportedly 60 times the aggregate figure of afforestation during the 35 years prior to 1949. In 1958, another 43 million acres of land were afforested. Five thousand afforestation centres had been set up (up to 1957), including 400 State-owned tree-farms.

According to a report of the late Dr. Liang Hsi, then Minister for Forestry, made on June 19, 1956, there were, in the main forest regions such as Kirin, Heilungkiang, Inner Mongolia, Szechun, Yunnan, Shansi, Shensi, Kansu and Sinkiang, 42 intermediary forest administrative agencies, and 352 basic-level forest management centres organized under the provincial forestry bureaus, with 8,335 staff members. They had, under their care, more than 31 million acres of forest land.[60]

One giant shelter belt of trees was near its completion at the end of 1958, which stretched along a total length of 1,000 miles. It begins at the western part of Kansu province, runs almost parallel to the Great Wall and ends up in Hopei province. An intensive effort was being made in 1959 to plant trees, shrubs and grass as well as to dig irrigation canals on an estimated 44,000 square miles (or 31 million acres) in the arid or semi-desert areas of Sinkiang, Ninghsia and Inner Mongolia—all now Autonomous Regions for minority groups.[61]

[59] *NCNA* bulletin, December 27, 1956.

[60] Liang Hsi, "Strive for a Better Conservation System, More Green Hills, and the Prevention of Natural Calamities," June 19, *HPYK*, 1956, No. 14, July 21, 1956, pp. 70–2.

[61] *The Times of India*, New Delhi, February 3, 1959, p. 6.

Equally important is the training of more than 14,000 specialists and technicians in forestry during the same period—as compared with 3,000 trained between 1927 and 1949. The afforested area on the Chinese mainland, as of July 1957, was larger than that of India, and said to rank fifth in the world after the USSR, Indonesia, USA and Canada.[62] Although Brazil is known to have a total forest area smaller only to the USSR, there seems to be little doubt that tremendous stride has been made in "making China green."

The overall plans, as laid down in the *Draft Programme for Agricultural Development in the Nation, 1956–67*, contain the following measures (now greatly accelerated after 1957):

> Cover all possible wasteland and denuded mountains with foliage in the 12 years starting from 1956. Trees should be planted in a planned way near houses, villages, along roads and rivers, as well as on wasteland and denuded mountains wherever possible. To achieve this aim, reasonably large tree nurseries for breeding saplings should be set up by agricultural producers' cooperatives, apart from the tree nurseries established by the state.
>
> In addition to developing forests for building purposes (including bamboo groves), trees of special economic value, such as the mulberry silk worm-feeding oak, tea trees, varnish and fruit trees, and also oil-yielding plants, should also be cultivated.
>
> The overall afforestation plan should include the creation of wind-breaks, sand-breaks and shelter belts to protect farmland, the headwaters of rivers, sea coasts and cities.
>
> The cultivation and management of trees along railways, highways and rivers should be taken up by local APCs and the income derived from this source should accrue to the cooperatives. Afforestation work along railways and highways should be carried out according to the specifications made by the Ministry of Railways and the Ministry of Communications.
>
> Active measures shall be taken to prevent insect pests and plant disease in the forests and to strengthen forest protection and forest fire fighting. (Article 21)

Qualitatively, there is room for improvement in the afforestation programme in China. During 1955 and 1956, the rate of survival of trees planted was only 60 per cent. In the spring of 1957, about

[62] *NCNA*, Peking, July 12, and September 25, 1957.

80 per cent of the saplings planted reportedly "came up to the quality standards stipulated by the government." According to a statement by the late Dr. Liang Hsi, then Minister of Forestry, in June 1956, the goal was to plant trees on 250 million acres of barren lands and mountains between 1956 and 1967. By then, the forest area will be 1·3 times of its size in 1956, and 70 per cent of the afforested area will consist of timber for various industrial uses.[63] The revised 12-year plan for the development of agriculture in the nation (1956–67), however, as above quoted passages show, does not specify any figure for afforestation.

Statistics (see Table VIII) indicate that both reclamation and afforestation programmes showed rapid development between 1956 and 1959. One reason is attributed to the popularization of cooperative farming and the communes, which resulted in better organization as well as utilization of manpower in rural China. According to Liao Lu-yen, 13 million acres would be added to China's farmland through the elimination of boundaries and unnecessary paths between fields as a result of organized farming. For 1959, 11·6 million acres of irrigated land and 46·6 million acres of afforested land were added up to September of that year.

Fertilizers

Chinese peasants are traditionally skilful utilizers of fertilizers —mainly in the form of human as well as animal manure and other forms of "natural" fertilizers like soybean cakes, green manure, bone meat (made from animal bones) and river mud. This is one of the reasons why after thousands of years of intensive farming, the productivity of the Chinese farms remains high. Peking's directives on agricultural production have repeatedly called for greater effort in the collection and more efficient use of these "natural" fertilizers, as they still constitute the bulk of the fertilizers used on Chinese farmlands. The various forms of traditional fertilizers have proved their utility by history. But what is more urgently needed is greater quantities of chemical fertilizers, the production of which came to 1·33 million tons in 1959.

One Chinese agronomist[64] estimated that the need for synthetic fertilizers of various indigenous crops in China, after experiments

[63] *JMJP*, January 18, 1956, p. 1. [64] Quoted in T. H. Shen, *op.cit.*, p. 37.

made at the National Agricultural Research Bureau before the war, as follows:

NUTRIENT DEFICIENCIES OF CHINESE CROPS

(Pre-war tests in selected counties of 14 provinces)

Percentage of Localities	*Rice*	*Wheat*	*Cotton*	*Rapeseed*	*Maize*
Percentage of the localities showing nitrogen deficiency	86	71	43	84	88
Percentage of the localities showing phosphorus deficiency	50	40	18	53	38
Percentage of the localities showing potash deficiency	14	9	11	17	20

It has been estimated that, on the average, the application of one ton of chemical fertilizer would result in the increase of five tons of grain.[65] Another writer estimated in an article in *Ta-kung pao* of October 27, 1957, that the use of one catty (1·1 pound) of ammonium sulphate would help to increase the production of the various crops as follows (in catties): rice, 3·6; wheat, 2·5; cotton, 0·93; and rapeseed, 1·75.[66]

H. T. Yieh of the National Agricultural Research Bureau in pre-war Nanking estimated, on the basis of his experiments, the possible increase in crop yields through the increased use of chemical fertilizers as below:

ESTIMATED INCREASE IN CROP YIELDS*

(In one thousand metric tons)

Crop	*Ammonium sulphate*	*Calcium superphosphate*	*Potassium sulphate*	*Increase in yield*	*Percentage increase*
Rice	4,015	2,081	166	15,900	30·9
Wheat	1,437	1,044	..	5,100	22·9
Cotton	509	199	119	750	26·4
Rapeseed	440	488	17	1,250	27·6
TOTAL	6,401	3,812	382		

* Quoted in T. H. Shen, *op.cit.*, p. 38.

[65] Chang Chen, *The Chemical Industry in the First Five-Year Plan*, Peking, 1956, p. 18.

[66] Wu Chien-sheng, "The Chemical Industry of Our Nation," *Ta-kung pao*, October 27, 1957, p. 3.

Although the use of chemical fertilizers in mainland China increased from 333,000 tons in 1952 to 1·22 million tons in 1955 and about 2·8 million tons in 1958 (see Table VIII; the peak pre-war figure was 400,000 tons in 1933), the average amount of chemical fertilizer applied to each *mou* was less than three catties (in 1958) compared to 120 catties for Japan and 66 catties for England.[67] One estimate puts the total amount of chemical fertilizer required for the farms in China at 15 million tons a year.[68] In resources, China is adequately equipped to tackle the problem. With rapid expansion of electric power, nitrogen can be extracted from the air in abundant quantities. The phosphorus deposits at Kunyang county in Yunnan province alone were estimated at 37 million tons with 34–37 per cent content of P_2O_5. The amount of potassium deposits at Ping-yang, Chekiang was estimated in excess of 175 million tons.[69] What is needed is a greater allocation of capital and technicians by the planners to develop more emphatically the production of chemical fertilizers.

Chemical fertilizer, if properly applied, can achieve impressive and immediate results in crop yield. It does not require too great an investment in capital or technical skill, nor advanced technology in application or maintenance. The manufacture of more chemical fertilizers and the careful studies for their effective application deserve top priority in the development programme of China. Recent reports from China indicate that increasing attention is being paid to the increase of production of chemical fertilizers which will probably run to more than ten million tons before 1963.[70]

There are several points which deserve attention in the promotion of use of chemical fertilizers in China. First is the need for careful studies of soil and crop conditions as well as water resources in various localities so as to arrive at the maximum efficiency in the use of specific kinds of synthetic fertilizers. Second, it is desirable to have a corresponding use in the amount of organic fertilizers to balance the chemical fertilizers, such as compost heaps. Third, the utilization and exploitation of local sources of fertilizers including animal and human excreta, oil-seed cakes, soybean cakes, green manures, pond or river mud, bones and bone products, ashes, waterweeds, and earth bricks from old heated beds (North China)

[67] *Ibid.* [68] T. H. Shen, *op.cit.*, p. 38. [69] *Ibid.*, p. 37.

[70] *Hua-ch'iao jih-pao* (*China Daily News*), New York, December 18, 1957, p. 1.

are quite important at the present stage.[71] The total amount of such native fertilizers used jumped from 1,500 million tons in 1957 to several billion tons in 1958.[72] A vigorous campaign to collect more manure was initiated in early 1959.

Rural cadres and peasants in China have often shown great ingenuity in developing these native sources of manure. In the "Accumulate Fertilizer" campaign during the winter of 1955–56, 70 million rural youths participated and made 400 million tons of native fertilizers.[73] The intensive efforts to increase the number of hogs during 1955–57 aimed not only to enhance pork supply but also to accumulate more hog manure. The attention paid to the local sources of fertilizer is illustrated by the following passage in Teng Tzu-hui's report to the National Conference of Agricultural Model Workers in February 1957 :

> For increasing fertilizers, the simplest and most effective measure is to make full use of human excreta and stable manure. On the basis of a per capita landholding of three *mou* which gives a family of four 12 *mou*, we may use half a metric ton of excrements on a *mou*. This, combined with stable manure and fowl dung, decomposed grass, ashes and river mud, will add up to 2–2·5 tons per *mou*, and there is no reason why production cannot be raised with this application. APCs in the various areas should set prices on excreta of different fertilizing value and buy them with cash or in partial cash payment from their members. . . . . In the past year, while we achieved unprecedented results in the accumulation of fertilizers, we meanwhile committed the error of emphasizing quantity without proper regard to quality. We ought to benefit by this lesson this year (1957).

The manure collected from one hog in a year, according to one estimate, can fertilize two or three *mou* of farmland. The number of hogs in China increased from 120 million heads at the end of 1957 to 160 million at the end of 1958, and 180 million in December, 1959.

[71] For discussion of many of these local sources of fertilizers, see T. H. Shen, *op.cit.*, pp. 32–6.

[72] Hu Yao-pang, "Lead the Youths toward the Noble Goal," *HPYK*, No. 21, November 6, 1956, p. 111.

[73] See *Link*, New Delhi, February 1, 1959, p. 34.

Modern Farm Implements

Many of the traditional types of farm tools in rural China were crude and inefficient. Also as a result of war from 1937 to 1949, a lot of farm implements were either destroyed or needed repairs. From 1955 to 1957, over three million pieces of new-type wheel plough were distributed among the Chinese peasants. In 1958 alone about 200 million pieces of farm tools were improved (including 20 million tools for irrigation and 40 million innovated implements). Over 41 million units of farm implements were equipped with ball bearings, and in 784 counties and municipalities (out of about 2,000) all the traditional transport media were fitted with ball bearings.[74] The number of new type water sheds increased from 1·8 million in 1957 to 2·6 million in 1958. A number of innovated instruments which particularly suit the local conditions or needs have been introduced. An illustration of this is the propagation of methane lamps and methane burners which can be made easily at low costs by the villagers with local resources. It has been estimated that one cubic foot of night soil mixture will produce methane which generates one horse-power, and one ordinary wind mill can produce 4 horse-power. Together with hydraulic power, the goal is to increase by tens of millions of horse-power in rural China within a few years.[75] However, the danger of too ambitious a programme for modern farm tools is seen in the reduction of the planned goal of five million double-wheel, double-blade ploughs for 1956 to one and a half million pieces (actual number sold). This points to the need for more thorough research on the practical conditions and needs regarding farm implements in the various rural regions in China.

A programme for more modern farm tools certainly includes tractors and combines, especially with the basic completion of collectivization after 1956. The Soviet Union, for example, imported about 5,000 tractors between 1924 and 1925 alone. Within a decade, she was importing 23,000 tractors a year, in addition to 10,000 tractors produced domestically each year.[76] The total number of tractors in all China in 1959 was 55,000 (15 h.p.). It has been estimated that about 52 per cent of the current 280 million acres of cultivated land

[74] *HPYK*, No. 24, December 25, 1957, pp. 83–5.
[75] Editorial *JMJP*, November 4, 1958, p. 1.
[76] Maurice Dobb, *Soviet Economic Development since 1917*, 1948, p. 213.

in China is on the plains, thus able to utilize machinery in varying degrees[77] This does not mean, however, that these lands cultivable by machinery will soon be using tractors. On the contrary, it would be utopian to expect spectacular results in mechanizing China's agriculture for the following reasons: First, it takes time to develop a modern farm machinery industry. The first tractor factory now under construction in China, scheduled to be completed in 1959, will have an annual production capacity of 15,000 TAT-54 type tractors equivalent to 36,000 tractors of standard type with 15-horse power. 400,000 TAT-54 tractors would be needed to plough 167 million acres of cultivated land. The number of harvester combines increased from 1,157 in 1957 to 3,500 in 1958. Second, even leaving aside the question of cost of buying tractors from abroad, there still remains the question of fuel supply. On the average, 10 tons of diesel oil a year would be required for one tractor of the TAT-54 type or one million tons for 100,000 such tractors. But the total amount of crude oil produced in China in 1959 was around 3·7 million tons. Third, there are the additional problems of training the technical personnel necessary to operate and to maintain these machines.[77a]

In view of the above, the argument that full mechanization must accompany organized farming in China seems to be an impractical one. Before industrialization is advanced sufficiently to create considerable numbers of job opportunities in secondary and tertiary occupations, a heavy displacement of farm labour by machinery will drastically worsen the employment situation in the Chinese countryside. Also according to Soviet experience, when chain-type tractors are used on a farm with an area of about 5·5 acres (or 200 metres by 100 metres), the utilization rate is only 64 per cent; but when run on 250 acres (or 2,000 metres by 500 metres), the utilization rate reaches 85 per cent.[78] These considerations may have been in the mind of Liao Lu-yen when he, in a speech of January 25, 1956, envisaged the eventual use of 1·2 million to 1·5 million tractors (15-horse power) with an annual replacement rate of 10 per cent but realistically set no time limit for such a goal. The establishment of communes will facilitate the employment of more tractors with greater efficiency, partly due to the shortage

[77] Chao Hsueh, "The Problem of Agricultural Mechanization in China," *Ch'i-hua ching-chi* (Planned Economy), (*CHCC*), No. 4, April 9, 1957.

[77a] For further discussion of these issues, see Chao Hsueh, *op.cit*, and *JMJP*, September 25, 1959, p. 4. [78] Quoted in Chao Hsueh, *op.cit.*

of labour power as a result of more intensive farming as well as the promotion of multiple rural development programmes.

F. *Other Agro-Technical Programmes*

China is vigorously promoting a number of other agro-technical measures which cannot be discussed fully here. These include the adoption of better cultivating methods (like close planting and deep ploughing), extension of multiple cropping areas, the popularization of advanced and tested farm experiences, the planting of high-yielding crops like corn and potatoes, pest control, the use of improved strains of seeds, and the development of scientific and technical training as well as research in agronomy. Peking's efforts in these fields are partly reflected in the data shown in Tables III, IV and VIII. For instance, the index for double cropping acreage increased from 100 in 1952 to 108·5 in 1957. The multiple crop acreage must have been further enhanced in 1958 and 1959, although details are not available. The planted area and production for potatoes increased, respectively, 57 per cent and 122 per cent between 1949 and 1956. The use of insecticides jumped from 90,000 tons in 1955 to over 450,000 tons in 1958. The crop acreage under pest control increased from 120 million acres in 1957 to around 300 million acres in 1958. The improving of tillage system in China centers on the expansion of multiple cropping area, close planting, deep plowing, and crop rotation—in addition to many previously discussed aspects such as amalgamation of parcelled plots and mechanization of farming. Most of these improvements do not entail large capital investment but are capable of obtaining immediate benefits.

The key areas which need greater attention at the moment seem to lie in the promotion of better seeds and agro-scientific research. Improved seeds were sown on 205 million acres of crop area in 1957 and on 278 million acres in 1958. However, there is still room for improvement in the development of better crop strains, although some 2,000 good crop strains were developed between 1949 and 1959. One Western agronomist estimated that improved strains of seeds alone could raise crop yields between 15 and 30 per cent in China.[79] In popularizing good seeds, the particular conditions and needs of different localities must of course be taken into consideration.

[79] Gerald Winfield, *op. cit.*, p. 290.

An editorial of *JMJP* of April 21, 1955 reported that more than 1,300 types of better crop breeds had been gathered from the rural areas for studies. Among the 32 types of better strains for 12 major crops of China were described in a report in April 1956 as follows:

IMPROVED CROP STRAINS (1956)*

Crop type	*Name of strain*	*Yield per mou (catties)*	*Highest yield*	*Characteristics*
Rice	Nan-teh	500–600	1,000 plus	Pest and disease resistant
,,	Ying-fan (Tientsin)	700–800	1,000	Strong stalk good quality
Wheat	Pima No. 1 (NW China)	200–300	700	Pest and drought resistant
,,	Kansu No. 96 (NW & NE China)	400	850	Disease resistant strong stalk
Corn	Chin-huang-hou (N. China)	500	1,757	Big cob, longer season for planting
,,	Fan-cha No. 2 (Shantung)	400	900	Disease resistant, hybrid growth period: 95 days
Soybean	Man-chang-chin (Heilungkiang)	200–240		2 per cent more in oil content; growth period: 125 days
,,	Hsiao-chin-huang (Kirin & Liaoning)	240		Drought resistant; high oil content
Millet	Hua-nung No. 4 (N. China)	300	600	Early ripening; drought resistant; large grain
,,	No. 811 (Hopei & Shantung)	300	600	Disease resistant
Kaoliang	Hsiao-pa-ko-cha (Liaoning)	800		Disease and pest resistant; strong stalk
,,	Yang-ta-li (Liaoning)	700		Drought and "water" resistant; more grain but weak wind resistance
Potatoes	Sheng-li No. 100	3,000	10,000	Early ripening; high starch content; may be planted late

IMPROVED CROP STRAINS (1956)—(Contd.)

Crop type	*Name of strain*	*Yield per mou (catties)*	*Highest yield*	*Characteristics*
Potatoes	Nan-jui-shao (Szechuan)	2,000 plus		Good taste; less fibre; low resistance to drought
Peanut	I-wo-hou (N. China)	300	1,000	Early ripening; drought resistant; large nut
Sesame	Pa-wang-pien	120		Strong; 45 catties of oil in 100 catties
Cotton	Sze No. 1 (Yellow River Region)			Fibre length 30 mm or more; high yield
,,	Tai No. 15 (Yangtze Region)	85		Fibre length 31 mm; pest resistant
Jute & Kenaf	Pai-lien-chih (Chekiang)			Disease resistant; high yield
,,	Hsin-hsien No. 1 (Kwangtung)	500		Disease resistant; high stalk
Sugarcane	Tai-t'ang No. 134 (S. China)			15 per cent sugar content; drought and pest resistant
Sugar beet	Yu-yi (NE China; from Poland)	5,000		20 per cent sugar content; drought and disease resistant
Tobacco	Yun-nan	500	800	Height: 300–400 cm; 120-150 leaves per plant; good quality

* Ch'un Li, "Good Strains of the Major Crops in Our Nation," *JMJP*, April 7, 1956, p. 2.

A new early-ripening, drought-resistant rice strain was introduced in 1958 by a Kwangsi peasant Chiang Shao-fang who succeeded in grafting rice scion on maize—after 62 failures.[80] The now famous "cotton mother" Chang Chiu-hsiang, by employing improved methods such as letting the cotton spouts grow closely together

[80] *China Today*, December 13, 1958, p. 13.

(30,000 to an acre) and allowing the cotton plant reach a greater height, she achieved an average yield of three tons of seed cotton per acre each year between 1955 and 1957. In 1958, this first peasant woman member of the National Institute of Agronomy, succeeded in yielding some 6 tons of seed cotton in a plot less than three-quarters of an acre. Throughout China, a movement to emulate Chang Chiu-hsiang swept the cotton-planting areas and in Shensi province alone there were 33,000 "Chiu-hsiang cotton growing teams" in 1958.[81] A description of the new, improved strains developed by hundreds of peasants in China in 1958 appears in the *Wen-hui pao* (Chinese daily in Hongkong) of November 27, 1958.

The selection of improved strains of seeds represents only the first step. To achieve higher yields on an extensive scale, careful studies must be done to ascertain which breeds suit what special localities and adequate amount of improved seeds must be supplied in time to the cultivators. The propagation of good breeds of crops can result in noticeable increase in production, without requiring too much capital investment. Like chemical fertilizers, it deserves top attention in the agricultural programmes in China. The introduction of better strains of crops also helps the pest control programme. Good results have been reported regarding Peking's effort to cope with locusts, cotton borers, rice blight, and wheat rusts.

One factor basic to all agro-technical improvements is scientific training and research. According to a report by Ting Ying, President of the Academy of Agricultural Science in Peking, made at the founding day of the academy on March 1, 1957, good progress had been achieved in the following fields of research: the control of locusts, the breeding of one improved strain of rice and another of wheat, which give a 10 to 20 per cent higher yield, prevention of damage by cotton borers, treatment of certain live-stock diseases, the manufacture of fertilizer from peanut or soybean nodules, and the planting of fruit trees on hilly lands.[82] But such research takes time to produce effects, and at the present, research in agro-science still seems to lag behind actual needs. The need for outstanding achievement in fundamental agro-technical studies was indicated by the fact that, out of 34 scientific awards granted by the Academia Sinica at Peking in 1956, only one was made in the field of agricultural science, and that one was a third-class

[81] *China Today*, January 24, 1959, pp. 13-15.
[82] *HCJP*, March 20, 1957, p. 3.

award given to a veterinarian for his work on a cattle disease.[83] In the past few years, there seemed to be a tendency on the part of many administrative leaders in China to emphasize agro-technical research projects which would yield quick results. Recent reports from China, however, indicate that there has been an increasing awareness of the importance of fundamental research in agro-science. In early 1957, in Szechuan province alone, more than one million peasant agro-technicians joined production work.[84]

Since 1957, a vast network of agro-technical institutes, research centres, training classes, and local agro-technical centres has been set up. Some findings of these efforts have already helped considerably agricultural development, particularly in the increase of yield per hectare. For example, it has been found that when the land is ploughed to a depth of 50 to 100 centimetres, the crops root system penetrates downwards and grows better, giving higher yields. A rice field in the Hsienfeng (Pioneer) People's Commune in Tientsin (Hopei province) area was ploughed to a depth of 150 centimetres and the rice plants roots penetrated to a depth of 166 centimetres. In two communes in Sip'ing County, Honan, two wheat fields which yielded a record harvest in 1958 were ploughed to 66 centimetres' depth and the fibrous roots of the wheat plants continued to grow well at a depth of 20 to 50 centimetres, penetrating as far as 100 to 200 centimetres. The combined use of large quantities of organic compost with proper proportion of chemical fertilizer has resulted in bumper harvests. In some rice plots, where the number of rice clusters reached even over 600,000 per acre and wheat ears 8 million per acre, the plants grew well and crops did not lodge. By planting the crops at slightly inclined degree in opposite directions at parallel rows and other improvements, a rate of 20 per cent or more photoenergy absorption has been achieved, compared to the usual rate of utilizing below 5 per cent of the sunlight that reaches the ground.[85]

The eight major tasks in the 1957 agricultural research plan, according to Yang Hsien-tung, Deputy Minister of Agriculture, were as follows:

[83] For details on the awards, see *HCJP*, February 14, 1957, p. 3.

[84] *JMJP*, April 7, 1957.

[85] See Hsiung Yi and others, "Scientific Importance of China's High-Yield Crops," *JMJP*, January 14, 1959, p. 1.

(1) To raise the annual yield per unit-area, emphasizing research on the (indistinct word), rotation, and fertilizing systems, research into the major problems of existing planting techniques, the prevention and control of major pests and diseases, and the selection of excellent strains. Special emphasis is laid on research into the solution of the problems of planting, and selection of strains for the double-cropping rice area. This is the most important task among the eight, and the largest portion of energy and resources must be devoted to it. The items selected for research for this task account for almost one-half of the total items in the plan.

(2) Wasteland reclamation, emphasizing research into the use of wasteland and the improvement of its soil, particularly the improvement and utilization of the red soil in the South.

(3) To make co-ordinated research into the estimation and exploitation of the resources in the sub-tropical regions, particular emphasis to be placed on research in rubber planting.

(4) To use atomic energy, starting with tracer atoms, for studying the nutritional problems of animals and plants.

(5) To study the improvement of old-type farm tools, the design of agricultural machinery, and the machine for transplanting water paddy.

(6) To raise the output and quality of animal husbandry, aquatic products and silkworms, emphasizing an increase in the output of feed, improving nutrition, and better care. The improvement of strains and the prevention and control of major diseases should receive attention, with particular emphasis on research in the development of hog raising.

(7) To study the division of economic areas.

(8) To study agricultural meteorology.[86]

Yang also remarked that "research in agricultural sciences must include the characteristics of regionality, rationality, complexity, and high precision. It is impossible to achieve marked results in a year. By this plan, however, the foundation can be laid for the future planning of the unified study of agricultural sciences."

The almost unlimited frontiers of agro-scientific researches may be seen in a California Institute of Technology's report on the world's food situation, issued in May 1956. The possibilities of producing entirely new edible crops or making synthesized foods or

[86] *NCNA*, June 20, 1957.

drastically reducing the production time and cost of certain food crops are becoming greater every day,[87] and successful exploits in these fields will open up unheard-of horizons in the world's food supply in particular and in rural economic development in general. The total number of scientific research personnel (including teachers) in the field of agro-technology was estimated as 11,000 in early 1957, of whom 1,340 were senior researchers.[88] The number of personnel available for agro-technical work in the rural areas has been greatly increased after the arrival of several millions of students and government functionaries in the villages after the autumn of 1957, and since the "big leap" in 1958. Equally important is the fact that valuable farming techniques of outstanding peasants are effectively utilized, and their experiences popularized throughout the nation where cultivating conditions fit.

G. *Programmes on Rural Finance and Market Control*

Agricultural Tax

The welfare of the peasants and the rate of capital formation in China today are both closely related to the amount of tax (primarily in the form of tax in kind) levied on the peasants. There are also historical and psychological reasons for the great importance assigned to the agricultural tax by many Peking leaders. During the eight years of the Sino-Japanese War (July 1937–August 1945), the agricultural tax (called *kung-liang*, or public grain) yielded around 80 per cent of the total revenue in the area of the Border Region (CCP-controlled) Government,[89] and success or failure in the collection of public grain often meant literally life or death to the guerrilla forces. Although the agricultural tax decreased from about 30 per cent of China's national budget in 1950 to some 8 per cent in 1958 and 7·4 per cent in 1959,[89a] it still is of great

[87] On this fascinating report by Dr. James F. Bonner of the California Institute of Technology, see *New York Times*, May 21, 1956, p. 19.

[88] BBC, "Summary of World Broadcasts," Part V, *Economic Supplement*, No. 247, January 3, 1957, p. 3.

[89] Li Ch'eng-jui, "Agricultural Tax System and the Peasants' Burden in Several People's Revolutionary Bases during the Anti-Japanese War," *CCYC*, No. 2, April 17, 1956, p. 101.

[89a] Li Hsien-nien, "Achievement of China's Finance in the Past Decade," *The Glorious Decade*, Vol. I, p. 350.

importance in government finance. There is also the possibility that the state purchasing prices of certain agricultural crops as taxes are set at a lower level than market prices, thus resulting in an under-valuation of the real weight of the agricultural tax in the nation's budgetary receipts. In monetary terms, the agricultural tax yields increased from an estimated 1·89 billion *yuan* in 1950 to 3·26 billion *yuan* (out of a total national budget receipts of 41·86 billion *yuan*) in 1958. (See Table VII.)

The two directives on agricultural tax work issued by the GAC on June 16, 1952 and on June 5, 1953, contained many of the basic provisions of the agricultural tax system prevailing in China up to 1958 and represented Peking's effort to unify the tax practices which had developed in a piecemeal fashion in the various liberated areas. The consolidation of power by the new government and the land reform programme gradually changed conditions over the whole country. Between 1950 and 1954 a number of directives on agricultural taxation were issued by the GAC in an intensified effort to secure as much uniformity as possible. About four years later, the *Regulations on Agricultural Tax* of the People's Republic of China was passed by the People's Congress on June 3, 1958, which replaced all the previous promulgations. The salient provisions in the new Regulations are as follows: First, the agricultural tax is collected on a proportional basis, with the average rate of tax for the nation fixed at 15·5 per cent and the maximum rate at 25 per cent. The higher rates are primarily applicable to economic crops and gardening yields. Second, agricultural surtaxes are limited to a maximum of 15 per cent of the regular tax, as compared to 22 per cent announced in 1956. Third, tax is leviable on four general categories of agricultural products: (1) foodgrain crops including potatoes; (2) economic crops; (3) income from gardening; and (4) other agricultural income ruled as taxable by the State Council. Fourth, the basis for calculating the taxable income is based on "normal yield," a term which will be discussed later on. Fifth, the agricultural tax is paid by the APC as the tax-paying unit. Individual farmers, who are not indigent, must pay an additional levy of 10 to 50 per cent of the amount of tax paid by the local co-operativized farmers. Peking leaders explain this additional tax for individual peasants partly on the basis that they do not have to make payment to the welfare fund of a co-operative, which benefits the entire village, but this provision is obviously also designed to encourage co-operative farming. Sixth, income from certain lands such as newly reclaimed land, newly developed orchards, experimental plots for agro-technical purposes, and tiny planted spots in between houses, is exempted from agricultural tax for the first 3 to 5 years. Seventh, income from certain lands such as poor hilly districts and backward areas where national minorities dwell, may be exempted from a part of the agricultural tax. Eighth, the "normal yield," once determined, will not be raised if the production is increased as a result of improved farming methods or agro-technical programmes for 5 years; nor will the "norm" be lowered if the production per unit of land is decreased due to wilful negligence of the cultivator concerned. Ninth, the agricultural tax may be collected either in two seasons, summer and autumn, or once in autumn only if the summer crop yields in the area in question are meagre. Tenth, agricultural tax is collected principally in the form of foodgrains (converted in term of the principal crop of the area); in case of difficulties, the tax-payer may submit other crops or cash as tax payment. Eleventh, tax grain (tax in kind) is to be delivered by the tax-paying co-operative (now the commune) to the tax agency without compensation if the round trip for delivering the agricultural tax will not take more than one day. When the journey for tax delivery takes more than one day (including returning time), suitable travelling expenses are offered. Twelfth, if any error or unjust assessment in agricultural tax collection is discovered, the tax-paying party may appeal to the *hsiang* and higher authorities for re-evaluation. Evasion of tax is punishable by levying of payment for the under-paid amount, or by court actions in the case of serious offences.[90]

The most important aspect of these new regulations on agricultural tax of June 1958 is of course the adoption of a nation-wide basis of the proportional tax system which had prevailed in North-east China. Although an agricultural tax system based on progressive scales is more egalitarian in nature, the decision of Peking to popularize a proportional tax for agriculture seems to be based on the following considerations: one, the basic completion of farm collectivization in early 1958 and the subsequent communization have prevented the income of peasant households within a locality from becoming too unequal and the danger of polarization of rural households in economic status is greatly reduced; two, a

[90] Chinese text of the *Regulations on Agricultural Tax of China* appears in *JMJP*, June 5, 1958, p. 2.

proportional tax system is much simpler in structure and easier to understand by the peasants; three, the proportional tax system is cheaper to administer; and the new system encourages agricultural production as the peasants can retain more than under a progressive scale when production is increased. It is difficult to ascertain at the present time to what degree the actual amount of agricultural tax has been increased for the agricultural sector as now no tax exemption base is retained for areas where the "progressive" agricultural tax system used to prevail between 1949 and 1957. Anyway, the specific amount of agricultural tax to be paid by the Chinese farmers is decided, in an overall manner, by the Peking planners each year. The planned figures for 1958 for the regular agricultural tax (in kind) and the agricultural surtax have been estimated as, respectively, 18·1 million and 2·5 million tons. This total of 20·6 million tons is said to represent a 4·6 per cent increase over the amount of agricultural taxes collected in the year 1957. The total "normal yield" of foodgrains in China in 1957 was fixed at 110 million tons, in terms of "fine grain." This represents 69 per cent of the actual production of foodgrains in the same year (1957), which was 174·05 million tons in terms of "fine grain."[91] These figures also indicate that when unprocessed grains (185 million tons of which were produced in 1957) were converted into "fine grains" which are the unit of calculating agricultural tax in kind, a "loss" of 6 per cent takes place. The "depreciation" rate for such conversion prior to the promulgation of these new tax regulations was usually around 10 per cent.

Another important provision in the agricultural tax system may be seen from a directive entitled "Methods of Calculating Agricultural Tax in the Northwest" issued in 1952.[92] This directive shows that agricultural tax in China is leviable on the entire proceeds of income-yielding land (e.g., farms for both food and industrial crops, fish ponds, woods, orchard, vegetable gardens, mulberry fields, bamboo groves), with the exception of a few minor items like stalks and fodder. Income from food crops is estimated as constituting a little less than two-thirds of such proceeds. The agricultural tax is

[91] Wu Po, "Explanations on the Agricultural Tax of China," *JMJP*, June 5, 1958, pp. 2–3.

[92] See *Nung-yeh shui-so cheng-ts'e wen-chien chi* (Compendium of Documents on Agricultural Tax Policies), Sian, 1952, pp. 93–102.

not leviable on income from non-agricultural subsidiary occupations, nor from livestock-raising.

When the agricultural tax is collected in the form of public grain, it is generally calculated in terms of the principal crop of the region, such as rice in areas south of the Yangtze River, millet in North China, *kaoliang* in the Northeast, and wheat in Northwest China. Sometimes the tax is paid in cash or in other agricultural products. So far, however, the bulk of the agricultural tax has been paid in the form of foodgrains (estimated at about 85 per cent of the total agricultural tax in 1955) and cotton (8 per cent in 1955). This has enabled the state to use the grain to control the market and stabilize food prices. Now the supply of foodgrains has become sufficient and when the transportation network is completed, an increased proportion of cash payment for agricultural tax may offer greater advantages to both the peasants and the government.

There are a few important provisions of the agricultural tax system that are not clearly spelled out. For example, the *1956 Agricultural Tax Regulations of Kwangtung Province* and *Provisional Regulations on Agricultural Tax in Newly Liberated Areas* of September 5, 1950 (Article 6)[93] stipulate that the agricultural tax in China is based as a rule not on the actual farm yield, but on the "normal annual yield," which is jointly determined, according to legal provisions, by the tax agent, the local villagers' representative body, and the tiller of the land. The "normal annual yield" is worked out according to the natural conditions of cultivation—with reference to the quality of the soil, weather, irrigation, manpower, animal power, number of harvests, and so forth—for a normal season of the land in question in a particular locality. According to the same regulations, if income in excess of the normal annual yield is obtained through more intensive cultivation, or other improvements, no extra tax will be levied. Tax reduction will be made if a loss of yield comes from natural calamities, but not if the harvest falls short of the normal annual yield as a result of the tiller's negligence or laxity.

The above provisions are designed to stimulate the cultivators to produce more than the "normal yield," but at the same time they seem to constitute a possible source of confusion, as the "normal yield" of a particular plot of land must be fixed by applying and interpreting the regulations. According to Chinese sources, the

[93] Text in *CYTC*, vol. II, pp. 301–11.

estimated normal yield is lower than that of the actual production. It is true that such estimates of yield are made only after discussions with local people, and a peasant is entitled to appeal to the district and *hsien* people's government if he is dissatisfied with a decision as to the amount of tax he should pay. But inaccurate evaluations do occur, and adjustments, when made, take time. Peking may be hoping that when the collectivization (and now communization) programme is consolidated throughout the nation, the problem of accurately ascertaining the size of a farm holding and of its normal yield will be effectively resolved. Since upon joining the collective or cooperative farm (now the commune), the land of the farmer is counted as his share in the common funds, the tendency of the farmer to under-report his farm yield or acreage is counteracted. Furthermore, under a jointly managed system of farming, the agricultural tax is generally paid collectively, and the opportunities for under-valuing the yield or concealing the true size of the plot are greatly reduced.

Another text of government directive on agricultural tax in China available at Harvard University is the *Enforcement Regulations for 1956 Agricultural Tax Levy in Kwangtung Province* promulgated on June 13, 1956.[94] Although these regulations are meant to be applied only in Kwangtung, they could not be too far apart from the rules laid down by the Central Government. This document is interesting because it provides procedural regulations on the collection of agricultural tax.

The directive instructs that the amount of tax levied on normal yield, should be in general maintained at the 1955 level (Article 7). This is consistent with Peking's announcement in 1955 that agricultural tax, on the main, would be the same as 1955 for the following three years. Thus, the increased portion of crop yield is free from tax. The APCs (now the communes) are asked to pay collectively the amount of tax paid by the cooperative members in 1955. Agricultural tax on the plot reserved for individual use (not to exceed 10 per cent of the APC landholdings) is borne by the respective members, but paid by the cooperatives in a unified manner (Article 6). The tax rates on different types of farms are stipulated as follows: State and public farms, 10 per cent of actual annual yield; Private farms and joint state-private farms capitalized by

[94] Chinese text appears in *Nan-fang jih-paa* (South China Daily), June 22, 1956, p. 1.

overseas Chinese, 12 per cent; Other private farms, 15 per cent; and on lands which are planted with bamboo, fruit trees, tea trees, and medicinal herbs, 8–13 per cent of normal income and the detailed rates are to be fixed by the *hsien* people's council (Articles 9 and 14). These provisions are designed to stimulate more investment of overseas Chinese and the planting of industrial crops. The following types of land are tax exempt: (*a*) Farms, groves, and plant nurseries for experimental purposes; (*b*) Groves owned by railways and highways for the purpose of afforestation; (*c*) Land on which trees are planted as protection belt; (*d*) Land cultivated by schools, orphanages, old-folks homes, hospitals, and labour reform farms; (*e*) Vegetables plots managed by members of government organs or servicemen for their own consumption; (*f*) Land near bridges and public ferries tilled for public welfare; (*g*) Urban or suburban land on which real-estate tax has been levied; (*h*) Land for dwelling purposes, graves, and wasteland (but no tax exemption is granted to land left in furrow due to the negligence of the owner); and (*i*) Land classified as tax exempt by the Provincial People's Congress. Certain types of land are made tax free for a specific period of time. For example, reclaimed new wasteland remains tax exempt for 3 to 5 years and reclaimed old wasteland (once cultivated, but not in the recent 3 to 5 years), one to 3 years. Reclaimed barren hills and wasteland for the cultivation of industrial and privately developed native crops are exempt from agricultural tax from 3 to 5 years (Articles 3 and 4). Additional income from newly irrigated land is tax exempt for 5 years. These provisions are obviously designed to encourage irrigation project, the reclamation of wasteland and the development of barren hills for industrial crops.

On the procedure of collecting agricultural tax, the Regulations contain the following provisions:

(1) The acreage of land, the estimation of tax income, land rental and the tax reduction or exemption of the APCs and the individual peasant households, are investigated, discussed, and registered by the *hsiang* people's committee, which reports the findings to the *hsien* people's council for examination. The *hsien* (or municipal) people's council calculates the tax amounts of various APCs and households, makes tax collection books, and issues circulars to the cooperatives and households for collection.

Farms are required to report to the *hsien* (or municipal) people's council within 10 days after reaping crop types in summer and autumn respectively, the acreage of land and the actual yields. The *hsien* people's council after carrying out examination, issues tax circulars for collection.

(2) Agricultural tax is calculated on a yearly basis and collected in summer and autumn. The percentage of the collection is based on the proportion occupied by the summer and autumn production figures in the annual production. This is stipulated by the *hsien* (or municipal) people's council and reported to the provincial people's council for approval. But tax is collected only in autumn in those areas where summer harvest was particularly poor.

(3) The agricultural tax collection takes the form of unprocessed rice in the locality, but in areas of industrial crops and the areas which do not produce rice, cash may be paid in lieu of the unprocessed rice, and the amount of the cash is fixed by the *hsien* (or municipal) people's council in accordance with the price of the rice in the locality concerned, and reported to the province for record.

(4) After the harvest of the crops, the APCs and farms and individual peasant households can, in accordance with the stipulations of the tax collection circular, deliver their grain or cash to the *hsiang* organization, which will in turn deliver to the designated granaries or banks according to schedule, and receive official receipts from the *hsien* (or municipal) tax collection organs. The grain to be delivered by the tax payers must be properly dried and cleared of foreign substances.

(5) If the tax payers regard the investigation as inaccurate, the decision as unfair and the calculation wrong, they may ask the *hsiang* people's committee for reconsideration and re-check, and should they be still not satisfied with the decisions, they may appeal to the *hsien* people's council for action. The *hsiang* people's committee and *hsien* people's council must conduct investigation immediately and the *hsien* people's council is required to pass judgment "in accordance with law."

(6) In case of flood, drought, and other natural calamities, or illness suffered by a member of the APC or individual peasant, partial or full exemption on agricultural tax is granted. (The scale of exemption for natural disasters may be found in a later section discussing the effect of flood and drought on China's agriculture.)

A survey of 26,935 APCs in early 1956 showed that agricultural tax (paid in grain in 1955) constituted, on the average, 12·8 per cent of the total grain production. The quantity of grain sold to the State was about 19·3 per cent of the total amount produced.[95] According to the *Report of the Indian Delegation to China*,[96] "as a rule, 60 per cent of the collection (of agricultural tax) is taken into the national budget, and 40 per cent is left to the provinces." The average amount of tax paid by the communes in 1958 came to around 10 per cent of the gross income of the communes and in 1959, about 8·6 per cent.[96a]

One Chinese source gave the average percentage of total agricultural tax (including surtaxes) to the actual output of agriculture (including food and industrial crops) for the past few years as follows: 1950, 12·29; 1951, 14·5; 1952, 13·2; 1953, 11·98; 1954, 12·47; 1955, 11·67; 1956, 10·17; 1957, 11; and 1958 (preliminary) 10.[97] Another mainland Chinese source made a comparison of the tax burdens of the peasants between the years 1952 and 1956 as follows:[98] (The total value of agricultural production for 1957 was estimated at 53·7 billion *yuan*; and that of 1958, around 67·1 billion *yuan*. Total peasants' income in 1957 was about 37·57 billion *yuan*.[99]) (See table on p. 205.)

In estimating the actual tax burden, we must also evaluate qualitatively a host of other issues. These may include: the relative price levels of daily necessity manufactured goods (the "scissors' differentials"); the quality of the tax administration, its actual procedures, local deviations and characteristics; additional burdens on the peasants in the form of contributions, such as those made during

[95] Li Hsien-nien, *Report on the Budget for 1956 and 1957*, June 29, 1957; 50 million *yuan* were later deducted from the original estimates of 2·99 billion *yuan* as estimated agricultural tax receipts in 1957.

[96] Ishikawa Shigeru, "The Burden of Agricultural Sector in the Socialist Accumulation of China," *Keizai Kenkyü* (Economic Research), 8·1, January 1957, p. 74.

[96a] *JMJP*, September 28, 1959, p. 2.

[97] Li Hsien-nien, *Report on the 1957 and 1958 National Budgets*, February 1, 1958, and other sources.

[98] Li Shu-teh, "Peasants' Burdens in 1956: Conditions and Problems," *Ts'ai cheng* (Finance), No. 8, August 1957; Chou En-lai, Report on the 1959 Economic Plan, August 26, 1959, and *Peking Review*, September 1, 1959, pp. 11–19.

[99] *People's Handbook*, 1958, p. 22; and Li Hsien-nien's report, February 1, 1958.

INCOME AND TAX OF CHINESE PEASANTS, 1952 AND 1956

	1952	*1956*	*Percentage change (1952=100)*
1. Net value of agricultural and subsidiary products (billion *yuan*)	32·276	38·416	119·0
2. Total of the peasants' tax burdens (billion *yuan*)	3·38	3·266	96·6
3. Percentage of peasants' tax burdens in net value of production	10·5	8·5	..
4. Total of the peasants' income (billion *yuan*)	28·896	34·86	120·6
5. Agricultural population (million persons)	491·91	532·20	108·2
6. Average per capita income (*yuan*)	58·7	65·5	11·6

Original Note:
The net value of agricultural and subsidiary production does not include the proceeds of self-supporting handicraft industry and primary processing industry for agricultural produce. The public reserve fund for the expansion of production totalling 290 million *yuan* in 1956 is not included in the peasants' income.

the Korean war, and the sale of bonds (138 million *yuan* worth of bonds were reportedly sold to the peasants in 1956)[100] or payment for items the sale of which is pressed by the government at various times; the pricing policy of the state for major crops, the purpose for which the collected tax (both in kind and in cash) is used; and other non-economic factors. The "scissors' differentials," according to Peking Statistical Bureau tabulations, decreased by 22 per cent from 1953 and 1959. It is calculated that between 1952 and 1957, as a result of the adjustments in scissors' differentials, the peasants were benefited by more than 17·87 billion *yuan.*[101]

A number of other important economic policies are being promoted by and coordinated with the agricultural tax policy. For instance, the latter is used in combination with price policy as a tool to adjust the ratio between food crops and industrial crops. When the cotton growers were granted preferential tax rates in 1950 and

[100] Ma Yin-ch'u, *New Approach to China's Population Problem,* July 3, 1957.

[101] Chang Ho-jan, "Are the Burdens of the Peasants Too Heavy?" *HH,* No. 16, August 18, 1957, p. 16 and *JMJP*, September 26, 1959, p. 5.

1951, acreage for cotton greatly expanded at the expense of food crops. The official price ratio between rice and ginned cotton (in catties), for example, was changed from 9·5:1 in 1951 to 6·75:1 in 1953, 7·25–8·25:1 in 1954, and 8·44:1 (Honan) in 1955.[102]

Even a well-legislated tax system may become abusive if it is administered defectively. In this respect, both the efficiency and honesty of the tax administration have greatly improved in comparison with the pre-1949 era. As one Western scholar pointed out, "the tax now collected goes to the national or local treasuries and is not embezzled in part or at all by the tax collectors" (as it often was during the Kuomintang period).[103] The types and procedures of taxation prevailing in rural China today, however, could perhaps be made simpler and defined more clearly.[104]

In addition to the agricultural tax levied directly on the income-yielding farmlands, there are other taxes which are directly or indirectly payable by the peasant households. For example, non-agricultural tax is levied on peasants (now the communes) who build houses or deal in side occupations.[105] In January 1957 the Ministry of Finance promulgated the *Provisional Regulations on Industrial-Commercial Tax in Rural Areas*, drawn up "to meet the new situation arising from the economic development and changes following the upsurge of agricultural cooperativization and to encourage the growth of multiple agricultural economy." Under these *Provisional Regulations*, all agricultural, forestry, fishery and pastoral products utilized by APCs were exempt from commodity-circulation or business tax. Handicrafts shops or service units like restaurants, barber shops, inns and sewing sections attached to APCs were free from income tax and all their vouchers, account books and contracts were exempted from stamp tax. But business income or profits made by service units attached to APCs would be subject to a 3 per cent business tax, payable each month.[106] The amount of indirect levies, as a major source of capital accumulation through involuntary savings in China, was also considerable. One Japanese

[102] *JMJP*, March 4, 1954. Also see Government of India, *Report of the Indian Delegation to China, op. cit.*, p. 76. A pre-war source gave the ratio between the wholesale price of rice and cotton in Shanghai in 1933 as 8 : 1.

[103] Charles P. Fitzgerald, *Revolution in China*, 1952, pp. 177–8.

[104] See Sung Chih-ho, "Adapt to New Conditions and Reform the Tax System in Rural Areas," *HPYK*, No. 21, November 6, 1956, pp. 72–3.

[105] See Kao Chang-jen, "Tax Work in the Rural Areas Should Be Improved," *JMJP*, November 24, 1956, p. 3. [106] *NCNA*, January 19, 1957.

economist estimated in 1957 that the total burden of the agricultural sector (including direct agricultural levies, bond sales, and indirect tax burdens) in the annual budgetary income of China as follows: 1950, 51 per cent; 1951, 44 per cent; 1952, 37 per cent; 1953, 41 per cent; 1954, 40 per cent; and 1955, 41 per cent.[107]

According to a decision of the State Council dated June 6, 1958, the average rates of agriculture tax vary from 13 per cent in the Sinkiang Autonomous Region to 19 per cent in Heilungkiang province. Most other provinces fall between the range of 15 to 16 per cent. The people's communes now assume the responsibility of paying taxes on a collective basis. The proportion of all these taxes in the gross income of communes in the Shensi province was estimated as between 8 and 14 per cent in 1959.[108]

A Chinese author wrote in August 1957 that in the coming few years the total amount of foodgrains to be collected (as tax) and purchased each year would be stabilized at 80 billion-plus *chin* (around 42·5 million tons). The amount came to 55·65 million tons in 1958-59.[109] Since the quantity of grains the Chinese peasants have to surrender to the government is unlikely to decrease while the population increases at the rate of 2·2 per cent per annum, whether the consumption of grain in China may be enhanced will depend greatly on the increase of agricultural production. In this connection the tremendous increase in agricultural yields as well as the expansion of subsidiary occupations during 1958–59 greatly lightened the relative tax weight of the peasants.

The burden of tax on the Chinese peasants cannot, naturally, be isolated from other related factors such as the amount of rural credit extended to the peasant households each year. These factors will be brought up in subsequent sections.

Rural Credit

The development of rural credit cooperatives in China in the past 10 years is indicated in Table VII. The total number of credit co-operatives in China reportedly expanded from about 7,000 in June

[107] Ishikawa Shigeru "The Burden of the Agricultural Sector in the Socialist Accumulation of China," *Keizai Kenkyü* (Economic Research) 8·1, January 1957, p. 74.

[108] *Compendium of Law of the PRC,* Vol. 7, 1958, p. 263, and *Ta-kung pao,* February 19, 1959, p. 2. [109] Ishikawa, *op. cit.* and *JMJP,* October 25, 1959, p. 6.

1953 to 120,000 in 1957. After 1958, there is a credit department in each of the 24,000 people's communes. The annual amount of credit extended to the peasants increased from US $85 million in 1950 to approximately 1·6 billion in 1958 and to about 2 billion in 1959.[110] More than 77 per cent of the total peasant households by early 1956 had joined credit cooperatives. Over 200 million *yuan* were paid up as share capital; the balance of deposits reached 500 million *yuan*, and loans extended amounted to 900 million *yuan* in these credit cooperatives. In 1957, there were 30,000 branch bank offices, plus 350,000 "savings assistants." The total savings deposited exceeded 2·8 billion *yuan*.[111] Deposits in credit cooperatives increased by 10 billion *yuan* between January 1958 and June 1959.[112] Interest rates on these loans were reduced several times in recent years. Reductions on monthly interest charges were made in October 1955 from between 1 and 2·4 per cent to between 0·4 and 0·9 per cent, with preferential treatment accorded to long-range agro-technical projects. The interest rates were again lowered on March 1, 1956. The interest rate on loans to poor peasants for investments in cooperatives remained unchanged at 4 per mille per mensem, and on loans to APCs and resettlement and reclamation projects the rate also remained unchanged at 4·8 per mille per mensem. Loans to individual peasants and individual members of APCs (including individual handicraftsmen) had their interest rate reduced to 7·2 per mille per mensem.

Interest rate on loans to credit cooperatives and on deposits made by credit cooperatives with the Bank was reduced in 1956 from 9 per mille to 5·1 per mille per mensem. Credit cooperatives with insufficient capital could also arrange for long-term loans from the Bank at a rate of interest reduced from 7·5 per mille to 4 per mille per mensem. Simultaneous with the reduction of interest rates for agricultural loans, the Agricultural Bank of China also directed rural credit cooperatives to reduce the rates of interests for loans and deposits as follows: 2·4 per mille per mensem for current savings deposits; 6·6 per mille per mensem for fixed savings deposits; and 7·2 per mille per mensem for loans issued by the cooperatives.[113]

[110] *TKP*, Peking, January 1, 1959, p. 2 and *JMJP*, September 26, 1959.

[111] Li Shao-yü, "Rural Banking Business since the Autumn of 1955 and the Future Tasks," report delivered at the National Conference of Outstanding Rural Bank Workers, *Chung-kuo chin-jung* (China Finance), No. 15, July 8, 1956.

[112] Tsao Chu-ju, "Money and Banking in New China," *China Today*, January 16, 1960, p. 12. [113] See *NCNA* bulletin, February 29, 1956.

At the end of 1958, the rates on industrial, agricultural and commercial loans were unified—all at 6 per mille per mensem. The interest rates for deposits were also adjusted as follows: current deposits, 1·8 per mille per mensem, fixed deposits of 6 months, 3 per mille; and fixed deposits of one year, 4 per mille.[114]

One Chinese writer summarizes the tasks of credit cooperatives in China as follows: The rural credit cooperative is, on the one hand, an organization which works from top to bottom, as an aid supplementing any inadequacies of the state banks, and as a bridge between and an assistant to state banks and farmers. Through business contracts, the rural credit cooperative will be consigned various bank operations (such as loans, savings, insurance), enabling the work of state banks to reach the broad masses. In addition, the cooperatives will educate and organize peasants in accordance with the state's banking policies. They will correct and prevent the peasants' tendency toward simplistic "economism" and the self-generation of agricultural capitalism; they will counteract the attitude of attaching too much importance to commodities and not enough to currency, or of hoarding goods in order to get a better price. On the other hand, the credit cooperative is a credit organization of the masses, working from bottom to top. The cooperatives are organized by the peasant masses themselves for mutual help and mutual benefit. They act as a coordinating agent for credit in kind. By transforming commodities into cash, the cooperatives can help the peasants in their problem of working capital, reduce the volume of bank personnel and funds, and centralize the scattered personal credits in rural areas, thus facilitating the linking of operations with state banks. At the same time, the credit cooperatives can educate peasants in a practical manner, and help them to realize that organization is better than being scattered, and that cooperative farming is better than individual farming. By these steps the credit cooperatives facilitate the cooperativization and collectivization of agricultural production and processing.[115]

[114] State Council Directive, *HPYK*, No. 1, January 10, 1959, p. 65.

[115] Chang Yuan-yuan, "Development of the Rural Credit Cooperatives Is Urgently Needed," *CCCP*, No. 8, February 28, 1952, pp. 149–51. For a discussion on the tasks and problems of rural banks, see Li Shao-yu, "Rural Banking Business since the Autumn of 1955 and the Future Tasks," *Chung-kuo chin-jung* (China Finance), No. 15, July 8, 1956.

The relationship between the credit cooperatives and the APCs is explained in an editorial of the *JMJP* of November 23, 1954. It emphasizes that

> the credit cooperative constitutes an important part in the cooperativization of rural areas. It coordinates with, but works independently of, the APC and the supply and marketing cooperative in a common effort to develop the socialist economy and gradually restrict the capitalist sector in rural areas until it is eliminated. The APC serves as the fundamental link in the cooperative movement, through which it is planned to gradually transform the system of individual ownership into that of collective ownership by the peasantry, to divert agriculture from the backward way of small-peasant production into the advanced method of collective production, and to gradually uproot from rural areas the economic foundation upon which depend hired-labour exploitation and the growth of capitalism. The supply and marketing cooperative and the credit cooperative perform their function by promoting and developing agricultural production and cooperativization through organization and control of the rural market and through regulation of rural finance and by tapping the financial resources of rural areas, until the commercial speculations and the usury of capitalism are gradually restricted and completely wiped out. The APC, the supply and marketing cooperative, and the credit cooperative are interrelated and none of them can be dispensed with.

Since 1950 the credit cooperatives in China have had a rapid development and shown many improvements in their business operations—like the lowering of interest rates on loans and the increasing cash loan extended to the peasant households instead of credit in kind. As a result, usurious activities in many rural areas have been arrested. For example according to investigations conducted by the People's Bank of China in 1955 among 159 *hsiang* and administrative *ts'un* in 7 provinces, the number of peasant households which had to contract loans at exorbitant rates was reduced from 2,570 in 1953 to 80 in 1954 after the extensive setting up of credit cooperatives. According to survey made in 57 *hsiang* in the provinces of Shansi, Kirin and other provinces in 1955, 287 usurers had deposited their capital in the credit cooperatives for lack of customers.[116] On the other side of the picture, as the need for credit among the peasants still exceeds the supply, the problem of how to encourage the better off rural households to increase their deposits with the credit department of the commune remains. It was reported that in 1958 the amount of cash deposits in rural areas of China came to 4·14 billion *yuan* (or 1·76 billion US dollars), which was 60 per cent more than that of 1957.[117]

Other problems of credit cooperatives in China may include the following: (1) A proper balance between long-term loans to the communes for productive purposes and loans to meet the cash shortage of operational funds by the communes and the immediate needs of the peasant households. Balance is also needed for loans to various types of enterprises in the rural areas including subsidiary occupations. (2) Better coordination between the credit programme and the government's advanced purchase of agricultural products and the agricultural insurance work. There were complaints by the peasants in 1956 that sometimes there was great pressure on the peasants who received money advanced by the state for later buying of crops to deposit the payment in the credit cooperatives. Five types of agricultural insurance were introduced in 1952, which covered livestock, cotton, wheat, tobacco and jute, and hogs and silk cocoon.[118] After the organization of communes, the insurance is now managed by the communes. (3) Peasant households which contracted loans from the credit cooperatives must be explained the necessity of repaying the credit on time, unless it is impossible for them to repay due to calamities of various kinds. Otherwise the operation of the credit cooperatives will be handicapped and it is unfair to those who repay their loans on time. (4) Closer supervision and checking of the projects carried out with the loans from the credit cooperatives are needed. Loans should be used for the purpose they are intended. (5) The above points are related to the general issue of inadequacy in the number of trained personnel who are competent managers and understand well the credit needs of various agricultural sectors in a particular locality. (6) The last and most important function is the supply of commodities needed by the rural community to back up the loans extended. Without timely

[116] *NCNA*, Peking, March 20, 1955.

[117] *Ta-kung pao*, Peking, January 1, 1959, p. 2.

[118] Chang Wen-hua, "Agricultural Insurance Work in East China," ***CCCP***, No. 4, 1952, pp. 876–8.

provision of items required by the peasants, large amount of rural credit will only lead to inflationary effects and confusion on the local market. Here a close coordination with the supply and sales cooperatives (now a part of the communes) in the villages is both desirable and necessary.

Rural Marketing

Credit cooperatives, together with the APCs, supply and marketing cooperatives, and handicrafts cooperatives[119] were described as four foundation stones of the Chinese rural economy. In many districts, these four cooperatives hold periodically joint conferences to plan programmes, coordinate activities, and resolve problems.[120] The supply and marketing cooperatives, for example, extended 180 million *yuan* (in terms of new currency or 76·4 million US dollars) in 1954 to the peasants as payment for the advanced purchase of cotton, foodgrains, peanut, jute, tea, wool, and silk cocoons, at an estimated value of 1·3 billion *yuan*. The total value of contracts made between the supply and marketing cooperatives and the handicrafts cooperatives came to more than 500 million *yuan*.[121] These four types of cooperatives, now incorporated in the communes, represent the core of the rural marketing system in China.

Rural marketing constitutes another key link in the chain of agrarian programmes of Peking. The major obstacles to better marketing conditions in pre-war China, as described very lucidly by Professor R. H. Tawney in his *Memorandum on Agriculture and Industry in China*,[122] were: poor transportation facilities, numerous abusive taxes, monopoly of the local market by usurers

[119] At the end of 1955, there were 3,100 handicrafts cooperatives with a total of 170,000 members. The majority of these cooperatives engage in blacksmith, carpentry, building, and bamboo work. See Teng Chieh, "Handicrafts Cooperatives Should Serve the Needs of the Peasants," *HY*, No. 5, May 28, 1955, pp. 151–2.

[120] Honan Cooperative Office, "An Analysis of the Changes in the Buying and Selling Needs of the Peasants after the Cooperativization," *CCYC*, No. 4, August 17, 1956, p. 70.

[121] Teng Fei, "The Basic Tasks and the Central Links in the Rural Supply and Sale Cooperatives," *HY*, No. 5, May 28, 1955, p. 174.

[122] R. H. Tawney, *A Memorandum on Agriculture and Industry in China*, 1931, pp. 44–9.

and landlords, pressure on the peasants to sell at very low prices immediately after the harvest, and high interest rates on loans. To these may be added: exorbitant charges by middle men, wide fluctuations in seasonal prices for agricultural products, the multiplicity of weight and measure units, unscrupulous trading practices, and corrupt or inefficient officials. Peking has instituted a host of measures to cope with these obstructive factors. Particular emphasis is assigned to the development of transportation facilities—railways, highways, and inland water barges—and impressive achievements are reported. Between 1950 and 1957, a total of some 10,000 kilometres (6,200 miles) of railroads and 260,000 milometres (160,000 miles) of highways were built in mainland China. In 1958, about 2,000 kilometres of railway and 150,000 kilometres of roads were built. More than 10,000 kilometres of inland river navigation and 6,000 kilometres of local civil air lines were added in the same year. There was a 70 per cent increase in the volume of goods transported by road, waterways, and air lines. The total quantity of freight moved by road, waterway and air between September and December 1958 came to 632 million tons.[123] In the railroad transport, the daily number of wagons loaded increased from 26,000 in August 1958 to 32,300 in December 1958. In 1959 the freight train turn-over rate was 2·52 days, the average daily run, 395 kilometres, and the weight of each freight car came to 39·4 tons. The average amount of freight per kilometre per annum reached 7·5 million tons.[123a] The number of locomotives introduced in 1958 doubled that of 1957, and that of passenger and freight wagons, increased by 60 per cent.[124] They had a great effect on rural marketing. For example, after the completion of the Chengtu-Chungking Railway in July 1952, the exchange value of one thermos bottle in western Szechuan dropped from 16 pounds of tobacco to 6·6. The cost of one pound of salt dropped from 11 pounds of rice to half a pound.[125] When the Yingtan-Amoy Railway was completed near the end of 1956, bamboo trunks which yielded no cash value in the hilly districts

[123] Wang Shao-tao, "Develop Transport by All the People," *Hung-ch'i* (Red Flag), No. 2, January 16, 1959, p. 20; *JMJP*, February 20, 1959, p. 1. Railway freight came to 350 million tons in 1958; and 520 million tons in 1959.

[123a] Lu Cheng-ch'ao, "Railway in the Past Decade," *The Glorious Decade*, Vol. I, p. 173.

[124] Lu Cheng-chao, "The Path for Our Nation's Railway Construction," *Hung-ch'i* (Red Flag), No. 2, January 16, 1959, p. 16.

[125] Wang Chih-feng, *The Chengtu-Chungking Railway*, Shanghai, 1954, 40 pages.

of western Fukien, began to sell for export at 60 *yuan* per 100. The cost of transporting bananas was reduced by about 60 per cent.[126]

Greater emphasis seem to be needed, however, in the development of local transportation facilities such as county and village roads, wagons or carts with rubber tires, and fuller utilization of inland rivers. According to a report by Wang Shao-tao, member of the CC, CCP in charge of Transportation and Communication, "twenty-six per cent of the counties at the end of 1955 were not reached by highways. 17 per cent of the *ch'ü* were outside the long-distance telephone system (in 1955)."[127] A similar observation was made by P'an Ch'i, Vice-Minister of Communications, at the National Conference on Local Transportation in December 1955. He pointed out that "while emphasis has been assigned to trunk lines, national roads, and modern means of transportation, branch lines, local routes, and traditional types of transportation means deserve greater emphasis. The problem of maintenance, after the roads are built, also calls for attention."[128] Situation improved after 1958. As a result of the expansion of major crops production in 1958, the question of storage facility has become an urgent one.

This transportation system is reinforced by an extensive local marketing network organized in various rural districts. In 1956 there were, according to Peking data, 1,427,000 trading establishments in the rural areas of China, including the following types: foodgrain, 42,000; cloth, 133,000; sundry goods, 225,000; medicines, 167,000.[129] These establishments had their bases in the *hsiang* (administrative villages), which numbered about 220,000 up to the middle of 1956, and were reduced to approximately 80,000 in early 1958. In Hunan province, for example, there was an average of three grain marketing stations in every *ch'ü* (district) in addition to the mobile market stations. In Hopei province, 3,700 market stations were set up in 1954 after the cotton harvest, to take care of the cotton trade.[130] Peking sources maintain that partly as a

[126] Shang Kai, "Travel Along the Yingtan-Amoy Railway," *JMJP*, December 10–3, 1956, p. 2.

[127] Wang Shao-tao, "Speed Up the Development of Local Transportation and Village Tele-Communications," *HPYK*, No. 4, February 21, 1956, pp. 84–6.

[128] P'an Ch'i, "Speed Up Local Transportation Development, Complete the Socialist Reform of Private Transportation Business," *HPYK*, No. 4, 1956, pp. 87–9. [129] "Basic Conditions in the Trading Network in Our Country in 1955", *HPYK*, No. 24, December 21, 1956, p. 82.

[130] *NCNA* bulletin, Peking, December 18, 1954.

result of these marketing improvements, the seasonal fluctuations in foodgrain prices on the mainland decreased from 21·76 per cent in 1950 to 18·99 per cent in 1951, 16·91 per cent in 1952, and to a still lower level in 1953 (all in weighted averages).[131] In 1954, the seasonal price gap in foodgrains in Hunan province was reportedly only 5·8 per cent, as against 30 and 40 per cent in the pre-war era.[132] The prices in China since 1953 have remained basically stable as the following table shows:

RETAIL PRICE AND WAGE INDICES IN CHINA (1952–57)*
1952 = 100

	1953	*1954*	*1955*	*1956*	*1957 (est.)*	*1958 (est.)*
1. Retail price index in 8 leading cities	103·7	104·1	105·5	105·8	107·7	107
2. Workers' living cost index in 12 leading cities	105·6	106·9	107·3	107·1	109·2	..
3. Index of purchasing prices of agricultural products (nation-wide)	110·1	113·8	113·2	116·6	122·4	125·1
4. Index of retail prices of manufacturing goods in the rural areas	98·5	100·2	101·4	100·4	101·6	101
5. Index of average annual wage income of non-farm workers	11·2	116·3	119·8	136·9	142·5	..
6. Item 5 in real wage terms	105·4	108·8	111·7	127·8	130·5	..

* *T'ung-chi yen-chiu* (Statistical Research), No. 4, 1958.

The total value of agricultural and subsidiary products purchased by the government through the supply and sale cooperatives in 1956 (not including the products bought directly by the Ministry of Agricultural Products) came to 2·9 billion *yuan*.[133] This illustrates the key role played by these cooperatives in rural finance.

[131] *JMJP*, March 1, 1954, p. 2.

[132] *NCNA* bulletin, Peking, December 18, 1954. Also see Chao Ch'ing-hsin, "The Boom and Slack Seasons in the Nation's Market after Agricultural Cooperativization," *CCYC*, No. 5, October 17, 1956, pp. 19–38.

[133] Data Section, *Tung-chi kung-tso* (Statistical Work, *TCKT*), No. 14, July 29, 1957, p. 12.

At the same time, the percentage of retail volume for daily necessity goods sold in 1956 as compared to 1955 was as follows: vegetable oil, 116; pork, 97; sugar, 119; cigarettes, 103; cotton cloth, 134; rubber shoes, 152; fountain pen, 140; bicycle, 143; radio, 159; kerosene oil, 118; and charcoal, 126.[134] Shortage in certain goods, like edible oil and pork, was reported both in 1956 and 1957. In 1957, prices for a number of commodities like vegetables, rapeseeds, sesame, handicrafts products, hogs, and vegetable oil, were raised—generally in favour of the agricultural sector. One of the contributing factors for pork shortage in 1956 was the low government purchase price for hogs. Shortage of certain subsidiary forms was also in evidence in some cities in 1958 and early 1959, but the total volume of retail sales of commodities in the first half of 1959 was 23 per cent greater than that of the corresponding period in 1958, estimated at 29·6 billion *yuan* or 12·57 billion US dollars.[134a]

Since 1949, the Chinese government has taken a series of measures to promote the "interflow of goods between urban and rural areas." These include the holding of exhibitions of goods, convocation of urban-rural coordination meetings, surveying of marketing conditions, re-organization of rural commercial agents like the peddlers, finding of sale outlet for new items, and the promotion of "triangle contract" among the cooperatives, state trading companies and state transportation agencies. The sale of daily necessities in the rural areas steadily increased in the past 10 years. Take one of the basic commodities, cotton cloth, as an example. Its volume of sale increased from 130·34 million bolts (one bolt equals to 36·58 metres) in 1953 to 128·70 million bolts in 1954, 128·85 million bolts in 1955, and 174·05 million bolts in 1956.[135] The production of cotton cloth increased from 5 billion metres in 1957 to 7·5 billion metres in 1959. The rate of commercialization of cotton increased from 74·9 per cent in 1952 to 80·1 per cent in 1955.[136] Collectivization and now the communes help market evaluation, the supply and sale of commodities in rural areas, and marketing control. Before 1958, there existed the problem of uneven

[134] S.S.B., *Communique on the Implementation of the National Economic Plan in 1956, op. cit.*

[134a] *Hung-ch'i* (Red Flag), No. 19, September 1, 1959, p. 5.

[135] Li Hsien-nien, *Report on the 1956 Final Account and the 1957 National Budget*, June 29, 1957.

[136] Tseng Ling, "The Rural Market at the Height of Agricultural Cooperativization," *CCYC*, No. 2, April 17, 1956, p. 13.

development in marketing facilities between rural and urban areas. In 1956 there were 6,132,000 employees in 3·3 million trading establishments with a total retail volume of 31·54 billion *yuan*. The rural areas, with 80 per cent of the 618 million people (1956) on the mainland and 53 per cent of the trade value, had only 1,427,000 trading establishments with 2,424,000 employees.[137] It is apparently desirable to increase the number, size, and business contents of the trading organs in rural China. More skilful utilization of traditional commercial media and personnel (peddlers, local merchants) would also help to promote a greater volume of rural trade and better marketing methods. There have also been qualitative changes in the market structure of rural China. For example, the proportion of means of production in the total sale of goods in the rural areas increased steadily during the past decade. According to a survey of 26,935 APCs in 1955, among the higher stage cooperatives their productive investment in agriculture constituted 28·5 per cent of the total agricultural income, and in subsidiary occupations, 40·4 per cent of income from side jobs was invested. The pattern of distribution of income among the communes assigns some 30 per cent as the average in investment.[138] The question, of course, is related to financial needs of commune members for daily living, and the quantity of means of production for sale in a given period in rural China. The composition of goods transacted in the rural market also underwent changes between 1950 and 1959. For example, the proportion of subsidiary products in the total sales by the peasant households declined before 1955, but showed an upward trend after 1956.

One of the major problems in the marketing of many agricultural products in China prior to 1958 concerned the unfavourable effects of too rigid centralized control of a number of rural products including vegetables, fruits, domestic fowls, and many other native

[137] "Basic Conditions in the Trading Network in Our Country in 1955," *HPYK*, No. 24, December 21, 1956, p. 82. In 1958, there were 6·4 million employees in commerce.

[138] "Survey on the Receipts and Expenditure of the APCs in 1955," *HPYK*, No. 24, December 21, 1956, pp. 63–5. Also see detailed data showing the increased sales of means of production between 1954 and 1956 in the 8 higher-stage APCs in Honan province, "Changes in the Purchase and Sale of Goods by Peasants After Agricultural Cooperativization," *CCYC*, No. 4, August 17, 1956, p. 59; Huang Chi-ming, "Deal Correctly the Relationship Between Accumulation and Consumption," *HPYK*, No. 13, July 10, 1959, pp. 22–4.

products, initiated in 1954 and 1955. As a result, "free markets under the state leadership" had been allowed to operate for many non-essential agricultural produce since the latter half of 1956. One Peking source lists four advantages of such free markets: (1) They provide greater incentive for both the peasants and the producers of manufactured goods to develop more variety and higher quality through the process of market selections; (2) They eliminate barriers in commodity circulation and increase the rate of turn-over; (3) They rectify the irrational aspects of the planned control measures, particularly as many subsidiary farm and handicraft products are diversified in quality and specifications, and (4) They encourage the state-operated and cooperative trading establishments to improve their work in management and in trade techniques.[139] After the end of 1957, many commercial and marketing agencies and facilities have been decentralized. Since mid-1958 trading and marketing functions have been included in the people's communes. Each commune now has departments dealing with the purchase of subsidiary products, distribution or sale of consumer goods, and the collection of those agricultural products which are under the unified purchase programme of the government. The principles governing rural finance and commerce are embodied in the following: Personnel and properties of State financial and trading agencies should be decentralized among the communes; there should be unification in programmes, planning, and capital; and the financial receipts and expenditures are to be the responsibilities of the communes.[140]

Since the autumn of 1959, rural fairs under State control have been established in many rural areas in China. Participants in these fairs are mainly people's communes, production brigades, and commune members. Special approval of the management of the fairs must be obtained if handicrafts industries, factories, mines, State enterprises, government organs, and other organizations wish to purchase commodities at the fair. Usually goods classified under Category III (which represent 20 per cent of subsidiary agricultural

[139] Kuan Ta-tung, "The Significance of Opening Up Free Markets Under the State Leadership," *HPYK*, No. 24, December 21, 1956, pp. 77–80; editorial, *JMJP*, November 22, 1956, Ching-yuan, "Why a Free Market Is Necessary," *CCHH*, No. 13, November 13, 1956.

[140] See *HPYK*, No. 22, November 25, 1958; *Ts'ai-cheng* (Finance), No. 10, October 9, 1958, pp. 6–10; and editorial "On the Cooperation Between Commerce and Industry and Agriculture," *Ta-kung pao*, July 30, 1959, p. 1.

products) are allowed to be transacted at these fairs, and the principal items within Category III have fixed prices (or price ranges) determined by the government. These village fairs are designed to facilitate interchange of goods, stimulate production of subsidiary products, and provide the peasants with greater variety of commodities. The "free markets" which existed in 1956 have ceased to operate after the development of the communes.[140a]

H. *Collection and Distribution of Agricultural Products*

The programmes of the Peking government for the purchase and distribution of major rural products are more comprehensive in scope, thorough in implementation, and diversified in purpose than in any previous period in China. They are designed to secure food supplies, to meet the industrial needs for a variety of raw materials, to provide a leverage for market stabilization, and to serve as a means to finance the overall industrialization of China.

The regulations dealing with the control and distribution of foodgrains form the central part of the whole programme. The State purchase and supply of foodgrains initiated in November 1953 was later developed into the "three fix" policy in March 1955—that is, the fixing of production, purchase, and sale of foodgrains. The basic governing documents are: *Directive on the Enforcement of Planned Purchase and Planned Supply of Foodgrains* issued by the GAC on November 19, 1953,[141] *Provisional Measures for Unified Purchase and Unified Supply of Grain in Rural Districts* promulgated by the SC on August 25, 1955,[142] *Provisional Regulations for Unified Purchase and Unified Supply of Grain in Cities and Towns* promulgated on the same date as the second Directive,[143] and *Directive on the Allocation of Foodgrain According to Persons in Rural Areas* issued jointly by the CC, CCP and the SC in August 1957.[144] The fixing of agricultural production norms follows in general the standards laid down in the land survey and production ascertainment campaigns of previous years. The major aspects

[140a] See P'eng Chien-fei "Development of Trade at Rural Fairs, Its Significance and Effects," *Ta-kung pao*, August 24, 1959; and *Kung-jen jih-pao* (Workers' Daily), July 30, 1959.

[141] Chinese text in *HY*, No. 4, April 1954, pp. 158–9.

[142] Chinese text in *HY*, No. 9, September 1955, pp. 160–2.

[143] Chinese text in *HY*, No. 9, September 1955, pp. 163–4.

[144] See *Hsin-hua jih-pao* (New China Daily), Nanking, September 2, 1957.

of the above four Directives all issued before the big leap in 1958, include the following:

One, grain-producing peasants (now the communes) should sell their surplus grain to the state according to the types of grain, purchasing prices and quotas of planned purchase fixed by the state. But after the APCs (now the communes) have delivered public grain and also grain to be bought by the state under planned purchase, they can freely keep and use their surplus grain. They may continue to sell it to state grain departments or cooperatives or carry on exchanges (with other communities) in small quantities in the countryside.

Two, control figures for planned purchase and planned supply are determined in accordance with the needs of the state and the people, as well as the food situation in the countryside:

(1) Control figures applicable to various regions are determined by the State Council on the basis of the national control figures fixed by the State Planning Commission.
(2) Control figures applicable to provinces, administrative districts and *hsien* are determined by government at the respective higher level.
(3) Control figures applicable to *ch'ü* and *hsiang* are determined by *hsien* governments. Control figures applicable to *hsiang* must be publicly announced to the masses, who should be directed and organized to carry out democratic discussions.

Three, all private grain merchants (now all in cooperatives since 1958) are not allowed to deal privately in grain, but may be commissioned by state grain departments to sell grain on their behalf under strict state supervision and control.

Four, grain output is calculated for each household according to the normal yield of grain per unit of land. The normal yield of peasants' cultivated plots is based on the production figures preliminarily fixed at the *hsiang* level before and after the spring ploughing of 1955 and fixed through discussions, according to land quality and natural conditions and in the light of peasants' conditions of management. For crop fields whose yield was normal in 1955, the normal yield is determined according to actual output; for crop fields whose yield was particularly good or poor, the normal yield is determined according to normal output. Where yield was already determined in 1954, the fixed output, if it generally corresponds to the actual output of 1955, may be used as the basis for fixing the normal yield while making appropriate adjustments when it is fixed too high or too low.

Five, the peasant household's consumption of grain generally includes seeds, food and fodder (no fodder is included in areas where grain is not used as fodder). The grain consumption standards are determined by the people's committees of provinces, autonomous districts and municipalities directly under the Central Government. Prior to 1958, State unified purchase of grain from surplus-grain peasant households, in general, accounted for 80–90 per cent of their surplus grain. Concrete rates of purchase are determined by the people's governments of provinces, autonomous districts, and municipalities directly under the Central Government.

Six, if important changes in the natural conditions that markedly affect the crop take place following the fixing of production, purchase, and sale of grain, the *hsiang* people's committees are required, according to the amount of crop loss, to readjust the quantity of grain delivery and sale to the state, or readjust the amount of grain supply originally fixed for the households which lost crops.

If, as a result of the above readjustments, the original balance between receipt and sale cannot be ensured within a province or an autonomous district, the government of a province or an autonomous region can appropriately increase the quantity of grain purchase in bumper harvest areas; if, as a result of increased purchase, the difference between receipt and sale can still not be ensured, the authorities concerned must submit their proposals to the State Council for assistance.

In case of serious natural calamities in one province or autonomous district or in several provinces, which hinder the balance of grain receipts and sales, the State Council may designate the bumper harvest provinces and autonomous districts to increase their purchase appropriately.

If, due to readjustment of purchase and sale figures, it is necessary to increase grain purchase from bumper harvest areas, the increased purchase is limited to a maximum of 40 per cent of the increased production gained by peasant households on account of the bumper harvest.

Seven, both surplus-grain households which have a surplus after delivering and selling the required quantity to the state, and self-sufficient households which have a surplus as a result of more production and less consumption are entitled "to dispose of their surplus grain freely without any interference, either by keeping it in storage, using it freely, selling it to the state or co-operatives, exchanging it for other commodities on the state grain market, or exchanging it with other peasants." But they are not permitted to use grain for speculative business. The quantities of grain supplies to grain-short households are fixed once every year.

Eight, between the autumn of 1957 and the summer of 1958 allocation of foodgrains in the rural areas (usually with APC as the unit) was done on the basis of actual needs of persons—instead of the former system of rationing according to the number of people in a household irrespective of their age or labour requirements. Details regarding the new method vary somewhat in different agricultural regions and even among local districts. But the general arrangements are more or less on this pattern: Persons in an APC are divided into 4 to 6 categories, according to the differences in actual needs in foodgrain consumption. For example, in the case of the New China APC in Kaoshun *hsien* in Kiangsu province, the system was (in 1957) like the following:[145] Children from 1–3 years were grouped into the first class, and the per capita ration standard was 200 catties (or 220 pounds) of rice a year. The second class consists of children between 4 and 5 with a per capita ration standard of 250 catties. Third class, 6 to 11 year olds, getting 380 catties. The fourth class includes the majority of the APC members from 18 to 50, working on a minimum of 120 work-days annually, and each was allocated 700 catties. The fifth class, with 440 catties a year ration, is composed of "wu-pao" or "five-guarantee" households. These are dependent members like widows, widowers, orphans, the disabled, the old aged, etc. whose minimum needs are provided free by the cooperative. (One estimate gives the total number of *wu-pao* households as 3·13 million in June 1958, with 5·19 million persons.) The last category consists of those who are not in any of the above five classes and its per capita grain allocation was fixed at 480 catties a year. The APC in question also decided that any surplus grain found after fulfilling the government production quota laid down in the "three-fix" policy should be partly sold to the state as additional procurement and partly distributed among members as remuneration of their labour. The maximum

[145] See *Hsin-hua jih-pao* (New China Daily), Nanking, September 2, 1957.

amount of grain a bachelor member with full labour power could get was limited to 800 catties a year.

These revised methods of grain allocation in the rural areas represent a more logical as well as equitable approach compared to the old system. According to Chinese sources, it also resulted in the decrease of the actual amount of foodgrain allocations in various areas during 1957 and early 1958, and removed a cause of complaint of some APC members who were childless or had few children as they got less grain allocation than those with large families. An indirect but very significant effect of this new system is the elimination of one source of encouragement for the Chinese peasants to have more children—thus helping the campaign to promote planned parenthood and birth control.

Since the second half of 1958, members of many people's communes have been supplied free food. But the standards set up in 1957 according to the above provisions are still used as a point of reference.

Nine, different standards of the monthly ration are laid down too for urban populace.

(*a*) In areas where rice is the staple food: (1 catty equal 1·1 lb.)

(1) 45–55 catties, with average not to exceed 50 catties—workers doing particularly heavy physical labour.

(2) 35–44 catties, with average not to exceed 40 catties—workers doing heavy physical labour.

(3) 26–34 catties, with average not to exceed 32 catties—workers doing light physical labour.

(4) 24–29 catties, with average not to exceed 28 catties—workers in government organs and (mass) organizations, employees of public and private enterprises, shop assistants, and other "brain" workers.

(5) 26–33 catties, with average not to exceed 32 catties—university and middle school students.

(6) 22–26 catties, with average not to exceed 25 catties—general residents and children over ten years.

(7) 16–21 catties, with average not to exceed 20 catties—children aged six years and under ten years.

(8) 11–15 catties, with average not to exceed 13 catties—children aged three years and under six years.

(9) 5–10 catties, with average not to exceed 7 catties—children under three years.

(*b*) In areas where miscellaneous cereals and wheat flour are the staple food:

(1) 50–60 catties, with average not to exceed 55 catties—workers doing particularly heavy physical labour.
(2) 40–49 catties, with average not to exceed 44 catties—workers doing heavy physical labour.
(3) 29–39 catties, with average not to exceed 35 catties—workers doing light physical labour.
(4) 27–32 catties, with average not to exceed 31 catties—workers in government organs and (mass) organizations, employees of public and private enterprises, shop assistants and other "brain" workers.
(5) 29–36 catties, with average not to exceed 35 catties—university and middle school students.
(6) 24–28·5 catties, with average not to exceed 27·5 catties—inhabitants in general and children of ten years and more.
(7) 18–23 catties, with average not to exceed 22 catties—children aged six years and under ten years.
(8) 12–17 catties, with average not to exceed 14 catties—children aged three years and under six.
(9) 6–11 catties, with average not to exceed 8 catties—children under three years.

Ten, the governments of provinces, autonomous regions and municipalities directly under the Central Government are empowered to, according to the following provisions and with reference to local conditions, determine the different standards for fixed quantities of grain for fodder, which are to be enforced in provinces, autonomous districts, and municipalities directly under the Central Government:

(1) 4–7 catties of unhusked grain per head daily—horses and mules.
(2) 2–4 catties of unhusked grain per head daily—donkeys and camels.
(3) 4–6 catties of unhusked grain per head daily—cows.
(4) Quantity of grain for hogs is determined within the limits of the food standards in surrounding villages.

The fodder includes wheat brans, rice brans and bean-cakes whose conversion rates are determined by the people's councils.

Eleven, peasants may appeal to state organs if they find inequity or irregularity in the grain output fixed, in the quantity of grain for delivery and sale, and in the amount of grain supply; state organs that take up the appeal are instructed to deal with the cases promptly and in a responsible manner. However, pending a new decision the peasants must still carry out the original evaluation.

In the *Detailed Regulations on the Carrying Out of Unified Purchase and Unified Supply of Grain in Rural Areas in Kwangtung*, promulgated on June 10, 1956, several supplementary provisions were announced. They include the stipulations that the APCs should serve as collective units in the foodgrain control programme; additional grain supply of 10–30 catties may be allocated to each household in case of marriages, funeral services, and celebrations; the state purchase programme should terminate in December so that peasants may sell their surplus grains on the state market after that date; and more than half a dozen kinds of grains other than rice may be sold to the state by the APCs to meet their quota. In the last connection, it is interesting to note that wheat, soybeans and other beans are calculated on a one-to-one ratio with processed rice, but wild corn, kaoliang and barley are equated (also on a one-to-one basis) with unhusked rice.[146] Potatoes are converted into foodgrains at a rate of 4 (pounds) to one. Regions generally with a great deal of surplus grain to export include Szechuan, Kiangsu, Hunan, Hupeh, and the three Northeastern provinces. However, a number of previously grain deficient provinces like Kweichow, Fukien, and Kwangtung had become grain exporting areas in 1957. After 1958, practically all rural areas in China no longer felt the shortage of foodgrains except in case of natural calamities.

The aims for introducing these controls regarding foodgrains are officially described as "to ensure supply of the grain required for the people's livelihood and for national construction, to stabilize grain prices, to eliminate grain profiteering and to strengthen further the worker-peasant alliance."[147]

[146] Chinese text in *Nan-fang jih-pao* (South China Daily), June 10, 1956.

[147] GAC, "Directive on the Enforcement of Planned Purchase and Planned Supply of Foodgrains," *HY*, April 1954, pp. 158-9.

The factors which prompted the adoption of the grain control measures in 1954 and 1955 may have included the following: (1) The indifferent food crop harvests in 1953 and 1954, when the planned targets were not fulfilled; (2) The extensive cultivation of industrial crops, particularly cotton; (3) The increasing urbanization on the Chinese mainland; (4) The effects of natural calamities and the Korean war (1950–1953); (5) Greater need for foodgrains as population grows, as more seedgrains are required as a result of expanded crop acreage, and as the number of livestock and domestic fowls multiply; (6) Higher per capita grain consumption as more people had become engaged in more active labour, especially due to the more intensive labour schedules of the APCs; and (7) Preference on the part of the state for tighter grain control over an increase in agricultural tax in kind.

Chinese sources give the amount of unprocessed foodgrain available on a per capita basis (for both human and other consumptions) as: 1949–50, 477 *chin* (one *chin* equals 1·1 pounds); 1950–51, 483; 1951–52, 523; 1952–53, 577; 1953–54, 574; 1955–56, 608; and 1956–57, 630, and in 1958 about 800 (estimates).[148] Grains available for human consumption have been given (in lbs.) as: 1953–54, 500; 1954–55, 510; 1955–56, 530; and 1956–57, 576.[149] According to one Chinese author, out of the per capita amount, 35 *chin* will be for seeds and 65 *chin* for livestock feed.[150] The amount of grain to be purchased for 1957–58 was reportedly a little less than that of 1956–57, and the export of grain was reduced from 1·32 million tons in 1956 to 0·78 million tons in 1957.[151] Another source describes the food situation in urban and rural areas of China in 1956 in these words:

> According to data gathered in 1954 and 1955, the average annual consumption of foodgrain for city and town residents is about 540 *chin* (or about 594 pounds). Scientists have estimated that each urban resident will need an average of 2,400 calories a

[148] Su Hsiu-lin, "Is There Enough Grain for the People to Eat This Year?" *Shih-shih shou-tse's* (Handbook on Current Affairs), No. 20, October 25, 1956; also Liang Chu-hang, "Grain Distribution in 1957 and 1958," *Liang-shih* (Foodgrains), No. 6, June 1957.

[149] Statistical Bureau data.

[150] Liang Chu-hang, *op. cit.*

[151] Po I-po, *Report on the Implementation of the 1956 Economic Plan and Draft Plan for 1957*, July 1, 1957.

day. 2,000 calories will be provided by the foodgrains, and the other 15 per cent can be obtained from other sources like fats, vegetables, meats, egg products, fish and nuts . . . . The current foodgrains problem in the cities concerns mainly the lack of variety in food supplies and certain management problems . . . . In the rural areas, out of a per capita amount of 610 *chin* of foodgrains in 1955, 540 *chin* are for human consumption, 30 *chin* are for use as seeds, and only 40 *chin* are left as livestock (including domestic animals) feed and for other uses.[152]

Several points may be usefully noted: First, the actual per capita consumption of foodgrain in urban China is probably larger than that of rural China, due to a combination of factors such as the greater need for non-human consumption of grain and inferior marketing facilities in the rural districts. Second, the supply of foodgrain in China does not depend solely on the amount of grain produced. Storage facilities, the amount of spoilage and waste, efficiency in transportation and distribution of grains, timely relief for famine areas, and absence of hoarding or speculation in grains, all affect the actual quantity of foodgrain that can be made available to the consumers. There are grounds to believe that notable improvements have been made in all these directions in present-day China, in comparison with the Nationalist period. Third, to offer variety and better nutrition in food for the people, additional sources of food supply other than grains must be effectively exploited. These may include the greater use of non-starch foods like vegetables, edible oils and marine products, and the speedier development of domestic fowls and livestock raising. Fourth, the effective tackling of the food problem in China after 1957 shows that the basic solution lies in the enhancement of crop production, particularly yield per acre.

Peking's programme to control the production, sale, and distribution of other important agricultural products besides grain is a complicated one. A *JMJP* editorial, dated June 2, 1956, stated that "the work of purchasing in advance cotton, tobacco, tea, jute and kenaf, and silk cocoons (for 1956) has been satisfactorily concluded. Only the plan to buy ramie has not been carried out well." However, reports in 1956 indicated that some local cadres indiscriminately

[152] Chu Hang, "Basic Conditions of Foodgrain in Our Country This Year," *HPYK*, No. 24, December 21, 1956, pp. 71–3.

deducted from such advance purchase funds certain loans previously contracted by the APCs or peasant households, or pressed the peasants to deposit too much in their accounts in the credit co-operatives. Some "advance purchase" contracts were improperly drawn up, partly as a result of the lack of trained personnel to handle these business arrangements. Government agencies at times evaluated incorrectly the prospective yields of the crops in question or the quality of different grades of the products. The procedures for collecting and pricing of agricultural products were, in some localities, too complicated or inefficient. Many APCs, after obtaining funds from the advance purchase programme, allotted too much of the income to farm investment (sometimes as high as 80 per cent), leaving an insufficient amount for the consumer goods needed by the members.[153]

One crucial aspect of the programme of government control of agricultural products concerns the prices offered for the foodgrains to be purchased. In the *Directive on the Planned Purchase and Supply of Foodgrains* issued by the GAC on November 19, 1953, it was stated that "prevailing official purchasing prices and official retail prices which are too high or too low and which are conspicuously out of line should be properly readjusted." (Article 4) It is clear that this calls for attentive studies of supply and demand conditions of foodgrains in a particular area.

To fix or adjust price scales which reflect the values of the various agricultural products or for the APCs (now the communes) to draw up suitable wage scales for the different types of work in subsidiary occupations is an extremely complicated task. As one Chinese writer points out, "the problem of production planning is closely related with the ratio of exchanges (values) among different agricultural products."[154] One of the reasons for the decline of the peasants' income from subsidiary occupations in 1955 was the low purchasing prices offered by the state for many agricultural side-products. For example, the price set for dried sunflower in

[153] See Editorial, *JMJP* (June 2, 1956); Sung Kai-fu, "Improving the Control Procedures for Vegetables and Other Native Products," *HPYK*, No. 21, November 6, 1956, p. 154; Chin Hsiang, "Keep the Tradition of Close Integration Between Agriculture and Subsidiary Occupations," *HPYK*, No. 23, December 6, 1956, pp. 69–70.

[154] Ta Sheng, "The Significance and Method of Investigation and Studying the Relative Prices of Agricultural Products," *Ta-kung pao*, Peking, August 18, 1957.

Fengchieh county, Szechuan province (in 1955) was 5 *yuan* per 110 lbs., which was only one-third the pre-war price. As a result there was a decline of 60 per cent in the total value of sunflowers sold by the peasants in 1955 as against 1954.[155] This low purchase price was an outcome of the policy of some government commercial agencies to make a profit at each administrative level. Some APCs tended to discourage the development of subsidiary products not only by setting relatively low wages for each work-day (in comparison to farm work),[156] but also through a comprehensive control of the members' working schedule, leaving them little or no time for subsidiary work. A contributing factor to the shortage of pork in 1956 and 1957 was the low price stipulated by the government for live hogs. After the hog price was raised in 1957 together with other measures, the number of hogs notably increased. (See statistical table in appendix.)

Between 1950 and 1955, prices (offered by the state purchasing programme) increased 15·7 per cent for grains, and 15 to 45 per cent for hemp, silk cocoon, tea, oilseeds, and cotton.[157] Another official source stated in the summer of 1956 that, when the government brought principal foodgrains like rice, wheat, and maize, the peasant sellers made a net profit of 10 *yuan* per *mou* (or 25 US dollars per acre) during good harvests.[158] In 1956, the purchasing price of state for agricultural products was raised by an average of another 3 per cent over 1955 or 113 per cent of 1952.[159] In the same year the volume of government purchases for important raw materials as compared to the previous year was as follows: vegetable oil, 85 per cent; cotton, 88 per cent; wool, 78 per cent; jute, 102 per cent; and cured tobacco, 113 per cent.[160] The index of agricultural purchasing prices in 1959 was 129 with 1952 as 100. In 1958, the purchase quotas on the whole were successfully fulfilled. The price adjustments since 1950 between agricultural commodities and manufactured goods have been in favour of the former—the

[155] Party Secretariat, Fengchieh county, Szechuan, "Problems in the Production of Special Native Products," *HPYK*, No. 19, October 6, 1956, p. 65.

[156] Party Secretariat, Ch'inyang county, "Why Profits Are Not Great, Although Many Subsidiary Occupations Are Developed," *HPYK*, No. 19, October 6, 1956, pp. 63–4.

[157] *Report of the Indian Delegation to China*, *op.cit.*, p. 76. [158] *Ibid.*, p. 132.

[159] Statistical Bureau, *Communique on the Implementation of the National Plan in 1956*, *op.cit.*

[160] *Jen-min shou-tse, 1958* (People's Handbook of 1958), Peking, p. 517.

"scissors' differentials" were reduced by 22 per cent between 1952 and 1959 according to Liao Lu-yen.[160a] Among the items which now remain under government control are: foodgrains, cotton, oil bearing plants, cured tobacco, jute, ramie, hemp, sugarcane, silk cocoon, tea, live hog, sheep wool, cattle hide, hand-made paper, hand-made sugar, scrap tin, scrap lead and several kinds of herb medicine, apples and oranges for export, and marine products from the major fishing areas for commercial sales. The Ministry for Purchase of Agricultural Supplies (abolished in November 1956) issued a directive on August 25, 1956, which dealt with the question of using the buying of agricultural products as an instrument to boost their production. This document pointed out, *inter alia*, that agricultural by-products and side occupations should be expanded and APCs should be encouraged to engage in semi-processing and short-distance transportation of agricultural products.

About three years after the introduction of the government unified purchase plans, the State Council ordered the opening of "free markets" in order to "enliven the trade in minor rural products and to promote greater urban-rural interflow of goods."[161] At that time, no detailed provisions were made on what were the exact items that could be transacted at these free markets. As a result, a number of major agricultural products were also sold by the peasants at these free markets, thus threatening the fulfilment of the state purchase plans for basic items like cotton, hemp, vegetable oil and foodgrains. On August 9, 1957, the SC issued another directive which contained the following three provisions: First, agricultural products under state planned purchase programmes such as foodgrains, cotton, and oil-bearing crops, when there are surpluses after the state purchases, must be sold to the state trading companies. Second, 22 items of agricultural products (including tobacco, flax, sugarcane, tea, bristle, etc.), 38 items of native herbs, exportable fruits (oranges and apples), certain types of fish supplied to cities, and used metals (copper, tin, lead, and steel) can only be sold to government-consigned shops or co-operatives. Third, any item of agricultural product which does not come within the above-mentioned categories such as domestic fowls,

[160a] Liao Lu-yen, "Achievement on the Agricultural Front in the Past Decade," *The Glorious Decade*, Peking, Vol. I, pp. 307 and 314.

[161] SC, "Decisions on the Control of Free Markets," *HPYK*, No. 18, September 25, 1957, p. 207.

fresh eggs, fruits, and cooking ingredients may be sold at the free markets. Fresh vegetables, although not listed, presumably come within the last category.[162] After 1958, these free markets in the rural areas mostly went out of existence, due to the popularization of the communes.

It is perhaps unavoidable when agricultural produce was not abundant that government should control the major agricultural products in order to attain the following goals: To keep prices stable, to prevent speculation or irrational distribution, to secure adequate amount of exportable rural products, to guarantee the supply of raw materials needed by industries, and most important of all, to provide the urban populace with a steady source of foodgrains. However, agricultural production will be adversely affected if the following happens: When the government purchase infringes upon the minimum foodgrain requirements of peasant households; when the purchase price of a specific produce is unreasonably fixed (either too high or too low); when the control is applied to items which are unsuited for such a purpose, like vegetables and fruits, or when the control machinery is defective. Since 1958, although the state control of major agricultural products has still remained thus far, the problem is greatly helped by the tremendous increase in foodgrains, economic crops, livestock (including fowls), and subsidiary products.

I. *Rural Organization and Administration*

There existed in the rural areas of China prior to mid-1958, four major centres for the planning and implementation of tasks handed down from the central or provincial government. They were: the local branch of the CCP; the *hsiang* administrative structure (the *hsiang* people's congress and the *hsiang* people's council); the cooperative system (APC, credit cooperative, and in some cases handicrafts cooperative); and the mass organizations, particularly the Youth League and the Women's Federation. The structure and functions of the many of these organizations such as the Party branch and the cooperatives, have been discussed in previous sections (see II D 3 and III 3 and 4). Here the discussion will deal in a summarized manner with the administrative set-up and its

[162] State Council, "Directive on the Control of Free Markets," *HPYK*, No. 13, September 25, 1957, pp. 207–8.

functions at the *hsiang* level and the major mass organizations. A *hsiang* (or nationality *hsiang*) is the basic (lowest) administrative unit generally comprised of several villages (or one very large village). Since the collectivization movement in 1955, the size of many *hsiang* has been enlarged through amalgamation, and the unit *ch'ü* (between the *hsiang* and the *hsien* or county) has been abolished in general. There were, in 1958, about 80,000 *hsiang* based on townships and 1,748 *hsien* or the equivalent units. After mid-1958, the *hsiang* administration has been combined with the people's communes.

The *hsiang* people's congress and the *hsiang* people's council are organized according to the Organic Laws governing these two bodies promulgated in September 1954. The people's congress of *hsiang*, consisting of 15 to 20 members if the *hsiang* has less than 2,000 in population and 20 to 35, if there are more than 2,000 people, is elected by direct ballot of all eligible voters 18 years old or above, either by secret voting or by show of hands. The tenure of the deputies of *hsiang* people's congress is two years, subject to re-election or recall by the congress. The power and functions of the *hsiang* people's congress include the following:[163]

(1) To ensure the observance and execution of the laws, decrees, and the resolutions of the people's congresses of the higher levels;

(2) To adopt and promulgate resolutions within the limits of their functions and power;

(3) To approve agricultural and handicrafts production plans and decide on concrete plans of mutual-aid and cooperative work and other economic work;

(4) To plan public works;

(5) To decide on enforcement plans for cultural, education, health, pension and relief measures;

(6) To examine financial receipts and expenditures;

(7) To elect members of the people's council of the *hsiang*;

(8) To elect deputies to the people's congress of the next highest level;

(9) To hear and examine work reports of the *hsiang* people's council;

(10) To revise or annul improper decisions and orders of the *hsiang* people's council;

[163] *Organic Laws of the Local People's Congresses and Local People's Councils*, September 21, 1954.

(11) To protect public property, maintain public order and safeguard civil rights;

(12) To ensure the equal rights of minority nationals; and

(13) To remove, in case of necessity, members or the chairman of the *hsiang* people's council.

The *hsiang* people's congress, according to legal stipulations, should be held once every three months. But it is not clear whether this provision is strictly observed in all the *hsiang* in China.

The legal centre of administrative power at the basic level of course is the *hsiang* people's council. It consists from 3 to 13 persons, depending on the size of the *hsiang*, all of whom are elected by the *hsiang* people's congress. The functions and power of the *hsiang* people's council are described as follows:

(1) To promulgate decisions and orders on the basis of the laws, decrees, the resolutions of the people's congress of the *hsiang* and those of the administrative organs of the state of the higher level;

(2) To sponsor election of deputies to the *hsiang* people's congress;

(3) To convene the *hsiang* people's congress and bring forward bills before it;

(4) To administer finance of the *hsiang*;

(5) To direct agricultural and handicrafts production and direct mutual-aid and cooperative enterprise and other economic work;

(6) To manage public works;

(7) To administer cultural, educational, health, pension, and relief work;

(8) To administer military service work;

(9) To protect public property, maintain public order and safeguard civil rights;

(10) To ensure the equal rights of minority nationals; and

(11) To carry out other business assigned by the people's councils of the higher level.

The *hsiang* people's council is stipulated to meet twice a month. It elects a chairman and several vice-chairmen. It may, according to needs, organize work committees of civil affairs, public security, military affairs, production and cooperation, finance and taxation, culture and education, and mediation. It can call on the deputies of the *hsiang* people's congress and "other suitable persons" to serve on such committees. These organizational divisions are subject to the approval of the people's council at the higher level.[164] After the establishment of people's communes in 1958, the *hsiang* administration is incorporated in the communes, as stated previously.

The question regarding the role and problems of the basic-level administrative system in China is a complex one. It cannot be deliberated fully here. A few observations which have a more direct bearing on the current agrarian programmes of the CCP may be made: First, after the basic completion of the communization movement at the end of 1958, major functions of the *hsiang* people's council such as the direction of agricultural and handicrafts production, the management of public works, and the administration of educational or health work have been taken up by the communes. This may be both advantageous and unavoidable, as the commune leadership is in more direct contact with the rural conditions and problems in a *hsiang*. Second, the economic and technical aspects have significantly become increasingly important at the *hsiang* level in China. Both in the *hsiang* administrative system and in the basic commune production teams, many new tasks have come to occupy important roles—such as the agro-technical study group, the accounting section, the rural credit department, the training class for new farm implements, and the work regarding the government purchase of agricultural products. In a survey of a *hsien* in southern Shantung in 1956, among the 3,900 cadres, 2,809 were engaged in economic and financial work.[165] Third, the existing organizational problems in the *hsiang* are both quantitative and qualitative. Quantitatively, there were, at least up to 1957, in many rural districts too many functionaries who had to be supported by the producing peasants. A survey of two counties in Shantung (near the end of 1956) revealed that on the average there was one cadre in every 200 rural inhabitants. That a similar problem exists in many villages is reflected by a speech of Teng Tzu-hui at the end of 1957 calling on the APCs to reduce their administrative staff from 1·5 to 2 per cent of the total membership to one per cent.[166] At the same time cadres in a number of

[164] State Council, *Organic Laws of the Local People's Congresses and the Local People's Councils*, September 21, 1954.

[165] "How Many Organs and Cadres Are There in a *Hsien*?", *JMJP*, December 11, 1956, p. 4.

[166] Teng Tzu-hui, *op.cit*; *Chung-kuo ch'ing-nien* (Youth of China), 22, November 16, 1957, p. 4.

localities were burdened with too many tasks assigned by the superior organs and by too many meetings. Qualitatively, the rapid development in many agro-technical fields increased the need for better trained men in the *hsiang* administration. The movement to transfer millions of students and urban government employees to the rural areas (started in the fall of 1957) was partly designed to cope with the above problem.

The important role played by the leading mass organizations like the Youth League (14 to 28 age group), the Women's Federation and the Children's Pioneer Corps (9 to 15 age group) in rural China has been discussed previously. It may be desirable to point out again their significance because they play a decisive as well as unique part in the organizational structure of China today. The activists in these mass organizations serve as a rule the nucleus and vanguard of many an agrarian programme in China (or in the cities, for that matter). The total membership of the Communist Youth League (in April 1958) numbered more than 25 million, and most of them belonged to rural branches. According to a report of Chang Yun at the Third National Congress of Chinese Women on September 9, 1957, half the number of *hsiang* in China were headed by women chiefs or deputy chiefs and 70 to 80 per cent of the APCs had women directors or women deputy directors who numbered more than 500,000. The Children's Pioneer Corps of China had a total membership of 35 million in 1959. The weighty part performed by these organizations is partly seen in the following examples. In 1955, under the initiation of the Youth League, an estimated 120 million young people participated in a nation-wide afforestation campaign which resulted in the planting of trees on six million acres of land. In the winter of 1955–56, 70 million rural youths joined the "accumulate fertilizer" movement and made 400 million tons of native fertilizer.[167] In 1956 the harvest-season nursery organizations took care of more than 6 million children and babies, thus helping considerably the agricultural production. Millions of "advanced agricultural workers" came into existence each year, most of them members of the youth and women organizations. Greater details of these mass organizations of China may be found in a volume of the author on this subject published by the Center for International

[167] Hu Yao-pang, "Lead the Youths Toward the Noble Goal of Socialism," *HPYK*, No. 21, November 6, 1956, p. 111.

Studies of M.I.T. (1954, 157 pages) and need not be repeated here.[168]

The various organizations at the *hsiang* (now the communes) level are often coordinated directly or indirectly by the Party branch of the CCP, which serves as the engineer, supervisor and adviser of almost all the major programmes. The role and functions of the Party in the rural areas have been discussed in section III. 4. Party cells were organized in 70 per cent of all *hsiang* in June 1954, 90 per cent at the end of 1955, practically in all the 80,000 *hsiang* in early 1958, and in about 24,000 communes in 1959.[169]

J. *Social and Cultural Programmes in Rural China*

The significance and achievements in the economic or agro-technical fields in Peking's agrarian programmes are easily recognizable. But of equal importance are the social and educational reforms that are being carried out in the Chinese villages, which complement and sustain many economic programmes. Take one example. In an APC in Shaokuan, Kwangtung province after a successful campaign in public health initiated in 1953 which practically eliminated malaria, dysentery, mosquitoes, flies, and breeding grounds for mosquitoes and developed a sanitary code for the villagers, the attendance rate in farm work for the cooperative members reached 98 per cent in 1956 and 1957. At the same time, the amount of manure accumulated increased from 1,900 tons in 1954 to 4,335 tons in 1956. (The total quantity of manures accumulated in China in the public hygiene campaigns came to tens of billion tons in 1958.[170]) Due to these and other improvements, the increase in annual food-grain production was: 45·5 per cent in 1955, and 50 per cent in 1956.[171] Also as an incentive for the peasants' morale, the availability of mass educational facilities or medical help could mean to a villager in China just as much as the material improvements. As a matter of fact, social and educational reforms such as the

[168] Also see author's "Mass Organizations in China," *American Political Science Review*, 48·3, September 1954, pp. 252–65; and "How Peking Reaches So Many," *The New Republic*, May 13, 1957, pp. 19–20.

[169] *Ta-kung pao* (Ta-kung Daily), Tientsin, November 25, 1955; and other *NCNA* bulletins.

[170] *HPYK*, No. 24, December 25, 1957, p. 119.

[171] Li Te-ch'üan, "The Patriotic Health Movement in 1958 and the Future Tasks," *HPYK*, No. 2, January 25, 1959, p. 54.

substitution of superstitious beliefs with scientific knowledge of natural forces and the ability to read basic characters are a prerequisite to the introduction of modern farming methods. The need for education becomes steadily greater in rural China as collectivization and the communes entail the employment of millions of managerial personnel, accountants, and agro-technicians.

By September 1956, there were in rural China 75 million peasants studying in spare-time classes, 360,385 village clubs, 23,091 village libraries, 2,558 cultural centres, and 78,087 public health stations. In 1954, peasants participated over 300 million times in various forms of educational programmes—exhibitions, lectures, slide demonstrations, and others. Near the end of 1958, there existed at least one school in practically every *hsiang*. At the end of 1958, there were one million clubs, 428,000 drama groups, and 473,000 libraries in China.[172]

Also there were in early 1955, 88 newspapers and 34 journals specially designed for the rural readers. The circulation of these journals was around 34 million in 1954, and that of leading newspapers increased from 2·2 million in 1955 to 4·4 million in 1956. In 1958 alone, 45,498 books were published with a total number of 2·38 billion volumes.[172a] The Ministry of Posts and Tele-Communications announced in Peking on September 6, 1959, that about 2,000 of China's county towns were on the telephone line and telegraph networks had connected all counties (*hsien*) and rural districts in China. There were, in June 1959, a total of 64,000 postal and tele-communication offices of which 53,000 were in the rural areas. Long distance telephone lines stretched over 300,000 kilometres (or 186,000 miles) and postal routes, over two million kilometres (1·24 million miles) in 1957. Another means of communication which gets great attention is the wired broadcasting network system. In Szechuan province alone, 36,000 lined broadcasting loudspeakers were installed in villages and towns as of November 1957, covering 120 out of 206 *hsien*. In 1960, practically all the people's communes were reached by telephones and telegraphic lines. One example serves to illustrate the close relationship between the development of industrialization, social communication, and agricultural production. When the pest of rice borers

[172] *JMJP*, November 30, 1958, p. 1.

[172a] Shen Yen-ping, "Achievement of Socialist Culture in New China," *The Glorious Decade*, Vol. II, p. 458.

was found in August 1957 in Hsintu *hsien* of Szechuan threatening the late rice crop, the CCP Hsintu *hsien* Committee used the wired broadcasting network to announce remedial measures to the peasants. In response to the call, over 70,000 peasants immediately plunged themselves into the fight to exterminate the insect pest. Within three days, the pest was basically brought under control. Media of communication like these are of course also utilized to disseminate government instructions, directions regarding various village programmes, propaganda, and weather forecasts. The rural film teams, numbering 2,300 in 1955, were organized to circulate among the villages. Films shown include those on the basic knowledge of modern farming, public sanitation, and management of the cooperatives.[173] It is significant to note that for the first time in China's history, athletic teams are being organized in the villages on a nation-wide basis. In Shantung province alone, there were in July 1957 5,241 ball teams. A volley-ball team comprised mainly of peasants, several times won the number three spot in the national volley-ball championship competitions during the past few years. In 1958, the number of people who qualified for national athletic standards reached 10 million, and there were 4 million students in 100,000 spare-time athletic schools.[174] One hundred and thirty million people took part regularly in some form of sports or other in 1958.[175]

Originally according to the Revised Programme for the Development of Agriculture 1956–67, announced in October 1957, in 5 to 7 years beginning from 1956 illiteracy in every locality would be basically wiped out according to specific local conditions. Spare-time training was to be set up in all *hsiang* to raise the cultural level of both the cadres and the peasants. Elementary education on a compulsory basis would be popularized within 7 to 12 years. Primary schools in the countryside were to be operated, for the most part, by the APCs. Also in 7 to 12 years, networks of film-projection teams, clubs, cultural stations, libraries, amateur dramatic groups and other cultural organizations were to be widely promoted in rural areas. Another goal was to have a sports field in every *hsiang* and to popularize sports in the countryside within 7 to 12 years.

[173] Data are gathered from the following sources: *SSST*, No. 5, March 6, 1957; *HCJP*, July 22, 1955, January 9, February 11, August 4, 1956 and January 28, 1958; and *Hsin Ti-Yu* (New Athletics), No. 15, August 6, 1957, p. 17.

[174] *JMJP*, December 25, 1959, p. 2.

[175] *China Today*, No. 3, January 17, 1959, p. 10.

The goal of basically eliminating many of the most serious diseases in China including malaria, smallpox, hook-worm infection, and schistosomiasis, originally set for fulfilment in 1967, now is envisaged to be attained around 1962. In 1958, 85 million public toilets were constructed, and 29·5 billion tons of rubbish removed.[176]

Socio-cultural transformation in rural China has been greatly stepped up since the "big leap" in 1958. The number of primary school students increased from 60 million in 1957 to 86 million in 1958, and that in secondary and technical schools from 7 million to 15 million during the same period. This new development obviously has more than social or cultural significance. By 1959, some 90 per cent of the school-age children were enrolled in schools. This also facilitates the promotion of agro-technical measures, thus contributing to the growth of rural economy. As these literacy classes are combined with political education, they help the government and the party to carry out political indoctrination and the strengthening of the concept of socialism.

With the help of new alphabets and the simplification of Chinese ideographic characters, it was found that peasants and workers could learn the alphabets and its use in spelling in an average of 12 hours. They can go on to complete the course for learning 1,500 words (a criterion of being literate) in about 45 hours. In the old days, some 400 hours were needed to complete such a course. 774 counties and municipalities out of about 2,000 had established colleges by 1958 and all villages in 1,546 counties had in 1958 their own secondary school.[177]

Universal opportunities for education enhance vertical social mobility, and build up higher morale or self-confidence among the peasants. When one examines the new elites in rural China, such as the agricultural model workers, village Party cadres, youth and women activists, and farmer technicians, one is able to see how the socio-educational measures are coordinated with economic programmes. There are certain common denominators about these new elitists: They all contribute in a notable way to rural production or to group welfare of the community. Their prestige status derives from their contribution towards what in economic terms is called marginal productivity which is helped by the enhancement in

[176] *HPYK*, No. 2, January 25, 1959, p. 54.

[177] *JMJP*, October 1, 1958, p. 10; also Wei Chueh, "Progress in Popularizing the Phonetic Alphabet," *Peking Review*, October 28, 1958, pp. 15–17.

marginal social productivity, but independent of their class or social backgrounds. Their recognition is accorded in both material and non-material ways—rewards in the form of some means of production (a cow, a farming machine, etc.) and in public honours such as the granting of the title of labour hero or invited to Peking to be personally congratulated by Chairman Mao Tse-tung. The social status as well as morale is also boosted by a number of recent measures such as the mobilization of government employees and students to take up jobs in the villages, the decentralization of industrial and commercial powers, and the admission of peasants into technical institutes or higher institutions of learning.

Many Western visitors to China have been struck not only by the speed and magnitude of social change going on in China, but also by its mass conviction and spontaneity. Simone de Beauvoir concludes in her report on China after her visit in 1955, that "this human factor happens to play a crucial role in present-day China. Techniques have reached that mid-point of development at which output depends in the strictest fashion upon the worker's free initiative. . . . A sulking and inert peasantry would completely undermine the system."[178] Dr. Gyanchand, a well-known Indian economist, points out after his extensive travel in China in 1957 that the new social mobility and liberalization of many traditional social institutions, including new status and opportunities made available to peasants, workers, and women, have stimulated the economic growth in China.[179] Mr. R. H. S. Crossman, in his eye-witness account of China in the autumn of 1958, observes: "A change of social behaviour of this kind cannot be achieved merely by compulsion from above. It is a product of a mass movement, inspired by a strong conviction of moral superiority. . . ."[180]

[178] Simone de Beauvoir, *The Long March*, 1958, pp. 490 and 491.
[179] Gyanchand, *The New Economy of China*, 1958, p. 395 and other passages.
[180] R. H. S. Crossman, "The Chinese Ironsides," *New Statesman*, September 27, 1958, p. 404.

CHAPTER V

AN EVALUATION OF THE CCP AGRARIAN POLICY

TO MAKE A comprehensive evaluation of the agrarian policy of the CCP, which stretches over a period of almost four decades is difficult as data available on a number of problems are not abundant. The issue is further complicated by the experimental nature of many agrarian programmes sponsored by the CCP at various periods. However, it is important that some general observations should be presented regarding the salient characteristics and problems of the CCP agrarian policy in order to have an overall view of an epic event. The emphasis will center on the recent period (1953–1959) for a number of reasons, such as the availability of more information and the fact that comments have been made on the historical periods at the end of each preceding chapter.

A. *Major Characteristics of the CCP Agrarian Policy*

The numerous programmes or experiments carried out by the CCP in China can be better understood or evaluated if we grasp some fundamental features of them. This may add more meaning to a number of seemingly unrelated moves on China's agricultural front. It also helps to lessen the danger of merely seeing the trees instead of the forest in the agrarian field of China.

The first important factor which makes the CCP agrarian programmes stand out among numerous other movements of rural reform in China in the past is its effectiveness and penetrating nature in its organization and leadership which reach right down to the village masses. During the past 38 years, the CCP leaders themselves admitted a number of mistakes in the agrarian policy. However history has shown that these occasional blunders have not kept them from achieving victory in the revolutionary movement which relied heavily on the peasantry and agricultural resources. A basic reason is because the CCP has come to understand well the needs and problems of the peasants, worked hard among the villagers, and demonstrated their discipline, devotion, and ability. These qualities are reinforced by the flexibility and realism in tackling thorny issues. This undaunting but practical leadership won them the support of the peasants during the trying days of guerrilla warfare against the much better equipped Japanese invading army. The same leadership accomplished the tremendous tasks of land redistribution, farm collectivization and currently communization throughout the nation in a short period of about 10 years. The strength of the CCP leadership, as embodied in the personality of its Chairman, Mao Tse-tung, lies not only in the understanding of the agrarian problems of China, but also in knowing when to change to a more realistic (sometimes longer) path in achieving the original goal. The adoption of the voluntary principle during collectivization movement and the allocation of much greater capital in the agricultural sector since 1957 are two of many examples.

By contrast, a few people in modern China who did go beyond the stage of writing or just talking about agrarian reform in a big city, their urban habits and manners prevented them from establishing a close rapport with the villagers. Their often condescending attitude was suspected or resented by the peasants who may be illiterate but certainly not unintelligent. The CCP cadres, however, lived and acted like peasants, because most of them were recruited from the peasant stock and followed the "mass line." When the Party sent students or "intellectuals" into the rural districts to work, they were always told to live among the poorest elements of a *hsiang* (See section on techniques in agrarian reform). Their sense of dedication to the revolutionary cause and strict Party discipline sustained them through long period of hardship or temporary setbacks which often were the undoing of bourgeois rural reformers. This Party line of "close identification with the masses," in addition to its propaganda value, helps to achieve close relationship between cadres who often came from another province and thus were "outsiders" to the local villagers. For example, when a group of Peking University students went to join the land reform work in a suburban village, they were told by a veteran cadre:

> Your coming here helps me tremendously. In the past, I had to lead land reform work in 3 villages all by myself. You must be wondering how I managed. Well, it's simple—just entrust the village cadres with the work. It is most undesirable that anyone who engages in mass work should distrust the masses. Don't be

afraid. The villagers make mistakes; so do we. The crux of the matter is that we must study and understand the situation, and check (their work) regularly. If any malady is found, we must cure it—and make them see how it is done so that they themselves may become doctors.[1]

This "mass standpoint," according to Liu Shao-ch'i, includes the following aspects:

(1) Serve the masses wholeheartedly, everything for the masses;
(2) Assume full responsibility for the masses;
(3) Have faith in the people's self-emancipation;
(4) Learn from the masses.[2]

Recently, the Peking government, together with the Party, is pushing vigorously several measures which are designed chiefly to further strengthen the organization and leadership in the rural areas, particularly in the APCs and communes. First is the despatching of students and excessive government employees in the cities to serve as functionaries in the APCs and local administrations—as previously mentioned. At the end of 1957 more than three million students were already settled in the rural areas and more are steadily being relocated. In early 1958, 280 agro-scientists or two-thirds of the staff of the Chinese Academy of Agricultural Sciences, moved into the farming areas throughout the country to promote agro-technical improvements in the villages and to combine their training with the experiences of the peasants.[3] The long-range impact (social, technical, and political) of the coming into being this new class of "educated peasants" can hardly be over-exaggerated.

Since the autumn of 1957, a new organizational form of rural work has been extensively promoted. This is the periodical visits of the leaders in a *hsien* government or Party secretariat, who are organized in the form of "circulating teams" to work (often in the fields) among the various *hsiang* and communes under their jurisdiction. The merits of this system were described as to include the following: (1) It enables the *hsien* leadership to make on the spot

[1] Chao Tsu-wang and Wu Hsin-hsiang, *op. cit.*, p. 28.
[2] Liu Shao-ch'i, "On the Party's Mass Line," *PC*, 2·1, July 1, 1950, pp. 7–10 and 31–2.
[3] *Peking Review*, 1·6, April 8, 1958, p. 4.

decisions after first-hand observations and discussions with village functionaries; (2) It provides opportunities for the *hsien* leaders to learn quickly detailed local needs and problems; (3) It facilitates direct communication between the *hsien* and *hsiang* thus cutting down red tape; and (4) It reinforces the principle of "collective leadership" advocated by the Party.[4]

Another basic-level organizational procedure in agrarian work widely publicized also since the fall of 1957 is the holding of meetings of APC or commune members or *hsiang* cadres in the fields during the rest periods or intervals of work, usually in small groups. The advantages of this method are said to be as follows: (1) It shortens or sometimes eliminates meetings at night, which are often long and tedious; (2) It helps to resolve many farming problems on the spot; (3) It results in higher attendance as the villagers are nearby in the fields; and (4) It enables the villagers to have more time for work and for sleep.[5] Leaders in the people's communes are encouraged to make bold innovations in farming techniques and consult closely with the members.

The above forms of organizing the cadres and peasants at the grass-roots level are being popularized in China today whenever local conditions permit. There are also other organizational forms or techniques designed to meet the particular requirements of a locality and are too numerous to be discussed here. The effective organization of manpower (also womanpower) and the innovations to meet new needs constitute a decisive factor in the development of agriculture in China—or would be in any underdeveloped area where capital and technology are far less available than labour.

The second salient characteristic in the agrarian policy of the CCP is its close coordination with other long-range, basic socio-economic programmes. As pointed out previously, land redistribution was utilized to remove the power of the landed gentry and the agrarian programmes are envisaged as a primary medium for capital accumulation to support the overall process of industrialization through the development of agricultural production and improvements in rival economy. A chief reason of the failure of many

[4] *JMJP*, September 23, 1957. This method was first introduced by the *hsien* cadres of P'ingshun county in Shansi.

[5] *JMJP*, September 27, 1957. This method was first popularized in Chining *hsien* in Inner Mongolia.

previous attempts at agrarian reform in modern China was the piecemeal and superficial manner by which a few well-meaning idealists attempted to cure the ills of rural China. The necessity of removing the grip of the landlord class or the conservative patriarchal clan heads for achieving lasting reforms is generally recognized. It would be difficult to fully develop the rural productive force if over half of the population of peasant women and youths remained fettered under traditional bondages. Equality of sexes is just empty words if the women peasants do not actually enjoy the same property rights or get equal reward with same work. In the words of Shen Chi-lan, woman labour hero and Vice-Chairman of the famous Golden Star APC in Shansi province:

> In the pre-liberation days, the woman was merely a household slave. Even ownership of property after the land reform (in 1948) did not make us fully equal. . . . After the organization of the APC (in 1951) we discovered if we were to do what we wanted, we needed to add one-third to the labour force. We (the women in her village) were essential. . . . When the wives brought home the grain they had earned themselves, the husbands finally began to understand that the women were equal—in the family as well as the cooperative.[6]

The close connection between agricultural development and non-economic reforms may be seen from the following case: A village in east China with 330 acres is conveniently located near a stream called the Dragon King. But in the old days no irrigation ditches were ever built because the various peasant households could not decide through whose fields the water channels should pass, or how to allocate labour or who would pay how much. After the APC was formed in 1955, the above problems ceased to exist, and 12,000 work-days were allocated for the job. In two months a two-mile canal was dug and the Dragon King was tamed to the benefit of the entire village. The production of the land which was used hitherto mainly for maize increased from 1,200 pounds per acre to 4,200 pounds per acre with the planting of rice. The average income of the members of that particular APC in 1956 reached 500 *yuan*

[6] Shen Chi-lan, "How We Became Equals," *China in Transition* (in English), Peking, 1957, pp. 313–17.

or seven times as much as that of pre-cooperative days.[7] This may be a "model case" used by Peking writers to propagate the collectivization movement, but the points raised in the report are applicable in numerous other areas of China.

Within the economic sphere, many of Peking's agricultural programmes are designed to fulfil simultaneously a number of coordinated functions in the different sectors of the economy. Take the recent all-out drive on encouraging hog raising, which already resulted in the increase of hogs from 88 million heads in 1955 to 146 million in 1957 and 180 million in 1959. This campaign serves at least three major purposes economically: It expands an important source of manure for fertilizing farmland; it increases the supply of pork which is one of the staple foods for the Chinese people; and it provides greater quantity of bristles, a major medium for acquiring foreign exchange. The obvious link between the enhancement in cotton production (from 444,000 tons in 1949 to 2,410,000 tons in 1959) and the expansion of the textile industry (from 3·8 billion metres of cotton cloth in 1952 to 7·5 billion metres in 1959) needs little elaboration. This problem of a suitable balance among various economic sectors is a very complicated one and will be discussed more in the next section.

One of the reasons why current agricultural development in China came as a great surprise to quite a few Western specialists is because often the evaluation is made from a limited approach, say, from purely economic factors. But organizational effectiveness plus mass determination can achieve unusual feats—the saving of the Wuhan city as well as tens of thousands of acres of farms from the unprecedented crest of the Yangtze River in 1955 is just one of such examples.

The third outstanding characteristic of the CCP's agrarian policy is related to the second one, but it is so important that it should be treated as a separate area of discussion. And this is the integration of many agricultural programmes with political objectives. As early as 1950 Teng Tzu-hui pointed out that,

> some comrades look upon agrarian reform as the simple matter of the distribution of land, which in turn is considered a simple technical job, and thus the problem of agrarian reform is

[7] Chou Ch'uan, "Today and Yesterday on China's Farms," *PC*, No. 8, April 1957, pp. 26–8.

> understood merely as a means for the development of production. This view is incorrect. It must be understood that agrarian reform constitutes the basic content of the New Democratic Revolution in China at the present stage.[8]

Both at the policy-making level and at the implementation level, changes in agrarian reform methods are often related to political requirements. Thus, from the spring of 1949 to the summer of 1950 when the CCP was consolidating their power in the "new areas," only a mild programme of rent and interest reduction was introduced. After the promulgation of the Agrarian Reform Law on June 28, 1950, holdings of the landlords in most of the "new areas" were redistributed. Before the summer of 1949, the surplus land and property of rich peasants were requisitioned, but the Agrarian Reform Law of June 1950 stipulated that "land owned by rich peasants and cultivated by them or by hired labour, and their other properties, shall be protected from infringement." (Article 6) The principal reason pointed out by Liu Shao-ch'i in his *Report on the Agrarian Reform Law* of June 14, 1950, was that "the present political and military situation has essentially changed."

CCP's agrarian policies at given periods were tied in with political goals such as the "resist-America aid-Korea" movement, the campaign "against waste, corruption and bureaucracy," and "be patriotic and produce more" movement. When peasants are taught to read and write, among the first lessons are included political slogans calculated to "awaken the class consciousness of the peasantry" and "teach the basic policies of new China." When a programme was found to be undesirable politically, it would be discarded or modified, even if it possessed certain economic advantages. One illustration is the discontinuation in the use of the "Get Prosperous" slogan in 1951, which was publicized after the Second World War to stimulate the peasants to greater production effort. After 1951, the phrase "fa-chia chih-fu" (make the family prosperous and rich) was dropped on the ground that "it strengthened the individualism of the peasants." The drastic acceleration of the collectivization process in 1955 and 1956 was in part, in the words of Mao Tse-tung, to nip in the bud the polarization of rural

[8] Teng Tzu-hui, "The Political Significance of the Agrarian Reform," *Chang-chiang jih-pao*, (Yangtze Daily), Hankow, December 27, 1950.

classes. Different treatments were accorded by the state to different rural households according to their class status. For example, in a speech of Teng Hsiao-p'ing on September 23, 1957, it was stated that,

> we must by means of reasoning and argument struggle against those well-to-do middle peasants who harbour deep-rooted capitalist ideology and engaged in capitalist activities. However, they should not be treated the same as landlords, rich peasants, counter-revolutionaries and bad elements. For the well-to-do middle peasants, the question remains one of persistently uniting with them, educating them, and reforming them.[9]

The adjustment of agrarian programmes with the changed or changing political conditions also reflects another characteristic feature of the CCP agrarian policy, namely, the realistic and flexible nature of its approaches.

Peking's directives and regulations on agriculture repeatedly exhort the cadres not to apply the provisions arbitrarily but to pay regard for the specific local circumstances. For instance, at the top level different time-tables were set for the implementation of land redistribution in different regions according to political and other conditions. A similar attitude could be found in Liu Shao-ch'i's report on the agrarian reform law of June 1950: "If deviations occur in some areas after agrarian reform is started and give rise to certain chaotic conditions which cannot be rectified quickly, land redistribution should be held up in these areas until next year." A directive on the "Active Preparation for Production Next Year" issued by the Ministry of Agriculture on September 8, 1956 emphasized, among other things, that in making arrangements for grain production and the promotion of the cultivation of high yielding crops, "local expediencies must be taken into account, and where conditions are not suitable, the general popularization of high-yield crops may turn such crops into low-yield crops and result in losses."[10] Teng Hsiao-p'ing, when reporting on the rectification campaign on September 23, 1957, stated: "The method of launching the movement of socialist education in the rural areas must also necessarily

[9] Teng Hsiao-p'ing, "Report on the Rectification Campaign," *JMJP*, September 23, 1957.

[10] *NCNA* bulletin, Peking, September 9, 1956.

be that of full and frank expression of opinions and general debate. It must be done by having faith in the majority of the masses.... There is no need to insist on identical methods in view of the different conditions in different localities. Notwithstanding the approaches taken, they should in no way restrict full and frank expression of opinions." The shift to a much greater emphasis on agriculture and its related industries in the second five-year plan (while still assigning priority to industrialization) is another example of CCP's sensitive response to practical needs.

At the implementation level, there are numerous examples in the actual agricultural programme which are indicative of this non-dogmatic approach. A few cases will serve to illustrate the point. Realizing the inadequate attention paid to subsidiary occupations in rural areas in the early years of the first five-year plan, Peking has encouraged the expansion of side occupations and the organization of handicraftsmen within the APCs and the communes into special groups since 1955. Another example of the elasticity in the CCP's agrarian policy is seen in the doubling of the amount of landholding (from 5 to 10 per cent) which was allowed to be set aside for private cultivation by APC members in 1957. In the current programme to increase the number of domestic animals, especially pigs and fowls, peasant households are permitted to raise them privately and keep the income derived from such efforts. When the CC, CCP issued a directive on the production management work in the APCs on September 14, 1957, it advised that "new science and technology of agriculture must be combined with the experience of local peasants. The history of agricultural development in a particular locality and the advice of old peasants must be given weight."

The basic characteristics of the CCP agrarian policy are of course not limited to the ones just mentioned. A number of others have been brought up in preceding chapters and need not be reiterated here. These include the increasing emphasis assigned to agro-technical measures (see IV.4), the effective use of the mass organizations, especially those of peasant youths and women (see IV.7), and the skilful utilization of propaganda media and techniques in promoting various rural programmes (see III.5). There are other important aspects such as the method of criticism and self-criticism regularly utilized by the CCP which serves a variety of political, psychological, and social functions.[11] But these complex issues call for detailed, separate studies and cannot be for practical purposes deliberated here. Certain general observations can also be found in the concluding section of the volume.

The recent few years have been an epic era in the annals of China's agrarian development. The increase in crop production in 1958 is outstanding in the modern history of China. Concomitantly, gigantic socio-economic changes like the organization of people's communes are being carried out in rural China. When these co-ordinated programmes such as the continued growth in agricultural production, expansion of local industries, popularization of agro-technical training, and elimination of illiteracy develop their full impact on the nation in general and on rural areas in particular, even greater development in agricultural development may be expected in China. Furthermore, many long-range projects such as soil conservation, irrigation, and other agro-scientific improvements will have their cumulative and causative effects in the future. These will raise still higher the level of agricultural production as well as the living standard of the peasants. As Prof. Charles Bettelheim wrote in his article on "China's Economic Growth" at the end of 1958: "One can expect future results to be in keeping with what People's China has already achieved."[12]

Some of the goals for the immediate future in the agrarian sector may be seen in the "Ten Proposals" made by the Conference of Model Workers of Socialist Agriculture held in January 1959. Among them are the following: first, to guarantee the fulfilling of the production targets of grain and cotton in 1959; second, to promote, in a coordinated manner, rapid expansion of agriculture, forestry, animal husbandry, subsidiary occupations and fishery; third, to further develop local industries by the communes, and to increase the value of product in such industries by 100 per cent; fourth, to enlarge marketing, trading and transport facilities, and to double the value of commercialized goods produced in the rural areas in 1959; and fifth, to achieve another big leap forward in the field of mass education, public hygiene, cultural activities, and scientific research.[13] Progress in the above goals will

[11] See author's "Criticism and Self-criticism as a Socio-Psychological Tool in China," *Nachrichten der Gesellschaft fur Natur-und-Volkerkande Ostasiens* (Hamburg, West Germany), 84, 1958, pp. 34-42.

[12] 4th article by Prof. Bettelheim, *The Economic Weekly*, Bombay, December 13, 1958, p. 1561. [13] *JMJP*, January 4, 1959, p. 5.

not only enable the Chinese villagers to live better in a more attractive environment, but will also close steadily the gap between the rural and urban workers, and between manual and "brain" workers. In this respect, it is interesting to note a statement made by Prime Minister Nehru in a New Delhi speech to the *padyatris* (voluntary village workers) of the Bharat Sevak Samaj on February 3, 1958: "Coming as most of you must be from cities, you must endeavour to narrow down the ominous gap between the rural and urban populations."[14] This problem is a basic one faced by many countries in the world today.

B. *Significant Aspects in the Current Agrarian Development*

Many aspects which are of major significance in evaluating the agricultural scene in China are a continuation of the trends of previous years—such as the increase in crop production, collectivization of farming, and agro-technical improvement. The meaning and impact of these have been discussed in preceding chapters of the book, and in this section discussion will centre on the unique aspects of the current (1957–59) agrarian development.

First is the exceptional increase in the productivity of major crops. As appended table at the end of the volume shows the yield in pound per acre for rice has increased from 2,400 pounds in 1957 to some 3,050 in 1958; that of wheat, from 740 to nearly 1,000; and that of cotton from 250 to about 350. This considerably changes the picture concerning limitations resulting from unfavourable land-labour ratio in China. It represents a most desirable way of solving the food supply problem, as the expansion of cultivated area is limited, costly and time-consuming. The reclamation of marginal, hilly land will, as previously pointed out, have adverse effect on soil conservation, thus increasing the possibility of floods in low lands. Internal migration (not to mention external emigration) for surplus agricultural populace to settle in more sparsely inhabited areas also poses many practical difficulties.

The ability to raise rapidly the productivity of major crops also dispels a traditional myth (often couched in the so-called law of diminishing returns) that farmland in China has been utilized to its maximum potential and that there could be little room to substantially enhance the yield per unit of land. The achievement in

[14] *The Times of India*, February 4, 1958, p. 1.

1958 has further strengthened the confidence of the Chinese farmers as well as the leaders to work for even higher yields in the future.

Related to the above is the second important point: viz., effective coordination between agricultural development and the "cultural-technical revolution" initiated near the end of 1957. The essential aspects of these measures have been discussed in previous sections (such as agro-technical training classes, experimental plots and mass education). Suffice it to say here that these played a decisive role in the stimulating of rural economic growth in general, and of crop yield in particular. Here it may be the place to remark that the "big leap forward" in agriculture in 1958 was not something materializing out of the blue; it was the cumulative result of various positive steps taken since 1949 by Chinese leaders, as the weather was not exceptionally good in that year. The significance of the technical-cultural progress is not limited to the agrarian field. It also enables the peasants to become more adept (and more conscious) regarding mechanical or scientific operations, hence making them better industrial workers when they are (and eventually many will be) transferred to the secondary and tertiary occupations.

The third major development on the current agrarian front in China is the skilful utilization of rural labour power. This has been accomplished through a variety of measures, such as more intensive farming methods, expansion of subsidiary occupations as well as local industries, and the promotion of labour intensive projects like irrigation, afforestation, and conservation. It tackles one of the basic problems in traditional China, that is, the low productivity of rural labour, which prevailed in many districts because of the high degree of underemployment and unemployment.

This effective use of agricultural labour offers a way out for a basic problem in the economic development of underdeveloped areas, particularly those with dense population. As is generally agreed, sustained growth of a nation's economy must be achieved in the long run through industrialization. But expansion in the industrial sector has to be capital-intensive, and at the initial stage it cannot offer immediate solution to the problem of unemployment or underemployment. In certain industries the installation of new machinery and the rationalization of operations in order to increase productivity actually result in the retrenchment of workers. Thus the main additional job opportunities during the first few years of industrialization in a populous, agricultural country must be found in the rural areas, not necessarily of course all in farming pursuit.

The Chinese experience has shown this question can be resolved. Aside from its obvious desirability, there are additional advantages in this approach such as the avoidance of over-loading of urban facilities (housing, transport, public utility capacities, etc.) and the indirect incentives given to the promotion of technical reforms and innovations. For example, the introduction of over 200 million improved-type farm implements in China in 1958 was stimulated by an acute shortage of labour power in many rural areas as a result of the promotion of multiple undertakings by the APCs and later the communes.

The fourth important aspect in the current agrarian programme of China is its effective use of indigenous resources, of which labour constitutes an important part. This takes various forms of divergent rural economic activities. The supplementation of chemical fertilizer with locally-made compost or manure has been mentioned already. The utilization of substitute materials (such as bamboo for timber in certain types of construction) to save scarce, essential items is another. Further illustrations may be found in the employment of renovated local transport equipment (carts fixed with rubber tyres and ball bearings, etc.), raising fish in paddy fields, propagation of technical know-how of experienced farmers, and the adoption of traditional folk art forms (with modifications) as mass media in propagating government programmes and socialist ideology.

This ability to utilize available local resources represents a major contributing element in the agrarian development of China. It enables China to expand rapidly her agriculture without too heavy a capital investment which is urgently needed for industrialization. The secondary and tertiary occupations also have raised the labour productivity and introduced numerous technical innovations, but most of them need to be capital intensive. The foodgrain production was increased by 35 per cent in 1958, but the increase in investment in agriculture by the state in the same year was only some three billion *yuan* (a 40 per cent increase over 1957), constituting about 9 per cent of the original budgetary expenditure. [One *yuan* equals 0·4246 U.S. dollar; actual expenditure in 1958 comes to 42 billion *yuan* or so, and receipts about the same amount.] The organizational approaches and techniques employed in China in making more effective use of indigenous resources (including rural manpower) deserve careful attention in the study of economic growth in underdeveloped areas where capital is generally in short supply.

The last but not the least important aspect in the rural development in China today is the coming into being of a new type of Chinese peasants freed from traditional superstitious beliefs and inferiority complex. Liberated from landlord-gentry dominance as well as magico-religious inhibitions, a positive, communal and enterprising spirit is becoming increasingly evident among the Chinese villagers. This dynamic spirit of self-confidence and self-reliance can be illustrated by a poem (out of millions) written by a young peasant who has become literate:

In heaven, there is no Jade God, the Ju-huang,
In the ocean, there is no Dragon King, the Lung-wang;
I am the Ju-huang,
I am the Lung-wang.
To the hills and dales, I pronounce:
Make way, here I come!

(*Author's translation*)

These simple yet powerful lines symbolize the prevailing mood of the Chinese people to fight for the betterment of their lot through the improvement of their environment. Instead of the toilers' former despondency and resignation, they are now proud and forward-looking. When, for instance, a drought lasted over three months in the spring of 1958 in two counties of Anhwei province, not a single peasant made offerings to the rain-god as was the custom in the past. Dr. Joseph Needham, renowned sinologist at Oxford University wrote in early 1959 that "extreme care is taken (in China) to foster all kinds of new ideas arising among the mass of the people, and to encourage originality. It was very moving to see in China last July the processions and rejoicing in honour of the local inventors and innovators. 'Kan hsiang, kan shuo, kan tso!' (Dare to think, dare to speak, dare to act!) was the catchword. . ."[15]

[15] Dr. Needham's letter to the editor of *New Statesman*, January 3, 1959, pp. 16–17.

At the same time, a new value in group spirit is fostered. Villagers are now encouraged, through education and collective living, to view the problems from the standpoint of the region or the nation, instead of emphasizing individual or local interests. This facilitates the promotion of large-scale projects like irrigation, conservation, and road building. For example, when one plain area in Shansi province needed assistance in farming work during harvest time in 1958, more than 7,000 persons came from neighbouring hilly districts to help. They asked for no remuneration, beside food and lodging. In the Nantung district of Kiangsu province when it was found that there was a shortage of 150 labourers for irrigation work in the spring of 1958, 646 people in an adjoining area volunteered their service, although the project would not yield any direct benefit for the latter district. This *esprit de corps* contributes to many national development programmes.

An Indian scholar, returning to India after three years' stay in China in the winter of 1958, wrote from his personal observations that "they (the Chinese people) go about their work cheerfully and merrily. . . . This mushrooming of small-scale heavy industry in the communes is having a great impact on this leap from agricultural backwardness to modern industrialization. Perhaps this explains the extraordinary self-confidence which one notices in the villages of China."[16]

C. *Salient Problems in Rural China*

Understanding the major characteristic of the agrarian policy in China also helps to achieve a fuller comprehension of many basic problems in the Chinese agriculture. For instance, without keeping in mind the essential feature of the present agrarian programme which is used as a primary means to accumulate capital to support industrialization as well as to socialize the countryside, one will not be able to achieve a balanced evaluation of such rural problems as a desirable rate of involuntary savings or how fast the standard of living of the peasants in China should be raised today. Peking's agrarian programmes are comprehensive and the issues involved extremely complex, thus the problems discussed here have to be by necessity selective. A number of specific points such as the operational problems

[16] Articles by Vidya Prakash Dutt on the people's communes, *The Hindustan Times*, New Delhi, March 3 and 4, 1959, p. 7.

faced by the APCs (now the communes), the need for more agro-technical personnel, the danger of indiscriminate land reclamation, questions regarding marketing and grain storage facilities etc., have been discussed in preceding chapters and need not be repeated here.

Greater Co-ordination and Accuracy in Planning [17]

The government control in all major economic sectors of China is comprehensive and the statistical data available to the Peking planners at least in the early stage were meagre. The situation is further complicated by the inexperience of many local cadres. Thus an editorial of the *People's Daily* of May 1, 1957 pointed out "there are many irrational constructions and waste during the first 5-year plan" due to "subjectivism, doctrinairism, formalism, and lack of experience."

Past reports in China seem to indicate there is a need for greater coordination between the agricultural and the industrial sectors, as well as among the three major components of China's agriculture —foodcrops, industrial crops, and subsidiary products. For example, cigarette factories in China operated at 30 per cent of the capacity in 1954 due to the shortage of tobacco supplies. In 1955, there was a shortage of cotton and only 76 per cent of the textile machinery was utilized. There was a bumper crop of cotton in 1957 (1·64 million tons) but the production of oil-bearing crops and soybeans fell short of the goal. Up to 1956, subsidiary occupations in many rural districts declined. In the report on the second 5-year plan, Premier Chou En-lai pointed out on September 18, 1956, that this factor (the neglect of agricultural side products), added to the low prices set for some subsidiary produce, had hampered the overall and full development of the agricultural economy, thus affecting the expansion of the entire economy as well as the peasants' income. A directive issued by the Ministry of Agriculture on September 8, 1957 reiterated the "need for rational allocation of proportionate acreages for different agricultural crops." Up to 1957, the gradual contractions of cotton sowing acreage was described as "the most striking gap in the ratios between foodcrop and cotton cultivation."[18]

[17] For more discussions on the mechanisms and problems of planning in China, see author's *Economic Planning and Organization in China, 1949–58*, 2 vols. Harvard University Press, 1959 and 1960.

[18] *JMJP*, editorial, September 7, 1957.

However, the planted area of cotton was stabilized in 1956–58—at about 15 million acres, and the record yield of cotton in 1959 came as a result of enhanced per-acre production (from 205 lbs per acre in 1956 to around 380 lbs per acre in 1959). That the problem of achieving a suitable acreage apportionment among various crops has not been totally resolved up to 1957 was reflected in a statement in a directive issued by the Ministry of Agriculture on September 8, 1957, which stated "the need for more rational allocations of proportionate acreages for different agricultural crops, so as to develop agricultural production in an overall manner. This way, the increased output of grain and cotton, as well as that of soybean and other economic crops may be ensured at the same time."[19] Up to 1958, the production of tea and silk cocoons in China had not reached their pre-war peak levels.

In the particular area of planning of agricultural crops for various areas, several technical problems were brought up in an article published in early 1957. The author pointed out that it was true that before setting down the control figures (for agricultural crops) the state had solicited the views of local areas. However, these views were generally submitted during the period from July to September—too early in many areas to make accurate crop estimations. The time gap between such reports and the actual planning, during which changes in natural conditions might occur, also affected the accuracy of the target figures. This may partly explain the original overestimation of 1958 crop yields.

The article maintained that due to the emphasis put on the state control figures, two sets of plans were generally prepared at the lower levels. In dealing with the higher levels, the regional authorities sought to reach and to exceed the minimum target figures, and in dealing with the lower levels, they demanded an increase in the targets provided in the plan, in order to stimulate enthusiasm in local production. Sometimes by concentrating on major foodcrops, the sowing of miscellaneous cereals and production of native products were edged out of the picture. Consequently, though originally the higher authorities had set down plans for different crops proportionately, and areas were reserved for flexible utilization apart from land devoted to grain and technical crops, in the actual implementation of the plans, the stipulated proportions

[19] *NCNA*, September 9, 1957.

were sometimes overruled.[20] The author recommended that planned production for foodgrains (but not for economic crops at the moment) should be gradually changed to planned purchase, and the state should not control the sowing acreage, but only issue to the cooperatives target figures relating to grain to be taxed and purchased. The state also should, it was suggested (before the issuance of these production goals), compile regional production plans for internal reference of the provincial cadres. These criticisms reflect the need for greater flexibility in the highly centralized control of agricultural programmes in China. In a speech on the economic plans for 1958 by Po I-po in August 1957, he too presented schemes to encourage smaller local enterprises. The planning chief remarked that "greater emphasis will be put on the co-ordination of large, medium and small enterprises and fuller use of smaller industrial undertakings and handicrafts."[21] Subsequently, the State Council issued three directives in November 1957, reassigning a number of industrial and commercial projects to local authorities, including greater power for regional administrations regarding foodgrains, forestry, and communications.[22]

One cause of adverse results in the agricultural programmes is sometimes due to the rigidity of planning. The planners in Peking cannot always be in touch with local circumstances nor can they unfailingly make prompt adjustments to altered local conditions. For example, an improved strain of paddy rice (Ch'ing-sheng No. 5) was introduced on 35,000 acres of land in Hunan province in 1956 without adequate preliminary investigations as to its suitability to this particular region. As a result, the yield on these fields was 22,550 tons less than that of the other paddy fields in the region which did not plant this particular strain.[23] The original intention was good; the defective implementation was the outcome of inadequate investigation of local farm conditions.

In planning, there is also the question of assigning priority to the proper key projects which would best facilitate the

[20] Yeh Chun, Chekiang Provincial Dept. of Agriculture, "An Inquiry into A Change for the Agricultural Planning System in China," *CHCC*, No. 2, February 1957, pp. 14–16. [21] *NYT*, August 12, 1957, p. 2.

[22] Chinese text in *HPYK*, No. 24, December 25, 1957, pp. 57–62.

[23] "Accept the Lessons in the Promotion of the Ch'ing-sheng No. Five Rice Strain," *JMJP*, October 12, 1956.

break-through in a backward agriculture. It is unfeasible to emphasize simultaneously all the programmes that are conducive to rural economic production. Hence preferences must be made among numerous agricultural development schemes, taking into consideration the long-term and immediate effects, resources (including technical know-how) available, the amount of capital investment required, and the degree of complexity in the application. There are, for example, many possible ways of carrying out agro-technical improvements in the Chinese agricultural system. The key projects here may include the use of more chemical fertilizers, extended pest control, and propagation of more improved seeds. The effects of such improvements which deserve greater attention could be immediate and substantial, without requiring too much capital allocation or technical skill in either application or maintenance. Another such example may be the development of the use of alternative or substitute materials either to meet shortages or to create new sources of wealth. For instance, it would be difficult to substantially increase overnight the supply of pork, and the killing of too many sows will handicap the situation in future. A more practical approach would be to encourage substitute consumption like mutton or beef, and to expand other channels of protein supply such as marine products or fowls, domestic and wild. In a similar manner, rice or wheat diet may be partially supplemented by corn or potatoes which are higher-yielding crops. To modify the food habits of a people is difficult, but not impossible. It is important to keep in mind the long-term benefits so as not to kill the goose that lays the golden eggs.

In attempting to carry out simultaneously and rapidly a myriad of agrarian programmes, certain local cadres have at times achieved quantitative results at the expense of quality, and short-term gains at the expense of long-range advantages. In Chekiang province, for example, some fields suitable for tea trees were used for planting food crops. Tea trees (for that matter, many other trees of commercial value) will take a few more years to yield utility value, but the help to the income of the local peasants is, in a long run, much greater. One Chinese deputy made the following remark in his speech at the third session of the First National People's Congress on June 21, 1956:

I observed (amidst positive accomplishments in the rural areas in Chekiang province) that reclamation of wasteland has taken place in the past few years. But the indiscriminate cutting down of trees in wrong spots has resulted in floods in a number of areas.[24]

As a contrast, planners at the national level show awareness of long-term needs. Thus out of the bumper production of wheat in 1958, over 7·5 million tons were reserved as seeds. This may account partly for the paradoxical result of shortage of flour in certain areas in 1958 after a good wheat harvest.[25]

A related issue in agricultural planning involves the compilation of statistical data. Among the more serious problems are the standardization of statistical methods and forms and the inadequacy of competent statistical workers. It was only in 1953 that the statistical reports on agricultural production in China were standardized. After minor changes between 1953 and 1955, the forms for these general agricultural reports were again simplified and systematized in 1956. The revised contents included 9 major forms and 8 appendices.[26] The steady improvements in the agricultural statistics in China since 1952 have been recognized by Western specialists.[27] The tightening up of statistical systems plus the preparation of overall analytical reports of accumulated data in 1956[28] have helped to narrow the time lag between the collection of data and the submission of statistical reports by the Central Statistical Bureau to the respective government organs. Extensive statistical survey among the communes on various aspects regarding production, accumulation, distribution and consumption are being conducted

[24] Ma Yin-ch'u, "Eight Impressions During My Recent Inspection Trip to Chekiang Province," *HPYK*, No. 14, July 21, 1956, p. 97.

[25] T'an Chen-lin, "Strive for Even Greater Harvest This Summer," *JMJP*, February 17, 1959, p. 3.

[26] Editorial, "Strive Vigorously for the Accomplishment of the Statistical Work Goals," *TKKT*, No. 1, January 14, 1958, pp. 2–5.

[27] For example, Dr. Alexander Eckstein wrote in May 1958: "There is no question that with the advent of the Chinese Communist regime, the efficiency of statistical organization and data collection was improved considerably. . . ." *The Review of Economics and Statistics*, vol. XL, No. 2, May 1958, Harvard University Press, p. 129.

[28] See Hsueh Mu-ch'iao, "Preliminary Experiences in the Statistical Work of Our Nation During the First FYP and Future Tasks," *TCKT*, No. 21, November 14, 1957, pp. 1–21.

in 1959.[29] The number of trained statisticians in China has multiplied in the last decade, but the shortage, especially at the local level still remains. Thus, serious over-estimations were discovered in the report of crop yields for 1958.

At the same time, it should be pointed out that the achievements in the agricultural sector in China since 1949 have been great—especially in view of the fact that resources available to the Peking planners at the beginning stage were very limited, and in numerous areas a trial and error approach was unavoidable. It is perhaps also unavoidable that the growth in the agricultural sector during the initial planning years was uneven or in spurts, as the agricultural production is still subject to unpredictable influences like weather. The concept of Peking leaders of a dialectical approach to economic development, that is, balance—imbalance—new balance is a realistic one. Nevertheless, economic development will be smoother and less costly if the degree of zigzagging in the agricultural (or industrial) growth is made less sharp. Helpful means in this respect may include more accurate planning, provision of safeguards or cushions against certain eventualities like natural calamities, and the securing of greater capital either by expanding trade or getting additional credit abroad.

Problems in Collective Farming

A number of operational and technical questions regarding the APCs and communes have been discussed in preceding sections. Here we shall only touch upon the more general issues connected with the collectivization movement in China today.

First is the question between the labour utilization rate of the commune (formerly the APC) members and their average income. Surveys of the APCs on the Chinese mainland in 1956 and 1957 indicate an increase in the number of labour days contributed by the cooperative members than in the days when they were engaged in individual farming. An investigation of 29 higher-stage APCs in the Chekiang province in 1956 showed the following changes in labour utilization rates.[30] (See table on next page.)

[29] For samples of statistical surveys among the people's communes, see *T'ung-chi Kung-tso* (Statistical Work), No. 23, December 14, 1958, pp. 16–18.

[30] Li Pei-kuan, "On the Distribution of Income in the Higher-Stage APCs," *HCS*, No. 7, July 1957, p. 4.

CHANGES IN LABOUR UTILIZATION RATES

Labour type	*No. of persons*	*Work-days*	*Percentage increase compared to the days of*		
			Individual farming	*mutual-aid teams*	*lower-stage APCs*
Male full-time labour	267	259	50	24·5	9·8
Male part-time labour	42	197	112	72·0	41·7
Female full-time labour	132	162	184	85·2	42·1
Female part-time labour	95	75	650	29·7	41·5

Survey of higher-stage APCs in Shansi province in 1956 also showed there was an increase of 30 to 40 per cent in the work attendance among the members compared to the time when these advanced APCs were not formed. These higher rates in labour utilization in the APCs led to increased production in varying degrees, but not necessarily in the higher per capita income proportionally for all who participated in these works. For instance, another survey of 118 higher-stage APCs in Kaishin, Chekiang, in 1956 indicated that when the annual number of days for each full-time labour was between 121 and 150, each labour day in these APCs (41) was valued at 1·29 *yuan*. In another 26 APCs the per capita number of days for full-time workers each year was between 151 and 200, but the monetary reward for each work-day decreased to 1·12 *yuan*.[31] There were APCs in other areas which showed a similar situation. The labour utilization is much more intensive in the communes, and it is not unusual for men and women members with full labour power to put in 300 days or more a year for various economic activities.

It is true, an increase in labour utilization generally resulted in expansion of production, thus raising the per capita income of the entire commune or APC in question (but not necessarily the actual expenditure of every member household). However, if greater utilization of labour is limited only to existing farm undertakings, it may reduce the average income (in monetary terms) for each work-day, thus causing the dissatisfaction of some members whose

[31] *Ibid.*

compensation may not be proportionally raised. As the increase in the rate of labour utilization has been a general development among the APCs and communes in China since 1955, it is important to avoid the above-mentioned shortcoming by developing additional productive jobs in the rural areas. This way, both the total income and the remuneration for each unit of work-day can be raised. The various new undertakings that could be developed in the Chinese agriculture are mentioned in the section on population.

Even when the net value of the unit work-day is raised, there still could be problems regarding the disposition of the income of an APC or a commune. The *Model Regulation for Higher-Stage APCs* (June 30, 1956) provided that 8 per cent of the total income of a cooperative should be reserved for common funds, and 2 per cent as welfare funds. But Peking directives on the APCs also called for the increase in income for 90 per cent of the cooperative members over the previous year whenever possible. It was difficult for quite a number of the APCs in 1956 and 1957 to fulfil both these conditions. An investigation of 11 representative APCs in Chekiang province showed the planned rate of 6 to 8 per cent of the total income of the APC for common funds had to be reduced to an average of around 5 per cent in 1956.[32] The number of productive enterprises has been expanded since the establishment of the communes, but the goal of accumulation rate has also been increased —from around 10 per cent for APCs (actual rate) in 1957 to 20 to 40 per cent for communes in 1959.[33] It seems the target of raising the income for 90 per cent of the commune members every year is a high one, at least for the present.[34] It would be more realistic to include the households which maintain but have not increased their annual income in this target figure of 90 per cent. The income of Chinese peasants rose about 10 per cent in 1958, according to a Peking source.[35]

There are problems which are not entirely within the communes, but connected with national issues. What is called in Chinese publications "the contradiction between the interests of the communes (or APCs) and the interests of the state" could include a number of basic questions such as the amount of agricultural tax

[32] *Ibid.*

[33] Yang Po, *op. cit.*; also see discussion in the section on communes.

[34] See *HPYK*, No. 3, February 10, 1958, pp. 79–80.

[35] Quoted in *NYT*, October 15, 1959, p. 3.

or agricultural products to be acquired by the government, the state pricing policy for major agricultural products, government planning in crop acreages and other agricultural programmes, the tendency of some peasants to divert their attention to private work from collective farming when they become well-to-do, and the policies of the state toward non-agricultural sectors such as the wages offered to unskilled industrial workers.[36] The first three questions have been touched upon in previous sections, and here the discussion shall center on the last two.

The "individualism" of the peasants is recognized as a major problem in the writings of China's leaders. Mao Tse-tung remarked in his *On People's Democratic Dictatorship* (July 1, 1949): "The grave problem is that of educating the peasants." It was later stated in the *Model Regulations for the APCs* of November 10, 1955, that "APCs should never resort to methods of coercion but should use the method of persuasion and set examples, so that those peasants who have not joined the cooperatives will realize that by joining they have everything to gain and nothing to lose and so will join voluntarily." (Article 2) Peking emphasizes the increase of agricultural production in order to improve the welfare of the peasants and to convince them of the superiority of collective farming.[37] There may also be other aspects to be considered in this connection—such as the avoidance of too crowded schedules so that peasants may have more free time, leaving greater leeway in agricultural planning to the APCs or communes, and the undesirability of over-ambitious goals.

As the people's communes combine economic functions with social, educational, and administrative roles, measures must be taken to meet new problems in these fields. For example, the *hsiang* (administrative village) government has been incorporated within the commune structure, but whether there should be separate administrative posts for these two units or not still needs to be studied. Another problem is how to strike a balance between the communization of individual families (in the forms of common dining halls, nurseries, community dormitories, etc.) and the providing of personal parental affection for the children. Under the present high enthusiasm for production among the peasantry, it is

[36] See Yang Po, *op. cit.*; also discussion in the section on people's communes.

[37] See Chu Chi-lin, "More Crops with Co-ops," *Peking Review*, March 4, 1958, pp. 13–15.

sometimes necessary to ensure the commune members to have adequate time for rest and recreation. In a directive promulgated in November 1958 by the Party secretariat of Hupeh province, which received high commendation from the CC, CCP, it contains detailed provisions on "performing well the work to take care of the people's living conditions." Its stipulations include (1) Villagers should have 8 hours' sleep, 4 hours' rest or recreation, 2 hours' study, and normally 8 hours' work. (2) Within collective living, certain personal freedoms should be permitted—such as individual households may keep cooking utensils so they may prepare meals during wintry days and old people, children, pregnant women may eat at home if they so wish. Commune members may raise hogs, fowls, and make pickled meat or fish at home, and (3) A sundry-item section should be set up within the common dining hall where people can buy meat, desserts, cigarettes, wine and other goods.[38]

The disparity between the income of rural and urban workers is not a new problem, but the fast development in the industrial sector of China accentuated the issue. Wage increases as well as fringe benefits given to industrial workers in 1956 further stimulated urban-bound migration from the rural areas. The seriousness of this question was reflected in a decree issued by the State Council near the end of 1957 which required that persons moving from villages into the cities must show documentary evidence to the authorities that they had legitimate grounds for doing so. In 1956 and 1957 especially during the "rectification" campaign when criticisms on government programmes were encouraged, there were complaints about "the sharp inequality between the incomes of peasants and industrial workers." Beginning from mid-1957, Peking has taken a series of measures aimed to improve the situation, such as the reduction of the salary scale for new apprentices in industries, raising prices for many rural products, and allocation of more capital for agriculture in 1957 and 1958. Equally important is the sending of excessive government employees and students into the rural districts since autumn 1957, which will not only help the villages administratively, but also culturally. One helpful move here would be the creation of a more attractive environment for the rural residents in China—such as the provision of more medical facilities, expansion of small-scale industries in rural areas, and the visits of first-rate cultural troupes to the villages. The

[38] See *JMJP*, December 20, 1958, p. 1.

formation of people's communes helps to bridge the gap between urban and rural populace, and between manual and "brain" workers, as previously brought out.

Improving the Welfare of the Peasants

It is both difficult and complex to evaluate the exact living standard of all the Chinese peasants on the mainland during the past 10 years for a number of reasons. First and the obvious hindrance is the impossibility to ascertain the exact conditions of each village among some 80,000 (1958) *hsiang* in China. Second factor is that there are considerable regional variations due to differences in natural endowment and the unpredictable changes in the forces of nature. Third, the needs of human beings are such that the "welfare" of a peasant must not exclude the "intangible" considerations as his or her educational opportunities, social status, and mental outlook on life and regarding the future. Finally, no matter how "objective" an analyst tries to be, he is limited by his background and his own values. The actual urgent needs of a villager in China may not coincide with what a writer thinks are the former's priority wants—especially when the latter has had no intimate contact with the rural community of China in recent years, where many basic changes have occurred.

Nevertheless, the question of the welfare of the peasantry in China today is too vital to be bypassed—it is one of the essential criteria to judge the agrarian policies of the Peking government. First we shall look at the material side of the picture. According to Chinese sources, the purchasing power in rural China increased from 8·1 billion *yuan* in 1950 to 19·1 billion *yuan* in 1956 and to over 28 billion *yuan* in 1958.[39] The living standard in 1958 was 9·7 per cent higher than in 1957. The prices of daily necessity goods remained basically stable between 1953 and 1959.[40] In 1957, there was a slight increase in the prices of some commodities, but the

[39] *HCJP*, October 29, 1957, p. 1; and *NYT*, October 15, 1959, p. 3.

[40] The retail price index of industrial products in rural areas, taking 1952 as 100, is as follows: 1953, 98·5; 1954, 100·2; 1955, 101·4; 1956, 100·4; and 1957 (est.) 100·4. The purchasing price index of farm products for the above respective years (also with 1952 as 100) is 110·1; 113·8; 113·2; 116·6 and (for 1957 estimates), 120·9. See Li Sen, "Develop Among the Peasants Another Convincing and Active Campaign of Socialist Education," *Cheng-chih hsueh-hsi* (Political Study), No. 8, August 13, 1957.

government purchasing prices for agricultural products were raised more than those of manufactured goods. As a result, it was estimated that the peasants would get an additional income of 560 million *yuan* in 1957 through upward adjustments in the prices of rural produce, and a net balance of 150 million *yuan* after deducting expenditures from higher prices for needed manufactured items.[41] According to data released by the Ministry of Commerce in August 1957, the total value of 51 major commodities supplied to the consumers by the Ministry in 1956 increased by 66·7 per cent over 1952. Specifically, watches increased more than 2·5 times; thermos bottle, charcoal, paper, fountain pen, and sewing machine more than 100 per cent; sugar, 80·9 per cent; cotton cloth, 77·3 per cent; and rubber shoes, 60·6 per cent. In the same period of five years, the number of bicycles sold exceeded 24·23 million. In 1950, 14 Chinese peasants shared one bolt of cotton cloth, but the same amount of cloth was shared by only 5 peasants in 1956. The per capita allocation of cotton cloth increased from 18 feet to 24 feet between 1957 and 1958. In 1953, the average annual expenditure on Western drugs by each peasant was 0·79 *yuan*, but it increased to 1·37 *yuan* in 1956.[42] The volume of sale of major consumer goods between 1950 and 1958 showed the following increases: foodgrain, 62 per cent; edible vegetable oil, 97·2 per cent; salt, 94·1 per cent; sugar, 3 times; marine products, 2·4 times; cotton cloth, 1·2 times; rubber shoes, 3·3 times; and machine-made paper, 2·7 times.[43] According to statistical data gathered from 15 provinces (Hopeh, Liaoning, Kirin, Heilungkiang, Shensi, Tsinhai, Shantung, Kiangsu, Anhwei, Chekiang, Yunan, Inner Mongolian Autonomous Region, and the three cities of Peking, Tientsin and Shanghai) and made public in July 1957, the conditions of food supplies in the rural areas were as follows: Grain-surplus households, 53·852 million households (half were lower middle or poor peasants) or 62·36 per cent; Self-sufficient households, 8·316 million or 9·63 per cent; Grain-short households, 24·187 million or 28·01 per cent (among them 15·911 million were poor peasants).[44] The total amount

[41] "Domestic Market Prices in the First Quarter of 1957," *TCKT*, No. 11, June 14, 1957.

[42] *HCJP*, August 13, 1957, p. 1. The per capita rate has been adjusted in accordance with population increases.

[43] SSB, *The Great Decade*, Peking, 1959, p. 142.

[44] Chou Po-p'ing, "The Policy of Unified Purchase and Sale of Grain Shall Not Be Frustrated," *Liang-shih* (Foodgrain), No. 7, July 1957.

of saving deposits in rural China increased from 1,190 million *yuan* in October 1957 to 4,150 million *yuan* near the end of 1959.[45]

Between 1950 and 1956 the government of China spent 3·07 billion *yuan* for basic construction in conservation, 1·31 billion *yuan* for relief, and 1·28 billion *yuan* for agro-technical improvements. This sum of 5·66 billion *yuan* constituted about 30 per cent of the total of all taxes paid by the Chinese peasants in these 7 years —amounting to 18·6 billion *yuan*. In 1957, 68·4 per cent of the tax receipts from the peasants was scheduled to be used for agricultural development—not including investment in rural education, medical service, and transportation.[46]

The household expenditure of the peasants in China in 1956 is partly reflected by a detailed survey of an average village household in Hunan revealed in a report by Politburo member T'an Chen-lin in May 1957:

LI YU-FANG'S CONSUMPTION IN 1956 AND THE COMPARATIVE COSTS FOR MAINTAINING THE SAME LIVING LEVEL IN PEKING AND SHANGHAI*

Actual consumption in Li's family of six during the year 1956				*Corresponding cost in Peking*		*Corresponding cost in Shanghai*	
Commodity	*Consumption (for six)*	*Unit cost (yuan)*	*Total cost (yuan)*	*Unit cost (yuan)*	*Total cost (yuan)*	*Unit cost (yuan)*	*Total cost (yuan)*
Rice	2,310 catties	0·076	175·56	0·148	342·00	0·121	279·50
Sweet potato	800 catties	0·013	10·40	0·04	32·00	0·04	32·00
Oil	24 catties	0·56	13·44	0·59	14·20	0·61	14·64
Salt	60 catties	0·15	9·00	0·2	12·00	0·15	9·00
Pork	40 catties	0·46	18·40	0·77	30·80	0·78	31·20
Beancurd, Sugar etc.			11·36		11·36		11·36
Vegetables				0·05	108·00	0·035	75·60

[45] *HCJP*, December 28, 1957, p. 3; *Ta-kung pao*, January 1, 1959, p. 2; and *China Today*, January 16, 1960, p. 12.

[46] Chang Hao-jan, "Are the Peasants' Burdens Really Heavy?" *HH*, No. 16, August 18, 1957, pp. 16–17.

LI YU-FANG'S CONSUMPTION IN 1956 AND THE COMPARATIVE COSTS FOR MAINTAINING THE SAME LIVING LEVEL IN PEKING AND SHANGHAI*—*Contd.*

	Actual consumption in Li's family of six during the year 1956			*Corresponding cost in Peking*		*Corresponding cost in Shanghai*	
Commodity	*Consumption (for six)*	*Unit cost (yuan)*	*Total cost (yuan)*	*Unit cost (yuan)*	*Total cost (yuan)*	*Unit cost (yuan)*	*Total cost (yuan)*
Coal Briquettes				0·012	43·20	0·0285	102·60
Cloth	72 feet	0·40	28·80	0·4	28·80	0·4	28·80
Socks	6 pairs	0·50	3·00	0·5	3·00	0·5	3·00
Hemp	3 catties		3·00		3·00		3·00
Overshoes	1 pair		4·50		4·50		4·50
Rent, Water, Power			1·00		72·00		124·56
Medical Expenses			12·00		12·00		12·00
Maternity Expenses			12·00		12·00		12·00
TOTAL			302·46		728·86		743·76

* T'an Chen-lin, "A Study of Peasants' Income in China," *JMJP*, May 5, 1957; *HPYK*, No. 11, June 10, 1957, p. 111.

NOTES:

1. No conversions have been made in respect of cloth, socks, hemp, medical expenses, and maternity (midwifery) expenses.
2. Shanghai prices for sweet potatoes taken as the same as in Peking.
3. Vegetables estimated at one catty per capita per day.
4. Coal briquettes estimated at 3,600 catties a year.
5. Rent and utility charges in Peking estimated at 1 *yuan* per capita per month; in Shanghai rent estimated at 1·19 per capita a month, and utility charges at 0·54 *yuan* per capita per month.
6. Firewood, and marine products, gathered by the household, are not included in the list.

T'an's report of May 1957 indicated that rural families paid much less for many commodities than the urban residents. It also showed that there existed considerable differences between the income of prosperous peasants and that of poor peasants, and among peasants of different regions (such as the double crop area in Kwangtung compared to a hilly district in the Northwest). As the chart below indicates, the average income per household of the peasants (4 to 5 persons in each household generally) in various provinces in 1955 was quite uneven:

Province (1955)	*No. of households surveyed*	*Average income per household (yuan)*
Kiangsu (South)	56,000	454
Shensi	328,432	306
Hopei (economic crop area)	93,000	399
Kansu	1,000	171

Income distribution in term of rural classes, according to a sample survey (1957) in Anyang *hsien* (county), Honan, was as follows:

*Rural class**	*Per capita net income in 1955 (yuan)*	*Per capita net income in 1956 (yuan)*	*Percentage increase*
Poor peasants	39·52	51·84	31·17
New lower-middle peasants	48·82	61·38	25·72
New upper-middle peasants	53·73	63·41	18·01
Old lower-middle peasants	54·59	62·70	14·85
Old upper-middle peasants	51·00	59·08	15·85
Former rich peasants	41·19	56·45	37·04
Former landlords	37·39	52·12	39·39
AVERAGE	49·53	59·63	20·30

* T'an, *op. cit.*, p. 108.

According to another survey of 19 APCs of various representative types (in grain areas, cotton areas, hilly districts, and backward areas, but not including isolated calamity districts) in the Anyang region of Honan province in 1956, the income of peasant households within different rural classes also showed considerable variations:

INCOME OF PEASANTS IN ANYANG COUNTY*

Rural class	*Percentage of households that increased income*	*Percentage of households that maintained same income*	*Percentage of households that reduced income*
Poor peasants	74·74	20·08	5·17
New lower-middle peasants	79·05	11·81	9·14
Old lower-middle peasants	72·22	16·74	11·04
New upper-middle peasants	82·22	9·42	8·36
Old upper-middle peasants	62·13	19·73	18·14
Former rich peasants	67·15	19·37	13·48
Former landlords	81·13	10·52	5·31
AVERAGE	75·50	14·72	9·87

* T'an Chen-lin, *op. cit.*, pp. 105–6.

The investigation in 1958 of an average people's commune in Pin-hsi county, Kwanghsi province showed that the middle peasants spent a per capita amount of 87 *yuan* annually. A typical household consumed in a year the following items: 3,000 pounds of foodgrains, 57 pounds of meat, 23 pounds of edible oil and 30 yards of cloth. It also spent, significantly, 9·6 *yuan* on educational stationeries, 2·4 *yuan* on books and periodicals and 14 *yuan* on medical expenses.[47]

To attempt a conclusive evaluation, we would need more comprehensive data than the above. A nation-wide survey of peasant household expenditure was initiated in 1956 and the results when published should be informative. But these limited reports still provide useful references. For example, as T'an Chen-lin pointed out, these figures indicated it would not be easy to realize the goal of enabling 90 per cent of the APC members to increase their income as advocated in government directives. Also it is significant that the poor peasant households and former landlords seem to be doing better than the middle peasants. After the "big leap" in 1958, the peasants in China have income sufficient for basic needs.

The above statistics do not necessarily mean that every peasant in China is leading an abundant life. Also due to the high rate of involuntary saving in the agricultural sector to support industrialization, the per capita increase in purchasing power among the peasantry during the first 5-year plan period was small, estimated

[47] *Ts'ai-cheng* (Finance), No. 13, November 24, 1958, p. 12.

about 70 *yuan* in 1950 and 78 *yuan* in 1956.[48] This figure may have been raised substantially in the second FYP period. But as previously pointed out, the welfare of the Chinese villagers cannot and must not be isolated from other non-economic factors such as the new social status enjoyed by the peasant men and women; an honest and effective administrative leadership; greater chances for education; internal peace and stability of the country; improved sanitary as well as medical conditions; and better cultural or recreational facilities. For example, more than 86 million children went to primary schools in 1958, an increase of 35 million over 1952 and the number of hospitals and clinics run by the communes exceeded 200,000 at the end of 1959, while the total number of hospital beds reached 440,000 in 1958.[48a] To an illiterate Chinese peasant who never had in the past any chance to enjoy modern medical treatment, the availability of educational and medical facilities for himself and his family may mean more to him than having an additional yard of cloth. The welfare of the peasantry in China is certainly closely related to the general economic development of the nation. This may include the growth in heavy and light industries, better marketing facilities, easier credit, expansion of exportable produce, stability of commodity prices, and greater supply of means of production for agriculture. Furthermore, consumptive power is more equally distributed among the people in China now instead of concentrated in a few million members of the privileged class during the pre-1949 era; thus, conspicuous consumption such as that enjoyed by the rich in cities like Shanghai in the prewar time is seldom in evidence. The shortage of certain goods could also come from the result of an expansion of consumption base. For instance, the peak prewar production of cotton cloth was achieved in 1936—at 45 million bolts (one bolt equals 40 yards or 36·58 metres) or about one tenth of a bolt for each person (or 3·6 metres) assuming the population then at around 450 million. The cotton cloth production in 1959 reached 7 billion metres which, even with the population growth (660 million) would give about a 200 per cent increase in per capita figure of cotton cloth. Yet there is still not enough cloth to satisfy all the demands, and the chief reason is due to the

[48] Chang Hao-jan, *op. cit.*, p. 17.

[48a] Li Te-chuan, "Ten Years of Public Health Work in New China," *China Today*, January 23, 1960, pp. 12-15.

fact that millions of people more can afford today to buy cloth in China and do buy more.

The improvement in the welfare of the Chinese peasants has been reported by many neutral visitors including Clement Attlee (1956), Rene Dumont (French agronomist, 1957), Joseph Nedham (1958), and Western journalists. A detailed report after extensive field studies (July–August 1956), was made by an Indian Agricultural Delegation to China. Among its general observations is the following: "As a result of increase in industrial and agricultural production in recent years and better distribution of incomes, there has been a noticeable improvement in the standard of living among the people in China."[49] This is especially so when compared to pre-1949 living conditions of the Chinese populace. For example, one survey showed that the average Shanghai worker, who was better off in income than the peasants in a relative sense, consumed only 300 pounds of grain and 6·4 metres of cotton cloth annually during 1929–30.[50]

The Population Growth

The welfare of the peasants is related, too, to the rate of population growth in China. The first census taken by Peking in 1953, which gave the total population on the Chinese mainland (as of June 30, 1953) as 582,603,417, is now generally accepted as the nearest approximate to reality.[51]

At the present rate of increase, estimated at 2·2 per cent per annum, the present population of China (650 million in 1958) will exceed 700 million in 1962—the end of the second 5-year plan. A rapid growth in the number of mouths to be fed will, in some ways, complicate the problem of raising the peasants' standard of living as well as other economic programmes. Premier Chou En-lai remarked to the Indian Agricultural Delegation on August 17, 1956 that the mere fact that the rate of increase of agricultural production (at 4 to 5 per cent per annum at that time) was outstripping the

[49] *Report of the Indian Delegation to China*, *op. cit.*, p. 41.

[50] Quoted in Su Chung, *op. cit.*, p. 10.

[51] Leo A. Orleans, member of the Reference Department of the Library of Congress, wrote in August 1957 issue of *The Journal of Asian Studies* that "there seems to be no reasonable alternative to the acceptance of the published data as the most current and the best information available on Chinese population and its distribution." Other Western demographers like Dr. Irene Tauerber who specialize on the study of Far Eastern population all seem to agree.

current rate of growth in population did not mean that population could continue to expand without any limit.[52] In 1956, Peking government began to take various measures to promote planned parenthood, and birth control methods were widely popularized in government directives as well as in all the leading publications in China. According to reports in late 1957, a supply network of contraceptives had been set up in both urban and rural areas—through the supply and marketing cooperatives, the medical supplies companies, the sundry goods companies, and the pharmaceutical companies which are required to carry items for birth control. For example, there were only nine stores selling contraceptives in the rural districts of Hopei province in 1955. The number of such stores increased to 3,500 in October 1957. Compared to 1954, the prices of condoms in 1957 went down 60 per cent, and quality had reportedly reached "the international standard." Forty-five million pieces of condoms were produced in 1957, about 450 times that of 1954, in addition to 300,000 diaphragms and 1·95 million tubes of contraceptive jelly. Another significant development is that approximately 40 per cent of the condoms supplies to Hopei province in the first half of 1957 went to the rural areas which absorbed 30 per cent of all the contraceptive drugs sold.[53] The price of condoms was reduced as just mentioned, and a diaphragm in 1957 cost only a few Chinese *fen* (cents).

Madame Li Teh-ch'uan, Minister of Public Health, reported on March 7, 1957 that:

> During the last year (1956) with the interest of various circles in contraception and under their guidance and encouragement, we have paid great attention to this problem and have done a great deal of work. We have actively and extensively developed propaganda on contraception, published popular pamphlets on the subject, printed many pictures for propaganda purposes in various places, given many speeches, held forums and exhibitions and shown projection slides, thus enabling many people to understand more about contraception.[54]

[52] *Report of the Indian Delegation, op. cit.*, p. 22. Also see Li Teh-ch'uan, "Birth Control and Planned Families," *JMJP*, March 9, 1957; and Ma Yin-ch'u, "A New Approach to the Population Problem," *op. cit.*

[53] *Kuang-ming jih-pao* (Brilliance Daily), Peking, October 25, 1957.

[54] Li Teh-ch'uan, "Birth Control and Planned Families," *JMJP*, March 8, 1957, p. 8.

In addition to the popularization of birth control knowledge and techniques, other means such as raising the legal marriageable ages (now at 20 for boys and 18 for girls) and the loosening of requirements for birth control surgical operations were being studied in China to better safeguard the health of the mothers.

At a large-scale birth control exhibition opened in the Chun-shan Park in Peking on March 8, 1957, a spokesman of the Ministry of Public Health reported that similar exhibitions were being held in many parts of the country. According to her, birth control was already beginning to show certain results. Peking's birth-rate in 1956 was down to 39 per 1,000 from 43 per 1,000 in 1954. In Shanghai, No. 9 Cotton Mill, birth rate among the 2,500 women workers decreased from 2·65 per cent in 1954 to 1·2 per cent in 1956.[55] So far information on the effect of the "planned parenthood" campaign in the rural areas is not available. It will take longer time to achieve nation-wide results in birth control among the villagers than in the urban populace. In the meanwhile, colonization programme of the sparsely populated areas in China like Heilungkiang and Sinkiang was greatly accelerated, and between 1955 and 1957, more than 700,000 people were reportedly settled each year in the areas in Northwest and Northeast China.[56] But as the annual increase of population is between 13 and 15 million, the issue remains. After 1958, when the expansion of various productive activities of the people's communes resulted in a shortage of labour power, the question of population control faded into the background. Nevertheless, planned parenthood, in the long run, is conducive to a quicker increase in living standard and better health of the mothers of China.

However, those determinist observers who maintain that rapid economic progress in China is unfeasible unless population growth is checked take a one-sided view. There were many factors causing economic stagnation or deterioration in traditional China which could be rectified even with population pressure — such as abusive land systems, concentration of people in treaty ports due to political instability in old China, negligence of conservation and afforestation, poor distribution or communication system, and ineffective administrative leadership. Furthermore, population is a relative matter, depending on the level of production of a particular country. For example, at the end of 1956 the per capita holding of arable land in Belgium was about half an acre and that of Belgian Congo

[55] *NCNA*, March 8, 1957. [56] *NYT*, December 16, 1957, p. 5.

was 9 acres, or 18 times as much.[57] The per capita holding of cultivated acreage in India (1955) was about 0·85, which is 170 per cent of that of Belgium. But there is no question which among the three areas is the more economically advanced or which has a greater population problem.[58] This illustrates the fact that population pressure in a particular country or area depends on the degree of resource utilization. And from a long-range view point, there are great potentialities in the development of food supplies for the world. As Dr. Robert Brittain wrote in 1952: "Human beings have reached a stage of technical development where they can produce from the available resources not merely subsistence, but abundance."[59] This view is supported by recent scientific progress (particularly in the Soviet Union) and by many leading scientists. Dr. James F. Bonner of the California Institute of Technology presented a fascinating paper in May 1956 on the possibilities of producing entirely new edible crops or making synthesized foods or drastically reducing the production time as well as cost of certain foodcrops. Among the possible new sources of food described in his report are: a meat beet or a fat plant, the cultivation of algae, chemical synthesis of essential meat proteins, and the conversion of woody stalks and leaves to edible sugar. The last three experiments had already been successfully tried at that time.[60] The rapid advancement in the peaceful application of nuclear energy and other forms of fuel have made within human reach, through the supply of cheap, abundant power, the conversion of regions on the earth (including marine resource) previously regarded as "useless" into direct or indirect sources of food supplies.

At the same time, these new scientific-technical exploitations in food resources and China's industrialization which will siphon off surplus labourers from the rural areas take time to realize. In the meantime, the additional employment created in China estimated at 1·3 million annually during the first five-year plan period was only one-third of the number of individuals who were reaching the labour age of 16 each year in China during the same period.[61] By 1967, seven

[57] Calculated from data in *1958 Information Please Almanac*, pp. 565–7 and 788.

[58] Also see "Malthusism," *Monthly Review*, December 1951, p. 251; quoted in Paul Baran's *The Political Economy of Growth*, 1957, p. 239.

[59] Robert Brittain, *Let There Be Bread*, 1952, p. 223.

[60] *NYT*, May 21, 1956, p. 19.

[61] *HH*, early September 1957, quoted in *NYT*, September 15, 1957, p. 28.

million will reach the working age of 16 each year. This population increase, plus fast urbanization under the impact of industrialization, has resulted in migration from villages to cities and the increase of non-productive personnel in urban centres. For example, while there were only five cities with a population of one million or more in China in 1950, the number had grown to 13 in August 1957.[62] During 1953 to 1957, it was estimated that 8 million people had found their way into the cities from rural China. A survey in 15 cities in 1957 by a correspondent of the NCNA news agency showed that 60 per cent of the population could be described as non-productive.[63] Urbanization and industrialization historically go hand in hand, but large influx of people to the cities intensifies many problems such as housing, transportation, and food supplies. At the same time, the rural labour force (on a full-time basis) estimated at 260 million in 1957, will reach 280 million by 1962.[64]

In view of the above, effective measures would still seem desirable to meet this situation. A number of counter-moves have been undertaken in China. They include the creation of more productive jobs in cities, greater use of human labour in additional enterprises, prevention of "blind migration" of peasants into the cities, transferring of urban residents into the villages and the development of China's hinterland.

The realistic means of offering extensive, *immediate* relief seems to lie in the creation of more opportunities for productive work in the rural areas themselves—until long-range programmes such as industrialization and planned parenthood can take full effect. There are a number of possible ways by which the additional labour power in rural China may be profitably utilized. These may include: (1) The development of both old and new subsidiary occupations such as local industries, handicrafts, breeding of domestic animals, fruits or vegetable growing, and the undertaking of side jobs like tea planting, raising silk cocoons, and fishing. (2) The expansion of labour intensive projects such as building irrigation or conservancy works, road construction, reclamation of wasteland, afforestation, and construction of means of transportation like junks, carts, and wagons. (3) Intensive cultivation and

[62] *NYT*, August 10, 1957, p. 3.

[63] Quoted in *NYT*, August 10, 1957, p.c.

[64] Wang Kuang-wei, "How to Organize Agricultural Labour Power," *CHCC*, No. 8, August 9, 1957.

the increase of multiple cropping, in order to raise the production per unit of land. (4) A greater rational division of labour so that the farmers may achieve higher efficiency and productivity, while concomitantly more facilities for social and cultural activities can be enjoyed by the villagers. These programmes, all being promoted in varying degrees in China and stepped up after the formation of communes in mid–1958, may entail a crowded schedule for the peasants, but hard work is requisite for a speedy development of an underdeveloped economy. The common people of China have always been diligent workers; with definite objectives under an effective leadership they now have something to struggle for, and the improvements already achieved serve as further incentives.

As mentioned before, since 1957, and particularly after the organization of the communes in the summer of 1958, there has developed a shortage of labour power in many rural areas in China. This unprecedented phonomenon resulted from a combination of factors: First, the more intensive farming methods engaged and the multiple economic activities undertaken by the communes call for a tremendous amount of labour. The expansion of irrigated land during the big leap year 1958 (totalling some 67 million acres) alone called for the work of about 100 million manpower. Second, the concomitant programmes for local industries, expansion of transport facilities (railway and road buildings, etc.), the making of fertilizers (both chemical fertilizers and native manures) and others, require a huge number of workers. The production of locally-made iron, steel, cement, and coal required some 100 million manpower during 1958. Third, the extensive social and educational programmes promoted in China's rural areas further tax the labour resources in the countryside. As a result, although the communes have succeeded in releasing additional labour force (through more rational organization and the adding of around 70 million full labour power by relieving peasant women from household chores), many rural districts are under heavy pressure for more labour power. It has been estimated that out of the 220 million full-time agricultural labour power available in 1959, only 80 million manpower would be available for foodgrain production. Thus labour productivity needs to be further raised.[65] This has relegated the population problem into the background, and represents a most encouraging development. However, the question of protecting

[65] *JMJP*, February 17, 1959, p. 3.

the health of mothers from having too many children and keeping the population increase slow to achieve more quickly an enhancement of living standard is not totally resolved.

The problem of population is not limited to the quantitative side of growth. There are also issues concerning the structural aspects of China's populace such as regional distribution, occupational divisions, internal as well as external migration, age breakdowns, and sex composition. These complex problems cannot be discussed here, partly due to the unavailability of detailed information.

Natural Calamities

Another major problem concerns the prevention or control of natural disasters. The scope of damage caused by natural calamities like flood, drought and water clogging from 1953 to 1959 (except 1957) was reported in Peking sources as follows:

DAMAGE BY NATURAL CALAMITIES (1953–59)*

Year	*Area affected (million acres)*	*Loss in grain production (million tons)*	*No. of persons affected (millions)*
1953	15·83	7·5	34·35
1954	30·25	8·85	62·23
1955	19·03	6·35	36·22
1956	38·33	12·20	74·34
1958	16·67	n.a.	n.a.
1959		n.a.	n.a.
1931 (flood alone)	26·30	n.a.	52·70

* *Liang-shih* (Foodgrains, Monthly), No. 7, July 1957; *JMJP*, February 17, 1959, p. 2; and *China Today*, January 30, 1960.

These statistics and the serious floods as well as drought occurring in 1959 indicate that a great deal remains to be done on the prevention of natural disasters in China. The long-range programmes like afforestation and conservation, which are being vigorously pushed by the Peking government, require time to take full effect. But it is also relevant to point out here that without these water and soil conservation efforts, the damages of natural disasters would be much greater. The effective organizational work in flood prevention and famine relief help to reduce the seriousness of the situation. For example, in the unprecedented floods of 1956, only a small number of people lost their lives, while in 1931 "about a quarter of a million persons died during the floods."[66] When the upper reaches of Yi and Shu Rivers in Shantung had the heaviest flow in the history of that province in 1957, about 550 lives were lost, while similar disasters in that region in pre-1949 days took away tens of thousands of human lives. According to one report, 62,000 pounds of freshly cooked foods were dropped by planes to the flood victims in those flooded districts in three days.[67] Equally important is the fact that thousands of tons of seeds for autumn crops were distributed by the Internal Affairs Ministry to peasants in these disaster areas so that production would not be interrupted.

There are also Government provisions for the reduction or exemption of agricultural tax for peasant households which suffer from natural calamities. The scales of exemptions as stipulated in the Regulations of August 1952 are as follows: For crop loss of 60 per cent or more, tax exemption, 100 per cent; 50–60 per cent losses, 70 per cent exemption; 40–50 per cent, 50 per cent; 30–40 per cent, 35 per cent; 20–30 per cent, 25 per cent; and 20 per cent or less, no exemption. The effective mobilization of local inhabitants in the case of flood or drought resulted in the successful coping with the threat of nature in many instances. For example, Wuhan in 1955 and Harbin in 1957 were threatened by the worst floods in the past 100 years, but both these cities were made safe by an all-out drive of the local people and the government. By contrast, Wuhan and its vicinity were inundated for several months in 1931, when the water crest of the Yangtze River of a lower height than that of 1955 hit the metropolis.

Development of Hilly Areas

It was estimated in 1957 that hilly and semi-mountainous districts constituted about two-thirds of China's total area. One-third of the population, cultivated acreage, and grain production of China is in these hilly or semi-mountainous districts.[68] Many important

[66] Kai-ming Ch'iu, "Agriculture," *China*, ed. by MacNair, 1946, p. 470.
[67] *NYT*, July 24, 1957.
[68] Chu Teh, "Speech at the Conference on Production in Mountainous Areas," *HPYK*, No. 24, December 25, 1957, p. 71.

items including timber, minerals, tung oil, tea, and fruits are produced in these areas.

In view of the above, it is not difficult to understand why Peking set up the development of China's hilly areas as a major task in the second five-year plan, and initiated an intensive campaign in 1957 to encourage the government functionaries and students to "go down to the *hsiang* (villages) and go up to the hills." This movement was in full swing by 1958. However, to successfully carry out this programme a number of problems need to be dealt with. The more impending ones include: the improvement in the transportation conditions, setting up of a better marketing network, provision of basic medical facilities, a coordinated soil conservation plan, and the development of local industries (including subsidiary occupations) in accordance with the special conditions in these hilly regions.

Agricultural production and the national economy as a whole will be helped greatly if a weak link in the rural economy, the hilly areas, could be strengthened. Teng Tzu-hui in a speech on developing hilly regions of November 29, 1957, asked that in each province one vice-chairman and one secretary in the CCP Secretariat of the province should devote to the work regarding these areas. A number of reports appeared in the issues of *People's Daily* in January 1958, describing successful programmes in certain such areas. The paper, at the same time, observed that "conservative thinking and inertia among cadres in hilly districts must be subjected to severe criticism."[69] To what degree this kind of reluctance on the part of some Chinese functionaries to engage in work in the hilly parts of the country may be overcome depends partly in a long run on how successfully the problems enumerated previously are coped with.

There are naturally other problems existing in rural China such as the relatively slow increase in livestock and domestic fowls, the need for more grain storage facilities, the development of new crop bases (e.g., cotton plantations in Sinkiang), the slow recovery of certain subsidiary occupations like silk cocoon and tea production, and the desirability of expanding additional food resources other than grain crops. But they do not have the same degree of magnitude or complexity as the previously discussed problems possess.

[69] Quoted in *NYT*, January 16, 1958, p. 13.

CHAPTER VI

CONCLUDING COMMENTS

EVALUATIONS OF the CCP's agrarian policy during various stages since 1921 have been made in preceding sections. The significant aspects include the close coordination between political and socio-economic objectives; emphasis on practical approaches in accordance with objective, changing conditions; priority on the raise of agricultural (particularly crop) production and productivity; skilful utilization of indigenous resources, including manpower; and the consistent attention assigned to the "mass line," that is, close liaison and consultation with the people.

Summing up the overall significance as well as implications of the agrarian policy of the CCP, we may now list the following points:

First is that thorough and sustained agrarian reform must be accompanied if not preceded by institutional changes in a backward, stagnant socio-economic system—such as the removal of the landlord-gentry domination in the countryside, greater social mobility through educational opportunities and equality of sexes, and the removal of superstitious or fatalistic beliefs among the peasants. Without eliminating those abusive or restricting institutional factors, agrarian reform programmes may remain on paper in the form of apparently progressive legislations or made impotent by the reactionary forces at the regional or local level.

Second is that to win the active support and participation of the villagers who constitute the most numerous class in most underdeveloped areas, the bulk of the peasantry (especially poor peasants and agricultural labourers) must be imbued with a sense of confidence and purposefulness. If the lower strata of the rural community are not helped, mobilized and enthused, the fruition of agrarian reform may be monopolized by a minority of upper-class peasants, resulting in further polarization of rural classes or frustration of the vast majority of the rural populace.

Third is that land reform (including redistribution of land holdings, tenurial reforms, removal of usurious loans, etc.) forms a prerequisite to general agrarian reform. In view of some adverse effects of the early Soviet Russian experience when land was nationalized outright in 1917, it seems desirable that peasants' ownership of land should not be abolished immediately. The Chinese experiment which effected a gradual process of organized farming through mutual-aid teams, cooperatives, collective farms and people's communes has achieved rapid progress in rural economy without serious disruption of the productive mechanisms. This does not mean that agrarian reform in other underdeveloped countries must go through the same four-stage transformation. It does seem to indicate that even if cooperative farming is introduced on a national scale, the legal right of cultivators to own land should not be denied at the initial stage.

Fourth is that the development of the agricultural sector through agrarian reform should not prejudice against the allocation of capital in the secondary and tertiary occupations (especially in capital industries). As a matter of fact, the programme of industrialization should have priority in resource allocations. Not only the success of modern farming depends largely on the industrial sector to supply means of production such as farm machinery and chemical fertilizers, but also many basic issues in the national economy—underemployment, economic self-sufficiency, higher labour productivity, raising of living standard, just to name a few —can only in a long run be resolved through industrialization. In this respect, as industrial expansion has to be capital-intensive, it is important that in the agrarian programmes the effective organization and use of manpower should get top attention. It is worth noting that in China, the agrarian development is coordinated with and serving the general plan of industrialization. Furthermore, the agrarian programme is not envisaged merely as an economic measure, but embodies concomitant steps to foster rural community improvement like mass education, public hygiene, technical training, and cultural development.

Fifth and lastly, an effective agrarian policy must be sustained by efficient, devoted leadership at the grass-roots level, in addition to direction and systematic planning from the Central Government To achieve this, mechanisms to offer opportunities and incentives for the active, capable elements among the masses must be devised. In China, the channelling of the energy and ability of the "activists' is often done through the mass organizations like the Youth League and the Women's Federation. Various incentives, including some ingenious methods of fanning popular enthusiasm such as labour emulation contest, public recognition in the form of agricultural model workers, etc., have been employed by the Chinese leaders. These organizational techniques involve no investment of large amount of capital, but get immediate results.

A general evaluation of agrarian policy and problems in China, however, involves more than the analysis of tangible factors. This is partly because the interpretation of facts is influenced by one's values or beliefs. Thus the reorganization of farm systems in China may be attacked by those who regard property ownership as an absolute right or may be supported by those who favour a more rational utilization of agricultural resources as well as manpower (like Prime Minister Nehru does in his *Discovery of India*, p. 376).[1] Then people may still hold divergent views on the specific manner in which organized farming is to be carried out, and at what speed.

Involved here too are the different stands on how far should individual rights go. Should an individual be entitled to everything his inheritance and efforts get him or should he be bound by considerations for the benefit of the entire nation, if not the world? Take a concrete case: Should some college or middle school graduates in present-day China who prefer to lead a more comfortable life in the large cities be free to do so, or must they take up tasks (by persuasion, preferably; and by government regulations, if necessary) in the rural areas or hinterland where they are needed most? Of course human beings are not machines and their personal aspirations should neither be ignored nor slighted unnecessarily. As the editorial comment of *Peking Review* (January 20, 1959) pointed out: "The satisfaction of personal tastes and preferences, the emancipation of the individual personality within the framework of the big collective, is a question that is receiving very much attention in the communes."[2] But men are also social animals and it would not be to their own ultimate interest if the welfare of the nation of which he is a member were being undermined. Besides, the term "individual right" in a highly competitive capitalist system centering on self-interests is often used as a rationalization of selfish deeds.

[1] Mr. Nehru wrote in 1951 that "The co-operative principle should be applied to the exploitation of land by developing collective and co-operative farms."

The Nagpur Conference of the Indian Congress Party in January 1959 resolved to promote cooperative farming gradually in the nation.

[2] *Peking Review*, No. 3, January 20, 1959, p. 4.

The Hoover era, advocating a brand of "rugged individualism," was also characterized by its financial irresponsibility, economic chaos, and resulting misery for the millions of not only Americans but also of innocent bystanders the world over during the Great Depression. And to what degree individual preferences should prevail depend, to no small extent, on the social and economic needs of a particular society at a given time, and the social consciousness of the people. Even in the United States, a growing number of State-planned programmes (e.g., limitations imposed by Washington on the planting acreages of major crops) are being implemented. Furthermore, there are now no more "unlimited frontiers" within the United States for expansion, and imperialistic exploitations overseas have become increasingly difficult. The American people have to bear, in the name of "national interests," restrictions on their basic constitutional rights as freedom to travel (to China, for instance). As to underdeveloped areas where there exists an impending need to develop resources and to accumulate capital in the quickest way possible there seems to be little practical choice that some individual privileges or comforts will have to subordinate themselves to the nation's welfare as a whole—so as to free themselves from the degrading backwardness as well as economic domination by foreign powers. A number of measures in Peking's current agrarian policy may appear to be too drastic even to some well-meaning Westerners. But as Dr. Benjamin Higgins of M.I.T. remarked in a paper on the economic problems in the Philippines at the 1957 Conference of the Association of Asian Studies: "To effect a take-off of a stagnant economy is like to start a stalled car—one cannot do it by leaning gently on it, it takes a vigorous push."[3] Take the question of the burden of the Chinese peasants as another example. Whether the emphasis is on the need for speedy economic development through a high rate of accumulation on a planned basis or on the rapid enhancement of *immediate* consumption level of the rural populace will lead to different evaluations of the agrarian policy of Peking. In examining the relative value in the apportionment of capital investment in the various economic sectors and the many reform measures to increase agricultural production, the following observations made by Prof. Kuznets of Johns Hopkins University are of relevance:

[3] Paper presented on April 3, 1957, at Boston.

In the older and more crowded countries, the main question is how to pull out of the vicious circle in which low productivity in the dominant industry—agriculture—means low real-capital formation (either in commodities or in the capacity of the working population) and hence a low base either for a technological revolution in agriculture or for productive employment of the idle labour force. The problem here is not what to do with a given substantial surplus arising in the primary industries but rather how to bring the economy to a point where adequate real surplus will flow into the proper channels to provide a widening base for sustained economic growth.[4]

To grasp more fully the overall significance and implications of the agrarian development in China, a brief discussion here on the Chinese experiment vis-á-vis the problem of economic growth in underdeveloped countries is perhaps in order. When one examines the interpretations of some Western economists regarding economic development in general and the growth problems of underdeveloped areas in particular, there are grounds to think that a careful re-appraisal of some aspects of their theories is needed. Just to mention a few examples: Lord Keynes' idea on creating effective demand through the "multiplier" formula assumes that capital, land, as well as labour are unlimited, while we all know that in most Asian and African countries capital is meagre and cultivable land often limited. Furthermore, the Keynesian approach of expanding demand through encouragement of consumption (e.g., by deficit financing) frequently is inapplicable in an underdeveloped country where the non-monetized sector is large and the institutional environment for productive investment unconducive. Thus in these countries, political and social reforms will have to accompany if not precede economic reforms. In the three major areas of production, distribution, and consumption in a stagnant or backward economy, it seems desirable for the first to get priority, the second to be managed on a planned basis and consumption to increase at a slow pace, at least during the initial stage. Take another example of the Schumpeterian concept of "creative, risk-taking entrepreneurship," which was described as a primary force in building up the Western economy. But the capitalists of underdeveloped areas today, dominated by a drive to make quick profits, handicapped

[4] Simon Kuznets, ed., *Economic Growth, Brazil, India, Japan,* 1955, p. 18.

by competition from advanced capitalist nations, and faced with changed conditions when foreign markets and raw materials can no longer be cheaply exploited, are often less well equipped than the government is in developing the sinews of economy like the capital industries. Prof. Ragnar Nurkse emphasizes the size of market as the limiting factor to investment inducement and the importance of foreign capital. The Chinese experiences have shown that well-laid and well-coordinated planning can effectively expand the market, without having to rely on huge capital from abroad. The weakness of the theorems of many Western economists, so far as the problem of developing the economy of underdeveloped country is concerned comes, in part, from the following factors: First, they generally apply the experiences of economic expansion of Western capitalist nations when the objective conditions which made it possible have changed today—such as getting indemnities from other countries by war or exploiting the colonies or semi-colonial areas. Second, they often assume the existence of "open frontiers" internally, an unregulated market economy, and free markets internationally, which is hardly the case today. Third, certain Western economists overlook or bypass some basic restrictive elements in an underdeveloped country, many of which are non-economic.[5] Again the Chinese experience particularly that in the agrarian field has illustrated the decisive role of social engineering, such as the skilful mobilization and organization of manpower and the introduction of non-material incentives.

The particularistic nature and problems of each underdeveloped economy are not identical, and no general panacea for economic development can be presented that will have a universal application. However, there do exist certain common denominators among most underdeveloped countries, and the following aspects could be of major importance in formulating policies to stimulate a rapid

[5] For discussions on the problem of economic development in underdeveloped areas, readers may refer to the following works in English: A. N. Agarwala and S. P. Singh, eds., *The Economics of Underdevelopment*, 1958 ; Paul Baran, *The Political Economy of Growth*, 1957 ; Charles Bettelheim, *Studies in the Theory of Planning*, 1959; H. C. Gupta, *Problems and Processes of Economic Planning in Underdeveloped Economics*, 1958; H. Arthur Lewis, *The Theory of Economic Growth*, 1955; Gunnar Myrdal, *Economic Theory and Underdeveloped Regions*, 1957; Ragnar Nurkse, *Problems of Capital Formation in Underdeveloped Countries*, 1952; and V. N. Singh, ed., *Keynesian Economics: A Symposium* (Part IV), 1956.

growth of their economy. The frame of reference might include the following: (1) Practical and effective utilization of indigenous resources, especially labour power. (2) While industrialization offers a long-range solution to many fundamental economic problems, top attention need be simultaneously paid to agricultural development (including labour-intensive methods) concomitant with the building of heavy industries which have to be capital-intensive. (3) Political-social reforms must accompany economic programmes, and techniques developed in mobilizing and organizing the masses and a conscientious leadership at the grass-roots implementation level are of basic import. (4) Even when extensive social-educational measures are promoted, they will take time to have their impact felt. In the meanwhile, the role of the government in mapping a systematic, coordinated plan, initially in a centralized manner, may be necessary. (5) Both the creation of additional wealth and the elimination of abusive factors in an underdeveloped economy such as waste, corruption, and conspicuous consumption are important. The significance of the last point is not only economic—but also psychological. The effectiveness of any move to induce the general public to save more or to exhort the populace to work harder will be greatly circumscribed if a minority of the privileged classes is callously indulging in ostentatious living or enjoying prerogatives. (6) The rate as well as the depth of economic growth in an underdeveloped area will in the long run also be influenced by the amount of "marginal social productivity" achieved. Thus mass education (including technical training programmes), health services and other social amenities deserve concurrent attention as the economic measures.

The above discussion leads to another basic question, i.e., "What criteria should be employed to measure economic growth in a country?" The Western yardstick as a rule is to analyze the change in per capita income in evaluating the level of economic development. Apart from the technical complications involved in accurately computing the national income (and the exact number of population) of a country, particularly for underdeveloped areas, neither the magnitude nor the forward momentum of economic growth in an underdeveloped economy is unfailingly gauged by using the per capita income concept as the sole criterion. Of course, national income divided by the number of population over a period of time does serve as a useful method in measuring economic development;

but there are several factors which make this approach an incomplete one. To mention a few: the per capita income figure is an average or abstract one. It does not necessarily mean an increment in the net national product will be utilized effectively to stimulate economic growth or to promote better welfare for the people. The per capita national income of Saudi Arabia may be higher than that of, say, India or even its rate of increase in a few specific years may be higher than India's (due, say, to a spurt in oil exploitation by foreign interests). This does not mean that the substantial enhancement of national income in such a country will be used properly to develop the nation's economy or to improve the livelihood of the masses. The ruling class may choose to build palaces or buy more Cadillacs. Another factor in the per capita income approach is that certain activities of a nation may not be *immediately* and *fully* reflected in the national income picture, such as long-range programmes of conservation and afforestation, investment in capital industries which take time to yield results, expansion of social overheads like schools, hospitals, housing, and cultural facilities, and the development of labour-intensive projects that often include a substantial amount of voluntary work such as road building. It seems that in addition to calculating (sometimes just guessing) the per capita income, other factors including the following need be taken into consideration in evaluating both the quantitative and qualitative nature of economic growth in an underdeveloped country: The quantitative (manpower) and qualitative (productivity) changes in labour utilization, the annual rate and amount of productive capital investment, the quantity as well as the rate of increase in both important capital and consumer goods, the amount of social overheads (services) made available to the people, and the productivity (yield per unit of land) of major crops—as most underdeveloped areas are primarily agricultural.

The question of working out a scheme to evaluate properly the growth patterns (economic and social) in underdeveloped areas is a complex one and calls for elaborate studies. Suffice it to say in this volume that the economic progress particularly the agrarian development in China in the past decade has indicated that a more refined methodology is needed to accurately gauge the magnitude and forwarding force of a dynamic economic transformation like China's. The "big leap" of the Chinese economy in 1958–59, which caught a great number of Western observers by surprise, can be better understood when one takes into consideration the fact that many measures taken by the Peking government between 1950 and 1957 have begun to take their cumulative effect—such as the conservation-afforestation projects, the training of vast number of agro-technicians and skilled workers, and the fostering of a spirit of self-confidence, enterprise and patriotism among the Chinese people. Economic growth which is something organic, after all, as W. Arthur Lewis points out, is the result of human effort. The recent development in rural China (together with progress in the secondary and tertiary occupations) indicates that China has pulled herself up economically by her own bootstraps, and a sustained growth is in evidence.[6] Its repercussions will not be limited to the domestic field, but also globe-wide, especially in Asian-African countries. The institutional environment and value systems in each country differ, and the Chinese agrarian experiment cannot and should not be transplanted *in toto*. However, there are elements such as the organizational skills and social engineering techniques developed by the CCP which could be of reference value to nations faced with similar problems as traditional China did.

[6] For an evaluation on the nature and tempo of economic growth in China in recent years in the English language, see Charles Bettelheim, "The Chinese Leap Forward," *The Economic Weekly Annual*, Bombay, January 1960, pp. 213–18; William W. Hollister, *China's Gross National Product and Social Accounts, 1950–1957*, M.I.T., 1958; Gyanchand, *The Chinese Economy*, 1958; Cheh-ming Li, *Economic Development of Communist China*, University of California Press, 1959; and T. J. Hughes and D. E. T. Luard, *The Economic Development of Communist China, 1949–1958*, Oxford University Press, 1959; Surendra J. Patel, "Planning in India and China," *The Economic Weekly Annual*, Bombay, January 1960, pp. 219–25; and Wilfred Malenbaum, "India and China: Contrasts in Development Performances," *The American Economic Review*, June 1959, pp. 284–309.

TABLES

(I to XI)

TABLE I

THE DEVELOPMENT OF ORGANIZED FARMING IN CHINA *

	1950	1951	1952	1953	1954	1955	1956	1957	1958	1959 (est.)
Mutual-aid teams (in 1,000)	2,700	4,760	8,030	7,450	9,930	7,150	..	none	none	none
Households in the mutual-aid teams (1,000)	11,313	21,000	45,364	45,637	68,478	60,389	..	none	none	none
Lower-stage APCs	19	300	3,640	15,000	114,000	633,000	681,697	..	none	none
Households in the APCs (1,000)	0·18	1·58	57	273	2,285	16,881	10,400	..	none	none
Higher-stage APCs (collective farms)	1	..	10	15	201	529	311,935	700,000	740,000 (June)	negligible
Households in the higher-stage APCs (1,000)	0·032	0·030	1·8	2·1	12	41	107,422	115,000	123,000	..
People's Communes								none	26,000	24,000
Credit co-operatives (1,000)	..	..	..	6·9 (June)	..	155	200 (est.)	..	..	..
Government farms (mechanized ones in parentheses)	1,215 (36)	..	2,336 (50)	2,376	2,415 (97)	2,242 (106)	.. (166)	.. ..	.. (1,440)	..
Total peasant households (1,000)	105,536	..	113,683	116,325	117,331	119,201	120,000	121,500 ?	123,250	..

* Data in this and other tables compiled from the First 5-Year Plan, 1955; State Statistical Bureau, Statistical Abstracts, *HPYK*, No. 17, 6 September 1956, pp. 39–50; *Report of the Indian (Agricultural) Delegation to China*, November 1956, *JMJP*, 22 and 24 February 1957, p. 2; Li Fu-ch'un, *Report on the Implementation of the First 5-Year Plan and Future Tasks in Socialist Construction*, 7 December 1957, (Ta-Kung Pao), Hongkong, 8 December 1957; Liao Lu-yen, "Report on the Agricultural Problem," *JMJP*, December 27, 1958; Editorial, *JMJP*, January 1, 1959; "Ten Recommendations of the Agricultural Model Workers' Conference," *JMJP*, January 4, 1959; Chou En-lai, "Report on the 1959 Economic Plan," *Peking Review*, September 1, 1959, pp. 11–19; Li Fu-ch'un, "China's Present Economic Situation," *China Today*, October 31, 1959, pp. 10–15; "The Progress of China's National Economy in 1959," *China Today*, January 30, 1960, pp. 11–15; Li Fu-ch'un, "Report on the Draft 1960 National Economic Plan," *Peking Review*, SSB, *The Great Decade*, Sept. 1959; April 15, 1960, pp. 5-21; and other sources.

TABLE II

FORMS OF ORGANIZED FARMING*

Type of organization	*Ownership of land, draught animals and farm implements*	*Average No. of households and acreage of land-holding*	*Type of work*	*Membership's income*
Mutual-aid teams (both seasonal and permanent)	Private	6 to 15 households; average landholding: no estimate	Farm operations	Each member gets the produce of his own plot, sometimes plus bonus for extra work
APCs	Private and cooperative	Households, 32; 92·5 acres	Farm operations and some subsidiary occupations	Dividends from co-operative shares (including land dividend) and labour compensation. Average income: 12,714 *yuan* per co-operative in 1955
Higher-stage APCs	Collective	Households, 160; 378 acres (June 1958)	Farm operations, subsidiary occupations and large-scale agro-technical projects	Mainly compensation for labour, with little or no compensation for land
People's Communes	Collective	Households, 5,000; 11,500 acres (1959)	Farming, forestry, fishery, animal husbandry, subsidiary jobs, local industries, etc.	From 20 to 30 per cent of income in free supplies of food, sometimes clothing; the rest in wages

* Figures taken from a report by the Statistical Bureau, "Data on the APCs", *HPYK*, No. 24, 21 December 1956, pp. 63–5; CC, CCP, *Resolutions on Some Questions Concerning the Communes*, December 10, 1958; Chou En-lai, "A Great Decade," *HPYK*, No. 19, October 12, 1959, pp. 10-18; and other recent sources.

TABLE III-A

FOODCROP ACREAGE, PRODUCTION, AND PRODUCTIVITY IN CHINA*

(In 1,000 metric tons or 1,000 acres)

	1949	*1952*	*1953*	*1954*	*1955*	*1956*	*1957 (1st 5-Year Plan goal)*	*1957*	*1958*	*1959 (est.)*	*1960 (goal)*
Rice											
Production	48,645	68,450	71,250	70,851	78,000	82,450	81,768	86,800	113,700	..	..
Acreage	64,272	70,955	70,803	71,805	72,933	83,260	73,259	80,603	81,861	..	..
Yield (lb./acre)	1,663	2,119	2,218	2,171	2,356	2,178	2,454	2,369	3,056	..	..
Wheat											
Production	13,808	18,100	18,300	23,350	22,950	24,800	23,725	23,650	28,950	..	..
Acreage	53,788	61,950	64,090	67,418	66,847	68,180	65,920	68,853	66,558	..	..
Yield (lb./acre)	568	647	627	759	759	799	792	752	957	..	..
Potatoes											
Production	9,850	16,350	16,653	17,000	18,900	21,851	21,300	21,900	45,400	..	..
Acreage	17,527	21,720	22,540	24,453	25,135	27,478	24,287	26,237	40,700	..	..
Yield (lb./acre)	4,937	6,626	6,494	6,098	6,626	6,996	7,733	7,339	9,821	..	..
Other Grains											
Production	35,800	51,500	50,700	49,250	54,950	53,400	54,800	52,650	61,950	..	..
Acreage	118,513	126,123	128,253	127,176	131,078	131,793	120,624	126,518	114,130	..	..
Yield (lb./acre)	667	898	871	851	924	891	1,000	917	1,195	..	..
Total grain production	108,100	154,400	156,900	160,430	174,870	182,500	181,590	185,000	250,000	270,500	297,500
Soybeans											
Production	5,100	9,500	9,931	9,080	9,121	10,223	11,220	10,050	10,500	11,500	..
Acreage	20,548	28,847	30,534	31,255	28,262	29,795	31,328	32,000	..	..	..
Yield (lb./acre)	545	726	716	639	710	755	788	700	..	..	..

* Data compiled from SSB, *The Great Decade*, Peking, Sept. 1959, and other sources.

TABLE III-B

FOODCROP ACREAGE, PRODUCTION, AND PRODUCTIVITY IN CHINA*

	1949	*1952*	*1953*	*1954*	*1955*	*1956*	*1957 (1st 5-Year Plan goal)*	*1957*	*1958*	*1959 (est.)*
Total foodcrop area	254,100	280,748	285,687	290,853	295,993	310,732	284,090	302,200	303,250	..
Total crop acreage	..	353,140	360,090	369,813	377,703	397,931	375,242	393,110	390,670	..
Total cultivated area	244,703	269,797	271,322	273,387	275,391	279,561	273,500	279,575	269,467	..
Irrigated fields								100,000	166,000	..
Multiple crop area index	..	130·9%	132·7%	135·3%	137·2%	142·3%	..	140·6%	145%	..

* Units: acreage, 1,000; production, 1,000 metric tons; yield, lbs. per acre; production of potatoes is calculated at the rate of four tons of potatoes to one ton of grain. One *mou* is equal to 0·1647 acre; one hectare, 2·47 acres; and one metric ton, 2,200 pounds. Data compiled from sources listed under Table I.

TABLE IV

PRODUCTION, ACREAGE, AND PRODUCTIVITY OF INDUSTRIAL CROPS*

	1949	1952	1953	1954	1955	1956	1957 (1st 5-Year Plan goal)	1957	1958	1959 (est.)	1960 (goal)
Cotton											
Production	444	1,304	1,175	1,065	1,518	1,443	1,635	1,640	2,130	2,310	2,540
Acreage	6,842	13,773	12,795	13,491	14,259	15,463	15,646	14,403	13,400	..	..
Yield	145	205	198	172	231	204	222	250	323	..	..
Jute and Kenaf											
Production	37	305	138	137	257	259	365	..	..	..	..
Acreage	69·2	390	195	178	287	335	342	..	..	..	..
Yield	1,176	1,721	1,557	1,693	1,970	1,706	2,350	..	..	..	..
Cured tobacco											
Production	43	222	213	232	298	399	390	300?	400?	440	..
Acreage	150·7	459	472	538	622	954	689	..	..	..	..
Yield	628	1,064	993	949	1,054	923	1,253	..	..	..	..
Sugarcane											
Production	2,642	7,116	7,209	8,592	8,110	8,666	13,180	10,393	13,525	..	..
Acreage	266·8	449·5	474	541	504	544	666	..	..	..	..
Yield	21,786	34,838	33,459	34,940	35,401	34,860	43,535	..	..	..	..

(Contd.)

TABLE IV

PRODUCTION, ACREAGE, AND PRODUCTIVITY OF INDUSTRIAL CROPS*

	1949	*1952*	*1953*	*1954*	*1955*	*1956*	*1957 (1st 5-Year Plan goal)*	*1957*	*1958*
Sugar beets									
Production	191	479	505	989	1,598	1,650	2,135	1,501	2,900
Acreage	3·95	86	121	180	284	371	348	..	..
Yield	10,638	12,253	9,182	12,088	12,379	9,787	13,515	..	..
Peanuts									
Production	1,268	2,316	2,127	2,767	2,926	3,335	..	2,571	2,800
Acreage	3,097	4,456	4,384	5,180	5,602	6,380	..	..	..
Yield	901	1,143	1,067	1,175	1,149	1,153	..	1,085?	..
Rapeseed									
Production	734	932	879	878	969	925	..	887	1,100
Acreage	3,742	4,602	4,117	4,214	5,775	535	..	..	..
Yield	432	446	470	458	369	380	..	..	..

* Units: Production, 1,000 metric tons; acreage, 1,000 acres; yield, lbs. per acre. Data compiled from sources listed under Table I.

TABLE V

PRODUCTION OF MAJOR SUBSIDIARY PRODUCTS IN CHINA *

(In 1,000 metric tons)

	1949	*1952*	*1953*	*1954*	*1955*	*1956*	*1957 (1st 5-Year Plan goal)*	*1957*	*1958*	*1959 (est.)*	*1960 (goal)*
Tea	41·1	82·4	84·7	92·1	108·0	120·5	111·9	111·5	140	..	..
Domestic cocoons	30·9	62·2	59·3	65·1	67·0	72·5	93·4	68	84·5	..	..
Wild cocoons	11·9	61·1	12·3	25·7	63·8	61·8	62·7	44	57	..	..
Marine products	447·9	1,663·3	1,899·7	2,293·5	2,517·9	2,640	2,802·6	3,120	6,000?	5,020	5,800

* Data from "Statistical Abstracts of the National Economy" (June 1956), *HPYK*, No. 17 (September 6, 1956), and *The First Five Year Plan*, pp. 81 and 89 and other recent sources. Production of wild cocoons, mainly in the Liaoning province, dropped sharply in 1953 and 1954 because of natural calamities.

TABLE VI

DEVELOPMENT IN LIVESTOCK RAISING IN CHINA *

(in 1,000 heads)

	1949	*1952*	*1953*	*1954*	*1955*	*1956*		*1957 (1st 5-Year Plan goal)*	*1957*	*1958*	*1959 (est.)*	*1960 (goal)*
Horses	4,875	6,130	6,512	6,939	7,312	7,385		8,340			7,600	
Cattle and Buffaloes	43,939	56,600	60,083	63,623	65,951	66,611		73,610			65,430	
Mules	1,471	1,637	1,645	1,717	1,723	1,706	83,760	1,970	83,900	85,000		100,000?
Donkeys	9,494	11,806	12,215	12,700	12,402	11,658		13,950			12,380	
Sheep and Goats	42,347	61,779	72,023	81,304	84,218	92,130		113,040	98,580	108,860	130,000?	..
Hogs	57,752	89,765	96,131	101,718	87,920	97,800		125,000	145,900	160,000	180,000	243,000
TOTAL	159,875	227,717	248,609	268,001	259,526	277,290		335,910	328,380	353,860	395,380?	..

* Data compiled from sources listed under Table I.

TABLE VII

FISCAL AND FINANCIAL PROGRAMMES IN AGRICULTURE IN CHINA *

(In million metric tons, if not otherwise indicated)

	1949–50	*1950–1*	*1951–2*	*1952–3*	*1953–4*	*1954–5*	*1955–6*	*1956–7*	*1957–8*	*1958–9 (est.)*	*1959–60 (goal)*
1. Total grain production, unprocessed grain. (Not including soybeans)	108·1 (1949)	124·7 (1950)	135·1 (1951)	154·4 (1952)	156·9 (1953)	160·43 (1954)	174·87 (1955)	182·5 (1956)	185 (1957)	250 (1958)	270·5 (1959)
2. Amount of public grain collected as tax (in terms of "fine grain" which contains some dehusked grain)	20·30	17·67	21·87	19·4	17·55	19	19	18·4	18·00	..	..
3. Tax grain in terms of unprocessed grain as in 1. (The average depreciation rate from 1 to 2 is about 10·3 per cent)	21·62	18·60	22·98	20·38	19·02	20·76	20·18	19·53	20·00	..	..
4. Grain purchased by state (unprocessed)	..	7·24	14·48	25·51	30·73	30·72	26·97	22·08	23·30	..	..
5. Total of 3 and 4	..	25·84	37·46	45·89	49·75	51·48	47·15	41·61	43·00	55·65	..
6. Value of agriculture tax (in billion yuan). One yuan equals US $0·4246)	..	1·890	2·168	2·601	2·905	3·277	3·05	2·965	2·94	3·26	..

(*Contd.*)

TABLE VII

FISCAL AND FINANCIAL PROGRAMMES IN AGRICULTURE IN CHINA *

(In million metric tons, if not otherwise indicated)

	1949–50	*1950–1*	*1951–2*	*1952–3*	*1953–4*	*1954–5*	*1955–6*	*1956–7*	*1957–8*	*1958–9 (est.)*	*1959–60 (goal)*
7. Percentage of agriculture tax in national budget receipts	..	29·63% (1950)	18·17% (1951)	17·08% (1952)	13·48% (1953)	12·4% (1954)	11·22% (1955)	10·17% (1956)	11% (1957)	8% (1958)	4·71% (1960)
8. Grain exported (soybeans figures in brackets)	..	(1950–2: 4–5 million tons)			·95 (·65)	·80 (·95)	1·0 (1·2)	1·32 (1·3)	0·78 (?)	.. ..	.. ..
9. Grain imported	..	..	none	none	none	0·40 (rice)	..	..	..	..	..
10. Rural credit extended to peasants (million US $)	..	85 (1950)	170 (1951)	454 (1952)	535 (1953)	357 (1954)	425 (1955)	1,400 (1956)	1,626 (1958)	2,028 (1959)	1,991 (1960)
11. Statement investment in agriculture, conservation, irrigation, forestry, and meteorology services (mill. US $)		..	..	..	499·7	583·8	628	969·8	866·2	1,020 (1959)	1,660 (1960)
		(Planned investment (mill. US $) 1953–57: 1,414·8)									

* Data compiled from sources listed in Table I; Li Hsien-nien, *1956, 1957, 1958, and 1959 Budget Reports; First Five-Year Plan*; and U.N. Economic Commission for Asia and the Far East, *Economic Surveys of Asia and the Far East, 1955-57* (Bangkok: 1956), 80–99.

TABLE VIII

AGRO-TECHNICAL DEVELOPMENT IN CHINA, 1950–60*

(In 1,000 acres, if not otherwise indicated)

	1950	*1951*	*1952*	*1953*	*1954*	*1955*	*1956*	*1957 (goal)*	*1957*	*1958*	*1959 (est.)*	*1960 (goal)*
Acreage newly reclaimed	..	1949–52:	280	1,525	2,061	2,165	4,833	..	..	..	..	..
Acreage newly afforested	316	1,126	2,713	2,780	2,915	4,276	14,308	7,500	10,889	43,650	46,600	33,330
Acreage newly irrigated	2,000	4,660	6,676	3,000	2,670	3,713	19,780	8,300(?)	7,181	66,700	11,660	10,000
Area sown with improved seeds												
cotton	19%	28·8%	51%	61·4%	67·7%	70%	89%	..	93%	97%	..	..
rice			5·4%	7·9%	12%	19%	41%	..	63%	82%	..	..
all foodgrains			4·7%	7·4%	15%	20·6%	36%	..	55%	77%	..	..
New farm tools distributed (1,000 pieces)	..	12	30	570	400	700	2,000	1,600 (all types)	..	210,000	..	..
No. of tractors (15 h.p. each)	1,286	1,410	2,006	2,719	5,061	8,094	19,367		24,629	45,330	59,000	..
Chemical fertilizer distributed (1,000 tons) (excluding soybean cakes in brackets)	160	220	300	600 (3,000)	820 (3,200)	1,030 (3,500)	1,620 (4,000)	..	2,000(?)	2,780	..	..

(*Contd.*)

Table VIII

AGRO-TECHNICAL DEVELOPMENT IN CHINA, 1950–60*

(In 1,000 acres, if not otherwise indicated)

	1950	*1951*	*1952*	*1953*	*1954*	*1955*	*1956*	*1957 (goal)*	*1957*	*1958*	*1959 (est.)*	*1960 (goal)*
Total capacity of power pumps distributed (1,000 h.p.)	..	..	..	..	137	227	390 (Sept.)	200	500(?)	1,600	2,800	5,000
Total number of agro-technical stations (1,000)	0·01	0·04	0·23	3·63	4·5	7·99	14·23	..	13·67	..	..	24(?)
Meteorological stations	158	191	317	357	511	715	1,377	..	1,647	2,755	..	..
Veterinary stations	251	576	1,005	1,734	1,343	1,266	2,257	..	2,930	..	..	..
Pest-observation posts (1,000)	..	..	..	..	..	..	4,000	..	..	..	..	..
Insecticides distributed (1,000 tons)	..	..	..	..	..	90	150	..	150	480	..	..

* Data compiled from sources listed under Table I.

TABLE IX

MAJOR FEATURES OF THE CURRENT (1953–59) AGRICULTURAL TAX SYSTEM IN CHINA *

Area†	*Tax Rates*	*Exemption Base*
East China (except Shantung province), Central-South China and Southwest China: 13 provinces	Progressive rates‡ from 7 per cent for a per capita income of 165–220 lbs. of grain (paddy) to 30 per cent for a per capita income of 2,145 lbs. or more of grain. Total tax classes: 24	165 lbs. of local staple grain (paddy) per person
Northwest China (Shensi, Kansu, Tsinghai provinces, excluding old liberated areas)	Progressive rates from 5 per cent for a per capita income of 165–209 lbs. of grain (wheat) to 30 per cent for 1,859 lbs. or more of grain. Total tax classes: 26	165 lbs. of local staple grain (wheat) per person
Northeast China (Kirin and Heilungkiang provinces; Liaoning province and 5 municipalities)	Proportional tax, 23 per cent of agricultural income 21 per cent	No exemption base
North China (Hopei and Shansi provinces)	Proportional tax 22 per cent	110 lbs. of grain (unhusked millet) per person
Northwest China (former Shensi-Kansu-Ninghsia border region)	Proportional tax: 18 to 20 per cent	165 lbs. of grain (wheat) per person

(*Contd.*)

TABLE IX

MAJOR FEATURES OF THE CURRENT (1953–59) AGRICULTURAL TAX SYSTEM IN CHINA *

Area†	*Tax Rates*	*Exemption Base*
Shantung province and Inner Mongolia	Proportional tax: rates unknown 1956 maximum rate for local surtaxes for all areas: 22 per cent of regular tax	165 lbs. of grain per person
Tibet, Sinkiang, and minority areas	Rates to be determined separately	
All China (except Tibet) (after 1958)	Universal proportional tax 15·5 per cent (maximum: 25 per cent) Agricultural surtax, 15 per cent of regular tax	Not mentioned

* Data compiled from GAC, and after 1954, the State Council *Directives on Agricultural Tax* (1951, 1952, 1953, 1954 and 1958), and Li Hsien-nien, "Report on the 1959 Final Account and the 1958 National Budget," *op. cit.*, and recent sources.

† Six regional administrative divisions were abolished in 1954. Regional names are used here to indicate the general area.

‡ These rates are not truly progressive as they are applicable to the entire agricultural output instead of the excess in total output which falls within a lower tax bracket.

TABLE X

SELECTED DATA ON RECENT INDUSTRIAL DEVELOPMENT IN CHINA

(In million metric tons if not otherwise indicated)

	Pre-1949 peak	*1949*	*1952*	*1957*	*1958*	*1959*	*1960 (goal)*
Steel	0·92	0·16	1·35	5·35	8·0	13·35	18·40
Pig iron	1·8	0·25	1·93	5·94	9·5	20·5	27·50
Electric power (billion kWh)	5·96	4·31	7·26	19·3	27·4	41·5	55·50-58·00
Coal	61·88	31	66·49	130	270	347·80	425·00
Crude oil	0·32	0·122	0·436	1·46	2·26	3·7	5·20
Cement	2·293	0·66	2·86	6·86	9·0	12·27	16·00
Machine tools (1,000)	5·4	1·58	13·7	28	50	70	90·00
Locomotive (1 unit)	nil	nil	20	167	350	350 (goal)	1,150?
Railway wagon (1 unit)	..	..	5,792	7,300	11,000	27,000 (goal)	59,000?
Automobile (1 unit)	nil	nil	nil	7,300	16,000	20,000	30,000?
Timber (million cubic metres)	..	5·67	10	27·87	35	41·20	47·00
Cotton yarn (million bales)	2·45	1·8	3·62	4·65	6·0	8·25	9·00
Cotton cloth (billion metres)	2·79	1·89	3·83	5·05	5·7	7·50	7·60
Sugar	0·41	0·20	0·45	0·864	0·9	1·13	1·30
Salt	3·92	2·985	4·945	8·28	10·4	11·04	14·00
Paper (machine-made)	0·16	0·11	0·37	0·84	1·2	1·70	2·80
Chemical fertilizer	0·227	0·027	0·18	0·63	0·81	1·33	2·80

TABLE XI

SELECTED DATA ON RECENT ECONOMIC DEVELOPMENT IN CHINA

(In billion US dollars, if not otherwise indicated*)

	1952	*1957*	*1958*	*1959*	*1960 (goal)*
I. Gross Value of Industrial & Agricultural Products	35·12	58·95†	78·18	102·46	126·53
1. Industry & handicrafts	14·57	33·33	49·68	69·21	89·17
2. Agriculture	20·55	25·62	28·50	33·25	37·36
II. National Budget					
1. Receipts	7·46	13·04	17·77	23·00	29·73
2. Expenditures	7·17	12·94	17·39	22·40	29·73
3. Investment for economic construction	(3·1)	(6·31)	(11·15)	(13·66)	(18·22)
4. Agricultural tax	(1·146)	(1·261)	(1·384)	(1·401)	(1·401)
(local surtax)			(0·187)	(0·187)	(0·187)
III. Commerce & Transportation (1,000 kilometres)					
1. Railway	24·20	29·86	31·20	36·00	43·00?
2. Roads	125	250	400	..	(plus 6·5)
3. Railway freight tonnage (in million tons)	na	275	380	542	720
IV. Employment (Workers & Staff in millions)	10·12	24·50	45	..	(plus 1·8)
V. Estimated Value of Foreign Trade	2·74	4·437	5·464	..	..
VI. Estimated National Income	26·66	40·337	54·05	65·725	..

* The official exchange rate, which has been maintained by China since 1953, is 2·355 *yuan* to one US dollar.

† This figure, 58·95 billion US dollars, is in term of 1952 constant prices. Calculated in term of 1957 prices, this figure should be 52·69. All the figures for 1958 and subsequent years are in term of 1957 constant prices.

APPENDIXES

APPENDIX I

NPC, MODEL REGULATIONS FOR ADVANCED AGRICULTURAL PRODUCERS' CO-OPERATIVES, JUNE 30, 1956*

CHAPTER ONE

GENERAL PRINCIPLES

Article 1. An agricultural producers' co-operative (the term as used in this document means the agricultural producers' co-operative of advanced type) is a socialist, collective economic organization formed by working peasants on a voluntary and mutually beneficial basis, with the guidance and help of the Communist Party and the People's Government.

Article 2. The agricultural producers' co-operative, in accordance with socialist principles, converts the chief means of production owned privately by its members into the collective property of the co-operative. The members are organized for collective work, and the co-operative applies the principle of "from each according to his ability, to each according to his work," giving equal pay for equal work, irrespective of sex or age.

Article 3. The co-operative shall, in the light of local conditions, steadily improve farming skills and, with the assistance of the state, bring about the gradual mechanization and electrification of agriculture, so as to promote the constant development of the rural economy. At the same time, with the expansion of productive activities, the income of members shall be steadily increased, and their material and cultural well-being improved.

Article 4. The co-operative shall properly integrate the collective interests of the co-operative with the personal interests of individual members. While members must observe and safeguard the collective interests of the co-operative, the co-operative must concern itself with and give consideration to the personal interests of its members.

Article 5. The co-operative shall properly integrate its own interests with those of the state. With the economic plan of the state as its guide, the co-operative shall be self-reliant in managing production. It must conscientiously fulfil its duties in delivering public grain and selling agricultural produce to the state.

Article 6. The co-operative shall be managed in a democratic way. Leading officers of the co-operative must be elected by members, and important matters must be discussed and decided upon by members. Leading officers of the co-operative must uphold the principle of collective leadership, keep in close touch with the rank and file, discuss things with them, and draw in all members to run the co-operative well.

* Foreign Languages Press, Peking, 1956. Chinese text in *Jen-min shou-Ts'e*, 1957 (People's Handbook, 1957), Peking, April 1957. pp. 173–8.

CHAPTER TWO

MEMBERSHIP

Article 7. All working peasants who have reached the age of 16 and other working people able to take part in the work of the co-operative may be admitted as members. Applications for membership must be voluntary and approved by a general meeting of members or a meeting of members' delegates.

The co-operative shall make active effort to take in as members the dependants of revolutionary martyrs, of soldiers and of government workers, and disabled as well as demobilized servicemen (including the military personnel who came over from the Kuomintang armed forces and those who accepted the peaceful liberation of the regions under their control but who have since been demobilized and returned to the countryside). The aged, the weak, the orphaned, the widowed and the disabled should also be admitted as members. New settlers should also be drawn into the co-operative.

Article 8. Former landlords and rich peasants who have given up exploitation may, depending on their conduct and work, be admitted individually as members or candidate members of the co-operative after their cases have been examined and approved by the township people's council.

Counter-revolutionaries in the countryside who have only committed minor crimes and have since repented, those who have committed relatively serious crimes but have since atoned for their crimes by rendering outstanding services during the suppression of counter-revolution, and those who behave well after serving their sentences and being released may, according to the degree of their repentance and service, be admitted as members or candidate members of the co-operative, after their cases have been examined and approved by the township people's council.

Former landlords, rich peasants and counter-revolutionaries who do not qualify for membership may, under the warrant of the township people's council, be admitted to take part in the work of the co-operative and thus enabled to reform and turn themselves into new men. These people shall receive payment according to the work they do in the same way as members of the co-operative, and the means of production they own shall also be dealt with in the same way as members of the co-operative. If they behave well, they may be admitted as members or candidate members of the co-operative after their cases have been examined and approved by the township people's council.

Candidate members may be changed into full members of the co-operative if they behave well and after their cases have been examined and approved by the township people's council.

Landlords' or rich peasants' dependants who have not themselves taken part in exploitation and counter-revolutionaries' dependants who have not themselves taken part in counter-revolutionary activities, may be admitted as members of the co-operative.

Article 9. Every member of the co-operative equally enjoys the right:

(1) to work in the co-operative and receive the payment which is his due;

(2) to make suggestions and offer criticism on co-operative affairs, take part in discussions, vote on co-operative affairs, and supervise the management of such affairs;

(3) to elect the leading officers of the co-operative and stand for election;

(4) to engage in subsidiary cottage occupations on condition that this does not interfere with the work of the co-operative; and

(5) to enjoy the benefits of cultural and welfare services run by the co-operative.

Former landlords, rich peasants and counter-revolutionaries do not have the right to stand for election and are not allowed to hold any important post in the co-operative for a certain period of time after becoming members. If they are candidate members, they do not have the right to vote or to elect either.

Article 10. Every member of the co-operative equally undertakes the obligation:

(1) to observe the regulations of the co-operative and to carry out decisions of the general meeting of members or of the meeting of members' delegates, and of the management committee of the co-operative;

(2) to take an active part in the work of the co-operative and to work in a disciplined way;

(3) to look after the property of the state and of the co-operative; and

(4) to strengthen the unity of the co-operative and resolutely oppose all activities aimed at undermining the co-operative.

Article 11. Members of the co-operative are free to withdraw from membership.

Members who wish to withdraw may do so, as a general rule, only after the harvest for the year is brought in. When a member withdraws he may take with him the land he pooled in the co-operative or land equal in size and quality to his own, and he may withdraw his contribution to the share fund and his investment in the co-operative.

Article 12. A member who gravely violates co-operative regulations and refuses to make amends after being repeatedly admonished and penalized, may be disqualified as a member by decision of the general meeting of members or of the meeting of members' delegates, following discussion of his case. A member so disqualified has the right of appeal to the township or county people's council if he disagrees with the decision.

A member so disqualified may still take part in the work of the co-operative, and should receive payment according to the work he does in the same way as members of the co-operative. If he wishes to leave the co-operative and work on his own, he may take with him the land he pooled in the co-operative or land equal in size and quality to his own, and he may withdraw his contribution to the share fund and his investment in the co-operative.

A member who has been disqualified but who has since made amends may be reinstated by decision of the general meeting of members or of the meeting of members' delegates, following discussion of his case.

CHAPTER THREE

LAND AND OTHER IMPORTANT MEANS OF PRODUCTION

Article 13. Peasants joining the co-operative must turn over their privately-owned land and other important means of production, such as draught animals, large farm tools, etc., to the collective ownership of the co-operative.

Household goods privately owned by members, and small holdings of trees, poultry, domestic animals, small farm tools and tools needed for subsidiary cottage occupations will not be made the common property of the co-operative.

Irrigation works such as ponds, wells, etc., on land owned by members should be turned over, together with the land, to the collective ownership of the co-operative. If these works are newly built and the owner has not yet derived any benefit from them, the co-operative shall pay appropriate compensation to the owner for the work done and expenses incurred. If loans have been contracted in building these works and have not yet been fully repaid, the co-operative shall assume responsibility for repaying them.

When lotus and fish ponds, reed beds, etc., owned by members are turned over to the collective ownership of the co-operative, the co-operative shall pay the owners reasonable compensation for the products in them.

Article 14. When land belonging to members is brought under the co-operative's collective ownership and dividends on land shares are abolished, members who are not able to do the more demanding work shall be assigned jobs which suit them, and given due consideration if they have difficulty in making a living; those who are entirely unable to work and depend on income from their land to meet their living expenses shall be given means of livelihood out of the co-operative's welfare fund, or may, if necessary, for a short time be given a suitable sum as a dividend on their land share.

Preferential treatment shall be given to dependants of soldiers and revolutionary martyrs, and to disabled servicemen, according to the special regulations for their treatment laid down by the state.

Article 15. People, who live and work in the city and have their families with them or those whose families live in the country but who themselves live and work away from home and have no one else in the family to work the land, may turn over the land they own in the country to the co-operative for its use. If they have difficulty in making a living and depend on income from their land to meet part of their living expenses, the co-operative shall give consideration to this and pay them a certain amount of compensation. If they return to the country and take up farming, the co-operative shall take them in as members, or, if they are not willing to join the co-operative, give them back their land or land equal in size and quality to their own.

Article 16. The co-operative shall set aside part of its land to be distributed to members for growing vegetables. The size of the plot for each household shall be determined by the number of persons in the household who are co-operative members, but, as a general rule, the amount of land so used by each person should not exceed 5 per cent of the average land-holding in the village in question.

Members need not turn the graveyards and building sites which they own over to the co-operative. The co-operative shall make over-all arrangements to meet members' needs for sites of new buildings or graveyards, and may, if necessary, appeal to the township people's council for help in making such arrangements.

Article 17. When draught animals, large farm tools, and tools for subsidiary cottage occupations which the members no longer use but which are useful to the co-operative are turned over to the collective ownership of the co-operative, the co-operative shall pay the owners compensation. The amount shall be discussed and fixed according to normal local prices to be paid by instalments. As a general rule, payments shall be spread over three years, and in no case more than five years. The question of paying interest on these instalment purchases shall be settled through consultation between the co-operative and the owners.

Small farm tools needed for production, such as sickles, hoes, etc., shall be provided and repaired by members themselves.

Article 18. Groves and orchards owned by members shall be dealt with according to the following rules:

(1) Small holdings of trees shall be retained by members.

(2) Saplings and seedlings shall be turned over to the collective ownership of the co-operative. The co-operative shall pay the owners a certain amount for the work done and expenses incurred.

(3) Large groves which have economic value, such as orchards, tea, mulberry and bamboo groves, tung oil trees, lacquer trees, etc., shall be turned over to the collective ownership of the co-operative and paid for. The amount of payment shall be determined by taking into consideration the income these trees will yield and whether their management will be easy or difficult, as well as the work already put into it, expenses incurred and benefits already received by the owners. Payment will be made by instalments out of the income from the property in question. When a co-operative is first set up, it need not immediately turn such trees into common property, but must bring them under its centralized management and pay the owners a certain proportion of the income from the property as compensation.

(4) Large timber-producing forests shall be turned over to the collective ownership of the co-operative. The prices to be paid by the co-operative will depend on the standards of timber at the time the purchase is made, and a price scale should be fixed accordingly. Payment will be made by instalments out of the income from the property in question. When a co-operative is first set up, it need not immediately turn such forests into common property, but must bring them under its centralized management and pay the owners a certain proportion of the income from the property as compensation.

Article 19. Large numbers of animals owned by members shall, as a general rule, be bought over by the co-operative at normal local prices and brought under the collective ownership of the co-operative. Payment will be made by instalments spread over several years. The question of how long should be taken to complete the payments and what interest should be paid on these instalment purchases should be settled through consultation between the co-operative and the owners.

When a co-operative is first set up, it need not immediately turn such animals into common property, but must bring them under the centralized management. The amount of compensation to be paid to the owners shall be fixed by consultation and according to local practice.

Chapter Four

FUNDS

Article 20. To raise funds to cover production expenses and buy means of production privately owned by members, the co-operative may collect a share fund from members according to the needs of production and the resources of members.

Article 21. Contributions to the share fund will be made by all able-bodied members of the co-operative.

If, when a co-operative was still in the elementary stage, members had already contributed to the share fund according to the amount of land they pooled or according to a fixed ratio between land and labour power, the original contributions should not be revised.

Members may pay their share fund in the form of means of production which the co-operative needs. If such payment in kind is not enough to cover the full share, members shall make it up by instalments. If the required contribution is exceeded, the co-operative shall, according to the provisions of Articles 17, 18 and 19 of the present Regulations, refund the surplus by instalments. Members, who are poor and still cannot pay up their shares even after they have received loans from the Poor Peasants' Co-operation Fund, may defer payment or pay less than the required amount provided the general meeting of members or the meeting of members' delegates agrees. No interest payments are to be added to the instalments or on the balance of the share fund in arrears.

Proceeds from means of production which a former landlord or rich peasant pools in the co-operative shall first go to pay up his contribution to the share fund. If there is a balance, it will be counted as his share of the reserve and welfare funds. If there is still a balance, it will be counted as an additional contribution to the share fund.

Each member's contribution to the share fund shall be registered under his own name. No interest is paid on it and it cannot be withdrawn unless the member withdraws from the co-operative.

Article 22. The co-operative shall set aside a certain amount of its annual income as reserve and welfare funds. The reserve fund shall be used for expanding production, for storing seed and fodder, and for increasing the fixed assets of the co-operative. It must not be diverted to other uses. The welfare fund is to be used for improving the co-operative's cultural and welfare services. It must not be used for other purposes.

A member who withdraws from the co-operative cannot make any claim on the reserve fund or welfare fund. New members (except those former landlords and rich peasants who own more than the usual means of production) are not required to contribute to such funds on joining the co-operative.

Article 23. When the co-operative is short of fund, members can make investments in it on a voluntary basis according to their means. However, the co-operative must not force its members to make such investments.

The co-operative shall repay investments made by members at a time agreed upon by the co-operative and the members concerned. The rate of interest on cash investments should, as a general rule, correspond to that paid on deposits by a credit co-operative. Investments in kind may carry no interest or a suitable rate of interest according to local practice.

Article 24. When several co-operatives merge there is no need to make any change in their members' contribution to the share fund. If a co-operative has collected less than the full share from its members because some of the means of production being used in the co-operative have not yet been turned into common property, it should, prior to the merger, turn them into common property and ask its members to make up their full contribution to the share fund.

When several co-operatives merge, their common property must not be divided up among the members.

Investments made by members and loans raised from outside the co-operative to increase its fixed assets shall be transferred, together with its other fixed assets, to the new amalgamated co-operative, which is responsible for repaying such loans and investments.

Chapter Five

MANAGEMENT OF PRODUCTION

Article 25. In organizing and developing production, the policy of the co-operative shall be to work in a thrifty and diligent way. It must make energetic efforts to extend the scope of production, develop a diversified economy by combining agriculture with other related pursuits, practise strict economy and reduce costs of production.

Article 26. The co-operative shall, in accordance with its economic resources and local natural conditions, make vigorous efforts along the following lines to raise the level of agricultural production:

(1) build irrigation works; conserve water and soil;

(2) use improved farm tools and gradually bring about the mechanization of agriculture;

(3) increase the supply of manure and other fertilizers by all possible means and make better use of them;

(4) use improved strains of crops;

(5) suitably and systematically enlarge the area under high-yield crops;

(6) improve the soil; level and terrace arable land;

(7) make rational use of all arable land and increase the area on which several crops a year are grown;

(8) improve farming methods: practise deep ploughing and intensive cultivation;

(9) eliminate and prevent insect pests, plant diseases and other natural calamities;

(10) protect and breed more and better livestock; and

(11) reclaim waste land and enlarge the area under cultivation according to plan if the work of water and soil conservation is not affected.

Every co-operative must make energetic efforts to learn the most efficient farming methods and do its utmost to find the best ways of increasing output and putting them into practice.

Article 27. The co-operative shall, in accordance with the state plan and local conditions, make vigorous efforts to increase the output of the principal crops such as grain and cotton, and at the same time promote the cultivation of such other industrial crops as mulberry, tea, hemp, oil-bearing crops, sugar-cane, beetroot, tobacco, fruits, medicinal herbs, spices, etc.

Article 28. Wherever necessary and possible, the co-operative shall actively develop forestry, animal husbandry, fishing, handicrafts, transport, sericulture, apiculture, poultry farming and other subsidiary occupations.

Provided that its normal production is not affected, the co-operative shall encourage and suitably help its members engage in subsidiary cottage occupations suited to individual management.

Article 29. The co-operative shall draw up a comprehensive production plan in order to organize production on systematic lines.

The co-operative shall draw up a long-term plan covering a period of three or more years and giving all-round consideration to the various productive and constructive tasks it will undertake during this period.

Before the beginning of the farming year the co-operative shall draw up its annual production plan under the following main heads: (1) sowing plans, output targets, and the necessary technical measures needed for ensuring fulfilment of these plans; (2) plans for forestry, animal husbandry, fishing and other subsidiary occupations; (3) capital construction plans; and (4) plans for employing all available manpower and draught animals.

To ensure fulfilment of the annual production plan, the co-operative shall draw up schemes for the progress of work in the various farming seasons and stages of work, set definite production tasks and definite dates for their completion.

Chapter Six

ORGANIZATION AND PAYMENT FOR WORK

Article 30. The co-operative shall organize members into field production brigades and subsidiary occupation brigades or groups in accordance with the scope of its production, division of labour and of occupations arising from the needs of production, and the conditions of its members. It shall appoint people to take charge of book-keeping, technical management, livestock, common property and other special jobs in order to implement the system of individual responsibility for production.

Article 31. The production brigade is the basic unit of labour organization in the co-operative and its members shall be organized on a permanent basis. The field production brigade shall assume responsibility for cultivating a definite area allotted to it and be given draught animals and farm tools for its regular use. The subsidiary occupation brigade or group shall be responsible for definite subsidiary occupations and be allotted, for its regular use, the tools employed in such occupations. In organizing members into production brigades and assigning work, the co-operative shall take into consideration the size of the land allotted to the brigade for cultivation, the location of this land, the crops suited to it, and the distance between it and members' homes. The co-operative shall also see to it that the labour power, the skill of the members and the ability of the leaders of the brigade measure up to the jobs given to it. Similar consideration should be given while organizing members into subsidiary occupation brigade or group, or assigning them work.

The management committee may, if necessary, transfer members, together with their draught animals, farm tools and other tools, from one brigade to another, or organize a temporary production brigade, to help fulfil a certain task.

Article 32. The co-operative must fix suitable norms for various jobs and rates of payment so as to put the piece-work system into practice.

The norm for each job should be based on the amount and quality of work which an average member working diligently under normal conditions can do in one day on that particular job. It should not be set too high or too low.

Payment for fulfilling the norm for a job is reckoned in units of work-days. The number of work-days a member earns for fulfilling the norm for each job is decided on the basis of the skill and intensity of labour involved and the importance of the job to the production of the co-operative as a whole. There should be suitable differences in the number of work-days awarded for fulfilling different kinds of norms. Such differences should be neither too small nor too great.

When working conditions change, the management committee may revise the norms of the different jobs accordingly.

Article 33. The co-operative shall put into practice a system of responsibility for output norms and of awards for overfulfilment of output norms. The field production brigades and subsidiary occupation brigades and groups must ensure that the output norms set are fulfilled and see to it that the products of some subsidiary occupations reach a certain standard of quality. Those who have overfulfilled their output norms shall be suitably rewarded with additional work-days. Those who fail to do their work well, and are so unable to fulfil output norms or fail to reach the required standard of quality shall, depending on circumstances, be penalized by being credited with less work-days. Output norms shall be suitably revised if an irresistible calamity occurs.

If the co-operative, as a result of good leadership, overfulfils its production plan, the officers concerned shall be credited with additional work-days as a reward.

Members who make innovations or inventions which increase productive skill, or who distinguish themselves in protecting common property or bringing about economies, shall be credited with additional work-days as a reward.

Article 34. The co-operative shall draw up a plan of work. At the same time as it works out annual and seasonal production plans and plans for particular stages of field work for the various production brigades, it shall calculate exactly how many work-days are needed to fulfil its production plans. It may introduce the system of responsibility for particular jobs by assigning such jobs with fixed numbers of work-days to the production brigades.

The co-operative shall lay down, according to the needs of production and the judgment of the members themselves, the number of work-days a member is required to put in in a year, a season, or during a particular stage of field work. In assigning work-days to members, the co-operative shall take into consideration their different physical conditions and make due allowance for women members and their actual need for doing household work.

When a member has finished the number of work-days he or she is required to do, the time left, if any, is at his or her own disposal.

Article 35. Those who do managerial work for the co-operative and are therefore unable to take a regular part in productive work will be credited with a certain number of work-days, the exact number to be decided by the general meeting of members or the meeting of members' delegates according to the amount and nature of the managerial work done. Members who do part-time managerial work for the co-operative or who are taken on only temporarily to do such jobs shall receive a suitable number of work-days as compensation according to the amount of work done and the time they are taken away from their normal work.

The number of work-days credited to the chairman of the co-operative for the year shall, as a general rule, be more than the number of work-days earned by the average member.

The co-operative shall not have too many persons involved in its managerial work. The number of work-days earned by all those engaged in managerial work for the co-operative, added to the number of work-days credited to members who temporarily take part in managerial work, shall, at most, not exceed two per cent of the total number of work-days earned by the co-operative as a whole.

Article 36. The co-operative shall organize emulation campaigns as a way of encouraging members to raise their efficiency and skill, overcome difficulties in their work and so fulfil or overfulfil their production plans.

The co-operative shall award prizes to individuals and units distinguishing themselves in such campaigns.

Article 37. The co-operative shall introduce a system of examination and checking to see if work is done well. The management committee and the production brigade leaders should make timely and thorough examinations to see if brigades or individuals have fully done the job assigned to them, reached the required standard of quality and completed it in the time set. If brigades or individuals fail to fulfil these requirements, the co-operative may either instruct them to do the job all over again, or, according to circumstances, reduce the number of work-days credited to them.

Article 38. Members of the co-operative must work in a disciplined way by

(1) not absenting themselves from work without good cause;
(2) carrying out instructions when at work;
(3) bringing their work up to standard; and
(4) taking good care of common property.

A co-operative member who behaves in an undisciplined way shall be criticized for his fault and taught to know better. For a serious offence the offender shall be penalized by reducing the number of work-days credited to him, requiring him to make good the damage done, removing him from his post if he holds any, or even disqualifying him from membership, as the case demands.

Chapter Seven

FINANCE AND DISTRIBUTION OF INCOME

Article 39. The management committee of the co-operative shall, at the same time as it maps out the year's production plan, draw up the year's budget covering income and expenditure, submit it to the general meeting of members or the meeting of members' delegates for adoption and then put it into effect.

The co-operative's budget should include: sources of funds (in kind and cash) and the year's plan of expenditure, a rough estimate of the value of the co-operative's production and an estimate of distribution of income.

Article 40. The co-operative must exercise the strictest economy and avoid waste in spending its funds. Its policy must be to run the co-operative diligently and thriftily. In the annual budget a ceiling shall be placed on all expenses for production, including those on seed, fertilizer, fodder, insecticide, repairing of farm tools, veterinary services, payments to tractor stations and stations providing animal-drawn farm tools for ploughing service and to pumping stations for irrigating the co-operative's land, on the revolving fund for subsidiary occupations, on costs of management, etc. Costs of management, excluding rewards and compensation paid to those engaged in managerial work for the co-operative, shall not exceed 0·5 per cent of the total annual value of the co-operative's production.

Article 41. The co-operative shall draw up rules and procedures for administering its finances.

All expenditure by the co-operative shall be examined and approved according to established procedure. General budget expenditure shall be approved by the chairman of the management committee. Large items of budget expenditure shall be approved by the management committee, and supplementary budget expenditure shall be approved after discussion by the general meeting of members or the meeting of members' delegates. Both the book-keeper and the cashier have the right to reject any item of expenditure contrary to established regulations and procedure.

Every item of income and expenditure in the co-operative must be accounted for by receipts or vouchers which must be demanded by the book-keeper before entering them in the books.

The work and responsibility of keeping accounts and handling money in the co-operative must be in separate hands.

The co-operative's accounts must be settled daily and monthly. Statements of income and expenditure must be made public quarterly and annually when the harvest for the year is brought in. The account of work-days credited to each member must be made public monthly.

Special persons must be designated to look after the common property of the co-operative. An inventory of common property must be made public when annual accounts are settled.

Article 42. The common property of the co-operative must be protected, and no member is allowed to misuse it. Any co-operative member guilty of corruption, theft or destruction of property belonging to the co-operative, or causing serious damage to common property through negligence, shall, depending on the merits of each case, be duly penalized and compelled to return the original property or make good the damage. Serious cases shall be handed over to the judicial organs.

Article 43. After paying the agricultural tax required by the state, and guided by the principle that members shall be enabled to get a higher personal income every year, and that the co-operative's accumulation of common property shall be increased, the co-operative shall distribute its income in kind and cash in the following manner:

(1) Costs of production for the current year shall be deducted. This sum shall be used to cover production expenses in the coming year, and to repay investments and loans contracted for the current year's production.

(2) After deducting such expenditure, the co-operative shall set aside a certain proportion of the remainder of its income as reserve and welfare funds. In general, the reserve fund, which includes repayments of loans and investments needed for capital construction, shall not exceed 8 per cent of this sum while the welfare fund shall not exceed 2 per cent; co-operatives engaged in growing industrial crops may increase the reserve fund to as high as 12 per cent.

(3) What is left of the total income in kind and cash shall then be distributed according to the total number of work-days credited to members, including work-days for agricultural production, subsidiary occupations, managerial work of the co-operative, and bonus work-days awarded to production brigades or individual members.

If the co-operative has not increased its income to any appreciable extent, it may put a smaller sum to reserve in order to increase the personal income of members. In case of crop failure, it may put only a small sum to reserve, or none at all. If there is a bountiful harvest, the reserve fund may be suitably increased, provided the personal income of members is increased. Measures concerning distribution of income shall be discussed and approved by the co-operative's general meeting of members or meeting of members' delegates.

Article 44. After setting aside a certain portion needed for the use of the co-operative, farm products harvested in the spring and summer should be distributed as advances to members on the basis of the number of work-days each has earned. The final settlement may be made when the year's harvest is in.

After setting aside a certain portion needed for its use, the co-operative may distribute by instalments to members its cash income including advance payments made by the state for the purchase of farm products. Such distribution shall be based on the number of work-days each has earned and actual needs. The final settlement may be made when the year's harvest is in.

Chapter Eight

POLITICAL WORK

Article 45. The co-operative shall carry on political work under the guidance of the Communist Party and the People's Government and with the help of the Youth League and the Women's Federation.

The purpose of political work is to ensure the completion of production plans, to see that the co-operative is run diligently and thriftily; to prevent waste and extravagance; to ensure that the principles of "to each according to his work," giving equal pay for equal work, irrespective of sex and age, are adhered to; to ensure a correct integration of the collective interests of the co-operative and the interests of the state with the personal interests of individual members, and to consolidate the co-operative both ideologically and organizationally.

Article 46. The co-operative shall arrange talks for members during their spare time so that they can learn about current affairs both at home and abroad, what the Communist Party stands for, and the policies, laws and decrees of the People's Government. It shall, in the course of the practical work and activity of the co-operative, educate members in the spirit of patriotism and collectivism and in the need for a still firmer worker-peasant alliance, constantly raise their understanding of socialism, and overcome survivals of capitalist ideas.

Article 47. The co-operative shall encourage members to be more active and creative in their work by organizing emulation campaigns, sending groups to visit other co-operatives and exchange experiences with them, promoting improvements in production techniques, giving awards for rationalization proposals, commending outstanding workers, and so on.

Article 48. The co-operative shall promote internal democracy, set its face against "commandism" and bureaucracy, encourage criticism and self-criticism, cement the unity between leading officers of the co-operative and the rank and file, between the members themselves and between one production brigade and another.

The co-operative shall strengthen its unity with other agricultural producers' co-operatives, handicraft co-operatives, supply and marketing co-operatives and credit co-operatives and pay attention to strengthening its ties with peasants working individually outside the co-operative.

Article 49. In areas inhabited by more than one nationality, the co-operatives shall pay special attention to fostering unity and mutual aid between different nationalities and respect for their different customs and habits. In co-operatives which are composed of two or more nationalities, attention should be paid to educating members in a spirit of giving consideration to the minority by the majority and of rendering help to the backward by the more advanced, so that unity is strengthened and the co-operative is run well.

In areas where returned overseas Chinese or the dependants of Chinese resident abroad are settled, the co-operatives shall pay special attention to rallying them to help run the co-operative well.

Article 50. The co-operative shall constantly heighten the revolutionary vigilance of members and see that its security work is efficiently done.

CHAPTER NINE

CULTURAL AND WELFARE SERVICES

Article 51. The co-operative must see to it that safety precautions are observed when members are at work, and that expectant mothers, the aged, and minors are not given work which involves arduous and excessive manual labour. It must also see to it that women members have adequate rest before and after childbirth.

The co-operative shall provide medical treatment for members injured or taken ill while at work and give them an appropriate number of work-days as compensation. It shall grant pensions to the dependants of those who lose their lives while at work.

Article 52. The co-operative shall steadily develop various cultural and welfare services according to the needs of members as production grows and the income of the co-operative as a whole and the personal incomes of members increase. Such cultural and welfare services shall include the following:

(1) Arrangements for members to raise their general educational level and study science after the day's work, and elimination of illiteracy by groups within a few years;

(2) The use of spare time and slack seasons to promote cultural, recreational and sporting activities;

(3) The fostering of public health and the promotion of sanitation in members' households;

(4) The encouragement of division of labour in members' households and mutual aid between neighbours and the organizing of child-care groups to help solve the domestic difficulties of women members who are working and to ensure the safety of infants;

(5) Provision of suitable material assistance to women members during childbirth; and

(6) Help to members in improving their housing conditions whenever possible.

Article 53. The co-operative shall give due consideration to and make proper arrangements as regards the work and livelihood of the aged, the weak, the orphaned, the widowed and the disabled who lack labour power or are entirely unable to work, and who are without means of support. It shall assure them a regular supply of food, clothing and fuel and see to it that the young have a chance of education and the aged a proper burial after death. In a work, it shall ensure that members have a means of livelihood in their life-time and a proper burial after death.

The co-operative shall, within reasonable limits, help members who find themselves in serious difficulties as a result of some misfortune.

Article 54. The co-operative shall organize members to gradually lay up a stock of grain within a few years, enough for one or two years' consumption, against any emergency.

Chapter Ten

MANAGEMENT

Article 55. The highest administrative body of the co-operative is the general meeting of members or the meeting of members' delegates.

The general meeting of members or the meeting of members' delegates elects a management committee to run the co-operative, a chairman to direct the daily work of the co-operative and to represent the co-operative in its dealings with other parties, and one or several vice-chairmen to assist the chairman in his or her work.

The chairman and vice-chairman (or vice-chairmen) of the co-operative also act as chairman and vice-chairman (or vice-chairmen) of the management committee.

The general meeting of members or the meeting of members' delegates elects a supervisory committee to supervise the operation of the co-operative.

Article 56. The functions and powers of the general meeting of members are as follows:

(1) to approve and amend the regulations of the co-operative;

(2) to elect or remove from office the chairman and vice-chairman (or vice-chairmen) of the co-operative and members of the management committee, and the chairman and members of the supervisory committee;

(3) to approve the prices fixed for draught animals, farm tools and trees brought under the collective ownership of the co-operative, and the plan for collecting the share fund;

(4) to examine and approve the production plan and budget drawn up by the management committee;

(5) to approve the proposals for payment and compensation to those engaged in managerial work;

(6) to examine and approve the plan drawn up by the management committee for distributing the annual income, and the measures for advance distribution and payment of the income;

(7) to examine and approve the reports of the management and supervisory committees on their work;

(8) to approve the admission of new members;

(9) to decide on important awards to members or on severe penalties on members; to decide on exclusions or reinstatements; and

(10) to decide on any other important matters.

Article 57. The general meeting or the delegate meeting is convened by the management committee, at least twice a year.

A simple majority of the co-operative members constitutes a quorum for the general meeting. In exercising its functions and powers as prescribed in items (1), (2), (3), (4), (5), (6) and (9) of Article 56 of the present Regulations, no resolution shall be valid unless approved by a two-thirds majority of those attending. In exercising other functions and powers, no resolution shall be valid unless approved by a simple majority of those attending.

Article 58. If difficulties occur in convening a general meeting because the co-operative's membership is very large or because members' homes are widely scattered, a meeting of members' delegates may be convened to exercise the functions and powers of the general meeting.

Members chosen to attend the delegate meeting shall, as a general rule, be elected by the production units. Except for big co-operatives with a membership of over a thousand, the number of delegates attending such a meeting should be not less than one-tenth of the members of the co-operative. Members doing specialized work, women members and young members shall be adequately represented at the delegate meeting. In areas where more than one nationality lives or where returned overseas Chinese or the dependants of Chinese resident abroad are settled, arrangements shall also be made for such members to be adequately represented at the delegate meeting.

No resolution of the delegate meeting shall be valid unless approved by a two-thirds majority of delegates.

Prior to the delegate meeting, meetings of members must be convened either by production brigades or by area to collect as many members' proposals as possible. These proposals should be brought to the meeting for discussion by the delegates. After conclusion of the delegate meeting, similar meetings of members must be convened for delegates to report back on its resolutions to members.

Article 59. The management committee of the co-operative shall run the co-operative in accordance with the regulations of the co-operative and the resolutions of the general meeting or the delegate meeting.

The management committee is composed of the chairman, vice-chairman (or vice-chairmen) and other members. As a general rule, the management committee shall have nine to nineteen members, depending on the size of the co-operative. Members of the management committee shall divide their work according to the needs of the co-operative.

Decisions of the management committee shall be valid only when they have been adopted by a majority of its members. The management committee must conduct its work in a democratic way; there must be no abuse of function or power.

The management committee may make the necessary appointments to the various posts in the co-operative. In appointing leaders of production brigades, or of production groups directly under its control, the management committee must secure in advance the consent of the membership of the production brigade or the production group in question.

Article 60. The supervisory committee of the co-operative shall see to it that the chairman and vice-chairman (or vice-chairmen) of the co-operative and members of the management committee abide by the regulations of the co-operative and the resolutions of the general meeting or the delegate meeting; that the accounts of the co-operative are in order; and discover whether there is any corruption, theft, or damage to the co-operative's property. It shall report on its work to the general meeting or the delegate meeting at regular intervals, and may make suggestions to the management committee at any time.

As a general rule, the supervisory committee shall have five to eleven members. If necessary, it may elect one or two vice-chairmen to assist the chairman in his or her work.

The chairman and vice-chairman (or vice-chairmen) of the co-operative and members of the management committee, book-keeper(s), cashier(s), and supply clerk(s) shall not simultaneously hold posts on the supervisory committee.

Article 61. The chairman and vice-chairman (or vice-chairmen) of the co-operative and members of the management committee, and the chairman and members of the supervisory committee shall be elected afresh every year. The same person or persons may stand for re-election and, when re-elected, may continue to hold their offices.

There should be a certain number of women members among the leading officers and other staff of the co-operative, and at least one woman member shall hold a post as chairman or vice-chairman of the co-operative.

If the co-operative is composed of members of different nationalities, the posts of leading officers and other staff shall be distributed in suitable proportions among members of the different nationalities. If there is a considerable number of returned overseas Chinese or the dependants of Chinese resident abroad in the co-operative, they too shall hold a suitable proportion of posts among the leading officers and other staff of the co-operative.

Chapter Eleven

SUPPLEMENTARY RULES

Article 62. Provisions of the model regulations for agricultural producers' co-operatives of the elementary type[1] may be applied to advanced co-operatives if they do not run counter to those of the present Regulations and if they are needed for advanced co-operatives.

Article 63. Each province or city may, according to local conditions and needs, make supplementary provisions on matters which are not provided for or not definitely provided for in the present Regulations.

Article 64. National autonomous areas may, in the light of the characteristics and actual needs of local nationalities, make supplementary provisions on matters which are not provided for or not definitely provided for in the present Regulations, or, on the basis of the fundamental principles of the present Regulations, draw up their own model regulations for co-operatives suited to local conditions.

[1] See *Model Regulations for an Agricultural Producers' Co-operative* 1956, Foreign Language Press.

APPENDIX II

CC, CCP, REVISED DRAFT PROGRAMME ON AGRICULTURAL DEVELOPMENT IN THE NATION, 1956–1967, OCTOBER 25, 1957*

THIS DRAFT programme, submitted by the CC, CCP in January 1956, has already played a positive role in actual daily life. In line with the changes of the past two years and based on experience in work, certain necessary amendments and additions have now been made to be submitted to the peasants and the entire people for discussion before further revision is made. This draft programme will be submitted to the CCP National Congress for approval and then to the SC for discussion and approval before its re-submission to the NPC for discussion and ratification to become an official document for promulgation. It is anticipated that certain revisions will still have to be made during the next 10 years with the coming into being of many new situations — Note of the CCP Central Committee, 25th October 1957.

INTRODUCTION

THIS PROGRAMME shall be a programme of struggle during the period of our country's first, second and third FYPs with a view to developing rapidly the agricultural production force so as to strengthen socialist industrialization and to raise the living standards of the peasants as well as of the entire people. Socialist industry is the leading force of our national economy. Nevertheless, the development of agriculture holds an important position in the socialist construction of our country. Grain for agricultural use, raw material supply for industry, and a countryside with a population of over 500 million have provided our country's industry with the world's largest domestic market. Speaking from the standpoint of these factors, in our country, if there is no agriculture there can be no industry. It is completely wrong, therefore, to neglect the importance of work in the agricultural field.

Agriculture can be developed along two roads. One is the capitalist road — under which the destiny of the peasants is in the hands of landlords, rich peasants, and speculative merchants, with a very few people growing richer and with the great majority of the people becoming poor and bankrupt. Another is the socialist road under which the peasants, led by the working class, master their own destiny, a road to common wealth and prosperity. This struggle between the two roads will continue to exist for quite some time in our country during the period of transition. However, with agricultural co-operation basically completed, the great majority of the peasants have left the former road and taken the latter. The task to be accomplished henceforth calls for the utmost effort to consolidate the co-operative system and, in the meantime, to continue to oppose the spontaneous influence of capitalism in the countryside.

*BBC translation, *Economic Supplement* No. 290, Oct. 31, 1957 Chinese text in *HPYK* No. 22, Nov. 25, 1957, pp. 127–32.

Agricultural cooperativization has opened a broad avenue for the development of our country's agricultural productive force. Without it, and under conditions of individual economy, it would be idle to envisage the call for achieving, with certain exceptions, the average per *mou* grain yield of 400 catties, 500 catties and 800 catties, respectively, within 12 years in the several major areas under varied conditions, or the call for the output and income of most co-operatives during the second FYP to keep abreast of or surpass that of the local well-to-do middle peasants when they work individually. With the realization of agricultural cooperativization, however, added to the great achievements made in socialist industrialization under the first FYP, and the continuous effort of all from this time forward, there exists the possibility of achieving all these goals called for in the programme.

Because our country has, in general, good natural conditions with an abundant labour force in the countryside and because the peasants are diligent and thrifty traditionally and have rich experiences in deep ploughing and intensive cultivation, the potentialities of agricultural economy are immense. A variety of positive and appropriate measures should be adopted on the basis of cooperativization to promote agricultural mechanization in a preparatory and systematic manner, to develop amply such latent potentialities, to oppose conservatism and to strive to attain the goals called for in the programme.

The increase of agricultural production and the living standards of the peasants depend primarily on the industrious labour of the peasants. However, the people's Government, led by the working class and the CCP will do its best to help the peasants. In future, the people's Government will step by step extend more substantial and necessary aid to the peasants for carrying out many of the measures provided in the programme for increasing agricultural production. In reality, this constitutes mutual assistance between workers and peasants as well as between the cities and the countryside.

The worker-peasant alliance led by the working class and the mutual assistance between workers and peasants constitute a guarantee for the emancipation of the peasants. In an effort to restore the landlord and capitalist systems, the bourgeois Rightists and feudal remnants have tried their best to sow discord between the workers and peasants and between cities and the countryside. They have failed in this abject attempt, and will continue to fail in the future.

The masses of peasants should be educated to integrate their love of their country, their co-operatives, and their homes. If the CPR, led by the Communist Party, had not been established, the masses of peasants would have continued to be dominated and exploited by the imperialists, landlords, rich peasants, and speculative merchants, they would not have been able to establish co-operatives, and many would have become bankrupt. For this reason, to love their homes, they should also love their country and their co-operatives. All egotistical and individualist views detrimental to the collective interests of the State and the co-operatives are wrong and, in reality, harmful to the interests of the families of persons holding such views. More difficulties may be encountered on the road of agricultural development. However, men are the masters of successes. To us — the liberated people — there is no difficulty that cannot be surmounted. It is one of the traditional greatest characteristics of our labouring people to fear no difficulties.

This programme is formulated from a national point of view. As conditions differ in many respects among different localities and co-operatives, the CCP and Government authorities and co-operatives of various provinces (municipalities and autonomous regions), special administrative areas (autonomous *chou*), *hsien* (autonomous *hsien*), *ch'ü* and *hsiang* (nationality *hsiang*) should, on the basis of this programme and following the mass line, formulate concrete plans for the development of their work, stage by stage and step by step in a practical way according to the specific conditions of their own localities and co-operatives. In the meantime, the various economic, scientific, cultural, educational, health, political and legal organizations of the State should also review their operational plans in the light of this programme.

Many of the tasks outlined in this programme, such as afforestation, the practice of diligence and thrift, the extermination of rats, flies, and mosquitoes, the elimination of the most serious diseases detrimental to the people's health, and the promotion of planned parenthood, should also be carried out by the urban people. These tasks can be fulfilled most effectively only through the co-ordination among the people both in cities and in the countryside.

THE PROGRAMME

1. *Consolidate the agricultural co-operative system*

THE AGRICULTURAL cooperativization of our country has, in the main, been completed in 1957. It is our future task to make an effort to consolidate all APCs during the second FYP or during a longer period. The qualifications of consolidated co-operatives are:

(*a*) The number of former tenant, poor and lower middle peasants — comprising mainly present poor peasants and lower middle peasants among the new middle peasants — should constitute a majority among members of the co-operative leadership. Care should be taken to let upper middle peasants also be appropriately represented in the leadership.

(*b*) The policy of practising democracy in operating co-operatives should be carried out fully. The management committee of the co-operative should make public the financial accounts regularly. Cadres should consult the masses in carrying out their work and should participate in productive work.

(*c*) The policy of operating co-operatives industriously and economically should be carried out fully. Effort should be made to combat idleness in labour, and to oppose extravagance and waste.

(*d*) Measures for increasing production should be adopted according to the economic conditions of the co-operative and local topographical conditions, and capital construction programme should be expanded gradually to ensure that State plans are carried out and fulfilled, and that the production cycle is expanded continuously, so that during the second FYP a great majority of the co-operatives reach or surpass the standards of local well-to-do middle peasants in production and income.

(*e*) The question of the distribution of income should be treated rationally. Equal attention should be paid to the interests of the State, the co-operative, and co-operative members, so that under normal conditions and under the condition that production will continue to develop, the accumulation of common funds and the incomes of the members of the co-operative will grow year by year. An effort should be made to make the income of the collective economy of the co-operative plus the income of the household subsidiary production of co-operative members reach or exceed the income of local well-to-do peasants on a per capita basis by 1962.

(*f*) Political and ideological work should be strengthened. An effort should be made to raise continuously the socialist consciousness of co-operative members, to surmount their capitalist ideology, to overcome their egoist and individualist ideology, which is contradictory to the interests of the State and the collective interests of the co-operative. In co-ordination with the rectification campaign among rural cadres and the overhauling of co-operatives, the work of the co-operative should be reviewed and summarized annually, and a concentrated course in socialist education given to all rural peasants. In areas inhabited by people of more than one nationality, attention should be paid to unity and mutual assistance between different nationalities.

The present small number of lower-stage APCs should, when conditions so warrant, be directed to transform voluntarily to advanced APCs. An effort should be made to intensify the education of the present small number of individual peasants and to strengthen leadership over them so that they will see their way to join co-operatives voluntarily. Those who do not want to join co-operatives should be permitted not to do so.

2. *Greatly increase the production of grain and other agricultural crops*

In the 12 years starting with 1956 in areas north of the Yellow River, the Ch'inling Mountains, the Pailung River, and the Yellow River in Chinghai the annual grain yield should be raised from the 1955 figures of over 150 catties per *mou* to 400 catties. South of the Yellow River and north of the Huai River the yield should be raised from the 1955 figure of 208 catties to 500 catties. South of the Huai River, the Ch'inling Mountains, and the Pailung River it should rise from the 1955 figure of 400 catties to 800 catties per *mou*. In districts of sandy fields, barren lands, drought-stricken areas, water-logged areas, mountainous areas of high altitude suffering from cold weather, areas where the frost-free period in a year is very short, sparsely inhabited areas and areas where large, scale wasteland reclamation is carried out, targets for production increases should be set according to actual conditions.

In the same 12 years, the average annual yield of ginned cotton should be raised from the 1955 figure of 35 catties per *mou* — the average for the whole of China — to 40, 60, 80 or 100 catties, depending on local conditions.

To develop grain production in priority, vigorous steps should be taken everywhere to develop a multiple agricultural economy, to ensure that output targets set in State plans for textile materials (cotton, hemp, silk), oil-bearing plants (soyabean, peanut, rape, sesame, tea-oil and tung-oil), sugar-producing crops (sugar-cane and sugar-beet), tea, cured tobacco, fruits, herb and other agricultural plants are reached. Furthermore, energetic measures should be taken to develop all other marketable industrial crops. In the various provinces of South China, where conditions permit, vigorous efforts should be made to develop tropical and sub-tropical plants.

APCs should encourage their members to grow vegetables and fodder on their own private plots. Agricultural co-operatives and State farms in the outskirts of cities or near industrial and mining districts should plant vegetables in adherence to the State plan, so that the abundant supply of vegetables to these places can be ensured.

3. *The development of livestock breeding*

Different development plans for co-operative livestock breeding in various districts should be mapped out in accordance with actual conditions. State livestock-breeding farms should be systematically developed. Cattle, horses, donkeys, mules, camels, pigs, sheep, rabbits, and other domestic animals should be energetically protected and bred, and all kinds of poultry should be raised. Special care should be taken to protect the females and young. Livestock-breeding stations should be established to improve breeds. In livestock-breeding areas, care should be taken to protect pastures, and to improve and grow grass. Special care should be taken to expand water supply. Livestock breeding co-operatives should gradually establish their own fodder and grass supply bases and encourage silage.

As far as possible, all areas should, within a period varying from seven to 12 years, practically eliminate the most serious animal diseases, such as rinderpest, hog cholera, Newcastle disease, contagious pleuro-pneumonia of cattle-foot and mouth disease, port cysticercosis, lamb measles, and sheep mange. During the period before 1962 veterinary stations should be set up in *hsien* or *ch'ü* in agricultural areas and in *ch'ü* or *hsiang* in livestock-breeding areas. Co-operatives should have personnel with basic training in the prevention and cure of animal diseases. Efforts should be made to develop fully the force of civil (traditional) veterinary workers who should be organized and guided to improve techniques and to participate in the work of preventing and curing animal diseases.

4. *There are two main ways to increase the yield of crops — taking steps to increase production and disseminating advanced experiences*

The chief measures to increase production are: (*a*) water conservancy projects; (*b*) increase of fertilizers; (*c*) use of improved farm tools and gradual introduction of new-type implements; (*d*) extension of the use of the best and most suitable seed strains; (*e*) extension of multiple cropping areas; (*f*) planting more high-yield crops; (*g*) intensive farming and improving farming methods; (*h*) soil improvement; (*i*) water and soil conservation; (*j*) protecting and breeding draught animals; (*k*) wiping out insect pests and plant diseases; and (*l*) opening up virgin and wasteland and extending cultivated areas.

The chief steps to popularize advanced experiences include the following: (*i*) provinces, municipalities, and autonomous regions should collect data on the experience of local co-operatives in increasing yields, compile them, and publish them in print, so as to spread this knowledge as widely as possible; (*ii*) agricultural exhibitions; (*iii*) conferences of model peasants called at regular intervals by governments of various levels, with awards and citations to peasants who distinguish themselves in increasing production; (*iv*) mutual visits and emulation campaigns between co-operatives to exchange experience for higher production;

(*v*) imparting technical knowledge and encouraging peasants and cadres to learn the advanced administrative experiences and technical knowledge of other *hsiang*, other *hsien*, and other provinces (autonomous regions).

5. *Development of irrigation and water conservancy projects and prevention of floods and drought*

Within 12 years starting from 1956 the development of water conservancy throughout the nation should emphasize the implementation of small and medium-scale water conservancy projects, and simultaneously the building of essential and feasible large-scale water conservancy works. Small-scale water conservancy projects — the digging of wells and ponds, and the building of irrigation canals, reservoirs, and dams — and the harnessing of small rivers should be carried out by local governments and APCs systematically and on a large scale. This work and the large and medium-scale water conservancy projects and the harnessing of the large and medium rivers undertaken by the State should virtually eliminate all ordinary floods and drought within 12 years. Energetic efforts should be made to drain water in heavily water-logged areas and to improve construction work in bog lands.

It is hoped that within 12 years, paddy fields and irrigated land will be expanded to some 900 million *mou* from the over 390 million *mou* in 1955. The capabilities of irrigation facilities in combating drought should be raised to 30 to 50 days, according to differences in local conditions. In areas where double-crop paddy can be raised, this ability should be raised to 50 to 70 days to ensure adequate harvests. To make full use of all available water resources, related authorities should intensify the study of underground water resources to guarantee the supply of necessary data to water conservancy authorities.

In building water conservancy projects for power generation, measures should be taken to build whenever possible medium and small hydroelectric power projects in co-ordination with large and medium electric power projects undertaken by the State in order gradually to bring electrification to the countryside.

6. *Energetic steps must be taken to increase output of fertilizers and chemical fertilizers*

APCs must employ all means to solve their own fertilizer needs. Special attention should be paid to hog-raising — in some localities sheep-breeding. With the exception of certain nationality areas which do not raise hogs for religious reasons, the number of hogs raised in the countryside by 1962 should reach the average of from 1·5 to 2 per household and from 2·5 to 3 by 1967. Pigs should be kept in pigstys, sheep in sheepfolds, cattle and horses in barns. Measures suitable to local conditions should be adopted actively to develop green manure crops of various types and to utilize fully human manure from the cities and the countryside, garbage which may be used for fertilizers, and other fertilizers.

Central and the local authorities should take vigorous steps to promote the chemical fertilizer industry which will turn out approximately from 5 million to 7 million tons of chemical fertilizers in 1962 and approximately 15 million tons of chemical fertilizers in 1967. Active steps should also be taken to promote the development of bacterial fertilizers.

7. *Old-type farm tools should be renovated and new-type farm tools popularized*

Renovated and new-type farm tools suitable to local conditions should be popularized according to the needs of production and after experiments in adaptability and renovation. Constant attention should be paid to the maintenance and repair of farm tools; technical guidance on the use of new-type farm tools should be strengthened. With the development of State industrialization, agricultural mechanization should be carried out systematically and effectively. Starting from 1956, machine-tool and agricultural departments concerned should, within the shortest period of time, carry out extensive experiments and research work and should draw up an agricultural mechanization programme adaptable to the conditions in our country in order to lay a good groundwork for the promotion of agricultural mechanization and for the manufacturing of machines suitable for use in various localities by the peasants; measures should also be taken to constantly improve and promote the use of such machines.

8. *Energetic steps must be taken to breed and extend the use of improved strains suitable to local conditions*

Before 1962 picked seeds of various crops should be in general use after testing their adaptability to local conditions in various areas. With regard to crops such as cotton, the picked seeds of which have been in general use, more work should be done in nurturing and selecting seeds as well as in the experimental planting of good seed from other localities and from abroad. All agricultural co-operatives should set aside land specially for growing seed as such and, in the meantime, should make efforts to strengthen seed selection work, as well as setting up a system for increasing the amount of selected seed and varying it. State farms at central and local levels should make themselves the centres for breeding good seeds of crops suitable to local conditions. Various provinces (municipalities and autonomous regions) special districts (autonomous *chou*), and *hsien* (autonomous *hsien*) should set up organs for handling seeds.

9. *Extend the area of multiple crops*

In the 12 years starting with 1956 the average multiple crop index set for various areas under varied conditions — including manure crops — will be raised to the following levels: (*a*) areas south of the Wuling Mountains — approximately 230 per cent; (*b*) areas north of the Wuling Mountains and south of the Yangtse River — approximately 200 per cent; (*c*) areas north of the Yangtse and south of the Yellow River, the Ch'inling Mountains, and the Pailung River — approximately 160 per cent; (*d*) areas north of the Yellow River, Ch'inling Mountains, and the Pailung River, and south of the Great Wall — approximately 120 per cent; (*e*) in areas north of the Great Wall, multiple crop areas should be expanded as much as possible by fully utilizing existing farmland and arable land as well as reducing fallow land acreage.

10. *Grow more high-yield crops*

All available water resources should be utilized and rice-cultivating areas expanded. In the 12 years starting with 1956 the areas under rice should be increased by 250 million *mou*. High-yield crops, such as maize and potatoes, should be properly developed according to the need and dietary habits of the people.

11. *Methods of cultivation should be effectively improved in accordance with local conditions*

All APCs must carry out deep ploughing, careful cultivation, rational application of fertilizers, effective irrigation, proper rotation of crops, inter-cropping and close planting, sowing and hoeing in good time, thinning and protecting young shoots, timely harvesting, and improving field work, in order to bring about good yields and good harvests.

12. *Improve soil*

APCs and State farms should try their best to improve and to make good use of saline and alkali soil, less productive lateritic soil, low-lying land, sandy and other less productive soils. Attention should be paid to prevent the salinization and alkalization of land. Active plans should be formulated for terracing hilly land. Exhaustive efforts should be made to turn less productive land into rich, fertile land.

13. *Carry out water and soil conservation work*

In areas suffering from loss of water and soil, APCs should be relied upon to mobilize the masses on a large scale to engage in water and soil conservation work step by step and in a planned way in co-ordination with local production work. It is requested that within 12 years, starting from 1956, noticeable results should be achieved in water and soil conservation work in all practicable areas, so that the damage caused by the loss of water and soil may be gradually reduced to the minimum. To achieve quick results in this work, agricultural, forestry, water conservancy, animal husbandry, scientific research, and other related organs should closely co-ordinate with one another under the unified leadership of local CCP and Government authorities to give active support to this work.

14. *Protect and breed draught animals*

In the seven to 12 years beginning 1956 each and every agricultural co-operative should own a sufficient number of serviceable draught animals. In this connection, it is necessary to produce sufficient fodder and forage and to raise high-yield fodder crops. APCs should continuously improve the breeding and control of draught animals according to their own conditions. APCs and the Government authorities should adopt correct measures to encourage the breeding of draught animals.

15. *Prevent, remedy and eliminate plant diseases and insect pests*

In seven to 12 years starting 1956, wherever possible, virtually wipe out insect pests and plant diseases most harmful to crops. These include locusts, cut works, rice borers, maize borers, aphides, red spiders, pink bollworms, wheat borers, wheat smut, wheat nematode and black rot on sweet potato. In addition, preventive measures should be taken against the infestation and spread of other dangerous plant diseases, insect pests, and weeds. Local plans should include any other serious insect pests and plant diseases that can be wiped out. Greater attention should be paid to plant protection and quarantine measures. The production of agricultural chemicals (insecticides) and their application should be developed in a planned manner. The quality of these products and their supply should be improved. In addition, technical guidance should be strengthened in their use to ensure that they are used safely and effectively.

16. *Reclaim wasteland to increase the acreage of cultivated area*

The State should reclaim wasteland in a planned manner. In 12 years starting in 1956 the acreage of cultivated land in State farms should be increased from the over 13 million *mou* in 1955 to approximately 100 million *mou.* Where practicable, migrants and co-operatives should be organized and encouraged to reclaim wasteland with their production teams and branch co-operatives. In reclaiming wasteland, attention should be paid to the co-ordination of this work with plans governing the conservation of water and soil and the development of animal husbandry, so that the loss of water and soil and the destruction of forests and indispensable grazing land can be avoided. In areas where forests have already been wiped out, an effort should be made to restore them.

APCs should make full use of all types of odds and ends of land, such as raised borders between crop fields, corners, pond and river banks, and unused courtyards. Lands in this category can be assigned to production teams or individuals co-operative members for cultivation.

In carrying out capital construction, factories, mines, commercial and agricultural enterprises, cultural, educational, public health, water conservancy, communications, and military departments concerned as well as mass organizations must do their utmost to economize in the use of land and to avoid the occupation and minimize the use of cultivated land.

17. *Development of the economy of hilly areas*

Agriculture, forestry, the livestock breeding industry, and the production of native and speciality products of various categories in hilly areas must be developed in accordance with local conditions whenever applicable and in line with the principle of promoting a multiple economy. Grain production should be developed in hilly areas under conditions which do not impede soil and water conservation. In areas where grain is still insufficient, efforts should be exerted to achieve grain self-sufficiency and to minimize the quantity of grain to be imported from other localities. In remote hilly areas, steps must be taken to develop forests for timber; nearby hilly areas should pay attention to the development of forests of economic value, woods for charcoal, fruit trees, and other native and speciality products. Hilly areas in the South must plant oil-yielding tea trees, tung-oil trees, bamboo groves, mulberry trees, and tea trees. Hilly areas in the North must take steps to grow walnuts, Mongolian oak, and wild pepper. Measures should also be adopted to expand the production of medicinal herbs, protect wild medicinal herbs, and, wherever possible, to take gradual steps to cultivate them.

In 12 years starting with 1956 measures should be taken to eliminate basically, damages by wild animals in all areas possible which endanger production in hilly areas and to protect and raise wild animals of economic value. Special districts, *hsien*, *hsiang*, and APCs in hilly and semi-hilly areas must draw up long-range production plans as well as measures concerning the appropriate use of land so as to promote the overall development of production. State departments concerned should extend vigorous assistance and co-ordination in communications, transport, supply and marketing, trade, and in cultural and educational, public health, and migration fields of work.

18. *Development of forestry and afforesting wasteland and denuded hilly areas*

In the 12 years starting with 1956 wasteland and denuded hills must be afforested whenever natural surroundings and manpower permit. Whenever possible, trees should be planted in a systematic manner near houses, villages, along roads and rivers. In this connection, afforestation work will have to depend on the APCs, which will practise the policy that trees planted by co-operatives belong to them. APCs should gather their own seeds and grow saplings and should adopt measures to effect division of work and responsibility in planting trees. Co-operative members should be encouraged to plant trees near their houses; they will retain ownership of trees they plant, and the income derived therefrom.

Besides developing forests for timber — including bamboo groves — manpower and vacant land in the city and the countryside should be fully utilized for planting fruit trees, mulberry, Mongolian oak, tea trees, trees for varnish, oil-bearing plants, and other trees of economic value. Vigorous steps should be taken to strengthen State afforestation. The State forest areas should devote attention to expanding forests for timber, and create, in a gradual and systematic manner, windbreaks, sandbreaks, and shelters to aid in water and soil conservation, and to protect sea coasts. Tree planting along railways, highways and rivers, and around large reservoirs and mines may be undertaken by railway, communication, and water conservancy departments as well as factories and mines concerned, with the income derived from this source accruing to the departments concerned; or it may be undertaken by APCs nearby, according to specifications set forth by the departments concerned, with the income derived from this source accruing to the co-operatives.

Cultivated land should not be occupied for afforestation. Within 12 years, all State forests should be properly set up and managed. The State may, for its own convenience, consign co-operatives to manage smaller State forests. Forest resources should be well taken care of and protected. Fire prevention work and the work of controlling harmful insects and diseases should be strengthened. Measures should be taken to halt random felling and wasteful felling and to restore forests after felling.

19. *Development of the production of ocean and fresh-water marine products and the breeding of marine life*

Measures should be taken to develop the latent potentialities of existing equipment in marine fishing on the basis of co-operativization so as gradually to improve fishing techniques. Attention should be paid to increasing the accumulation of public funds, replenishing as well as improving equipment, and the step-by-step expansion of motorized junks and other fishing vessels. Steps must be taken to strengthen safety measures and to strive to expand fishing activities in deep seas. Waters suitable for fish-breeding should be fully utilized to develop fresh-water fish-breeding. Steps should be taken to cultivate good-quality stock and to prevent ichthyological diseases, to expand the shallow-sea fish-breeding industry, and to strengthen the breeding of fish, crustacea, and seaweeds.

20. *Proper management of State farms*

All State farms must unite and assist APCs around them in production and technical fields and to play an exemplary role. State farms should undertake varied production and should raise the utilization rate of the labour force, continue to improve production techniques and labour management, and raise labour productivity. State farms must practice strict economy, consistently implement the principle of operating farms on the basis of industry and thrift improve the wages system, and endeavour to increase output while reducing production costs.

21. *Improve agro-scientific research work and technical guidance*

Wherever necessary and possible, efforts should be made to establish and improve organs undertaking research in agricultural science and those providing technical guidance. These include colleges of agricultural science, regional and other specialized institutes of agricultural science, provincial agricultural experimental stations, model *hsien* breeding farms, and district agricultural instruction centres. In this way agricultural research and technical guidance will be of better service in developing agriculture.

Agricultural research and technical guidance should be carried out in close co-ordination with the production and experiences of the peasants. It should be of service in summarizing the special characteristics of the peasants in a locality and promoting the experiences of old peasants in increasing production and the study of advanced production experiences of other localities. Personnel of the *hsien* agro-technical stations should select their farms and APCs as bases to participate in agricultural production.

In the 12 years from 1956 peasants with certain production experience and a certain level of education will be trained as technicians of primary and intermediate grades for agricultural co-operatives so as to meet the needs of the co-operative economy.

22. *Strengthen meteorological and hydrological work*

Within 12 years from 1956 a meteorological and hydrological network will be basically established; weather forecasts, particularly those of bad weather, will be intensified and weather forecasts for rural areas will be established. Various localities should pay attention to radio weather forecasts so as to prevent damage by flood, drought, wind, frost and other natural calamities.

23. *All APCs should apply the principle of industry and thrift*

Industry means giving full encouragement to APC members to work conscientiously, to branch out into new fields of production, to develop a multiple economy and to exercise minute care over all undertakings. Thrift means being strictly economical, lowering production costs, and opposing extravagance and waste. In all capital construction plans co-operatives should make the fullest use of their own manpower and the material and capital at their disposal. It is necessary to educate the peasants in how to be industrious and thrifty in household management so that they can plan their household expenses. In rural areas, women's organizations should consider industry and thrift as an important topic in educating women. They should introduce those who are outstanding in careful spending and saving, and correct the erroneous attitude of those who indulge in spending. All festive entertainments should be minimized and unreasonable customs involving expense corrected.

24. *Raise the utilization of the labour power, labour productivity, and develop a many-sided economy*

If agriculture, forestry, livestock-breeding, fisheries, subsidiary production, the rural handicraft industry are to be developed to the full, if the national wealth and the income of the peasants is to grow, APCs must make fuller use of manpower and raise labour productivity. In the northern part of China, production activities in winter should be encouraged. There should also be improvements in production technique, labour organization, and labour management. In the seven years beginning with 1956 every able-bodied man in the countryside ought to be able to put in at least 250 working days a year.

Reasonable organization and arrangements should be formulated so as to draw women into labour production according to their skills. Within seven years, every able-bodied woman in the countryside should, besides the time she spends on household work, be able to give at least 80 to 180 days to agricultural and subsidiary production — including subsidiary cottage occupations — according to various districts and actual conditions of the locality. In addition, all those in the countryside who can contribute only half the labour of an able-bodied man or who are fitted only for light work should be encouraged to do well at whatever work they are fit for and suited to.

25. *Food storage*

All APCs except those deficient in food or which deal mainly with forestry or economic crops, should, within 12 years beginning in 1956, store enough grain for emergency use for three months, half a year, one year, or one and a half years, according to local conditions. All APCs should draw up concrete plans to meet this requirement. In areas where crop harvests are unstable and transport is poor, special attention should be given to storage of grain after a bumper harvest to prevent food shortages in time of poor harvest. Within 12 years starting in 1956 the State should store enough grain for emergency use for one or two years.

26. *Improvement of living conditions*

With the development in production of the co-operative and the increased income of members, APCs should, based on needs and potentialities, encourage and assist their members to make plans for repairing and building houses by groups and in separate stages in line with the principle of willingness, mutual assistance, economizing expenses and minimizing the use of land, so as to improve the living conditions of members.

27. *Elimination of the "four evils"*

In the 12 years starting with 1956 measures should be taken to wipe out rats, sparrows, flies and mosquitoes in all possible places. The elimination of sparrows is to protect crops, and sparrows in cities and forest areas may be spared.

28. *Vigorous steps should be taken to eliminate the most serious diseases*

In the 12 years starting with 1956, measures should be taken to eliminate the most serious diseases in all possible places; these include schistosomiasis, small-pox, bubonic plague, malaria, kala-azar, hookworm, filariasis, tetanus, and venereal diseases. Steps should also be taken to prevent and cure other diseases such as measles, dysentery, typhoid fever, contagious encephalitis, poliomyelitis, diphtheria, pulmonary tuberculosis, leprosy, thrachoma, goitre, hypertrophic osteoarthritis, and Kaschin-Beck's disease. Every effort should be made to train medical and public health personnel, including traditional Chinese doctors. Popular and permanent patriotic sanitation campaigns should be carried out actively to draw popular attention to hygiene and to cultivate the habit of cleanliness. The fundamental spirit calling for cleanliness is to eliminate diseases and to inspire the people to change old habits in order to reform the country.

29. *Protection of women and children*

The principle of equal pay for equal work should be strictly applied to women engaged in productive labour. APCs, when necessary and according to requirements and potentialities, may set up creches during the busy farm season. When work is given out, the health and physique of women members must be taken into consideration. Suitable regulations should be mapped out. taking into consideration the age and physique of children who help in auxiliary work during the busy season. Public health departments concerned should train midwives for rural areas and should actively promote the use of modern delivery methods, provide post-natal and infant care, and take steps to cut the incidence of maternal diseases and the infant mortality rate. Except in a few nationality areas, birth control and planned parenthood should be publicized and encouraged so as to avoid placing too heavy a burden on living expenses in order to give the children a better education and good opportunities for employment.

30. *Practice the "five guarantees," give preferential treatment to martyrs' dependants and disabled revolutionary military personnel, and support and respect parents*

APCs should work out a unified plan to assign production groups or teams to see that those members who lack manpower or who are widows or widowers with no close relations to depend on, are given productive work and a livelihood; that they have enough food, clothing and fuel; the children are educated properly, and the dead are decently buried. This way they are assured of help during their lifetime and a decent burial at death. As for martyrs' dependants who lack manpower and disabled ex-servicemen who cannot maintain livelihood after receiving compensatory funds, the APC must assist them according to the measures for preferential treatment stipulated by the State so that their livelihood will not be lower than the average co-operative member.

Young people and adults, both male and female, should be taught to support and respect their parents so that the livelihood of the old and the weak will be taken care of materially and comforted spiritually.

31. *Elimination of illiteracy and development of rural cultural education*

Within the 12 years beginning with 1956 illiteracy among young people and adults should be wiped out completely. Efforts must be made to establish spare-time cultural schools in the *hsiang* or co-operative so as to raise the cultural standard of rural cadres and peasants. Apart from those which are State-operated, the establishment of schools should be encouraged among the masses. Establishment of private schools is permitted in order to disseminate primary school education. Following the development of agricultural production, APCs should, according to local conditions and the principle of industry and thrift, develop their cultural and recreational activities step by step.

32. *Development of rural broadcast network*

Beginning in 1956, in the next seven to 12 years, depending on local circumstances, the radio network will be extended to all rural areas. Most co-operatives in agriculture, forestry, fishery, livestock-breeding, salt production, and handicrafts will be able to tune in to broadcasts.

33. *Development of rural telephone and postal services*

In seven to 12 years from 1956, in accordance with local circumstances, a telephone network will be established in the *hsiang* and some APCs. Radio telephone-telegraph equipment will be installed in some localities. During the same period, all villages are to be provided with post and telegraphic services.

34. *Development of rural communication and transportation*

In a matter of seven to 12 years, starting from 1956, depending on various local conditions, the whole countryside must be provided with networks of roads. All roads between one province (municipality or autonomous region) and another, between administrative regions (autonomous *chou*), *hsien* (autonomous *hsien*), districts and *hsiang* (nationality *hsiang*) shall be built in accordance with the needs of the locality and on the basis of economy and practical use. At the same time, all roads must be constantly and carefully maintained. Special attention should be paid to road-building in hilly districts. In places served by waterways, navigable channels should be dredged and kept in good order under whatever conditions are possible to improve communications.

35. *Reorganization of rural commercial network*

In order to cope with this new development following agricultural co-operativization, commercial bodies and supply and marketing co-operatives should complete the reorganization of their buying and selling machinery within the next few years, improve the circulation of goods, strengthen control over primary markets, ensure that all rural areas receive good service in the supply of goods and the purchase of agricultural products, struggle against capitalist influences and promote production in the rural areas.

36. *Development of rural credit co-operatives*

Credit co-operatives in rural areas should be strengthened so as to provide credit for APCs and peasants whenever necessary and to encourage saving.

37. *Develop the initiative of demobilized military personnel in building socialism in rural areas*

Demobilized military personnel in rural areas should preserve the traditions of the PLA on the socialist production front, practice thrift, closely unite with the masses, and adhere to the policies, decrees, and labour discipline of the State so that they become activists in agricultural production. *Hsiang* people's councils and APCs must make suitable arrangements for the production activities of demobilized military personnel and help them promote their studies and improve production techniques. People's governments at all levels must conduct political and ideological education among demobilized military personnel and constantly pay attention to their progress.

38. *Heighten the enthusiasm of rural youth in socialist undertakings*

Rural youth should be taught to love their fatherland ardently, to love the countryside, to love to take part in labour and to love their co-operatives as own families. They should be given every encouragement to show initiative in learning to read and write, studying agro-scientific techniques, and the production experiences of the old and adult peasants. They should become the spearhead, the shock force in productive, scientific and cultural work in the countryside. Primary and middle school graduates in urban areas, with the exception of those who can enter higher schools or find local employment, should actively respond to the call of the State and take part in agricultural production and the great task of socialist agricultural construction. Eighty-five per cent of our population is in the rural areas and unless our agriculture is developed we cannot develop our industry. Therefore, to work in the rural areas is an extremely essential and most glorious task.

39. *Reform of landlords, rich peasants, counter-revolutionaries, and other bad elements and the safeguarding of the socialist order in rural areas*

Former landlords, rich peasants and counter-revolutionaries in the rural areas shall, according to their conduct, be admitted as members or candidate members of APCs in accordance with the "Model Regulations for Advance-stage APC." Those unqualified for admission to agricultural co-operatives shall be allowed by the *hsiang* people's council to work in the co-operatives under supervision. The APCs should, depending on various circumstances, intensify education of and control over the peasants inside and outside the co-operatives so as to heighten their vigilance against any possible subversive activities. Former landlords, rich peasants, and counter-revolutionaries who have become co-operative members shall be demoted to candidate members or work under supervision if they behave badly or fail, after repeated exhortations, to make attempts to improve. Similarly, candidate members shall be demoted to working under supervision. Anyone engaging in subversive activities shall be punished according to the law. Gambling and activities under secret societies or the guise of Taoism should be strictly prohibited. Thieves, swindlers, hooligans, secret agents, and other undesirable elements who undermine the social order are subject to punishment according to law.

40. *Workers in the cities and peasants in the co-operatives must give each other every support*

Workers must turn out more and better industrial goods which the peasants need, and the peasants must grow more and better grain and industrial raw materials which industry and town dwellers require. Workers and peasants should also arrange joint meetings, mutual visits, and write to each other. They should keep in touch, give each other encouragement, and exchange experiences so as to promote the development of industry and agriculture and help consolidate the alliance between the workers and the peasants led by the working class.

APPENDIX III

RESOLUTION ON SOME QUESTIONS CONCERNING THE PEOPLE'S COMMUNES*

Adopted by the Eighth Central Committee of the Chinese Communist Party at Its Sixth Plenary Session, December 10, 1958

IN 1958, a new social organization appeared fresh as the morning sun above the broad horizon of East Asia. This was the large-scale people's communes in the rural areas of our country which combines industry, agriculture, trade, education and military affairs and in which government administration and commune management are integrated. Since their first appearance the people's communes with their immense vitality have attracted widespread attention.

The movement to set up people's communes has grown very rapidly. Within a few months starting in the summer of 1958, all the more than 740,000 agricultural producers' co-operatives in the country, in compliance with the enthusiastic demands of the mass of peasants, had reorganized themselves into over 26,000 people's communes. Over 120 million households, or more than 99 per cent of all the peasant households of various nationalities in China, have joined the people's communes. This shows that the emergence of the people's communes is not fortuitous; it is the outcome of the economic and political development of our country, the outcome of the socialist rectification campaign conducted by the Party, the Party's general line for socialist construction and the great leap forward of socialist construction in 1958.

Although the rural people's communes were only established a short while ago, the mass of the peasants are already conscious of the obvious benefits they have brought them: labour power and means of production can be brought under unified management and deployment on a larger scale than before to ensure their still more rational and effective use and, consequently facilitate the development of production. Under the unified leadership of the commune, industry, agriculture (including farming, forestry, animal husbandry, side-occupations and fishery), trade, education and military affairs have been closely co-ordinated and rapidly developed. In particular thousands, and tens of thousands of small factories have mushroomed in the rural areas. To meet the pressing demands of the masses, the communes have set up large numbers of community dining rooms, nurseries, kindergartens, "homes to honour the aged" and other institutions for collective welfare, which have, in particular, completely emancipated the women from thousands of years of drudgery in the kitchen and brought broad smiles to their faces. As the result of the bumper crops many communes

* *China Today*, III, 13, Dec. 27, 1958. Chinese text in *HPYK*, No. 24, 1958, Dec. 25, 1958, pp. 3–11.

have instituted a system of distribution that combines the wage system with the free supply system; the mass of peasants, both men and women, have begun to receive wage and those families, which in the past constantly worried about their daily meals and about their firewood, rice, oil, salt, sauce, vinegar and vegetables, are now able to "eat without paying for it." In other words, they have got the most important and most reliable social insurance. For the peasants, all this is epoch-making news. The living standards of the peasants have been improved and they know from practical experience and the prospects of the development of the communes, that they will live a still better life in the future.

The development of the system of rural people's communes is of even more profound and far-reaching significance than this. It has shown the people of our country the way to the gradual industrialisation of the rural areas, the way to the gradual transition from collective ownership to ownership by the whole people in agriculture, the way to the gradual transition from the socialist principle of "to each according to his work" to the Communist principle of "to each according to his needs," the way to the gradual diminution and final elimination of the differences between rural and urban areas, between worker and peasant and between mental and manual labour, and the way to the gradual diminution and final elimination of the domestic functions of the state.

All this has proved that the resolution on the establishment of people's communes in the rural areas adopted in August, 1958, on the basis of the creativeness of the masses, by the Political Bureau of the Central Committee of the Chinese Communist Party at its Peitaiho meeting, is correct and is of historic significance.

People's communes have now been set up as a general rule in all rural areas inhabited by peoples of various nationalities (except in Tibet and in certain areas). Some experiments have also begun in the cities. In the future, the urban people's communes, in a form suited to the specific features of cities, will also become instruments for transformation of the old cities and construction of the new, socialist cities; they will become the unified organisers of production, exchange and distribution and of the livelihood and wellbeing of the people, social organisations which combine industry, agriculture, trade, education and military affairs and in which government administration and commune management are integrated. There are, however, certain differences between city and countryside. Firstly, city conditions are more complex than those in the countryside. Secondly, socialist ownership by the whole people is already the main form of ownership in the cities, and the factories, public institutions and schools (except part of the family members of workers and staff) under the leadership of the working class have already become highly organised in accordance with socialist principles; therefore, the switchover of cities to people's communes inevitably raises some requirements different from those in the rural areas. Thirdly, bourgeois ideology is still fairly prevalent among many of the capitalists and intellectuals in the cities; they still have misgivings about the establishment of communes—so we should wait a bit for them. Consequently, we should continue to make experiments and, generally speaking, should not be in a hurry to set up people's communes on a large scale in the cities. Particularly in the big cities, this work should be postponed except for the necessary preparatory measures. People's communes should be established on a large scale in the cities only after rich experience has been gained and when the skeptics and doubters have been convinced.

The rural people's communes which have already been established have not had time to consolidate their organisations, perfect their working systems, systematically settle the new questions concerning production, distribution, livelihood and amenities, management and administration which have arisen with the establishment of the communes. This is because the communes were only recently set up and most of them immediately after their establishment threw themselves into the heavy work of the autumn harvest, ploughing and sowing and the nation-wide campaign for iron and steel. There is as yet insufficient experience of successfully running and developing the people's communes. Different approaches to certain questions are unavoidable. The urgent tasks at present are to quickly achieve a unity of views on the communes among all members of the Party and among the people, strengthen the leadership over the communes, check-up and consolidate their organisation, define and perfect their working systems, and improve the organisation of production and life in the communes. Energetic efforts must be made to strengthen those communes which have already set up their basic structure, so that they will be in a position to carry out ever more successfully their great mission of promoting the development of the productive forces and the relations of production.

II

The people's commune is the basic unit of the socialist social structure of our country, which combines industry, agriculture, trade, education and military affairs; it is, at the same time, basic unit of organisation of socialist state power. Marxist-Leninist theory and the initial experience of the people's communes in our country enable us to foresee now that the people's communes will quicken the tempo of socialist construction and constitute the best form for realizing the following two transitions in our country: firstly, the transition from collective ownership to ownership by the whole people in the countryside; and secondly, the transition from socialist to Communist society. It can also be foreseen that in the future Communist society, the people's commune will remain the basic unit of social structure.

From now on, the task confronting the people of our country is: through such a form of social organisation as the people's commune, and based on the general line for socialist construction laid down by the Party, to develop the social productive forces at high speed to advance the industrialisation of the country, the industrialisation of the communes, mechanisation and electrification of agriculture and to effect the gradual transition from socialist collective ownership to socialist ownership by the whole people, thus fully realising ownership by the whole people in the socialist economy of our country, and gradually building our country into a great socialist land with a highly developed modern industry, agriculture, science and culture. During this process, the Communist factors are bound to increase gradually and these will lay the foundation both in material and spiritual conditions for the transition from socialism to Communism.

This is a gigantic and extremely complex task. In the light of experience already gained, and under the concrete conditions obtaining in our country, it is possible that socialist ownership by the whole people may be fully realised at a somewhat earlier date, but it will not be very soon. Though the pace at which we are advancing is fairly rapid, wide-spread realisation of the industrialisation of our country, industrialisation of the communes and mechanisation and electrification of agriculture and the building of a socialist country with a highly developed modern industry, agriculture, science and culture will still take a very long time. The completion of this whole process will take 15, 20 or more years counting from now.

The imperialists and those who parrot them say that this time is too short for us to build a highly developed modern industry, agriculture and science and culture, and that we won't be able to achieve our aim. We have got used to such tunes; there is no need to pay any attention to them; it is inevitable that the facts will batter these people down time and time again. But there will be other people who will say that this time is too long. They are good-hearted people from our own ranks, but they are over eager. They think that the building of a highly developed modern industry and so on, full realisation of socialist ownership by the people as a whole, or even the attainment of Communism, is something quite easy. They think that ownership in the rural people's communes is even now of the nature of ownership by the people as a whole, and that very soon or even now they can dispense with the socialist principle of distribution according to work and adopt the Communist principle of distribution according to needs. That is why they cannot grasp the fact that the socialist system will have to continue for a very long time. This view, of course, is the result of misunderstanding and such misunderstandings must be cleared up.

It should be pointed out that the switch from agricultural producers' co-operatives to people's communes, the transition from socialist collective ownership to socialist ownership by the people as a whole and the transition from socialism to Communism are processes which are inter-connected but are, at the same time, distinct from each other.

First of all, the switch from the agricultural producers' co-operatives to the people's communes has expanded and enhanced the original collective ownership and contains certain elements of ownership by the whole people, but this does not mean to say that collective ownership in the countryside has been transformed into ownership by the whole people. Now the whole Chinese countryside has switched over to people's communes, but a certain period of time will have to pass before ownership by the whole people is realised throughout the countryside.

True, the establishment of the people's communes has indeed added certain elements of ownership by the whole people to the collective ownership economy. This is because the rural people's communes and the basic organisations of state power have been combined into one; because the banks, stores and other enterprises owned by the whole people originally existing in the countryside have been placed under the management of the communes; because the communes have taken part in establishing certain industrial and other constructive undertakings which are by nature owned by the whole people; because in many counties federations of communes exercising a unified leadership over all the people's communes in the given counties have been formed and have the power to deploy a certain portion of the manpower, material and financial resources of the communes to undertake constructive undertakings on a county scale or over (this has already started in many areas), and so on. But at the present time the means of production and products of the rural people's communes are in the main still collectively owned by the communes and differ from those of the state-owned enterprises which belong to the whole people. Both collective ownership and ownership by the whole people are socialist ownership; but the latter is more advanced than the former because the state representing the whole people can directly make a unified and rational distribution of the means of production and products of enterprises owned by the whole people according to the requirement of the national economy as a whole, while this cannot be done by enterprises run under collective ownership, including the rural people's communes of the present type. To say that ownership by the people's communes as they now exist in the countryside is already ownership by the whole people does not conform to reality.

To gradually promote the transition from collective ownership to ownership by the whole people, federations of communes in a county should be established widely throughout the country. In the coming years, and on the basis of the energetic development of production and enhancement of the people's political understanding, such federations should take suitable steps to increase gradually the proportion of their means of production which come under ownership by the whole people and the proportion of their products which are subject to unified distribution by the state, and, when conditions mature, change collective ownership into ownership by the whole people. If timely steps are not taken to promote and complete this change and if the existing collective ownership be left intact with the result that commune members confine their attention to a relatively narrow scope of collective interests, the continuous development of the social productive forces and the continuous enhancement of the people's political understanding will be impeded. This is not proper. However, it must be pointed out that collective ownership still plays a positive role today in developing production in the people's communes. How soon the transition from collective ownership to ownership by the whole people will be effected is determined by the objective factors—the level of development of production and the level of the people's political understanding—and not by mere wishful thinking that it can be done sooner or later. Thus, this transition will be realised, by stages and by groups, on a national scale only after the lapse of a considerable time. Those who, because of failure to understand this, confuse the establishment of people's communes with the realisation of ownership by the whole people and make any impetuous attempt to negate collective ownership in the countryside prematurely and hastily carry out a change-over to ownership by the whole people, will be doing the wrong thing and therefore cannot succeed.

Furthermore, the change from socialist collective ownership to socialist ownership by the whole people is not the same thing as a switchover from socialism to Communism. Still less is the change from agricultural producers' co-operatives to people's communes the same thing as the change from socialism to Communism. The change from socialism to Communism will require much more time even than the change from socialist collective ownership to socialist ownership by the whole people.

True, the free supply system adopted by the people's communes has in it an embryo of the Communist principle of distribution according to needs; the policy of running industry and agriculture simultaneously and combining them carried out by the people's communes has opened up a way to reduce the differences between town and countryside and between worker and peasant; when the rural people's communes pass over from socialist collective ownership to socialist ownership by the whole people, these Communist factors will grow further. All this must be acknowledged. Moreover, with social products becoming increasingly plentiful thanks to the continuous advance of industry and agriculture throughout the country; with the proportion of what is supplied gratis under the distribution system of the people's communes gradually growing larger and the standards of free supply being gradually raised; with the consistent raising of the level of the people's political understanding; with the constant progress of education for the whole people; the gradual reduction of the differences between mental and manual labour; and the gradual diminution of the domestic function of the state power, etc., the conditions for the transition to Communism will also gradually mature. It is of course not proper to ignore or even impede this course of development and relegate Communism to the distant future.

Nevertheless, every Marxist must soberly realise that the transition from socialism to Communism is quite a long and complicated process of development and that throughout this entire process society is still socialist in nature. Socialist society and Communist society are two stages marked by different degrees of economic development. The socialist principle is "from each according to his ability and to each according to his work"; the Communist principle is "from each according to his ability and to each according to his needs". The Communist system of distribution is more reasonable, but it can be put into effect only when there is a great abundance of social products. In the absence of this condition, any negation of the principle of to each according to his work will tend to dampen the labour enthusiasm of the people and is therefore disadvantageous to the development of production, to the increase of social products, and hence to speeding the realisation of Communism. For this reason, in the income of commune members, that portion of the wage paid according to work done must occupy an important place over a long period and will, during a certain period, take first place. In order to encourage the labour enthusiasm of commune members and also facilitate satisfaction of their complex daily needs, the communes must strive to increase the wages of their members gradually and, for a number of years to come, must increase them at a rate faster than that portion of their income that comes under the heading of free supply. Even after the transition from collective ownership to ownership by the whole people, the people's communes will, over a necessary historical period, retain the system of distribution according to work done owing to the fact that there is not as yet an abundant enough supply of social products to realise Communism. Any attempt to negate prematurely the principle of distribution according to work and replace it with the principle of distribution according to needs, that is, any attempt, when conditions are not mature, to enter Communism by over-reaching ourselves—is undoubtedly a utopian concept that cannot possibly succeed.

Both the transition from socialist collective ownership to socialist ownership by the whole people and the transition from socialism to Communism must depend on a certain level of development of the productive forces. Production relations must be suited to the nature of the productive forces and only when the productive forces develop to a certain stage will certain changes be brought about in production relations—this is a fundamental principle of Marxism. Our comrades must bear in mind that the present level of development of the productive forces in our country is, after all, still very low. Three years of hard battle plus several years of energetic work may bring about a great change in the economic face of the country. But even then there will still be a considerable distance to go to reach the goals of a high degree of industrialisation of the entire country and the mechanisation and electrification of the country's agriculture; and there will be an even longer distance to go to reach the goals of an enormous abundance of social products, of a great lightening of labour and of a sharp reduction of working hours. Without all these, it is, of course, impossible to talk about entering a higher stage of development in human society—Communism. Therefore, since we are devoted to the cause of Communism, we must first devote ourselves to developing our productive forces and working energetically to fulfil our plan for socialist industrialisation. We should not groundlessly make declarations that the people's communes in the countryside will "realise ownership by the whole people immediately", or even "enter Communism immediately", and so on. To do such things is not only an expression of impetuosity, it will greatly lower the standards of Communism in the minds of the people, distort the great ideal of Communism and vulgarise it, strengthen the petty bourgeois trend towards equalitarianism and adversely effect the development of socialist construction.

On the question of transition from socialism to Communism, we must not mark time at the socialist stage, but neither should we drop into the utopian dream of skipping the socialist stage and jumping over to the Communist stage. We are advocates of the Marxist-Leninist theory of uninterrupted revolution; we hold that no great wall exists or can be allowed to exist between the democratic revolution and the socialist revolution and between socialism and Communism. We are at the same time advocates of the Marxist-Leninist theory of the development of revolution by stages; we hold that different stages of development reflect qualitative changes and that these stages of different quality should not be confused. The Political Bureau of the Central Committee has pointed out clearly in its August resolution on the establishment of people's communes in the rural areas that: in the case of the people's communes, "the transition from collective ownership to ownership by the whole people is a process, the completion of which may take less time—three or four years—in some places, and longer—five or six years or even longer—elsewhere." Even with the completion of this transition, people's communes, like state-owned industry, are still socialist in character, where the principle of "from each according to his ability and to each according to work" prevails. After a number of years, the social product will increase greatly, the Communist consciousness and morality of the entire people will be raised to a much higher degree, universal education will be instituted and developed, the differences between worker and peasant, town and countryside and mental and manual labour—legacies of the old society that have inevitably been carried over into the socialist period, and the remnants of unequal bourgeois rights which are the reflection of these differences—will gradually vanish, and the function of the state will be limited to protecting the country from external aggression but will play no role internally. At that time Chinese society will enter the era of Communism where the principle of "from each according to his ability and to each according to his needs" will be practised. In order to clarify misunderstandings about the people's communes and ensure the healthy development of the people's communes movement, extensive and repeated publicity and education based on this Marxist-Leninist point of view must be seriously carried out throughout the Party and among all the people of China.

III

The people's communes must have plans for their production, exchange, consumption and accumulation. Their plans should be subordinated to the state plans and to the administration of the state. In working out their plans, the people's communes should, at the same time, fully develop their own characteristic features and their initiative.

Development of production is the key to the consolidation and advance of the people's communes. The correct policy of the people's communes for the development of production should be: to ensure the simultaneous development of industry and agriculture, and of production for their own consumption and for exchange in accordance with the principles of unified state planning, of adaptation to local conditions and of running the communes industriously and thriftily. In every aspect of production and capital construction, thrift must be observed, careful plans worked out, and manpower, material and financial resources used as rationally as possible; production costs must be reduced, expenditures cut down and income increased. Extravagance and waste among some functionaries of the communes following a bumper harvest should be prevented and opposed.

In agricultural production, shallow ploughing, careless cultivation, and "big acreage, small output" should be gradually replaced by deep ploughing, intensive cultivation, and "small acreage, big output." Farming should be carried on with the finesse of gardening, and agricultural production should be mechanized and electrified to bring about a big increase in yields and labour productivity and to gradually reduce the acreage under cultivation and manpower engaged in agriculture. We should strive to raise a yearly average of two to three thousand catties, or one ton to one and half tons of grain per capita within a comparatively short period. Along with the solution of the grain problem, the proportion of the total agricultural output occupied by cotton, flax and jute, silk, soybeans, oil-bearing crops, sugar-bearing crops, tea, tobacco, medicinal and other industrial crops must be increased step by step. In addition, great attention should be paid to accelerating the development of forestry, animal husbandry, farm side-occupations and fishery. In short, as on the industrial front, a great revolution must be carried out on all the fronts of agriculture, forestry, animal husbandry, farm side-occupations and fishery so as to bring about a thorough transformation of the face of agriculture.

People in the past often worried about our "over-population" and the relatively small amount of land available. But this idea has been overturned by the fact of 1958's bumper harvest. In so far as we succeed in seriously popularising the experience gained in getting high yields through deep ploughing, intensive cultivation, layer-by-layer fertilisation and rational close planting, it will be found that the amount of arable land is not too little but quite a lot and it is not a question of over-population but rather shortage of manpower. This will be a very big change. In the next several years, local conditions permitting, we should try to reduce the area sown to various crops to about one-third the present acreage. Part of the land so saved can lie fallow or be used for pasturage and the growing of grass fertilisers; the rest can be used for afforestation, reservoirs and the extensive cultivation of flowers, shrubs and trees to turn the whole land with its plains, hills and waters into a garden. By these means, firstly, it will be possible to greatly economise the use of water, fertiliser and manpower, and considerably increase the fertility of the soil. Secondly, it will make full use of every mountain, river and forest and the pasture land and greatly develop the comprehensive management of agriculture, forestry, animal husbandry, farm side-occupations and fishery. Thirdly, it will transform our natural environment and beautify the whole country. This is a great ideal that can be realised. People's communes throughout the land should work to realise this aim.

People's communes must go in for industry in a big way. The development of industry by the people's communes will not only accelerate the industrialisation of the whole country but also promote the realisation of ownership by the whole people in the rural districts, and reduce the differences between town and countryside. According to the differing conditions in each people's commune, an appropriate part of the labour force should be switched, step by step, from agriculture to industry to develop, according to plan, the production of fertiliser, insecticides, farm implements and machinery, building materials, the processing and many-sided use of agricultural produce, the manufacturing of sugar, textiles and paper, mining, metallurgy, electric power and other light and heavy industries. Industrial production in the people's communes must be closely linked with agricultural production; it should, first of all, serve the development of agriculture and the mechanisation and electrification of farming; at the same time it should serve to meet the demands of commune members for daily necessities, and serve the great industries of the country and the socialist market. The principles of adaptation to local conditions and obtaining raw materials locally should be fully taken into consideration; in order to avoid increased costs and waste of labour power, industries should not be set up in places where there are no raw materials or where they have to be brought from places very far away. With regard to production techniques, the principle should be carried out of linking handicraft with mechanized industry, and crude methods with modern methods of production. All handicraft industries which have good foundations and prospects for expansion must continue to be developed, and gradually carry through the necessary technical transformation. The mechanized industries must also make full use of iron, steel, lathes and other raw materials and equipment produced by native methods and employ native methods themselves; and gradually advance from crude to modern industries, from small to large enterprises and from a low to a high level.

Whether in industry or agriculture, people's communes should develop self-supporting production which directly meets their own needs, and they should also develop commodity production on as wide a scale as possible. Each according to its own characteristics, and under the guidance of the state, every people's commune should carry out the necessary division of labour in production and exchange of commodities with other people's communes and state-owned enterprises. Only in this way can the economy of the whole society expand at a faster rate, and every commune get through exchange the machinery and equipment required for the mechanization and electrification of farming and the consumer goods and ready cash required to meet the needs of commune members and pay them wages, and enable wages to increase year by year. To ensure fulfilment of plans for exchange, an extensive system of contracts should be set up between the state and the communes and among the communes themselves.

It must be stressed that during the course of a necessary historical period commodity production by the people's communes and the exchange of commodities between the state and communes and among the communes themselves must be greatly developed. Such production and exchange of commodities are different from those under capitalism, because they are conducted in a planned way, on the basis of socialist public ownership and not in an anarchical way on the basis of capitalist private ownership. Continued development of commodity production and continued adherence to the principle of "to each according to his work" are two important questions of principle in expanding socialist economy. The whole Party should have a unified understanding of them. Some people, while attempting to "enter Communism" prematurely, have tried to abolish the production and exchange of commodities too early, and to negate at too early a stage the positive roles of commodities, value, currency, and prices. This line of thinking is harmful to the development of socialist construction, and is therefore incorrect.

IV

To speed up production, the proportion of accumulation should be appropriately increased, after production costs, administrative expenses and taxes have been deducted from the gross income. But on the basis of the development of production, the portion of income used to meet the individual and collective expenses of commune members (including the portion spent on public welfare, culture and education) should be increased annually, in order to improve the livelihood of the people year by year.

The introduction of a distribution system which combines the wage system and the free supply system in that part of the income allotted to commune members for their own consumption, is a form of socialist distribution created by China's people's communes and at the present time it represents the earnest demand of the broad mass of members. As stated above, this distribution system embodies an embryo of Communism but in essence it is still socialist — based on the principle of "from each according to his ability and to each according to his work".

The proportions of wages and free supplies in the total amount allotted to members should be determined in the light of the varying conditions of development of production in the communes. At present, in fixing the ratio between wages and free supplies, care should be taken to avoid as far as possible reducing the income of households which have relatively few members but are strong in labour power; in general, it should be made possible for more than 90 per cent of the members to increase their income compared with the previous year while the rest should get no less than in the previous year.

At present, the scope of free supply should not be too wide. The application of the free supply system is not to make the life of the people uniform. Under the systems of socialism and Communism, the needs of the people are on the whole similar while varying according to the individual. Therefore, in the future, as well as at present, care should be taken to ensure as far as possible that members have suitable freedom of choice within the framework of the free supply system.

Wages must be increased gradually as production expands. At present after deducting the items freely supplied, the wage scale in the rural areas can be divided into six or eight grades. The highest grade may be four or more times as much as the lowest grade. But the differences should not be too great, for then they would not conform to the actual differences in the skill of labour now existing in the rural areas. Certain differences between the wage levels of different areas are permissible. At present differences between wage grades in the city are greater than those in the countryside, and this is necessary. In the future, as a result of the tremendous rise in production, everyone will be much better off, and whether in city or countryside such differences between wage grades will be unnecessary and gradually disappear. That will be nearing the era of Communism.

The reasons that wage levels in the city are generally higher than those in the countryside are many-sided (including the factor that living costs are higher in the city), and this is also a temporary situation which should be explained to the peasants. Some commune members, apart from working in the villages, also receive money sent home by other family members who are away in cities or elsewhere (such as workers, armymen, functionaries and overseas Chinese). Work should be done to dissuade other members from wrangling about this. In distribution within the commune, such members should be treated the same as others without discrimination in regard to free supplies and wages allotted, and they should not be urged to make special investments or contributions to the commune. If they rely on their family members away from home for the whole of their livelihood, the commune should not interfere, but it may stop supplying them with the usual allotments. Those who leave home for study, apart from those whose needs are covered by the state or can be covered by their own families, should be supported by the county federation of communes, according to the standards laid down by the schools.

The more the cause of socialism develops and the more abundant social products become, the more abundant too will become the means of livelihood allotted to each individual. Some people think that the switch over to communes will call for a re-distribution of existing personal consumer items. This is a misconception. It should be publicized among the masses that the means of livelihood owned by members (including houses, clothing, bedding and furniture) and their deposits in banks and credit co-operatives will remain their own property after they join the commune and will always belong to them. When necessary, the commune may borrow the surplus housing space of members with their consent, but the ownership still belongs to the owners. Members can retain individual trees around their houses and small farm tools, small instruments, small domestic animals and poultry; they can also continue to engage in some small domestic side-occupations on condition that these do not hamper their taking part in collective labour.

Debts still owned when the people's communes were established should not be declared cancelled irrespective of whether these are between individuals, between the commune and its members, or debts contracted by commune members with banks or credit co-operatives. These debts should be repaid where conditions permit and where the conditions do not allow of them being repaid for the time being, they should be held over.

V

The people's commune is the organiser of the production and life of the people and the fundamental purpose of the development of production is to satisfy to the maximum extent the constantly growing material and cultural needs of all members of society. In leading the work of the commune, the Party must give all-round attention to the ideological development, production and livelihood of commune members. It must care for the people and correct the tendency of seeing only things and not men. The greater the labour enthusiasm of the masses, the greater attention should the Party pay to their well-being. The more the attention paid by the Party to the livelihood of the masses, the greater will be their enthusiasm in work. It is wrong to set production and people's livelihood against each other and imagine that attention to the livelihood of the masses will hamper production. Of course, it is also wrong to put a one-sided and improper stress on improvement of the people's livelihood without regard to the raising of their level of political consciousness and the development of production, and not to advocate hard work for long-term interests.

Communists have always held that in a Communist society labour will be changed "from a heavy burden into a pleasure and will become the primary necessity of life." There is no doubt that the working day will be greatly shortened in future. With the development of mechanization and electrification, we must strive to introduce the six-hour work day within several years. Our intensive work at the present time is creating conditions precisely for the six-hour work day and even shorter working hours in future. At present, the system of eight hours' actual work and two hours' study should be put into effect in both city and countryside. During the busy farm season or when other work in the rural areas is particularly heavy, working hours may be appropriately extended. But, at any rate, eight hours for sleep and four hours for meals and recreation, altogether twelve hours, must be guaranteed every day and this must not be reduced. It is true that there is a labour shortage at present, but a way out must be found in stressing the successful implementation of tools reform and improving labour organisation and not in extending working hours. Special attention must be paid to safety in production and labour conditions must be improved where possible in order to reduce to the minimum or completely avoid work accidents. Sufficient rest must be ensured to women both before and after childbirth and they should also get the necessary rest during menstruation when they should not be asked to do heavy work, to get their feet wet in cold water or work at night.

Community dining rooms should be well run. All commune members must be assured of enough to eat and good and clean food suited to their national and local habits. Community dining rooms should have dining halls, and they should run efficiently their own vegetable gardens, beancurd mills, bean noodle mills, and condiment shops; they should raise pigs, sheep, chickens, ducks and fish. The main food and dishes should be varied and appetizing. Nutrition specialists should be consulted to make sure that the food contains enough calories and with the nutriment needed by the human body. Where necessary and possible, special food should be provided for the aged, children, invalids, pregnant women and nursing mothers. Certain commune members may cook at home. Community dining rooms should be managed democratically. Their administrative staff and cooks should be chosen from among those who are politically reliable. It is best that they be elected democratically.

Nurseries and kindergartens should be run well so that every child can live better and receive a better education there than at home, and so that the children are willing to stay there and the parents are willing to put them there. The parents may decide whether the children need to board there, and may take them back home at any time they wish. In order to run nurseries and kindergartens well, communes should train a large number of qualified nurses and teachers.

The "homes to honour the aged" should be run well so as to provide better dwelling places for those old people who have no children to rely on (those who enjoy the "five guarantees"— food, clothing, fuel, the bringing up of children and burial).

Communes must ensure the successful running of primary and secondary schools and adult education. Universal primary school education should be instituted in the rural areas throughout the country. Full-time secondary schools and half-time secondary agricultural schools, or other secondary vocational schools, should be well run and universal secondary education should be introduced step by step. Earnest efforts should be made to eliminate illiteracy, organise various kinds of spare time schools and carry on political education, literacy classes and technical education for adults. In reducing the differences between manual and mental labour, the institution of universal education among the working people and the gradual raising of their educational level is an important step which must be carried out conscientiously. The communes, in addition, must also select and send a number of young people to study in senior secondary schools, secondary vocational schools and institutions of higher learning in the cities so as to train fairly highly educated working personnel for the state and the communes. The principle of combining education with productive labour must be carried out thoroughly in all schools, without exception. Children above the age of nine can take part in some kinds of labour to an appropriate extent so as to cultivate the habit of work in childhood and stimulate their physical and mental development; but strict attention must be paid to the health of the children, they must only be assigned light work in short spells and suited to their physique and their interests.

Ideological and political work among the staffs in community dining rooms, nurseries, kindergartens, homes to honour the aged, primary schools, public health centres, clubs and shops must be strengthened and efforts made to give positive guidance to public opinion so that the whole of society and all in the communes regard the successful running of community dining rooms, nurseries, kindergartens and other collective welfare undertakings and satisfactory work in the catering services as a lofty task of service to the people. The attitude of the exploiting classes in looking down on work which concerns the daily life and welfare of the masses and work in the catering services, must be criticised and corrected.

The old existing houses must be reconstructed step by step; new, picturesque townships and village settlements must be built by stages and in groups; these will include residential quarters, community dining rooms, nurseries, kindergartens, the homes to honour the aged, factories, threshing floors, livestock sheds, shops, post and tele-communications offices, warehouses, schools, hospitals, clubs, cinemas, sports grounds, baths and latrines. The construction plans of townships and village settlement should be thoroughly discussed by the masses. We stand for the abolition of the irrational patriarchal system inherited from the past and for the development of family life in which there is democracy and unity. This stand has been warmly received by the masses. Therefore, in building residential quarters, attention must be paid to making the houses suited to the living together of men and women, and the aged and young of each family.

There is a considerable number of stupid fellows in the world, including Mr. Dulles of the United States, who frantically attack our people's communes. This Dulles knows nothing about our country but he pretends to be a China expert and feverishly opposes the people's communes. What makes him particularly heart-broken is that, as is alleged, we have smashed that very, very wonderful family system that was handed down over thousands of years. It is true that the Chinese people have broken the feudal patriarchal system. It must be known that this patriarchal system has long since ceased to exist in capitalist society and that this is a matter of capitalist progress. However, we have gone a step further to establish democratic and united family something that is rare in general in capitalist society. Only in the future in those places where the socialist revolution has been carried out and the capitalist system of exploitation of man by man has been eliminated will it be possible to establish such families universally. As to nurseries, kindergartens and workers' canteens in the factories, these also first appeared in capitalist society. But under capitalism, all such undertakings established by the bourgeoisie are capitalist in nature and are aimed to facilitate the exploitation of men and women workers by the capitalists. On the other hand, such undertakings run by us are socialist in nature and they facilitate the development of socialism and the liberation of the individual personality of man. They have truly and completely emancipated the mass of women and enabled the children to receive better education and care. That is why they are warmly welcomed by all the working people, and primarily by the mass of women.

VI

The organisational principle of the people's commune is democratic centralism. This principle must be applied in the management of production, in distribution of income, in the livelihood and welfare of commune members and in all other aspects of work.

Unified leadership and differentiated management at different levels should be put into effect in the people's commune. The administrative set-up of the commune in general can be divided into three levels, namely: the commune administrative committee, the administrative district (or production brigade) and the production team. The administrative district (or production brigade) is in general the unit which manages industry, agriculture, trade, education and military affairs in a given area and works on a basis of economic accounting, with its gains and losses pooled in the commune as a whole. The production team is the basic unit of labour organisation. Under the unified leadership of the commune administrative committee, necessary powers should be given to the administrative district (or production brigade) and the production team over such matters as the organisation of production work and capital construction, finances and welfare amenities, in order to bring their initiative into full play.

The various levels of organisation of the county federation of communes and the people's commune must learn to make reasonable distributions and shifts of manpower between the different branches of production (agriculture, industry, transport) and between routine production work, shock production tasks and service work, in order to avoid situations where there is work without men in one place and men without work in another. The organisation of labour must be constantly improved, the system of responsibility for a given task at a given level must continue to be applied and reinforced in production and other tasks, the system of labour inspection and labour awards must be perfected and there must be effective guarantees that labour efficiency and the quality of work are steadily improved.

There must be both discipline and democracy in the labour organisation in the people's commune. What we call getting organised along military lines means getting organised on the pattern of a factory. It means that labour organisation in the people's commune should be as organised and disciplined as in a factory or the army; this is necessary in large-scale agricultural production. The forces of large-scale agricultural production, like the forces of large-scale industrial production, are an industrial army. The modern industrial army was organised by the bourgeoisie, each factory being like a military camp. The discipline for the worker standing before the machine is as rigid as that in the army. The industrial army in socialist society is an industrial army of a single class, the working class, which has got rid of the capitalist who exploited surplus value and which has put into force in the working class a vigorous and lively democratic centralism based on voluntariness. We are now applying this system to the rural areas, thus establishing a socialist industrial army for agriculture based on democratic centralism, which is free from exploitation by the landlord and rich peasant and raised above the level of small-scale production.

Militia organisations should be set up at corresponding levels of production organisations in the people's commune. The leading bodies of the militia and production organisations should be separate and, in principle, the commanding officers of the various levels of the militia, such as regimental, battalion and company commanders, should not be concurrently directors of communes and administrative districts (leaders of production brigades) and leaders of production teams. These commanders should take part in the administrative organisations of the same levels in the commune as their members, and they will receive dual leadership: from the administrative organisations of the same levels and the superior commanding organisations of the militia. The militia should be equipped with necessary arms produced by arsenals set up locally. The basic units of the militia should undergo military training according to a set schedule, while the ordinary militia-men should also get appropriate training after work; this is to prepare conditions for turning the whole nation into soldiers. The broad mass of working people in our country greet the militia system warmly, because, in the course of their protracted revolutionary struggle against imperialism, feudalism and their running dogs, the Kuomintang reactionaries, they came to realise that only by arming themselves would they be able to overcome the armed counter-revolution and become masters of the land of China; and after the victory of the revolution, they have come to see further that there are still imperialist pirates abroad who are clamouring every day about wiping out this people's state; therefore, the whole of our people are determined to continue to arm themselves, and they declare: be warned, you pirates bent on plundering us; do not dare to make a vain attempt to harm our people engaged in peaceful labour; we are fully prepared! If the imperialist should dare to unleash an aggressive war against our country, then we will turn the whole nation into soldiers; the militia will co-operate with the People's Liberation Army and at any time replenish it to utterly crush the aggressors.

There should be both centralism and democracy in all organisations of the people's communes, including the militia organisations. The people's communes should not only organise the people's production work but the people's livelihood as well. In order to do their work well, the communes must practise a high level of democracy, consult the masses on all matters, faithfully represent their interests and reflect their will. Therefore, while "organising along military lines, working as if fighting a battle and living the collective way," the communes must implement democratic management. It is absolutely not allowed to use "getting organised along military lines" as a pretext or make use of the militia system which is directed against the enemy to infringe in the least on democratic life in the commune and the militia organisations. The people's commune is the basic organisation of our country's state power; only by ensuring democracy in the commune will it be possible to create throughout the country a vigorous and lively political situation in which there are both centralism and democracy, both discipline and freedom, both unity of will and personal ease of mind.

VII

In running a people's commune well the fundamental question is to strengthen the leading role of the Party. It is only by strengthening the Party's leading role, that the principle of "politics in command" can be realised, that profound socialist and Communist ideological education among the cadres and commune members and struggle against all kinds of erroneous tendencies can be conducted, and that the Party's line and policy can be put into execution correctly. There are some people who think that with the emergence of the commune the Party can be dispensed with, and that they can practise what they call "merging the Party and commune in one." This kind of thinking is wrong.

In its work in the people's commune, the Party, besides its essential task of ensuring that the correct line and policy are put into effect, should also pay attention to educating the commune staffs to develop good styles of work—first of all the mass-line and a business-like style of work.

Following the 1957-1958 rectification campaign, the Party's mass line achieved a new, great victory. The great leap forward in socialist construction and the setting up of people's communes throughout the rural districts are two signal marks of this victory. The mass-line working method of the Party is the life blood of the people's communes. The setting up and consolidation of the people's communes is impossible without the mass line, without the full faith of the people in the Party and in the People's Government, and without an upsurge in the revolutionary zeal of the masses. Therefore, leading functionaries of all levels in the commune must put the mass line thoroughly into practice in every type of work tackled. They must look upon themselves as ordinary toilers, and treat the commune members with a comradely attitude. Kuomintang and bourgeois styles of work which coerce the masses are strictly prohibited. Because of the big leap forward in production and the victory in setting up communes, some cadres are beginning to get dizzy with success and, unwilling to do the patient work of educating the masses by persuasion, they are exhibiting certain rude attitudes. Though these are individual cases, they should make us keenly vigilant.

In all its work, the Party should hold fast to the principle of combining revolutionary zeal with a scientific spirit. The great leap forward in 1958 has achieved an unprecedented victory for socialist construction in our country. Now, even our enemies find it impossible to deny the significance of this victory. But we must never overlook our small weak points because of big achievements. On the contrary, the bigger the achievement the more we need to remind our cadres to keep cool-headed and not be carried away by the flood of news of victory and become unable or even unwilling to see the weak points in their work. One tendency meriting attention in the present work of socialist construction is exaggeration. This is incompatible with the practical working style of our Party, and is harmful to the development of our socialist construction. We must do our economic work in a more thorough-going way. Our leading personnel at all levels must be good at differentiating between the real truth and false appearances and between demands which are justified and those which are not; in assessing conditions they must strive to keep close to objective reality. Only by doing so can we work out and carry through our plans on a reliable and solid basis.

VIII

In order to promote the consolidation of the people's communes and ensure an ever bigger leap forward in industry and agriculture in 1959, the Communist Party committees of the provinces, municipalities and autonomous regions should, in compliance with the requirements put forward in this resolution, make full use of the five months from December 1958 to April 1959 to tidy up the people's communes in their areas by doing educational propaganda, checking over and consolidating them.

In the course of checking over the communes, it is necessary in the first place for leading personnel to make earnest self-criticisms and listen with modesty to other's opinions, and on this basis, mobilise the masses with great daring to air their views freely and frankly, carry out debates and post up tatzupao (written opinions in big Chinese characters posted on the walls for everybody to read), cite good examples of both men and things, criticise wrong ideas and bad styles of work, sum up experience, point out correct directions and develop a thorough-going socialist and Communist ideological education movement.

In the course of checking over the communes, it is necessary to carry out an overall and thorough check-up of the production plan, distribution, welfare facilities, management, financial work, organisation and leadership in the communes. The organisations of the Communist Party and communes should be carefully checked over at the same time to guarantee that the leading personnel of the Communist Party and communes at various levels are activists loyal to the interests of the people and to the cause of Communism. In addition, the finest people who have been tested in the big leap forward and people's commune movement and are qualified for Communist Party membership, should be enrolled in the Party.

Problems related to the style of work of Communist Party members and cadres should be dealt with through Party education and frank airing of views by the masses. In dealing with these problems attention should be paid to safeguarding the zeal and initiative of the cadres and masses and the principles of "unity-criticism-unity" and "taking warning from the past in order to be more careful in the future" and "treating the illness in order to save the man" must be observed. Those who have committed errors but are willing to correct them should be criticised seriously but treated with leniency. The masses should be mobilised to purge out of the leadership those alien class elements who have smuggled themselves into the leadership and those who show a very bad style of work and have never corrected their errors even after being repeatedly admonished.

Serious and complex class struggles are going on not only abroad, in the capitalist world, but also here at home. It is necessary to educate the masses to increase their revolutionary vigilance to prevent disruptive enemy activities. Whether former landlords, rich peasants and counter-revolutionaries and other people deprived of political rights should be accepted as members or probationary members of the communes, or remain to work under supervision, should be discussed and decided by the masses dealing with each case on its merits in the course of checking over the communes.

The work of checking over the communes should first be carried out in one or two communes as an experiment in each county. That is to say help should be given to the comrades in one or two people's communes to get things going well in a fairly short space of time, so as to acquire experience, set examples and then popularise the experience gained. Every province, municipality and autonomous region should organise its investigation group composed of a thousand, several thousands or 10,000 people for the check-up, and the first secretaries of the Communist Party at the provincial, regional and county levels should personally lead the work of checking over the communes. These investigation groups should draw comparisons between different regions, counties and communes, organize mutual visits, call on-the-spot meetings to develop the good points found and overcome the shortcomings discovered, mobilise enthusiasm for the work, and find out ways of concretely solving current problems and promptly popularizing successful experience. In short, through these check-ups, the work of the people's communes in the country must be generally carried one step forward.

APPENDIX IV

GOVERNMENT OF CHINA, FAST PROGRESS IN WATER CONSERVANCY IN CHINA, JANUARY 1960*

CHINA completed more than 11,600 million cubic metres of earthwork in the construction of water conservancy projects in the last two months of 1959. The amount of earth shifted, if built into a dam one metre high and one metre thick, would circle the equator about 290 times.

At the present time, China is building 1·5 million water conservancy projects, not including those concerned with water and soil erosion.

Most of them are small and medium-size projects mainly undertaken by the people's communes. But there are also a number of huge schemes such as the Sanmen Gorge project and six others on the main course of the Yellow River, and the Tankiangkow dam on the biggest tributary of the Yangtze River.

A great number of the small and medium water conservancy schemes have been completed and put in use for winter irrigation. The work quota for 1959 on many of the huge projects has been finished ahead of schedule. The flow of the unruly Yellow River in its lower reaches was successfully barred by the completion of the Weishan dam in early December. The Han River, the biggest tributary of the Yangtze, has also been cut off by the newly built cofferdam of the Tankiangkow reservoir project which, when completed, will have a storage capacity of 28,300 million cubic metres of water.

An outstanding feature of this winter's water conservancy construction is the simultaneous building of reservoirs, irrigation canals and ditches. When a project is completed, the whole irrigation system is completed at the same time and can be put to use promptly. The waterway network in the Huai River plain in Central China built in the past few years is being strengthened while new ones are added.

The work being done this winter is marked by high speed and high quality. The numerous small iron and steel smelting plants and other industrial undertakings built by the people's communes since the great leap forward in 1958 have contributed greatly to the promotion of tools innovations at the construction sites. A campaign to replace spades and shoulderpoles with machines and semi-mechanized implements to lighten labour and raise working efficiency is now sweeping all water conservancy construction sites throughout the country. National average working efficiency this winter is much higher than last year.

Immense operations are going on in Hupeh Province in the Yangtze River valley to harness the local rivers, mostly tributaries of this river, China's biggest.

The aim is to control these local rivers for irrigation and hydro-electric power generation and to terrace, cultivate and transform the hilly parts of the province in the basins of the tributaries.

* This contains the latest available data on the utilization of water resources in China, which constitutes a major cause for the rapid development of Chinese agriculture. English text appears in *China Today*, New Delhi, January 23, 1960, pp. 10-11.

This work is in addition to the giant undertakings along the major tributaries of the Yangtze River, such as the Tankiangkow reservoir along the Han River and the Chelin reservoir along the Hsiushui tributary in neighbouring Kiangsi Province.

Work is in hand on no less than one million water control, irrigation and soil conservation projects in Hupeh Province. Several hundreds of these are of considerable size. The rest are medium and small ones which are being built by the people's communes.

All the six major tributaries of the Yellow and Haiho Rivers in hilly Shansi Province in North China are being harnessed on a long-term basis. This is in order to end their centuries-old scourge and use their water for irrigation, power generation and other useful purposes.

More than 60 large and medium reservoirs are being built on the six tributaries and waterways connected with them, a greater number than the total built in any previous year. Except for a few giant reservoirs being built with government investment, most of them are being undertaken by the people's communes, in many cases with government financial aid.

The 914 people's communes in the province were also constructing numerous smaller projects to extend irrigation, check soil erosion and prevent the silting of the big reservoirs being built on the Yellow and Haiho Rivers and their tributaries. In the past three months, 50,000 canals have been completed and the soil erosion on 13,000 square kilometres of land has been put under initial control.

Through joint efforts by 27 people's communes in Pingtu County, Shantung Province a 30-metre wide and 65-kilometre long canal has been completed in just 10 days.

The canal, running east-west, cuts across and connects 10 bigger rivers and 80 small streams in the county. The canal plus over 50 bigger reservoirs and 3,000 small reservoirs, ponds and irrigation ditches will form an integrated system to bring irrigation to practically all the farmland in the county. Most of these works are now being built.

The canal with its numerous reservoirs, ditches and sluice gates can regulate, store and drain water throughout the county. Over 200 small hydro-electric power stations can be built of which 33 have been or will be completed. Fishery and water transportation will be developed.

An integrated network of canals and reservoirs stands out on the map of the Sanmiaochien People's Commune in Poyang County, Kiangsi Province.

Bounded as it is by a lake and two rivers on three sides, the commune has radically solved the age-old problem of water-logging in spring and dryness in autumn by building two trunk canals intersecting at right angles and measuring 20 kilometres in length and by crisscrossing them with 23 ditches. On the hilly side, seven reservoirs of different sizes hold practically all the water on the high ground. In the lowland, four reservoirs have been dug to receive the water on the plain. All the reservoirs, canals and ditches are interconnected.

During the rainy spring season, four drainage channels lead off excess water to the rivers and lakes, but the reservoirs and seven sluice gates store up as much water as possible for the dry season. Most of the farmland in the commune are thus irrigated by gravitation.

The commune is now building water mills and small hydro-electric power stations on the waterways.

APPENDIX V

JMJP, PRESS COMMUNIQUE ON THE PROGRESS OF CHINA'S NATIONAL ECONOMY IN 1959, JANUARY 22, 1960*

THE 1959 plan for the development of the national economy was overfulfilled because the whole nation adhered to the general line for building socialism, the big leap forward and the people's communes and launched a vigorous mass campaign to increase production and practise economy.

The major targets of the Second Five Year Plan were successfully reached three years ahead of schedule by opposing rightward tendencies and exerting full efforts, as was urged by the great call of the Eighth Plenary Session of the Eighth Central Committee of the Chinese Communist Party.

The value of the 1959 output of industry and agriculture totalled 241,300 million *yuan*, an increase of 31·1 per cent over 1958, according to preliminary figures compiled by the State Statistical Bureau.

Of this, the value of industrial output totalled 163,000 million *yuan*, an increase of 39·3 per cent; that of agricultural output 78,300 million *yuan*, an increase of 16·7 per cent.

Breakdown figures of the principal items follow:

Steel (excluding that produced by simple, local methods)—13,350,000 tons, an increase of 67 per cent over 1958;
Pig iron (excluding that produced by simple, local methods)—20·5 million tons, an increase of 115 per cent;
Coal—347·8 million tons, an increase of 29 per cent;
Electricity—41,500 million kWh, an increase of 51 per cent;
Crude oil—3·7 million tons, an increase of 63·4 per cent;
Cement—12,270,000 tons, an increase of 32 per cent;
Timber—41·2 million cubic metres, an increase of 18 per cent;
Chemical fertilizer—1,333,000 tons, an increase of 64·4 per cent;
Metal-working machine tools—70,000 in number, an increase of 40 per cent;
Paper—2,130,000 tons (of which machine-made paper was 1·7 million tons), an increase of 31 per cent;
Sugar—1,130,000 tons, an increase of 26 per cent;
Salt—11,040,000 tons, an increase of 6 per cent;
Cotton yarn—8·25 million bales, an increase of 35 per cent;
Cotton piece goods—7,500 million metres, an increase of 32 per cent;
Grain—540,100 million catties (270,050,000 tons), an increase of 8 per cent;
Cotton—48·2 million piculs (2,410,000 tons), an increase of 14·76 per cent.

Budgetary outlay for investment in capital construction totalled 26,700 million *yuan*, an increase of 24·5 per cent over 1958. 1,341 above-norm construction

* This Communique is included in its entirety here as agricultural development cannot and should not be isolated from development in other economic sectors or from the general growth patterns. English text appears in *China Today*, New Delhi, January 30, 1960, pp. 11-15; and *Peking Review*, January 26, 1960, pp. 9-13.

projects were undertaken, of which 671 went into full or partial operation during the year.

Below-norm projects undertaken by governments at or above the county level numbered 75,000, of which 54,000 were completed during the year.

In addition, great numbers of small construction projects were undertaken by people's communes. The gross volume of goods handled by various means of transport amounted to 2,212 million tons, an increase of 67 per cent over 1958. Of this, railway freight reached 542 million tons, an increase of 42 per cent. Retail sales amounted to 63,800 million *yuan*, an increase of 16·4 per cent over 1958.

The total value of stocks of goods in various commercial departments at the end of the year exceeded that at the end of 1958 by 26 per cent. Trade was brisk and commodity prices were stable.

The supply of a small number of commodities was tight during the first half of 1959 owing to rapidly increased purchasing power but for quite some time this tight situation has ceased.

The big expansion of industrial and agricultural production brought about a 21·6 per cent increase in national income in 1959 compared with 1958.

The 1959 revenue of the state reached 54,000 million *yuan*, an increase of 29 per cent over 1958.

All this shows that the readjusted targets of the 1959 plan adopted by the Standing Committee of the National People's Congress last August were exceeded by a wide margin. On the basis of the 1958 big leap forward, the Chinese people attained a better, all-round big leap forward of the national economy in 1959.

The continuous big leap forward of 1958 and 1959 made for the successful accomplishment three years ahead of schedule of the Second Five Year Plan (1958-1962) for the Development of the National Economy proposed by the First Session of the Eighth Congress of the Chinese Communist Party in September, 1956 and endorsed by the State Council in February 1957.

The Second Five Year Plan provided that in 1962 the total value of industrial and agricultural output should go up by around 75 per cent over 1957. In 1959, it was already 94·4 per cent above 1957.

The total value of industrial output was to have gone up by around 100 per cent. It already went up by 131·5 per cent.

The total value of agricultural output was to have gone up by around 35 per cent. It already increased by 45·8 per cent.

The national income was to have risen by around 50 per cent. It already shot up by 62·86 per cent.

Breakdown figures in the output of the major items of heavy industry, light industry and agriculture are listed in the table on page 367.

The table on page 367 shows that the 1962 targets of the Second Five Year Plan were reached or exceeded in 1959 in the case of such major industrial and agricultural items as steel, coal, electricity, metallurgical equipment, power-generating equipment, metal working machine tools, timber, cotton yarn, cotton piece goods, salt, machine-made paper, grain and cotton, and that only those for crude oil, aluminium ingots, chemical fertilizer, cement, edible vegetable oil, sugar, soybeans, pigs, cattle, horses and sheep were not yet reached.

Classification of products	*1962 Targets of Second Five Year Plan*	*Production in 1959*
I HEAVY INDUSTRY		
Steel	10,500,000 to 12,000,000 tons	13,350,000 tons
Coal	190,000,000 to 210,000,000 tons	347,800,000 tons
Electricity	40,000,000,000 to 43,000,000,000 kWt	41,500,000,000 kWt
Crude oil	5,000,000 to 6,000,000 tons	3,700,000 tons
Aluminium ingots	100,000 to 120,000 tons	70,400 tons
Chemical fertilizer	3,000,000 to 3,200,000 tons	1,333,000 tons
Metallurgical equipment	30,000 to 40,000 tons	205,000 tons
Power generating equipment	1,400,000 to 1,500,000 kWt	2,150,000 kWt
Metal working machine tools	60,000 to 65,000	70,000
Timber	31,000,000 to 34,000,000 cubic metres	41,200,000 cubic metres
Cement	12,500,000 to 14,500,000 tons	12,270,000 tons
II LIGHT INDUSTRY		
Cotton yarn	8,000,000 to 9,000,000 bales	8,250,000 bales
Cotton piece goods	7,290,000,000 to 8,060,000,000 metres	7,500,000,000 metres
Salt	10,000,000 to 11,000,000 tons	11,040,000 tons
Edible vegetable oil	3,100,000 to 3,200,000 tons	1,460,000 tons
Sugar	2,400,000 to 2,500,000 tons	1,130,000 tons
Machine-made paper	1,500,000 to 1,600,000 tons	1,700,000 tons
III AGRICULTURE		
Grain	around 500,000,000,000 catties (around 250,000,000 tons)	540,100,000,000 catties (270,050,000 tons)
Cotton	around 48,000,000 piculs (around 2,400,000 tons)	48,200,000 piculs (2,410,000 tons)
Soybeans	around 25,000,000,000 catties (around 12,500,000 tons)	23,000,000,000 catties (11,500,000 tons)
Pigs	around 250,000,000	180,000,000
Cattle	around 90,000,000 head	65,430,000 head
Horses	around 11,000,000	7,600,000
Sheep	around 170,000,000	112,530,000

The 1959 output of all products that have decisive importance for the development of the national economy surpassed the original 1962 targets by a wide margin.

For instance, steel output exceeded the target by 1,350,000 to 2,850,000 tons, coal by 137·8 million to 157·8 million tons, metallurgical equipment by 165,000 to 175,000 tons, power-generating equipment by 650,000 to three quarters of a million kilowatts, metal working machine tools by 5,000 to 10,000 and grains by 40,000 million catties (20 million tons).

In 1959, the national economy made an even better, all-round big leap forward as a result of the thorough implementation of the policy of simultaneous development of industry and agriculture and of heavy and light industry, giving priority to heavy industry. A high-speed, proportionate advance was registered in all departments of the national economy in that year. The rate of development of heavy and light industry and agriculture was all very high. These facts demonstrate powerfully that the proportionate relationship between these departments and within each is harmonious.

Compared with 1958, industrial production increased by 39·3 per cent and agriculture by 16·7 per cent last year. Agriculture grew at a relatively faster rate (the ratio between the rates of industrial and agricultural growth was four to one during the First Five Year Plan period, 2·65 to 1 in 1958 and 2·35 to 1 in 1959).

In the industrial field, heavy industrial production went up by 43·3 per cent and light industry by 34 per cent in 1959 compared with the preceding year. The rate of increase was relatively more rapid in light industry. (The ratio between the rates of growth of the heavy and light industry was 1·98 to 1 during the First Five Year Plan period, 3·06 to 1 in 1958 and 1·27 to 1 in 1959).

Certain weaker links in the national economy had an even more rapid development. In the field of transportation, for instance, the volume of freight carried by modern means of transport increased 59 per cent and that by simple, local means of transport increased by 74 per cent. Both exceeded the rate of growth of industry and agriculture. This improved, to a certain extent, the condition where transport had lagged behind the needs of the development of production.

In the field of the power industry, electric output in 1959 reached 41,500 million kilowatt-hours, an increase of 51 per cent compared with 1958. The output of power-generating equipment totalled 2,150,000 kilowatts, or 2·69 times the 1958 figure. Both surpassed the rate of aggregate industrial growth. This improved the power supply situation.

During the great leap forward of 1959, while State-run, big and modern enterprises showed a tremendous advance, so also did locally-run and medium and small enterprises and those operated by simple local methods. The total value of the output of local industry last year was 39·7 per cent more than in 1958. The overwhelming majority of the small enterprises using simple, local methods, which had been built in 1958, expanded their production and improved their technique after a check-up.

In 1959, the small and medium-sized enterprises produced 11·05 million tons of pig-iron, or more than half of the national total (20·5 million tons, excluding pig iron produced by simple, local methods). The figure was 1,520,000 tons more than China's total output of pig iron produced with modern equipment in 1958 (9,530,000 tons). Of the 13·35 million tons of steel produced in China last year, the output of small and medium-sized converters accounted for more than one-third, i.e. 4·72 million tons.

The widespread development of small and medium-sized enterprises greatly accelerated the advance of industry, improved the geographic distribution of industrial enterprises, trained large number of skilled workers and management functionaries and brought about even closer relations between industry and agriculture.

Factory and office workers in all spheres in 1959 continued to develop the communist style of work, combining a practical spirit with daring in thinking, speaking and action, and displayed energy, perseverance and ingenuity in work. They engaged in mass campaigns for technical innovations and the technical revolution on an even wider scale, bringing not only greater and faster but also better and more economical results both in production and construction. Labour productivity of industrial workers taking part directly in production increased by 15·5 per cent. Tens of thousands of new products were successfully trial produced. The quality of products showed a general improvement. The quality of iron produced by small blast furnaces approximated to that by big blast furnaces.

At the same time, a general reduction of costs was registered by all departments. Industrial departments cut costs by 6 per cent, enterprises under the Ministry of Building by 13·5 per cent and the transport and communications departments by 14·6 per cent. The cost of commodity circulation was also lowered.

Simultaneous with the big economic growth, education, science and culture developed greatly.

Full-time institutions of higher learning accepted 270,000 new students in 1959. Total enrolment reached 810,000, an increase of 23 per cent over 1958 and approached the original 1962 targets of 850,000 stipulated in the Second Five Year Plan.

Total enrolment in all types of secondary schools reached 12·9 million and that of primary schools 90 million.

Total enrolment in spare-time secondary schools and colleges reached 10 million, an increase of 94 per cent over 1958.

There was a big expansion in scientific research institutes, both independent ones and those belonging to institutions of higher learning, economic departments and enterprises.

Press, broadcasting, films, the theatre and other cultural undertakings all expanded rapidly. Considerable achievements were made in the fields of sport and public health.

The living standards of the people were raised on the basis of the continued big leap forward of industry and agriculture and increased labour productivity.

The average wages of factory and office workers (not including new factory and office workers) rose by around 5 per cent compared with the previous year. State outlay for labour insurance funds, medical expenses, welfare funds and collective amenities for factory and office workers went up by more than 16 per cent.

The average income of members of rural people's communes was around 10 per cent higher than in 1958.

Among the consumer goods provided to the people by the State through the commercial departments, grain increased by 6·5 per cent, cotton piece goods 23 per cent, knitted goods 38·7 per cent, machine-made paper 13·7 per cent and cigarettes 15·9 per cent. The supply of the overwhelming majority of other daily necessities also increased to varying degrees. Only supplies of meat and eggs will need some time to achieve a relatively big increase.

The people's communes played a tremendous role in the continued big leap forward of the national economy in 1959. This year witnessed the gravest natural calamities China encountered in decades. A total of 650 million *mou* (43⅓ million hectares), or 30 per cent of the total sown area in the country, was affected. A dry spell lasted for three to four months last summer in eight provinces, causing serious drought on nearly 400 million *mou* (over 26·6 million hectares) of farmland.

However, agricultural production still made big headway because the people's communes, being large in scale and having a high degree of collectivism, effectively organized the members to wage a heroic struggle against the natural calamities and put into effect the "eight major measures" for increasing agricultural production.

Apart from the good harvests of grain and cotton, the output of soybeans, vegetables, peanuts, sugar cane, sugar beet, fruit, tobacco and tea also increased to varying degrees. Forestry, stock raising, rural side-occupations and fishery all made progress.

An additional 280 million *mou* (more than 18·6 million hectares) of land were afforestated in 1959.

The total number of pigs in the country reached 180 million at the end of 1959, 20 million more than in 1958. The number of cattle, horses and larger livestock reached 85·38 million, which is also higher than in 1958. Poultry breeding registered a big expansion.

The campaign to collect wild vegetation after the autumn harvest was highly successful. In all, the output value of rural side-occupations was more than double that of 1958.

The total output of aquatic products was 23·6 per cent higher than in 1958.

Large-scale water conservancy work was continued in 1959 through the organized efforts of the people's communes. The total earth and stone work completed in the year ending last September amounted to 13,000 million cubic metres. An additional 70 million *mou* (more than 4·6 million hectares) of land were brought under irrigation and large numbers of existing irrigation systems were improved. Water conservancy work on a still larger scale has been undertaken since last October.

The superiority of the people's communes also manifests itself in the big expansion of industry in the rural areas. The total output value of commune-run industry rose by 70 per cent in 1959 compared with 1958.

The big growth of commune-run industry made for the improvement of farm implements and rural means of transport, the expansion of semi-processing facilities for agricultural and subsidiary rural products, the raising of labour productivity in agriculture and the increase of accumulation by the communes and the income of their members.

The people's communes also account for the vigorous growth of cultural, educational and public health undertakings in the countryside. By the end of 1959, commune-run agricultural and ordinary middle schools numbered 25,000 and commune-run primary schools 270,000. There were nearly one million cultural centres, libraries and clubs run by communes. The number of commune-run hospitals and clinics exceeded 200,000.

Community dining rooms run by the communes totalled 3·9 million and nurseries and kindergartens totalled 3·69 million.

After the 1959 check-up, the people's communes set out along the road of consolidation and healthy development.

The continued big leap forward in the national economy in 1959 has given further confirmation of the high-speed, proportionate big leap forward situation that began to emerge in 1958 in the development of China's national economy. Owing to the rapid growth of production and the continued improvement in livelihood, the political consciousness of the people of all nationalities in the country has risen higher than ever, their unity has become stronger than ever and they are happy and full of vigour.

The great achievements of 1959 powerfully testify to the absolute correctness of the general line for building socialism, the big leap forward rate of development and the people's commune form of organization, all of which were proposed by the Chinese Communist Party and Comrade Mao Tse-tung.

On the basis of the great triumph of 1959, the workers, peasants and revolutionary intellectuals are confidently striving for a continued leap forward in the national economy in 1960, for catching up with the level of Britain, within ten years, in the output of major industrial items and for the realization far ahead of schedule of the 1956-1967 national programme for the development of agriculture.

LIST OF ABBREVIATIONS

Major Sources

CCCC *San-nien-lai Chung-kuo ching-chi ti ch'eng-chiu* (Economic Achievements of New China in the Past Three Years, Peking: Oct. 1952), 192 pp.

CCCP *Ching-chi chou-pao* (The Economic Weekly), Shanghai.

CCHH *Cheng-chih hsüeh-hsi* (Political Study), monthly, Peking, Shanghai, Mukden and Chungking.

CCYC *Ching-chi yen-chiu* (Economic Research), bi-monthly, Peking.

CHCC *Chi-hua ching-chi* (Economic Planning), monthly, Peking.

CKCC *I-chiu wu-ling nien Chung-kuo ching-chi lun-wen hsuan* (Collected Essays on China's Economy in 1950), compiled by the Editorial Committee, *Collected Essays on China's Economy*, Peking: San-lien Book Co., Sept. 1951). Series 2 (Agrarian policy), 441 pp.; 3 (Industry and commerce), 362 pp.; 5 (Light industry), 208 pp.; 6 (Trade), 163 pp.; 7 (Communications), 243 pp.

CKNP *Chung-kuo nung-pao* (Agricultural Journal of China), monthly, Peking.

CMR *China Monthly Review*, English, Shanghai, 1951–June 1953.

CSM *Christian Science Monitor*, Boston.

CW *Chang-wang* (Outlook), Semi-monthly, Shanghai, 1948–1950.

CWR *China Weekly Review*, English, Shanghai, (predecessor of *CMR*), 1947–1951.

CYTC *Chung-yang ts'ai-ching cheng-ts'e fu-ling hui-pien* (Compendium of Laws and Regulations Regarding Financial and Economic Policies of the Central [People's] Government, compiled by the Financial and Economic Committee, GAC, Peking: Hsin-hua Book Co.). First series (Aug. 1950), 824 pp.

DH Conrad Brandt, Benjamin Schwartz, and John King Fairbank, *A Documentary History of Chinese Communism*, Harvard University Press, 1952, 552 pp.

FES *Far Eastern Survey*, Semi-monthly, New York.

FKHP *Chung-hua jen-min kung-ho-kuo fa-kuei hui-pien* (Compendium of Laws and Directives of the People's Republic of China), Vols. 1 to 5, Peking, Sept. 1954 to 1959.

HI *Hung-ch'i* (Red Flag), semi-monthly, Peking, successor to *HH*, from July 1, 1958.

HCJP *Hua-ch'iao jih-pao* (China Daily News), New York.

HCS *Hsin chien-she* (New Construction), monthly, Peking.

HF *Hsin-Chung-kuo fu-nü* (Women of New China), monthly, Peking.

HH *Hsueh-hsi* (Study), semi-monthly, Peking, succeeded by *HC* from July 1, 1958.

HKC *Hsin kuan-ch'a* (The New Observer), semi-monthly, Peking.

HPYK *Hsin-hua pan-yüeh-k'an* (New China Semi-monthly), Peking, successor to *HY* since Jan. 1956.

HY *Hsin-hua yüeh-pao* (New China Monthly), Peking, Oct. 1949 to Dec. 1955, predecessor of *HPYK*.

JMJP *Jen-min jih-pao* (People's daily), Peking.

JMST *Jen-min shou-ts'e* (People's Handbook), Tientsin-Peking: Ta-kung pao, issued annually since 1950.

KC *Kuan-ch'a* (The Observer), semi-monthly, Shanghai, 1947–1950, predecessor of *HKC*.

KWCP *Kuo-wen chou-pao* (Kuo-wen Weekly), Shanghai, 1922–1937.

Mao *Mao Tse-tung hsuan-chi* (Collected Works of Mao Tse-tung), published by Tung-pei Book Co., Harbin, May 1948, 999 pp. Revised versions in 4 volumes, first three already published between Oct. 1951 and Feb. 1953, by Jen-min Pub. Co.; totalling 1144 pages.

MT *Ming-chien i-shu yu i-jen* (Folk Artists), edited by Chou Yang, Hsin-hua Book Co., Kalgan, 1946, 101 pp.

NCNA New China News Agency bulletins, daily releases in Peking, London and Hongkong.

NYT *New York Times.*

PA *Pacific Affairs*, Quarterly, New York.

PC *People's China* (in English), semi-monthly, Peking, predecessor of *PR*.

PR *Peking Review* (in English), semi-monthly, Peking, successor to *PC* from 1958.

SSST *Shih-shih shou-ts'e* (Current Events Handbook), monthly, Peking.

TC Liu Shao-ch'i and others, *T'u-kai cheng-tang tien-hsing ching-yen* (Typical Experiences in [the work of] Agrarian Reform and Party Purification), published by Chung-kuo Publishing Co., Hongkong, April 1948, 58 pp.

TCKT *Tung-chi kung-ts'o* (Statistical Work Bulletin), semi-monthly, Peking.

TK *Chung-kuo Kung-ch'an-tang yu t'u-ti ko-ming* (The CCP and the Agrarian Revolution), a collection of 12 items on land policy of the CCP, pub. by Cheng-pao-she, Hongkong, 1948, 78 pp.

TKP *Ta-kung pao* (Ta-kung Daily), Tientsin and later Peking, also Hongkong.

TKWC *T'u-ti kai-ke chung-yao wen-hsien hui-chi* (Compendium of Important Documents on Agrarian Reform), Peking: Jen-min Pub. Co., March 1951, 27 items, 145 pp.

TPST *Tu-pao shou-ts'e* (Handbook for Newspaper Reading), pub. by *Yangtse Daily*, Hankow, 1950, 1118 pp.

TT *Wei Ch'ung-chieh tang ti tsu-chih erh tou-cheng* (Struggle for the Purification of Party Organization), Cheng-pao-she, 1947, Hongkong, 85 pp.

TU *T'u-ti kai-ke shou-ts'e* (Handbook on Agrarian Reform), Hsin-hua Book Co., Shanghai, Oct. 1950, 164 pp.

WNTC *Wu-nien-lai ti ts'ai-cheng ching-chi kung-tso* (Financial and Economic Work in the Past Five Years), Peking, March 1955, 93 pp.

Abbreviations of Titles of Chinese Government Organs and Organizations

ACDWF: All-China Democratic Women's Federation, ACFW after 1958
ACFDY: All-China Federation of Democratic Youth, ACFY after 1958
ACFL: All-China Federation of Labour
ACFTU: All-China Federation of Trade Unions (Changed from ACFL on May 10, 1953)
ACFW: All-China Federation of Women, successor to ACDWF
ACFY: All-China Federation of Youth, successor to ACFDY
ACSF: All-China Students' Federation
APC: Agricultural Producers' Cooperative
CC: Central Committee
CCP: Chinese Communist Party
CEC: Central Executive Committee
CPG: Central People's Government
CPPCC: Chinese People's Political Consultative Conference
CYL: Communist Youth League
FEC: Financial and Economic Committee
GAC: Government (or State) Administrative Committee, now the State Council
KMT: Kuomintang (The Nationalist Party)
MA: Ministry of Agriculture
NCNA: New China News Agency (Hsin-hua she)
NDYL: New Democratic Youth League, now the Communist Youth League
PA: Peasants' Association
PC: People's Commune
PLA: People's Liberation Army
PRC: People's Representatives Conference
PRG: People's Representatives Congress
RAC: Regional Administrative Commission (abolished in 1954)
SC: State Council
SCH: Shansi-Chahar-Hopei (Border Region during the Sino-Japanese War)
SKN: Shensi-Kansu-Ninghsia (Border Region during the Sino-Japanese War)
SPC: State Planning Commission (Set up on Nov. 20, 1952)
SSB: State Statistical Bureau

CHINESE UNITS OF MEASURE AND WEIGHT AND THEIR WESTERN EQUIVALENTS

chin	(catty)	0·5 kg. or 1·1 lbs.
chih	(Chinese foot)	0·3333 metre or 14·1 inches
kung-ch'ing or *shang*	(hectare)	2·47 acres
li	(Chinese mile)	0·5 km. or 0·3107 mile
ma	(yard)	0·9144 meter or 3 feet
mou	(Chinese acre)	0·066 hectare or 0·1647 acre
pi	(bolt)	40 yards or 120 feet
tan	(picul)	50 kgs. or 110 lbs.
tun	(metric ton)	1,000 kgs. or 2,200 lbs.*
yuan†	(Chinese dollar)	U.S. $0·4246 or 0·143 pound sterling

* Not 2,204·6 pounds, because of rounding.

† This is the "new *yuan*," which replaced the old *yuan* by a directive from the State Council on Feb. 21, 1955 at the exchange rate of 10,000 old *yuan* to one new *yuan*.

SELECTED BIBLIOGRAPHY*

Primary Sources[1]

(Arranged Chronologically)

1. CC, CCP, **Manifesto of the First National Congress of the CCP on the Current Situation*, June 10, 1922.
2. CC, CCP, **Manifesto of the Second National Congress of the CCP*, July 1922.
3. CC, CCP, **Manifesto of the Third National Congress of the CCP*, 1923.
4. CC, CCP, **Fourth Manifesto of the CCP on the Current Situation*, January 1925.
5. Mao Tse-tung, **Report on An Investigation of the Peasant Movement in Hunan*, February 1927.
6. Ch'u Ch'iu-pai, *Some Debatable Problems in the Chinese Revolution*, April 1927.
7. CC, CCP, **Resolutions of the Fifth National Congress of the CCP*, May 1927.
8. CC, CCP (August 7, 1927 Emergency Conference), **Circular Letter to All Party Members*, August 1927.
9. CC, CCP, **Resolutions of the Emergency Conference of August* 7 (1927), August 1927.
10. Ch'u Ch'iu-pai, *Chinese Revolution and the CCP*, June 1928.
11. CC, CCP, **Political Resolution of the Sixth National Congress*, September 1928.
12. CC, CCP, **Resolution on the Peasant Movement of the Sixth National Congress*, September 1928.
13. CC, CCP, *Resolution on the Land Question of the Sixth National Congress*, September 1928.
14. CC, CCP, *The Political Work of the CCP after the Sixth National Congress*, September 1928.
15. Soviet Republic of China. *Provisional Land Law of the Soviet*, May 1930.
16. Ch'u Ch'iu-pai, "Chinese revolution and the Peasant Movement" *Pu-erh-sai-wei-k'e* (Bolshevik), 3·4–5, May 15, 1930, pp. 111–149.
17. Li Li-san, **The New Revolutionary Rising Tide and Preliminary Successes In One or More Provinces*, June 11, 1930.

* Journal articles which are too numerous to be included in the Bibliography may be found in the footnotes of the book.

[1] These primary sources, all in Chinese and arranged chronologically here, are found in the following Libraries: The Hoover Library, Stanford University; Harvard-Yenching Library, Harvard University, and the Library of Congress, Washington, D.C. Those with asterisk marks have been translated into English, and may be found in the following sources: *The Collected Works of Mao Tse-tung*, 4 vols.; Conrad Brandt and others, *A Documentary History of Chinese Communism*; Chao Kuo-chun, *Agrarian Policies of China*, 1949-1956; Chao Kuo-chun, *Economic Planning and Organization of China*, 1949–1958, all published by the Harvard University Press; and other publications.

18. Chou En-lai, **Report of Shao Shan, Reference Item Number Nine of the Third Plenum of the CC, CCP*, September 24, 1930.
19. CC, CCP, **Resolution of the Enlarged Fourth Plenum of the CC, CCP*, January 1931.
20. Soviet Republic of China, *Land Law of Hunan-Kiangsi Border Soviet*, December 1928.
21. Soviet Republic of China, *Land Law of Hsin-kuo hsien* (county), April 1929.
22. Soviet Republic of China, **Constitution of the Soviet Republic*, November 1931.
23. Soviet Republic of China, **Land Law of the Soviet Republic*, December 1, 1931.
24. CC, CCP, "The Present Peasants Struggle and Our Tasks," *Pei-fang hung-ch'i* (Red Flag of North China), 13–14, October 15, 1932, 66–79.
25. Soviet Republic of China, *How to Analyze Class Status in the Countryside*, 1933.
26. Soviet Republic of China, *Decisions Concerning Some Problems Arising From Agrarian Reform*, 1933.
27. CC, CCP, "Chinese Communist Party and the Agrarian Revolution," *Chung-kuo k'e-min* (The Revolution of China), January 1933, 171–179.
28. Mao Tse-tung, **Report to the Second All-China Soviet Congress*, January 22, 1934.
29. CC, CCP, **The Ten Great Policies of the CCP for Anti-Japanese Resistance and National Salvation*, August 15, 1937.
30. CC, CCP, **The CCP's Public Statement on KMT-CCP Cooperation*, September 22, 1937.
31. Mao Tse-tung, **On New Democracy*, January 19, 1940.
32. CC, CCP, **Decision of the CC on Land Policy in the Anti-Japanese Base Areas*, January 28, 1942.
33. CC, CCP, *A Compendium of Important Documents Since the Outbreak of the War of Resistance* 1937–1942, Yenan, 1944.
34. Lin Tsu-han, *Summary of the Work of the SKN Border Region Government in the Last Year*, January 6, 1944.
35. SKN Border Region Government, *Collected Policies and Regulations of the SKN Border Region*, supplementary volume, August 1944.
36. Mao Tse-tung, **On Coalition Government*, April 24, 1945.
37. CC, CCP, **Constitution of the CCP*, June 11, 1945.
38. SCH Border Region Government, *A Compendium of Current Policies and Regulations*, 2 vols., December 15, 1945.
39. CC, CCP, **Documents on the Correction of Undesirable Tendencies in Learning, the Party, and Literature*, 1946.
40. CC, CCP, *Regulations on the Compulsory Purchase of Excess Land From the Landlords*, December 21, 1946.
41. CC, CCP, *The Land Law*, October 10, 1947.
42. Mao Tse-tung, *Present Situation and Our Tasks*, December 1947.
43. Jen Pi-shih, *Some Problems in the Agrarian Reform*, January 12, 1948.
44. Liu Shao-ch'i and others, *Typical Experiences in the Work of Agrarian Reform and Party Purification*, a collection of nine items on agrarian

reform during the late 1947 and early 1948, published by Cheng-pao-she, Hongkong, 1948, (?) 85 p. (abbreviated as *TT*).

45. CC, CCP, *Directive on Agrarian Reform*, February 22, 1948.
46. Mao Tse-tung, **Speeches at the Cadres' Conference of the Shansi-Suiyuan Liberated Area*, April 1, 1948.
47. CC, CCP, *Directive on Agrarian Reform and Party Purification*, May 25, 1948.
48. Central Plain Bureau, CCP, *Program on Rent and Interest Reductions*, October 8, 1948.
49. Northeast Bureau, CCP, *Directive on Land Reform in the Newly-Liberated Areas*, December 23, 1948.
50. CC, CCP, **Resolution of the Second Session of the Seventh Plenum*, CC, CCP, March 13, 1949.
51. Mao Tse-tung, **On the People's Democratic Dictatorship*, July 1, 1949.
52. Political Bureau, Kwangtung, Kwangsi and Hunan Border Area, *Program on Rent and Interest Reductions in the Kwangtung, Kwangsi and Hunan Border Area*, June 1949.
53. East China Bureau, CCP: *Regulations on Rent Reduction in the East China*, September 15, 1949.
54. People's Political Consultative Conference, **Common Program of the CPPCC*, October 1, 1949.
55. Military and Political Committee, Central-South China: *Regulations on Rent and Interest Reductions of the Central-South China Area*, February 25, 1950.
56. Government Administrative Council, *Directive for Dealing with Agricultural Land in the Suburbs of the Cities in Old Liberated Areas*, February 25, 1950.
57. GAC, *Directive on Agrarian Reform and Taxation in kind in the new Liberated Areas*, February 28, 1950.
58. Mao Tse-tung, **Opening Address to the Third Session of the 7th Plenum of the CC, CCP*, June 6, 1950.
59. Liu Shao-ch'i, **Report on the Agrarian Reform Problem*, made at the Second Session of the National Committee of the PPCC, June 14, 1950.
60. Central People's Government Council, **The Agrarian Reform Law*, June 28, 1950.
61. GAC, **General Regulations for the Organization of the Peasants' Association*, July 14, 1950.
62. GAC, **Decisions Concerning the Differentiation of Class Status in the Countryside*, August 4, 1950.
63. GAC, *Provisional Regulations on Agricultural Taxation in the New Liberated Areas*, September 1950.
64. GAC, *Regulations on the Land Reform in Suburban Areas*, November 10, 1950.
65. GAC, *Regulations for the Disposal of Land and Property of Overseas Chinese During the Implementation of Agrarian Reform*, November 6, 1950.

66. GAC, *General Regulations for the Organization of Ch'u and Hsiang People's Governments and the Ch'u and Hsiang People's Representatives' Conferences*, December 8, 1950.
67. GAC, *Decisions Regarding Agricultural Production in* 1951, Feb. 1951.
68. GAC, *Directive on the Guarantee of the Relative Value Between Cotton and Grain*, March 7, 1951.
69. GAC, *Directives on the Three-Anti and Five-Anti Movements*, March 11, 1952.
70. GAC, *Decisions on the Fees for Title Deeds of Land and Houses*, March 1951.
71. GAC, *Directive Regarding the Work of Public Grain Collection in the Summer of* 1951, May 25, 1951.
72. Ministry of Finance, CPG, *Outline for Carrying Out the Work of Land Survey and Production Evaluation in Agricultural Tax Work*, July 5, 1951, *JMJP*, July 7, 1951, 1.
73. GAC, *Decisions Regarding Agricultural Production in* 1952, Feb. 15, 1952.
74. GAC, **Directive Regarding the Work of Agricultural Tax in* 1952, June 16, 1952.
75. Administrative Commission, Central-South China, *Regulations on the Control and Reformation of Former Landlords*, August 1952.
76. CC, CCP, **Decisions on Mutual Aid and Cooperation in Agricultural Production*, February 1953.
77. GAC, **Directive on the Enforcement of Planned Purchases and Planned Supply of Foodgrains*, Nov. 19, 1953.
78. CC, CCP, **Decisions on the Development of the APC's*, Dec. 16, 1953.
79. Teng Tzu-hui, **Report on the Rural Work Conference*, *NDYL*, July 15,1954.
80. PRC, **The National Constitution of China*, Sept. 20, 1954.
81. SSB, Chekiang Province, *Talks on Rural Statistical Work*, Sept. 1954.
82. MA & CYL, **Joint Directive on the Education and Training of Accountants and Technicians for the APCs*, Jan. 5, 1955.
83. MA, **Directive on the Work of the Agro-technical Popularization Stations*, April 1, 1955.
84. Mao Tse-tung, **On the Cooperativization of Agriculture*, July 31, 1955.
85. SC, **Provisional Measures for Unified Supply of Grain in Cities and Towns*, August 25, 1955.
86. CC, CCP, **Resolution on Agricultural Cooperativization*, Oct. 11, 1955.
87. SC, **Draft Model Regulations of the APCs*, Nov. 10, 1955.
88. CC, CCP. ed., *High Tide of Socialism in the Rural Areas of China*, Jan. 1956, 3 vols., 1,360 pages.
89. MA, **Provisional Regulations on the Prize-Awarding to Model Agricultural Workers*, Jan. 12, 1956.
90. Ch'en Po-ta, *The Socialist Reform of China's Agriculture*, Feb. 2, 1956.
91. Mao Tse-tung, **On the Correct Handling of Contradictions Among the People*, Feb. 27, 1956.
92. NPC, **Model Regulations for Higher-Stage APCs*, June 30, 1956.
93. CC, CCP & SC, *Directive on Strengthening the Leadership, the Production Activities of the APCs, and on Strengthening construction of the APCs*, Sept. 12, 1956.

94. Chou En-lai, *Report on the Suggestions Regarding the Second Five-Year Plan for the Development of National Economy, Sept. 16, 1956.
95. SC, *Directive on the Rural Financial Work, Oct. 30, 1956.
96. CC, CCP & SC, *Directive on the Work of the Purchase and Supply of Foodgrains, Nov. 21, 1956.
97. T'an Chen-lin, A Study of Peasants' Income in China, May 5, 1957.
98. CC, CCP, *Directive on Carrying Out Well the Work of Production Management in the APCs, Sept. 14, 1957.
99. CC, CCP, *Revised Draft Programme on Agricultural Development in the Nation, 1956–57, Oct. 25, 1957.
100. Teng Hsiao-p'ing, *Report on the Rectification Campaign, Oct. 1957.
101. SC, *Regulations on Improving the Commercial Management System, Nov. 15, 1957.
102. Ko Ch'ing-hih, *On "Treating the Nation as One Chess Board," Feb. 16, 1958.
103. NPC, Regulations on Agricultural Tax of China, June 3, 1958.
104. CC, CCP, *Resolution on Some Questions Concerning the People's Communes, Dec. 10, 1958.
105. SC, Measure on Certain Problems Concerning Credit Work in the People's Communes, Dec. 20, 1958.
106. CC, CCP, Decisions on the Improvement of Rural Financial and Trading Systems After the People's Communes, Dec. 20, 1958.
107. Tseng Hsi-sheng, "Some Problems in Directing Agricultural Production," Hung-ch'i (Red Flag), No. 12, June 16, 1959, pp. 1–8.
108. Tao Ch'u, Report on a Survey of the Hu-meng People's Communes, Jan. 28, 1959.
109. Editorial, JMJP, Implement the "8-item" Agricultural Code and Raise the Quality of Planting, March 19, 1959.
110. SSB, *Communique on the Fulfilment of the First FYP for the Development of National Economy (1953–57), April 13, 1959.
111. Chou En-lai, *Report on Government Work, April 18, 1959.
112. Teng Tzu-hui, Manage Well the Common Dining Halls and Carry Out Strictly the Principle of Voluntariness, June 1959.
113. Wang Kuang-wei, "Strengthen the Support of Agriculture by Industry," Hung-ch'i (Red Flag), Aug. 16, 1959, pp. 4–12.
114. CC, CCP, *Communique of the 8th Plenary Session of the 8th CC, CCP, Aug. 26, 1959.
115. Chou En-lai, *Report on Adjusting the Major Targets of China's 1959 National Economic Plan and Further Developing the Campaign for Increasing Production and Practising Economy, Aug. 26, 1959.
116. Liao Lu-yen, *"Glorious Achievements on the Agricultural Front during the Past Decade," JMJP, Sept. 26, 1959.
117. Chou En-lai, *"A Great Decade," JMJP, Oct. 6, 1959.
118. Li Fu-chun, *"Big Leap Forward in China's Socialist Construction," HPYK, Oct. 12, 1959.
119. Po I-po, "Struggle for the Speedy Realization of the Task of Technical Reform in Agriculture," Hung-ch'i (Red Flag), Oct. 16, 1959, pp. 24–30.

120. NCNA, **Press Communique on the Progress of China's National Economy in 1959*, *JMJP*, Jan. 23, 1960.
121. M. of Agri. Machinery Industry, * "Acceleration of Technical Transformation of Agriculture," *China Today*, Feb. 27, 1960.
122. Li Fu-ch'un, **Report on the Draft 1960 National Economic Plan*, March 30, 1960.
123. Li Hsien-nien, **Report on the Final State Accounts for 1959 and the Draft State Budget for 1960*, March 30, 1960.

Books, Monographs, and Pamphlets (*in Chinese*)

1. CC, CCP, *High Tide of Socialism in the Rural Areas of China*, Peking, Jen-min Pub. Co., January 1956, 3 vols., 1,360 pages.
2. Central-South Bureau, CCP, *The Present Mutual-Aid and Cooperative Movement*, Chung-nan People's Publishing Society, July 1946, 96 pages.
3. Chao Lien-chih, *Labour Cooperatives in the Villages of the New Democracy*, Ch'iang-hsueh Pub. Society, July 1946, 96 pages.
4. Cheng Pei-pin, *The Functions of Government Loans in the Promotion of Agricultural Cooperation*, Shanghai, 1956, 56 pages.
5. Chou Yang and others, *Folk Art and Artists*, Hsin-hua Book Co., Kalgan, 1946, 101 pages (abbreviated as MI).
6. *Chung-kuo fu-nu*, (Women of China) *Women on the Agricultural Front*, Peking, 1956, 63 pages.
7. Dept. of Agriculture, Northeast Regional Government, *Reference Materials for Agricultural Producers' Cooperatives*, Northeast Agricultural Pub. Co., Kukden, 1952, 98 pages.
7*b*. Hsu Ti-hsin, *Analysis of the National Economy During the Transitional Period in China*, Peking, Science Publishing Co., rev. ed., 1959, 331 pages.
8. Hu Hua, ed., *Source Materials on the History of New Democratic Revolution in China*, Commercial Press, Shanghai, 1951, 494 pages.
9. Hu Ming and Lu Shih-kuang, *Export of Native Products and the Nation's Industrialization Programme*, Peking, 1956, 78 pages.
10. Huang Yen-p'ei, *Return From Yenan*, Tung-pei Book Co., Changchun, 1946, 35 pages.
11. Joint Committee on Rural Reconstruction, *Ways and Means to Improve the Agriculture of China*, Commercial Press, Shanghai, 1947, 369 pages.
12. *Labour Cooperatives in the Border Region*, Yenan, 1944, 94 pages.
13. *Labour Heroes of the 8th Route Army*, Published by the 8th Route Army, Yenan, 1944, 117 pages.
14. Li Jen-liu, *Agricultural Cooperatives of the New Democracy*, Chung-hua Book Co., Aug. 1950, Shanghai, 106 pages.
15. Li Ken, *The Production Movement in the Liberated Areas*, Chung-kuo Pub. Co., Hongkong, July 1947, 31 pages.
16. Liaotung Provincial Bureau, CCP, *How the Village Party Cell Should Lead the Masses in* (*Agricultural*) *Production*, Hsin-hua Book Co., Nov. 1949, 77 pages.

17. Lin Hsing, "How to Practice the System of Fair Compensation within the Mutual-Aid Teams," Jen-min Pub. Co., Shanghai, Feb. 1954, 32 pages.
18. Lin Tung-pei, *Land Reform and Literary Works,* Hsin-hua Book Co., Shanghai, Nov. 1950, 74 pages.
19. Liu Ch'ung-wu, *Agricultural Production in New China,* Peking, San-lien Book Co., May 1953, 54 pages.
20. Liu Shao-sh'i, *On the Party,* Hsin-hua Book Co., 1946, 105 pages.
21. Mao Tse-tung, *Selected Works of Mao Tse-tung,* Tung-pei Book Co., 1948, 999 pages (abbreviated as *Mao*).
22. Meng Nan, *The Problem of Land Reform in China,* Hsin-min-chu Book Co., Hongkong, 1948, 93 pages.
23. Meng Hsien-chang, *Textbook on Modern Economic History of China,* Shanghai, Chung-hua Book Co., 1951, 404 pages.
24. Mu Hsin, *A Bird's-Eye View of the Shansi-Suiyuan Liberated Area,* Luliang Cultural and Educational Pub. Society, April 1946, 138 pages.
25. *Mutual Aid in the SCH Border Region,* Kalgan, 1946, 72 pages.
26. National Committee, PPCC, *Collection of Agrarian Reform Reference Materials,* Wu-chih nien-tai Pub. Co., Feb. 1951, Peking, 148 pages.
27. Northeast Bureau, CCP, *Village Cadres Must Participate and Lead Production Work,* Mukden, Hsin-hua Book Co., May 1953, 54 pages.
28. Northeast People's Pub. Co., *New Experiences in the Agricultural and Patriotic Production-Increase Movement in Chao-yuan County,* Jan. 1953, 51 pages.
29. Pao, Sha-ying, *Experience of Teaching in the Villages,* Hsin-hua Book Co., Yenan, 1949, 84 pages.
30. SCH Border Region Government, *Typical Experiences of the Mutual-Aid* (*Movement*), n.d. 50 pages.
31. Shu Jen, *Democratic Management in the Agricultural Mutual-Aid and Cooperative Organizations,* Hua-tung Pub. Co., Jan. 1954, 36 pages.
32. *Sketches of the fan-shen Movement of the Rural Women in the Liberated Areas of China,* A Collection of 9 Articles, Hongkong, 1949, 53 pages (abbreviated as *NF*).
33. Tao Tuan-yu, *The Primary School of Yang-chia-way,* Hsin-hua Book Co., 1945, 36 pages (abbreviated as *Tao*).
34. *Textbook for Peasants,* compiled by the Peasants' Association of the SCH Border Region, September 1945, 38 pages.
35. Ti Ch'ao-pai, *Peasant Problem in Post-war China,* Nan-hai Pub. Co., Hongkong, 1948, 52 pages.
36. *Village Cadres Must Participate in and Lead Agricultural Production,* Hsin-hua Book Co., Mukden, Aug. 1950, 81 pages.
37. Wang Yu, *How to Develop Cultural and Recreational Work in the Rural Areas,* Hsin-hua Book Co., Shanghai, Dec. 1950, 88 pages.
38. Wu Wen-hui, *Land Problem of China and Its Solutions,* Commercial Press, Shanghai, 1944, 1947, 287 pages.

Books, Monographs, and Pamphlets (*in English*)

1. Adler, Solomon, *The Chinese Economy,* New York, Monthly Review Press, 1957, 276 pages.

2. Agarwala, A. N. and Singh, S. P., ed., *The Economics of Underdevelopment*, London, Oxford Univ. Press, 1958, 510 pages.
3. Band, Claire and William, *Two Years With the Chinese Communists*, New Haven, 1948, 347 pages.
4. Baran, Paul, *The Political Economy of Growth*, N.Y., Monthly Review Press, 1957, 308 pages.
4*b*. Barnett, A. Doak, *Communist China and Asia*, Harper Brothers, 1960, 575 pages.
5. Beauvoir, Simone de, *The Long March*, tr. by Austryn Wainbouse, N.Y., The World Pub. Co., 1958, 513 pages.
6. Belden, Jack, *China Shakes the World*, Harper and Brothers, New York, 1949, 524 pages.
7. Bodde, Derk, *Peking Diary*, New York, Henry Schuman, 1950, 292 pages.
8. Brandt, Conrad, Schwartz, Benjamine and Fairbank, John K., *A Documentary History of Chinese Communism*, Harvard University Press, 1952, 552 pages (Abbreviated as *DH*).
9. Buck, John Lossing, *Land Utilization in China*, University of Chicago Press, Chicago, 1937, 494 pages.
10. Chao Kuo-chun, *Agrarian Policies of China, 1949–1956*, Harvard University Press, 1957, 276 pages.
11. Chao Kuo-chun, *Economic Planning and Organization in China, 1949-1957*, Harvard Univ. Press, 2 vols., 1959 and 1960, 550 pages.
12. Ch'en, Han-seng, *Agrarian Problems in Southernmost China*, Kelly and Walsh, Ltd., Hongkong, 1946, 144 pages.
13. Ch'en, Han-seng, *Landlord and Peasant in China*, International Publishers, N.Y., 1938, 144 pages.
14. Ch'en Po-ta, *A Study of Land Rent in Pre-Liberation China*, Foreign Languages Press, Peking, 1958, 101 pages.
15. Compton, Boyd, Ed., *Mao's China, Party Reform Documents, 1942-1944*, Univ. of Washington Press, Seattle, 1952, 278 pages.
16. Cressey, George B., *Asia's Lands and Peoples*, McGraw-Hill Book Co., New York, 1944, 608 pages.
17. Crook, David and Isabel, *Revolution in a Chinese Village*, London, Routledge and Kegan Paul, 1959.
18. de Castro, Josue, *The Geography of Hunger*, Little, Brown & Co., Boston, 1952, 337 pages.
19. Elegant, Robert S., *China's Red Masters*, Twayne Publishers, New York, 1951, 264 pages.
20. Epstein, Israel, *The Unfinished Revolution in China*, Boston, 1947, 442 pages.
21. Fairbank, John K., *The United States and China*, Harvard University Press, rev. ed. 1958.
22. Fei, Hsiao-t'ung, *China's Gentry, Essays in Rural-Urban Relations*, University of Chicago Press, 1953, Issued in cooperation with the International Secretariat, I.P.R., 287 pages.
23. Fei, Hsiao-t'ung, *Earthbound China*, University of Chicago Press, 1945, 319 pages.
24. Feis, Herbert, *The China Tangle*, Princeton University Press, 1953, 445 pages.

25. Fitzgerald, Charles P., *Revolution in China*, Praeger, New York, 1952, 290 pages.
26. Fitzgerald, Charles P., *Floods in China*, Praeger, N.Y. 1958, 285 pages.
27. Foreign Languages Press, Peking, *People's Communes in China*, November 1958.
28. Forman, Harrison, *Report from Red China*, Henry Holt & Co., New York, 1945, 250 pages.
29. Ganguli, B. N., *Land Reform in New China*, Ranjit Printers and Publishers, New Delhi, 1954, 74 pages.
30. Gupta, H. C., *Problems and Processes of Economic Planning in Underdeveloped Economics*, Allahabad, Kitab Mahal, 227 pages.
31. Gyanchand, *The New Economy of China*, Bombay, Vora & Co., 1958, 429 pages.
31*b*. Ho Kan-chih, *A History of the Modern Chinese Revolution*, Peking, Foreign Languages Press, 1959, 627 pages.
32. Hollister, William W., *China's Gross National Product and Social Accounts, 1950–1957*, M.I.T., 1958, 161 pages.
33. Hu Ch'iao-mu, *Thirty Years of the Communist Party of China*, Foreign Languages Press, Peking, 1951, 94 pages.
33*b*. Hughes, T. J., and Luard, D.E.T., *The Economic Development of Communist China, 1949-1958*, Oxford Univ. Press, 1959, 223 pages.
34. Isaacs, Harold, *The Tragedy of the Chinese Revolution, 1923–1937*, University of Stanford, Palo Alto, 1951, 382 pages.
35. Kuo Ping-Chia, *China, New Age and New Outlook*, Alfred A. Knopf, N.Y., 1956, 231 pages.
36. Levy, Marion J., Jr., *The Family Revolution in Modern China*, Cambridge, Harvard University Press, 1949, 390 pages.
37. Lewis, H. Arthur, *The Theory of Economic Growth*, Illinois, Richard Irwin, Inc., 1955, 453 pages.
38. Li, Choh-ming, *Economic Development of Communist China*, University of California Press, 1959, 284 pages.
39. Lindsay, Michael, *The Tax System in a Communist Area*, for limited distribution, (1948 ?), 45 pages.
40. MacNair, H. F. (ed.), *China*, University of California Press, 1946, 574 pages.
41. Mao Tse-tung, *Selected Works*, People's Publishing House, Bombay, 4 vols., 1955, 1,282 pages.
42. Moraes, Frank, *Report on Mao's China*, The MacMillan Company, New York, 1953, 212 pages.
43. Myrdal, Gunnar, *Economic Theory and Under-developed Regions*, London, Gerald Duckworth and Co., 1957, 168 pages.
44. North, Robert C., *Moscow and Chinese Communists*, Stanford University Press, 1953, 306 pages.
45. Nurkse, Ragnar, *Problems of Capital Formation in Underdeveloped Countries*, N.Y., Oxford University Press, 1953, 163 pages.
46. Payne, Robert, *Mao Tse-tung, Ruler of Red China*, Henry Schuman Inc., New York, 1950, 293 pages.
47. Rosin, Jacob and Eastman, Max, *The Road to Abundance*, McGraw-Hill Book Co., New York and London, 1953, 166 pages.

48. Rosinger, Lawrence K., *China's Crisis*, Alfred A. Knopf, New York, 1945, 259 pages.
49. Rostow, W. W., *The Prospects for Communist China*, Wilby, 1954, 379 pages.
50. Schwartz, Benjamine, *Chinese Communism and the Rise of Mao*, Harvard University Press, 1951, 258 pages.
51. Shabad, Theodore, *China's Changing Map*, Praeger, 1956, 295 pages.
52. Shen, Tsung-han, *Agricultural Resources of China*, Cornell University Press, 1951, 407 pages.
53. Singh, V. N., ed., *Keynesian Economics : A Symposium* (Part IV), Delhi, People's Publishing House, 1956, 233 pages.
54. Smedley, Agnes, *Battle Hymn of China*, Alfred A. Knopf, New York, 1945, 528 pages.
55. Snow, Edgar, *Red Star Over China*, Modern Library, 1938, 1944, 529 pages.
56. Stein, Gunther, *The Challenge of Red China*, McGraw-Hill Book Co., New York, 1945, 490 pages.
57. Steiner, H. Arthur, *Maoism, a Source Book :* selections from the writings of Mao Tse-tung. Introduced and edited by Steiner, University of California at Los Angeles, Los Angeles, 1952, 142 pages.
58. Strong, Anna Louise, *China's Millions, The Revolutionary Struggle from 1927 to 1935*, New York, 1935, 457 pages.
59. Sung Ch'ing-ling (Mme. Sun Yat-sen), *The Struggle for New China*, Foreign Languages Press, Peking, 1952, 398 pages.
60. Tawney, Richard Henry, *Land and Labour in China*, Harcourt Brace & Co., New York, 1932, 207 pages.
61. Tawney, Richard Henry, *A Memorandum on Agriculture and Industry in China*, Institute of Pacific Relations, Honolulu, 1931, 128 pages.
62. Thomas, S. B., *Government and Administration in Communist China*, Institute of Pacific Relations, rev. ed., 1955, 196 pages.
62*b*. Tuang Ta-lin, *Agricultural Co-operation in China*, Peking, Foreign Languages Press, 1959, 179 pages.
63. United Nations, *Land Reform, Defects in Agrarian Structure as Obstacles to Economic Development*, N.Y., 1951, 101 pages.
64. United Nations, *Measures for the Economic Development of Underdeveloped Countries*, N.Y., May 1951, 108 pages.
65. Wales, Nym, *Red Dust, Autobiographies of Chinese Communists*, Stanford University Press, Palo Alto, 1952, 238 pages.
66. Weber, Max, *Religion in China*, The Free Press, Glencoe, Illinois, 1951, 308 pages.
67. White, Theodore and Jacoby, Annalee, *Thunder out of China*, William Sloan Associates, Inc., New York, 1946, 331 pages.
68. Winfield, Gerald, *China, the Land and the People*, William Sloan Associates, Inc., New York, 1948, 437 pages.
69. Wu Yuan-li, *An Economic Survey of Communist China*, Bookman, Ass., 1956, 366 pages.
70. Yakhontoff, Victor H., *The Chinese Soviets*, Coward-McCann Inc., New York, 1934, 296 pages.
71. Yang, Martin, C., *A Chinese Village*, Columbia University Press, New York, 1945, 275 pages.

INDEX

INDEX

(Index entries have been made under the key word of spelt-out names of organizations and not under the initials extensively used in the text. Thus the Chinese Communist Party is entered as "Communist Party, Chinese", not as "CCP." A list of abbreviations used in the text with their expansions is given on pp. 373–5.)

ADMINISTRATION and Organization, rural, *see* Organization and Administration, rural
Advanced purchase programme, 227–8
Afforestation and forests, 41, 62, 182–4, 235, 303, 337
Agrarian Reform Law (1950), 95, 100–01, 114, 122, 124, 138, 141, 247
Agricultural Bank of China, 208–9
Agricultural Producers' Cooperatives (APCs), 149, 150, 243, 344
  consolidation, 330–31
  —credit cooperatives coordination, 210
  private holdings in, 249
  surplus produce, 220–22
  for higher stage APCs, *see* Collective Farming; *see also* Cooperatives
Agro-technical education, research and improvements, 62–3, 167–8, 176–96, 237, 243, 252, 259, 268, 303–04, 335, 338, 351; *see also* Technique
Airlines, 213
"Almanac for Peasants", 134
Alphabet, reformed, 239
Athletics and games, 238
Autumn Harvest Insurrection, 17

BANK OF CHINA, 208–9
Bank rates, 208, 209
Birth control, 274, 275, 279
Birth rate, 275
"Blind Actionism", 19
Books, 237
Border regions
  administration, 65–6
  agricultural programme, 41–2
  agro-technical improvements, 62–3
  cooperatives, 55
  credit, 57–8
  cultivated area, 72
  education, 68–9
  immigration to, 41
  interest reduction and debt relief, 44–5, 51–2
  labour force, 61, 72
  land legislation, 42
  land redistribution, 51
  marketing, 59
  mutual-aid teams, 55
  population, 62
  production and productivity, 60–62, 72
  reclamation and irrigation, 55
  rent reduction, 42–4, 51
  subsidiary industries, 59–60
  transport and communications, 59
  see also Yenan
Bourgeois and bourgeoisie, 40
Broadcasting, 134–5
Budget, national, 149, 301–02, 308

CADRES, 115, 116
  and collectivization, 159
  eight disciplines, 126
  identification with peasants, 242
  modest living standards, 54, 155–6
  recruitment and training, 125–7
  shortage and excess, 73, 84–5, 234–5

Capital formation, 11, 147, 169, 255, 286, 353
Capitalism and capitalists, 40
Cartoon books, 133
Central People's Government (CPG), 6, 114–15
Cheng-feng (Rectification) Movement, 125, 127–30, 265
Ch'en Tu-hsiu, 14, 15–16
Chiang Kai-shek, 16, 71
Children, 68, 235, 340
Chou En-lai, 20, 106, 125, 149, 256, 273
Ch'u Ch'in-pai, 16, 19, 19n
Chu Teh, 33
Cinema, 134
Cities, 265, 270, 277
Clan land, 47
Classes, rural, 18, 26, 90, 101–2
  changes in status, 30–31
  definitions, 25–6, 79, 96, 97
  effects of CCP war-time policies on, 63–5
  income distribution, 270
  meetings to determine, 122, 123
Clubs, 170, 237
Collection of agricultural products, 219–31
Collective farming, 148–50, 151–61
  aims, 149, 317–18
  defined, 152–3
  establishment of, steps in, 153–6
  finance, 316–17, 321–2
  income distribution, 321–2
  management, 317–18, 325–7
  means of production, surrender of, 314–16
  membership, 150, 312
  preconditions for, 94, 96, 99, 150, 210
  private property in, 314–15
  political work of, 323
  problems of, 158, 159–60
  regulations, model, 311–27
  social effects, 159, 324
  wages, 318–21
  see also Agricultural Producers' Cooperatives and People's Communes
"Commandism", 130
"Common Programme", 94–5, 141, 148
Communes, *see* People's Communes
Communications, *see* Transport
Communism, transition to, 345, 346–51
Communist Party, Chinese (CCP)
  administration and, 114–17
  agrarian policy of, 241–51; pre-soviet period (1921–7), 14–17; soviet period (1927–37), 17–38; Sino-Japanese war period (1937–45), 38–74; post-war transitional period (1945–9), 74–93; land reform period (1950–53), 94–7, 113–7; current (1953–9), 147–240, 241–81
  cities, centre shifted to, 92–3
  collectivization policy, 151–2
  communization policy, 162–4, 236
  composition, 71, 96
  confiscation policy, suspended, 38
  Congress, National, 6th (1928), 19
  expulsion from, 130
  hsiang organization, 236
  landlords, attitude to, 100
  land question, theory of, in soviet period, 18–22; in Japanese war period, 38–41; in post-war transitional period, 74–6
  land reform technique, 117–24
  Leftward swing, 16
  mass organizations, coordination of, 236
  nationalism of, 71, 142
  peace and prosperity offered by, 141–2
  peasantry, initially assigns subsidiary role to, 14–15
  propaganda techniques, 130–46
  "Ten Great Policies" (1937), 41
  "United front" policy, 38–9
Communist Party, Chinese, Central Committee (CC, CCP)
  agrarian programme (1927), 19
  Agricultural Development, Revised Draft Programme on (1956–67), 328–43

class struggle, on avoidance of, in rural areas, 15
on communes, 171 (1958 resolution), 344–62
collective farming, directives on, 158–63
on interest reduction, 44
on land policy, 39, 44, 79–81
on Li Li-san's policy, 20–21
Mao removed from office by, 17, 19
on nurseries, 172
on rent-reduction, 42–3
Confucianism, 139
Conservation, 250, 268
land, 62, 177–80, 335
projects, development of, 333
technical, administrative and organizational problems, 179–80
water, 177–80, 335, 363–4
Conservatism, 140, 137–9, 143–4
Constitution, National (1954), 148
Consumers' goods, 59, 60, 65
Consumption
household, 221, 222
urban, individual, 226–7
Contraceptives, 274
Controls, 41–2
purposes and effects, 231
see also Procurement, Purchase, *and* Rations
Cooperative farming, *see* Agricultural Producers' Cooperatives
Cooperatives, rural, 32, 40, 50, 56, 57, 59, 99, 211, 212, 342-3
credit, 207–12; functions of, 209; coordination with APCs, 210
see also Agricultural Producers' Cooperatives
Corruption, 129–30
Cottage industries and handicrafts, 4
Cotton, 246, 256–7, 272–3; *for under* Yield, Production, Crops, etc. *see under those headings*
Councils, Village, *see* Organization and Administration
Crèches, 170, 172, 235, 356
Credit, rural, 47, 57–8, 88–9, 168–9, 207–12, 302, 342
Crops
acreage, production and productivity, 295–8, 304
area under, 61, 62
high yield, 334
improved, 34, 63
nutritional deficiences, 185
see also Yield
Cultivated area, 61, 62, 72, 141
Cultural centres, 237

DEBT, *see* Indebtedness
"Democratic centralism", 164, 357–8
Dictatorship (pressure) against hostile elements, 144–6
Discussion groups, 136–7
Disease, *see* Health and Hygiene
Distribution of agricultural products, 219–31
Drama, village, 69, 111–13, 132–3, 170, 237

ECONOMIC GROWTH, theory of, 11, 252–3, 253–4, 255, 261, 285–6, 286–90, 328–30
Economy, rural, 1–6
Education, 35, 68–9, 109–11, 170, 272, 356
adult, 237, 238, 239, 341
agro-technical, 178, 183, 193–6, 239, 250, 304
compulsory, 238, 239
effects of, 239–40
expansion of, 236–40
traditional, 10
see also Schools
Eighth Route Army, 61–2, 71n; *see also* Red Army *and* People's Liberation Army
Election Law (1953), 106
Employment, underemployment and unemployment, 12–13, 252, 276–7, 308

Erh-liu-tze (loafer) reform, 68
Exhibitions, 216, 218–19, 237

Fairs, 216, 218–19
Family, 341
 council, 144
 in commune, 264–5, 357
 old style, 10
 planning, 274, 275, 279
Farms, size of, 8, 29, 30, 64
Fertilizers, 1, 42, 168, 184–7, 235, 303
 and public hygiene, 236
 output, 333n
Films, 238
Fisheries, 337–8
"Five-anti" (*wu-fan*) movement, 129
"Five-guarantee" (*wu-pao*) households, 222, 340
Five-year plans, 365–71; *see also* Plans and Planning
Foodgrains
 consumption, town and country, 227
 distribution, 143, 166, 169
 exports, 226, 230
 per capita availability, 226
 procurement prices, 228–31
 procurement (purchase and collection), 169, 215, 219–31
Forests, *see* Afforestation
Free markets, 218, 220, 230–31
Fragmentation, 8; *see also under* Farms and land (holdings)

Games and Athletics, 238
Gentry, landed, *see* Landlords
Government Administrative Council (State Council after 1954), 258
 directives on foodgrain purchases, 228
 directives on tax work, 197
Government servants, drafted to countryside, 158–9, 235, 243, 265
Grains, exports and imports, 302; *see also under* Foodgrains
Grazing, 41

Health and Hygiene, 236, 239, 272, 340
Health Stations, 237
Hilly areas, 270, 280–81, 336–7
Hogs, 246
"Houses of Culture", 137
Huai River Project, 178

Illiteracy, 238, 239, 250, 341
 and new alphabet, 239
Implements, farm, 1–2, 42, 63, 188–9, 253, 303, 334
Income, national, 308
Income, peasant, 166, 167, 245, 267
 collectivization enhances, 157
 in communes, 167, 169, 223, 345, 353–4; and labour utilization, 261–4
 prices, fall of, lowers, 229–30
 compared with urban, 265, 270
Indebtedness, peasant, 5, 24, 45, 210, 355; *see also* loans
Indemnity payments, 7
Individualism, peasant, 264–5, 283–4
Industrialization, 147, 252, 255, 283, 307, 352
 landlordism as obstacle to, 139–40
Industry, rural, 47–8, 59–60
Insecticides, 304
Inspection Teams, 126–7
Intensive farming, 334
Interest, reduction of, 38, 39, 41, 75–6, 247
 in Border Regions, 44–5, 51–2
 by credit cooperatives, 208
 in post-war (post-1945) period, 81, 87
Investment, 308
 in agriculture, 253, 302
 in conservation, irrigation, forestry and meteorology, 302
 see also Capital formation
Irrigation, 41, 42, 55, 168, 177–80, 250, 303, 333

JEN PI-SHIH, 75
definitions of rural classes, 79, 85–6, 91
on extreme measures in land reform, 85–6, 91
on middle peasants, 91
Justice, 106, 107–8, 120, 144–5

LABOUR, AGRICULTURAL, 75
in Border Regions, 61, 64
in collective farms, 157
in communes, 261–4, 339
defined, 26, 79, 97
land distributed to, 77, 78, 98
productivity, 2–3, 339
shortage, 157, 168, 278–9
in soviet areas, 27, 30, 37
utilization, 252–3
Labour exchange system, *see* Mutual-aid teams
Labour heroes, 69, 116, 142–3
Land
certificates, 28
clan, 47, 81
compulsory purchase of landlords', 77–8
committees, 27, 28
confiscation, 16, 23, 36, 38, 39, 75, 76, 78, 82
conservation, 62, 177–80, 335
holdings, size of, 8, 29–30, 64
institutional, 98
laws, (1928) 22; (1929) 22; (1931) 23–5, 37, 42; (1946) Draft, 77; (1947) 75, 78; (1950) Agrarian Reform Law, 95, 100–01, 114, 122, 124, 138, 141, 247
question, CCP theory of, 18–22
of religious groups, 47, 78, 81, 98
redistribution, 39; in soviet period, 24, 25, 27–8, 29; in anti-Japanese war period, 51; in post-war (post-1945) period, 77–8, 79–80, 85, 94; excesses in course of, 90; *see also* Land Reform (1950–53) *and* Agrarian Policy, current (1953–9)
scarcity, 36
school, 47, 78, 98
suburban farm, 82
system, 8–9
uncultivated, 47
utilization and management, 9
Landlords, 3, 4, 10, 18, 30, 31, 37, 39, 54, 85, 90, 100, 139–40, 145
absentee, 4, 47
confiscation of property of, 75, 92, 97, 247
conservatism of, 10
defined, 25–6, 79, 96
income, 270, 271
purchase, compulsory, of land of, 77–8
reform of, 342
Land Reform (1950–53)
excesses in execution, 99–100, 124
and industrialization, 283
inspection teams, 126–7
institutional changes essential for, 282
leadership in, 283
mass media in, 130–37
meetings in, 119–24
opposition to, 106–7
per capita receipts under, 99
principles of, 94–8
procedure of, 117–24
progress, year to year, 98–9
sociological and psychological factors, 137–46
see under Land *for redistribution in earlier periods and* Agrarian policy, current, *for* 1953–9
Law and order, 106, 107–8, 120, 144–5
Leadership, organizational, 6–13, 283–4
Libraries, 170, 237
Li Fu-ch'un, 177, 181
Li Li-san, 16, 20, 21, 23, 36
Literacy, 238, 239, 250, 341
Liu Shao-ch'i, 101, 114, 135, 139–40, 243, 247, 248
Livestock, 61, 63, 300, 332, 335
Loafers (*Erh-liu-tze*), reform of, 68

Loans, 31–2, 41
Local government, *see* Organization and Administration, rural

MANURES, *see* FERTILIZERS
Mao Tse-tung, 14, 16, 29, 31, 32, 52, 55, 60, 65, 70, 76, 127, 151, 161, 242, 247, 264
 on armed rebellion, 17, 18, 35–6
 on credit, rural, 58
 differences with CCP hierarchy, 19, 20, 21
 on industrialization, 92–3
 on land question and policy, 18, 38, 40
 leadership consolidated, 21–2
 on loafers, reform of, 68
 on peasant problem, 39
 on poor peasants, 83–4
 on pressure and persuasion (people's democratic dictatorship), 138–9, 144–5
 removed from CPB of CCP, 19
 on rich peasants, 114
 on 6th Congress of CCP (1928), 19–20
 on soviet regions, 33–5
 on united front, 38–9
Market, rural and marketing, 47, 72, 89, 168–9, 212–19, 341
 free, 218, 230–31
Mass media, 130–37
Mass organizations, 50, 67, 102, 148, 235–6, 283
Mechanization, 189
Meetings, village, 119–24
Merchants, grain, 220
Migration, 41, 181–2, 251
 to cities, 265, 277
Model workers, 69, 116, 142–3
Musical forms, propaganda use, 131–2
Mutual-aid teams, 47, 50, 55–6, 72, 150

NATIONAL INCOME, 147, 308
Nationalism, 71, 142
Nationalization, 282–3
National People's Congress, 106
Natural disasters, 2, 221, 236, 279–80
Navigation, inland, 213
"New Democracy", 39, 247
Newspapers, 237
 blackboard and wall, 133
Nurseries, 170, 172, 235, 356

ORGANIZATION and Administration, rural
 in anti-Japanese war period, 48–51, 65–6
 CCP and, 114–16
 communes and, 163–7, 170–71
 current, 231–6, 264
 inefficiency of, 6–7, 9
 in land reform period, 102, 105–6
 personnel shortage for, 84–5
 in post-war period (1945), 83–5
 in soviet period, 26–9
 "three-thirds" system in, 65–6
Organized farming, 293–4; *see also* Agricultural Producers' Cooperatives; Collective farms; *and* People's Communes
Output, *see also* Yield
 agricultural, 1, 141
 per household, 220

Pai-mao-nü (The White-Haired Woman), 131–2
P'eng Chen, 73–4
Peasant Associations, 19, 26, 28, 48, 50, 78, 81, 83, 84, 102–05, 122
Peasantry, 1, 4–5, 7, 11, 12, 33, 35, 39, 96, 148, 208, 210, 254–6, 264–5
 classes among, 18, 25–6, 62–5, 79, 90, 96, 97, 101–2
 expenditure, household, 268–9, 271
 land reform and, 140–43
 middle, 30, 33–4, 54, 63–5, 84, 85, 86, 91, 97, 151–2, 248, 270–71; defined, 26, 79, 96

poor, 27, 30, 33–4, 52, 54, 63–5, 75, 83, 85, 98, 151–2, 270–71; defined, 26, 79, 97
role, pivotal, in revolution, 14–16, 18, 40
rich, 2, 23, 28, 30, 31, 37, 54, 63–5, 75, 78, 97, 114, 270, 342; defined, 26, 79, 96
standard of living, 266–73, 339; *see also* Income, peasant
subsidiary occupations, 175–6, 206, 228, 249, 256
superstition and conservatism of, 5, 11, 33, 35, 138, 140, 245
surplus grain of, 220–22
tax burden on, 204–05, 207
People's Bank of China, 89, 210
People's Communes, 147–8, 149, 150, 161–72, 243, 250, 278, 345, 352, 355–60
accumulation in, 147, 169
basic unit of socialist structure, 346–51
CC, CCP Resolution on (1958), 344–62
CCP organization in, 236
consolidation of, 360–62
economic and technical aspects, 163–4, 168–70, 172
effects of, 167–71
family life in, 264–5, 357
income distribution in, 167, 169, 223, 345, 353–4
labour utilization and average income, 261–4
marketing and credit functions of, 168–9, 212, 216–17, 218
organizational aspects, 164–67, 171
plans of, 351–3
political and administrative aspects, 163, 234, 357–8
private property in, 166–7
problems of, 171–3, 261–6
production and productivity, 173–6, 351–3
social and cultural aspects, 164, 170–71, 172
surplus produce of, 220–22
spread of (figures), 162, 171, 344
wages in, 166, 167, 345, 353–4
People's Consultative Conference, 115
People's Council, *hsiang*, 232, 233–4, 244–5
People's Liberation Army (PLA), 107, 342; *see also* Red Army *and* Eighth Route Army
People's Militia, 48, 67, 68, 83, 106, 107, 358–9
People's Representative Conferences, 84
People's Representative Congress, 108; *hsiang*, 232–3
People's Tribunals, 106, 107–8, 120, 144–5
Pest Control, 63, 174, 236, 237–8, 335–6, 340
Planned parenthood, 274, 275, 279
Plans and planning, 149, 155, 168, 256–61; Five Year Plans, 365–71
Po I-po, 87, 258
Poor Peasants' Corps, 75
Poor Peasants' League, 83, 84
Population and overpopulation, 1, 12–13, 96, 101–2, 252, 273–9
Posters, 134
Prices, 33, 34, 215
of daily necessities, 266–7
policy and taxation, 205–6
for procurement of foodgrains, 228–31, 264
Procurement and distribution of agricultural products, 219–31
Production and productivity, 32, 36, 41, 47–8, 55, 60–61, 62, 63, 72, 88, 147, 156, 157, 168, 169, 173–6, 219–20, 236, 250, 251–2, 253, 257–8, 295–8, 301, 308, 331–2, 351–3; industrial, 365–71; *see also* Output; Labour, agricultural; *and* Yield
Production Brigades, 154–5, 165
Propaganda media and techniques, 130–46
Pumps, 304

Purchase of agricultural products, 219–31, 258, 301
advance, 227–8

RADIO, 134–5
Railways, 213–14, 308
Rations, standard, 222–5
urban, 223–4
fodder, 224–5
Reading groups, 136
Reclamation, 41, 42, 55, 61–2, 180–82, 251, 303, 336
Rectification Movement, 125, 127–30, 265
Red Army, 18, 24, 27, 33, 47, 65, 71n; *see also* People's Liberation Army *and* Eighth Route Army
Rent, 9, 31, 38, 39, 42–4, 51, 75–6, 80–81, 86–7, 247
Research, agro-technical, 193–6
Resources, utilization of, 253–4
Rights, individual, 284–5
Roads, 169, 213, 214, 308
Rural problems, current, 255–81

San-fan (three-anti) movement, 129
Schools
village and winter, 109–11, 170, 237, 239, 272
secondary and technical, 239
see also Education
Seeds, improved strains of, 42, 190–93, 258, 303, 334
Socialism, transition to, 345, 346–51
Socialization, *see* Collective farming *and* People's Communes
Social reform, 33, 35, 67–8, 159, 164, 170, 236–40, 244–5, 272, 278
Sanmen Gorge Project, 177–8
Soviets, 14, 17, 18, 19, 20, 22n, 23–5
agricultural production under, 32
changes in class status under, 30–31
cooperatives under, 32
Land Law during period of, 23–5, 36
land redistribution under, 29
rent, usurious loans, and sur-taxes abolished, 31–2
rural organization and administration under, 26–9
Soybean, 256, 257; *see also references under* Yield and Output
State Council, 258; *see also* Government Administrative Council
State Farms, 338
State Planning Committee (Commission), 220
Statistics, 260–61
Students, drafted, 158–9, 235, 243, 265, 284
Subsidiary occupations and products, 175–6, 206, 228, 249, 299
Sun Yat-sen, 40n
Superstition, 5, 10–11, 35, 138

T'AN CHEN-LIN, 268–71
Taxation, rural, 4–5, 7, 9, 25, 31, 32, 45–7, 52–4, 82, 87, 101, 124, 169–70, 196–207, 263–4, 268, 280, 301–2, 305–6, 308
Technique, agricultural, 41, 42, 48
backwardness of, 2, 6
improvement in and unemployment, 12–13
improvement in and production, 36
see also Agro-technical improvements
Telegraph, telephone and radio, 134–5, 214, 237–8, 341
Tenants and tenancy, 4, 9
Teng Hsiao-p'ing, 248
Teng Tzu-hui, 95, 152, 159, 178, 234, 246, 281
"Three-anti" movement, 129
"Three-fix" policy, 219–20, 222
"Three-responsibility" system, 155
"Three-thirds" system, 65–6
Tobacco supplies and manufactures, 256; *see also references under* Production *and* Yield
Tools, *see* Implements, farm

Tractors, 188–9, 303
Trade, foreign, 308
Traditions and values, 140
  conflict between old and new, 137–8, 139
  utilized by CCP, 143–4
Transport and communications, 59, 134–5, 169, 172, 213–14, 237–8, 308, 241

UNDERDEVELOPED ECONOMY, 11, 252
Unemployment, *see* Employment
United front, 37, 38–9, 71

VALUES, *see* Traditions and values
Village administration, *see* Organization and administration

WAGES, 166, 167, 245, 267, 345, 353–4
Warlords, 7
War, Sino-Japanese, and CCP land policy, 38–40
Water conservation, 177–80, 335, 363–4
"White-Haired Woman" (*yangko* drama), 131–2
Winter Schools, *see* Schools
Women, emancipation of, 35, 67, 159, 164, 168, 172, 245, 340
  in administration and organization, 235
"Work team" group, 117–19
Wu-fan ("five-anti") movement, 129
Wu-pao ("five-guarantee") households, 222, 340

Yangko dance, 69, 104, 111, 113, 120, 131–2, 144
Yenan, 41, 62, 63; *see also* Border Regions
Yield, 2, 29, 61, 101, 168, 175, 185, 332-3, 334; *see also* Crops *and* Output
Youth, 68, 235, 342
Yu-shien project, 179

1253